MORE MAC
PROGRAMMING
TECHNIQUES

DAN PARKS SYDOW

M&T Books
A Division of MIS:Press, Inc.
A Subsidiary of Henry Holt and Company, Inc.
115 West 18th Street
New York, New York 10011

© 1995 by M&T Books

ISBN 1-55851-405-8

Printed in the United States of America

Limits of Liability and Disclaimer of Warranty

The Author and Publisher of this book have used their best efforts in preparing the book
and the programs contained in it. These efforts include the development, research, and
testing of the theories and programs to determine their effectiveness.

The Author and Publisher make no warranty of any kind, expressed or implied, with
regard to these programs or the documentation contained in this book. The Author and
Publisher shall not be liable in any event for incidental or consequential damages in connection with, or arising out of, the furnishing, performance, or use of these programs.

All products, names and services are trademarks or registered trademarks of their respective companies.

Editor In Chief: Paul Farrell
Managing Editor: Cary Sullivan
Editor: Michael Sprague
Production Editor: Stephanie Doyle
Technical Editor: Pete Ferranti
Copy Editor: Suzanne Ingrao

DEDICATION

To my wife, Nadine . . .

Dan

Contents

More Mac Programming Techniques

Chapter 2: Custom Controls and the CDEF.... 57

Chapter 3: More Custom Controls: Sliders 127

Chapter 4: Control Panels and cdevs 189

Chapter 5: Resources................................ 261

Chapter 6: Resource Files 303

Appendix A: Errors 501

Index 519

ACKNOWLEDGMENTS

Michael Sprague, Development Editor, M&T Books, for keeping things rolling smoothly.

Stephanie Doyle, Production Editor, M&T Books, for a page layout effort that resulted in a great looking book.

Peter Ferrante, Apple Computer, for another helpful technical edit, and for taking the time to test the software.

Michael C. Amorose, Alamo Computer, for including his mach resource template on this book's disk.

Jason Anderson, Beyond Midnight Software, for including his PictSize utility on this book's disk.

Alessandro Levi Montalcini, for adding his shareware cdevEloper utility to the book's disk.

John Holder, for including his shareware utility Resource Handler FKEY with this book's disk.

Carole McClendon, Waterside Productions, for making this book happen.

Introduction

More Mac Programming Techniques

Chapter 1 covers the MDEF—the menu definition procedure. An MDEF is a code resource, that is, compiled code that can be used by other applications. Because the first four chapters of this book all deal with code resources, you'll read a thorough description of code resources and definition procedures in general, and then menu definition procedures in particular. This chapter has a detailed walk-through of the creation of an MDEF that displays patterns rather than text items, and of the test application that makes use of this MDEF.

Chapters 2 and 3 describe the CDEF, or control definition function. This type of code resource can be used to add 3-D buttons of your own creation to any Mac program. In Chapter 2, you'll see an example that does just that. Chapter 3 continues the discussion of the CDEF using sliders in the example programs.

Chapter 4 covers the cdev, or control device function. After building a cdev you'll have what's more commonly known as control panel—just like those under the Apple menu of any Mac.

Chapter 5 discusses resources. Here the focus is on using multiple DITL resources in a single dialog box. This is a technique that you'll find useful in any program—especially tutorial or educational software that allows the user to move through screens of information as if flipping through the pages of a book. Also covered in this chapter are custom resource templates—the tool to creating your own resource types.

Chapter 6 describes resource files. You're already familiar with the resource file that's a part of almost every Macintosh project, but there are other uses for resource files as well. In this chapter, you'll see how to write programs that use resources found in resource files, create new resource files, and copy resources from one file to another. Finally, this chapter includes and in-depth discussion and example of the very important topic of preferences files.

Chapter 7 discusses files. Here you'll see how to open an existing PICT or TEXT file, and how to save your own application documents as new PICT or TEXT files. To do any of these tasks, you'll make use of the standard dialog boxes that the Toolbox provides for selecting or naming files.

Chapter 8 covers printing. Here you'll read about the functions that make up the Printing Manager, and you'll see how to use them in a very short program that prints some graphics to your own printer—regardless of the type of printer you have connected to your Mac. After that, you'll see how to print a PICT file (like the one created in Chapter 7) and how to print the contents of a dialog box.

WHAT'S ON THE DISK

The disk that comes bundled with this book has a single folder on it. Within that folder are three more folders: Metrowerks Examples f, Symantec Examples f, and Utilities f.

The Symantec Examples f holds the source code files and project files for the every example program that is covered in this book. If you have the Symantec C++ or THINK C compiler, you'll find that everything is all set up for you. If you have the Symantec compiler, you'll find that you'll save a lot of typing by using these projects.

The Metrowerks Examples ƒ contains the source code files and project files for each of the examples discussed in this book. All of the Symantec examples are repeated here in CodeWarrior format—you won't have to make any changes to the source code or project files.

The Utilities ƒ folder contains several third-party programs and utilities that compliment the topics covered in this book.

WHAT YOU NEED

To understand the contents of this book, you should be familiar with a higher-level language—preferably C or C++. All source code listings are given in C. You should also be familiar with basic Macintosh programming concepts such as programming with the Toolbox.

All you need to run the example programs included on the disk is a Macintosh compiler. Either the Metrowerks CodeWarrior compiler, the Symantec C++ compiler, or the THINK C compiler will do. If you have one of these compilers, you can compile all of the source code from either a 680×0-based Macintosh or a Power Macintosh.

WHY THIS BOOK IS FOR YOU

Most Macintosh books cover the basics of Mac programming: the event loop, displaying windows and dialog boxes, and the primary resource types, such as the WIND and the DLOG. While very valuable to the new Mac programmer, they leave an information void that the intermediate Macintosh developer has no way of filling. To develop a real, nontrivial Macintosh application, you need to move beyond the basics.

After reading this text and working through the numerous example programs, you'll be able to write Macintosh programs that include any or all of the following features:

- Fancy controls like buttons that have a slick, three-dimensional look to them and sliders that have a look like the sliding volume control on a stero receiver.

- Menus that hold more than just text items. Some applications call for menu items that are graphical, not text based—like a graphics program that allow the user to change patterns by choosing a new pattern from a menu.

- Multiple resource files so that your application can remain small. Upgrades to the application are quick and leave the resources untouched.

- A preferences file so that the user of your application will be able to save program options and dialog box settings.

- File-handling capabilities. To be complete, your Mac application should allow the user to open files and save documents as new files.

- Document printing. A truly polished application allows the user to print the document that he or she created.

- Control panels. If your program will be small, and will affect system-wide settings, such as the speaker volume, make it a control panel rather than an application.

If you would like to know about any of these topics, this book is for you. In general, if you've programmed the Mac, but aren't sure how to go about turning your very basic program into a full-blown application that's ready to be distributed to others, this book is for you.

More Mac Programming Techniques covers all of the above-mentioned topics, and several others. There's plenty of example C language source code in the book—and on the included disk. And if you own either the Metrowerks CodeWarrior compiler, the Symantec C++ compiler, or THINK C, you'll also find the disk contains project files all set up for your immediate use.

Chapter

1

CUSTOM MENUS AND THE MDEF

The behavior of a menu is controlled by the Menu Manager. As you've worked with Macintosh applications you've certainly noticed that most menus behave in the same way. A click of the mouse button while the cursor is over a menu drops that menu down and displays its menu items. The menu items are listed in the Chicago font, and each item occupies the same height in the menu. Macintosh menus look similar to one another because the Menu Manager uses the same code to display different menus. That code is stored in the System file in a resource of type MDEF.

While most menus do have the same look to them, some applications implement menus that are anything but standard; graphics programs are a prime example. Most have a menu that, when dropped down, displays an array of colored squares. Selecting one of the squares changes a color setting within the graphics applications. A program that uses a nontraditional menu, such as the one just described, doesn't use the system MDEF code. Instead, that application contains its own MDEF and instructs the Menu Manager to use its code rather than the system code.

In this chapter you'll see exactly how to create your own MDEF resource. Once you know the basics of how to write an MDEF, the look of the menus that your applications use will be limited only by the bounds of your imagination.

The MDEF and Menu Definition Procedure

Most Mac programmers are familiar with the MENU resource—it defines the text of the items that appear in a single menu. But many of these same programmers don't realize that all Macintosh menus also make use of an MDEF resource that defines the look of the menu when it appears on the screen. This MDEF resource, with an ID of 0, is found in the System file that is present on every Mac. You can verify that this resource exists in the System file of your own Mac by opening a copy of the System file using a resource editor such as ResEdit (see Figure 1.1).

Figure 1.1 shows that ResEdit displays the MDEF resource using the ResEdit hex editor. There's nothing to view graphically because the MDEF simply consists of code—the code of a *menu definition procedure*. This procedure is responsible for the drawing of all menu items in a menu. It also provides the code to handle user actions in a menu. Because each Mac has a copy of this resource in its System file, it is available to every program. That means that menus typically have a consistent look and consistent operation in all Macintosh applications.

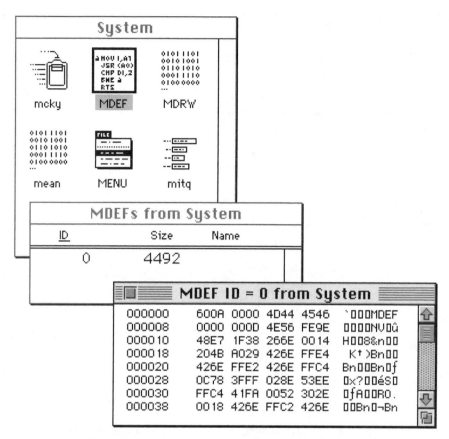

FIGURE 1.1 THE SYSTEM FILE CONTAINS AN MDEF RESOURCE WITH AN ID OF 0.

Setting the MDEF ID of a MENU Resource

When you define a MENU resource in a project's resource file, you give that resource a menu ID, and you specify which MDEF resource that menu should use. If you're like most Mac programmers, you might not be aware of this fact. That's because your resource editor by default specifies that each new MENU uses the system MDEF with ID 0. You can, however, change this specification.

Figure 1.2 shows a typical MENU resource in ResEdit. When this resource is on the screen, the ResEdit menu bar will look like the one pictured in Figure 1.3. If you select the **Edit Menu & MDEF ID** menu item from the MENU menu, you'll see the dialog box shown in Figure 1.3. Here you can either leave the MDEF ID at 0, telling the Menu Manager to use the system menu definition procedure, or you can set the ID to a different MDEF resource, thereby telling the Menu Manager to use a different menu definition procedure.

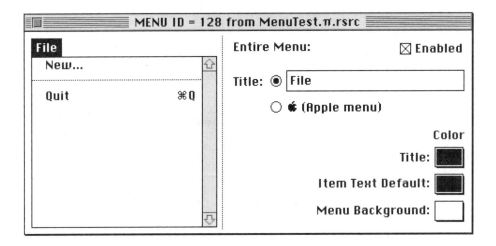

FIGURE 1.2 THE MENU RESOURCE THAT DEFINES A TYPICAL MENU.

How many other menu definition procedures are there to choose from? That depends on how many MDEF resources you've created. You'll create one or more menu definition procedures and save each as an MDEF resource. Then you'll copy any or all of your own MDEFs to the resource file for the project your working on. Any MDEF that is in the project's resource file is available for use by that project.

The MDEF Defines the Look and Actions of a Menu

An MDEF controls how a menu looks and acts. Figure 1.4 shows the look of a typical Macintosh menu, as defined by the system's MDEF resource.

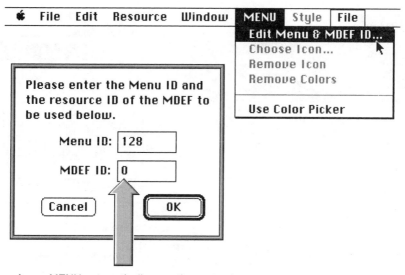

A new MENU automatically uses the system's
menu definition procedure—MDEF 0

FIGURE 1.3 EACH **MENU** RESOURCE SPECIFIES AN **MDEF** RESOURCE
THAT WILL CONTROL THAT **MENU.**

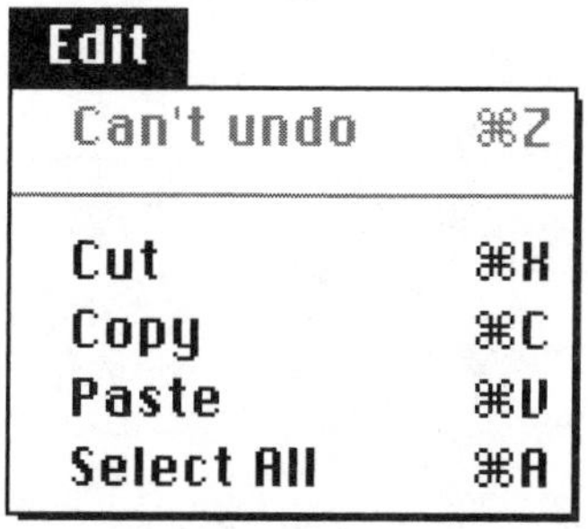

FIGURE 1.4 A TYPICAL MENU, AS CONTROLLED BY THE SYSTEM **MDEF.**

Occasionally, a Macintosh program will require a menu with a completely different look than the one supplied by the system MDEF resource. Figure 1.5 gives a couple of examples. In cases such as those shown in Figure 1.5, the application will use its own MDEF resources rather than the system MDEF.

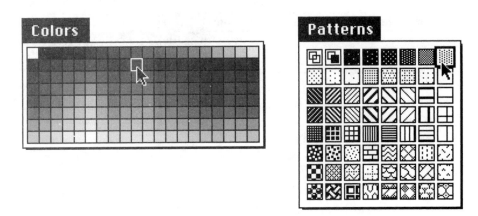

FIGURE 1.5 NONSTANDARD MENUS CONTROLLED BY **MDEFs**
OTHER THAN THE SYSTEM **MDEF.**

Programmer-defined MDEFs aren't used only to create menus that display graphics. A single MDEF can be created to change the overall look of each of an application's menus. In Figure 1.6 you see how using an MDEF resource other than the system's MDEF 0 causes an application's Edit menu to take on a whole new look.

FIGURE 1.6 AN **MDEF** CAN BE USED TO CHANGE THE LOOK OF A MENU
THAT DISPLAYS ITEMS AS TEXT.

In this chapter you'll learn how to create your own MDEF resource. You'll also develop a simple application that serves but a single purpose—to test your new MDEF.

Once you specify that a MENU resource is to be controlled by your own MDEF resource, the system MDEF will not come into play—for that one menu. So while your primary purpose in creating an MDEF is usually to create a more graphical menu, you'll also have to give your menu definition procedure the ability to handle the routine tasks that the system menu definition procedure normally handles. These tasks include

- Calculating the menu's boundary (for display purposes)
- Displaying the menu items on the screen when the menu is clicked on
- Handling proper highlighting of menu items as the user moves the cursor over items
- Noting which menu item is selected by the user

Creating and Using an MDEF Code Resource

Your menu definition procedure will start out as source code. You'll write code that defines the look of a menu and code to handle all of the previous tasks—the tasks normally handled by the system menu definition procedure. Then, instead of turning the source code into an application, you'll use your development environment to compile the code into a *code resource*. A code resource, as its name implies, is simply compiled code stored in a resource.

When you tell your development environment to turn code into a code resource, you'll be given the opportunity to save that resource to a resource file. Your development environment will create a new resource file, compile your menu definition source code, and save the compiled code as an MDEF resource in the new resource file. Figure 1.7 shows a menu definition procedure I've created and saved to a resource file named MyMDEF.rsrc. Because the resource is compiled code, opening it in a resource editor will result in the display of meaningless hex characters. You'll notice in the figure that instead of giving the MDEF an ID of 0, which would conflict with the system's own menu definition procedure, I've given my MDEF a different ID. In this example I've arbitrarily given my MDEF an ID of 1000.

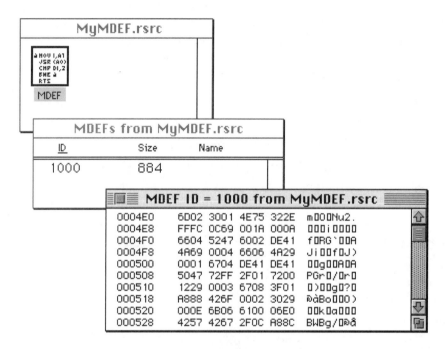

FIGURE 1.7 LIKE THE SYSTEM **MDEF**, YOUR **MDEF** WILL BE COMPILED CODE SAVED AS A RESOURCE.

Once an MDEF is created and saved to a resource file, it can be used with any menu in any application. First, you'll open the resource file that holds the MDEF and copy the MDEF resource. Next, you'll use the resource editor to open the resource fork of the application that will be using the MDEF. Then you'll paste the MDEF resource into that application. I've shown an example of this in Figure 1.8, where I'm using my MDEF with ID 1000 and an application named MyTestApp that I've already developed.

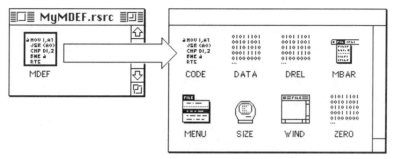

Copy an 'MDEF' from its resource file and
paste it into the resource fork of an application

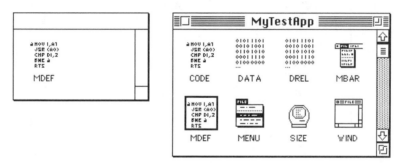

Then the 'MENU' resources in the
application will have access to the 'MDEF'

**FIGURE 1.8 FOR AN APPLICATION TO USE AN MDEF, THAT MDEF MUST BE
PASTED INTO THE APPLICATION'S PROJECT FILE.**

Once an application contains an MDEF resource, any MENU resources
that have been designated to be users of that MDEF will have access to it.
Figure 1.9 shows an application project's resource file with two MENU
resources in it. One of them—MENU 128, the Edit menu—will use the
standard system MDEF. The other MENU—MENU 129, a menu titled
Fill—will be using my own MDEF.

When a MENU will be using a custom menu definition procedure—as
my Fill menu is doing—you generally won't add any menu items to the
MENU. Instead, the MDEF itself will be responsible for adding the individual menu items. Figure 1.10 shows what both the Edit and Fill menus might
look like when controlled by their respective menu definition procedures.

N O T E I say "generally" because there are times when you'll add menu items. For an MDEF that displays graphical items, like patterns, you won't add the items in the MENU resource. If your MDEF doesn't use graphical items, however, you will add the items in the MENU resource. An example of this is shown back in Figure 1.6. The MDEF that controls that menu changes the look of the menu and the text that the items are displayed in, but it still uses text for each item.

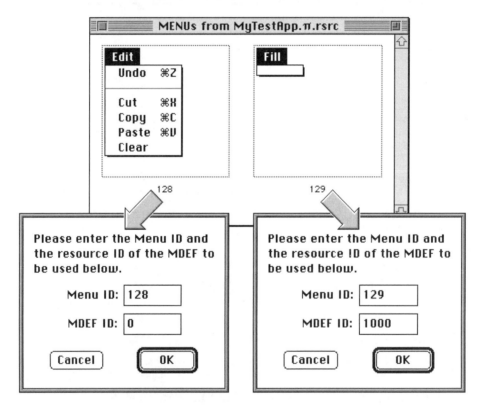

FIGURE 1.9 DIFFERENT **MENU** RESOURCES CAN USE DIFFERENT **MDEF** RESOURCES.

THE MDEF SOURCE CODE

In this section you'll see the source code for an example MDEF code resource. The MyMDEF code resource displays a menu that holds five menu items. Rather than using text for the menu items, each menu item is a rectangle with a different pattern in it. Figure 1.11 shows what this menu looks like. Both the MyMDEF source code file and the MyMDEF project file appear on the included disk. I'll introduce the source code for MyMDEF.c piecemeal, explaining each part of it as it is introduced. The entire listing appears at the end of this section.

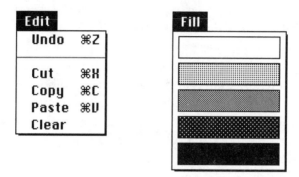

FIGURE 1.10 BOTH STANDARD AND NONSTANDARD MENUS MAY APPEAR WITHIN THE SAME MENU BAR OF ONE APPLICATION.

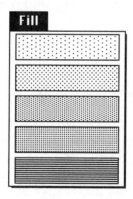

FIGURE 1.11 THE MENU THAT IS DISPLAYED BY THE MYMDEF MDEF CODE RESOURCE.

The Menu Definition Procedure Entry Point

When a user clicks the mouse button while the cursor is on a menu in a menu bar, the Menu Manager invokes the code in the system's menu definition procedure (MDEF = 0). That procedure is then responsible for drawing the text that makes up each menu item. It is also responsible for handling actions in the dropped menu. If the MENU resource that defines a particular menu specifies an MDEF other than the system MDEF, the Menu Manager will instead use the code within that other MDEF.

When the Menu Manager uses your menu definition procedure, it will first look for a function named `main()` in the MDEF code, which serves as the Menu Manager's *entry point* into your MDEF code. This function named `main()` is a callback routine. A *callback routine* is a programmer-defined function that gets called by the Toolbox. Since a Toolbox function (not one of your own functions) will be calling your menu definition procedure's `main()` function, the declaration of your `main()` routine must adhere to a strict calling convention.

The Toolbox expects callback routines to follow Pascal calling conventions, not C conventions. So your declaration of `main()` must start with the pascal keyword. That tells the compiler to load the function parameters on the stack in the proper sequence. You, the programmer, do not have to be concerned with the differences between Pascal and C calling conventions.

For the MDEF `main()` routine, the Menu Manager expects no return value. That means you'll follow the `pascal` keyword with the `void` keyword, and then the function name. While some compiler environments allow the MDEF `main()` routine to have a variable number of parameters, traditionally the `main()` routine has five parameters. While you can give these parameters the names you'd like, their data types should be as shown in this snippet from the `main()` declaration of this chapter's MyMDEF example:

```
pascal void  main( short       message,
                   MenuHandle  the_menu,
                   Rect        *menu_rect_ptr,
                   Point        hit_point,
                   short       *which_item_ptr )
```

When the Menu Manager calls the `main()` function, it will place values in the function parameters. That will allow `main()` routine to take care of whatever menu-related task needs handling. And how will the menu definition procedure know what type of task the Menu Manager wants handled? The very first parameter to main() will hold that information. The message parameter will hold one of four constants, each of which represents a Menu Manager request for the handling of a different task :

mDrawMsg   Draw the menu on the screen (drop the menu)
mChooseMsg   Tell which item was selected, and highlight it
mSizeMsg   Calculate the dimensions of the menu
mPopUpMsg   Calculate the rectangle of the pop-up menu box

An understanding of this first parameter to main() gives you enough information to follow just what main() does:

```
pascal void  main( short       message,
                   MenuHandle  the_menu,
                   Rect        *menu_rect_ptr,
                   Point       hit_point,
                   short       *which_item_ptr )
{
   switch ( message )
   {
      case mSizeMsg:
         // determine the size of the menu
         break;

      case mDrawMsg:
         // draw the menu on the screen
         break;

      case mChooseMsg:
         // determine which item was selected, highlight it
         break;

      case mPopUpMsg:
         // determine the size of the pop-up box
         break;
   }
}
```

As the user moves the cursor over a menu that uses the MyMDEF menu definition, the Menu Manager will invoke this MDEF code repeatedly. It will call it once, passing an mSizeMsg message, to determine the size of the nonstandard menu. Then it will call it again, passing an mDrawMsg message, to draw the menu. And as the user moves the cursor over the items in the menu, the Menu Manager will call the code several times, each time passing an mChooseMsg message.

The message parameter tells the main() function which task should be handled. The remaining four parameters provide information the menu definition procedure will need in order to handle that task.

The second parameter, the_menu, is a handle to the menu record of the clicked-on menu. This handle will be used to set some of the fields of the menu record.

The third parameter, menu_rect_ptr, is a pointer to the rectangle that is the boundary of the clicked-on menu. If the value of message is either mSizeMsg or mPopUpMsg, menu_rect_ptr won't point to a valid rectangle. Instead, it will be your job to calculate the size of the menu rectangle. If the value of message is either mDrawMsg or mChooseMsg, this pointer will point to a valid rectangle. Where do these dimensions come from? A call to main() with either of these messages will be preceded by an earlier call to main() with either a message value of mSizeMsg or mPopUpMsg. That call will set the menu boundary and make the Menu Manager aware of the size.

The fourth parameter to main(), hit_point, is the point in the menu at which the cursor is currently located. The menu definition procedure needs this information when the value of message is mChooseMsg. The menu definition code will respond to a message of this type by highlighting and unhighlighting menu items as the user drags the cursor over the menu. The hit_point will be used to determine which item the cursor is currently over. Again, it should be obvious that as the user moves the cursor over a dropped menu, the menu definition procedure will be repeatedly called by the Menu Manager.

The last parameter to main(), which_item_ptr, is a pointer to the last item selected from the menu. This parameter will be used when message has a value of mChooseMsg. As the user drags the cursor over the dropped menu, the menu definition code will highlight an item that the cursor covers. But at that time it must also unhighlight whichever menu item was previously highlighted. The which_item_ptr will be used for that purpose.

Typically, main() is used as a branching point. Depending on the value of the message parameter, main() will call one of the programmer-defined routines to handle the task at hand. Here's the main() routine for MyMDEF, which handles three of the four possible message values:

```
pascal void  main( short         message,
                   MenuHandle  the_menu,
                   Rect          *menu_rect_ptr,
                   Point         hit_point,
                   short         *which_item_ptr )
{
   switch ( message )
   {
      case mSizeMsg:
         Do_My_Size_Of_Menu( the_menu );
         break;

      case mDrawMsg:
         Do_My_Draw_Menu( the_menu, menu_rect_ptr );
         break;

      case mChooseMsg:
         Do_My_Choose_Item( menu_rect_ptr, hit_point, which_item_ptr );
         break;
   }
}
```

In this chapter I'll be working with menus that drop down from the menu bar—not with pop-up menus. So I'll omit any mPopUpMsg code from the remainder of this discussion. Pop-up menus are a subject worthy of quite a few pages of explanation. For more information on creating an MDEF that uses a pop-up menu, refer to *Inside Macintosh: Macintosh Toolbox Essentials*.

Taking Care of the Preliminaries

While a menu definition procedure isn't an application, it is code, and it does contain functions. So, like application code, you'll need to use function prototypes to give the compiler's preprocessor information about each function you define. The MyMDEF menu definition procedure will consist of four functions. The first three each handle one message type, and the fourth is a simple utility routine that will be used to invert the highlighting of a menu item.

```
void  Do_My_Size_Of_Menu( MenuHandle );
void  Do_My_Draw_Menu( MenuHandle, Rect * );
void  Do_My_Choose_Item( Rect *, Point, short * );
void  Invert_My_Item( short, Rect * );
```

To eliminate the scattering of numbers throughout my source code, I'll use #define directives to establish a half dozen constants. Figure 1.12 shows just what each of the first four constants refers to. In that figure I've taken the liberty of changing the scaling of the menu items a little so that it becomes clear just what some of these pixel dimensions are referencing.

```
#define      TOP_BOT_SPACE          2
#define      SIDE_SPACE             5
#define      MENU_PAT_WIDTH       100
#define      MENU_PAT_HEIGHT       25
#define      NUM_MENU_ITEMS         5
#define      SYS_PAT_LIST_OFFSET   20
```

NOTE While at this point it may seem like overkill to be so concerned with these menu dimensions, you'll soon find out that they are important. When your menu definition procedure receives an mChooseMsg message, it will be your responsibility to highlight and unhighlight menu items. You can't accurately do that without knowing these dimensions.

The System file of every Macintosh contains a PAT# resource with an ID of 0. This system pattern list holds 38 patterns that are readily available for your program's needs. Figure 1.13 shows all 38 of the system patterns. My example MDEF will use five of these patterns—one for each of the five menu items. An index is used to access any pattern from the list. My menu items will use patterns 21 through 25, so I defined a constant named SYS_PAT_LIST_OFFSET with a value of 20. Later, you'll see how this constant is used when the menu is drawn to the screen.

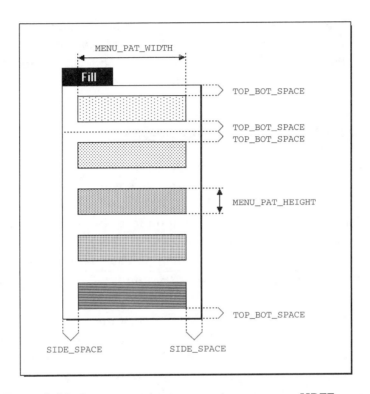

FIGURE 1.12 CONSTANTS DEFINE THE DIMENSIONS OF THE MDEF MENU.

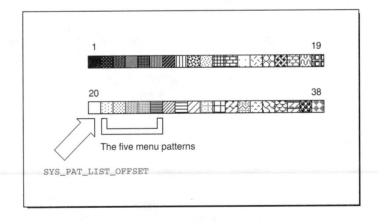

FIGURE 1.13 MYMDEF WILL USE FIVE OF THE 38 PATTERNS
IN THE SYSTEM'S PATTERN LIST.

A menu definition procedure can have functions, function prototypes, and #define **directives, but it can't contain global variables. Since the code for an MDEF is seldom very complex or very lengthy, this shouldn't be a hindrance.**

T I P

Handling an mSizeMsg Message

When the main() routine of a menu definition procedure receives an mSizeMsg, it means the Menu Manager needs to know the size of the menu that is defined in the MDEF. For a standard menu, the Menu Manager can calculate this information on its own. That's because it can use the size of the Chicago font—the standard menu font—to determine the height and width of each menu item in a standard menu. A custom menu, however, may consist of patterns, graphics, or different sizes of fonts, so the Menu Manager needs some help.

When main() receives an mSizeMsg, call the MDEF function that calculates the menu's size. The menu's size is the rectangle that it occupies when it is dropped down. In my example, the width is the width of one pattern that will be drawn in the menu, plus the small buffer area I'll add to either side of the pattern:

```
MENU_PAT_WIDTH + (2 * SIDE_SPACE)
```

You can refer back to Figure 1.12 to see how the constants in the previous equation, and the following equation, are defined. The height of a single menu item is the height of one of the patterns, plus the buffer area that appears above and below the pattern. That means the height of the entire menu is the number of menu items times the height of one item:

```
NUM_MENU_ITEMS * (MENU_PAT_HEIGHT + (2 * TOP_BOT_SPACE))
```

As the values are calculated they should be stored in the menuWidth and menuHeight fields of the menu's menu record. Recall that the second parameter to main() is a handle to the menu. The Menu Manager is responsible for obtaining a handle to the menu and passing it to your main() function. You are responsible for setting the two menu size fields in this menu record. To do this, dereference the handle twice using the * operator. Here is the complete Do_My_Size_Of_Menu() routine for the MyMDEF example:

```
void  Do_My_Size_Of_Menu( MenuHandle the_menu )
{
   (**the_menu).menuWidth  = MENU_PAT_WIDTH + (2 * SIDE_SPACE);
   (**the_menu).menuHeight = NUM_MENU_ITEMS * (MENU_PAT_HEIGHT +
                             (2 * TOP_BOT_SPACE));
}
```

Once the menuWidth and menuHeight fields of the menu record are set, the Menu Manager knows the size of the menu. That information is necessary for the process of drawing the menu to the screen—the topic I'll cover next.

Handling an mDrawMsg Message

The Menu Manager can draw a standard menu by simply using the Chicago font to draw the text of each menu item. For a standard menu, the Menu Manager takes the menu item information that has been defined in a MENU resource and stores it in the menu's menu record. For a custom menu, things are not that simple. The Menu Manager doesn't know what each menu item in a custom menu looks like, so it counts on the custom menu's menu definition procedure to supply that information in a draw function. To access this information, the Menu Manager will send main() an mDrawMsg message. That message should be handled by a routine that does the actual drawing. I've named the MyMDEF version of this routine Do_My_Draw_ Menu().

To draw the menu items you'll set up the location of the first item and then enter a loop. The body of the loop should draw an item and then change the location to the area that will hold the next menu item. For the MyMDEF example, the loop will draw each of the five pattern-filled rectangles that make up the menu items. The following snippet shows how the MyMDEF example determines the location of the patterned rectangle that will serve as the first menu item:

```
Rect   the_rect;

the_rect.top = menu_rect_ptr->top + TOP_BOT_SPACE;
the_rect.left = menu_rect_ptr->left + SIDE_SPACE;
the_rect.bottom = the_rect.top + MENU_PAT_HEIGHT;
the_rect.right = the_rect.left + MENU_PAT_WIDTH;
```

Recall that `menu_rect_ptr` is a pointer to the rectangle that is the boundary of the clicked-on menu. This pointer doesn't always point to a valid rectangle. The Menu Manager is able to supply a valid rectangle only after it sends the menu definition procedure an `mSizeMsg` message. Before a menu definition procedure ever receives an `mDrawMsg`, you can safely assume that an `mSizeMsg` has already been handled and that the `menu_rect_ptr` now points to a valid rectangle.

The rectangle that `menu_rect_ptr` points to holds the pixel boundary of the entire menu and holds these numbers as global coordinates. Since the menu definition procedure will be drawing to the screen—not a window—global coordinates are desired. The top of the first menu item rectangle will be at the coordinate held in `menu_rect_ptr.top`, plus the small pixel buffer value `TOP_BOT_SPACE`:

```
the_rect.top = menu_rect_ptr->top + TOP_BOT_SPACE;
```

Figure 1.14 shows how this value is obtained. The bottom of the first patterned rectangle is then simply the top plus the height of the menu item rectangle:

```
the_rect.bottom = the_rect.top + MENU_PAT_HEIGHT;
```

The coordinates of the left and right sides of the first patterned rectangle are determined in the same manner as the coordinates for the top and bottom:

```
the_rect.left = menu_rect_ptr->left + SIDE_SPACE;
the_rect.right = the_rect.left + MENU_PAT_WIDTH;
```

With the coordinates of the first patterned rectangle established, it's time to draw that rectangle. That's done in loop:

```
short     i;
Pattern   the_pat;
short     item_height;

for ( i = 1; i <= NUM_MENU_ITEMS; i++ )
{
   GetIndPattern( &the_pat, sysPatListID,
                  SYS_PAT_LIST_OFFSET + i );
   FillRect( &the_rect, &the_pat );
   FrameRect( &the_rect );

   the_rect.top += item_height;
   the_rect.bottom = the_rect.top + MENU_PAT_HEIGHT;
}
```

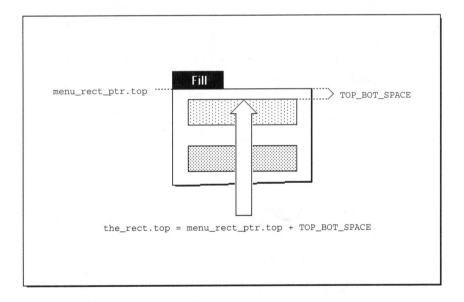

FIGURE 1.14 **THE TOP OF THE FIRST MENU ITEM RECTANGLE IS THE SUM OF THE TOP
COORDINATE OF THE MENU AND THE PIXEL BUFFER.**

The loop begins with a call to GetIndPattern(). The first parameter,
the_pat, will be assigned a pattern by the Toolbox when the function has
completed. The second parameter specifies the ID of the PAT# pattern list
resource to use. I am using the system PAT# pattern list discussed earlier, so

I'll pass in the constant sysPatListID here. Finally, GetIndPattern() needs a value that serves as an index into the pattern list. There are 38 patterns in the system list, and MyMDEF will be using patterns 21 through 25 for the five menu items. Setting this last parameter to SYS_PAT_LIST_OFFSET + i results in the proper pattern being used in each iteration through the loop.

Drawing the patterned rectangle to the menu requires just two Toolbox calls. A call to FillRect() draws the rectangle with the system pattern, and a call to FrameRect() provides a thin black frame around the rectangle.

The loop ends by incrementing the top and bottom coordinates of the_rect in preparation for the drawing of the next menu item. Notice that the top coordinate must be incremented by the height of the entire menu item, not by the height of a patterned rectangle. The following line of code shows how item_height is calculated, and Figure 1.15 points out the difference between the height of a menu item and the height of a patterned rectangle.

```
item_height = MENU_PAT_HEIGHT + ( 2 * TOP_BOT_SPACE );
```

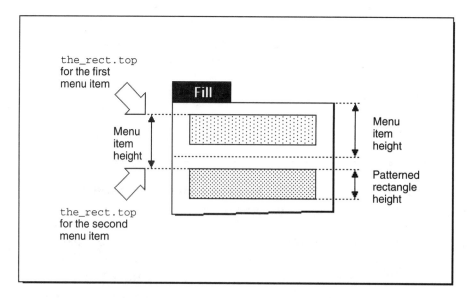

FIGURE 1.15 THE HEIGHT OF A MENU ITEM DIFFERS FROM THE HEIGHT OF A PATTERNED RECTANGLE WITHIN AN ITEM.

Every time the user clicks the mouse while the cursor is in the menu bar on the title of the menu that uses the MyMDEF code, main() will be called twice. The first call will send main() an mSizeMsg message to get the boundaries of the entire menu. The second call will send main() an mDrawMsg message to draw the entire menu, hence giving the appearance of the menu dropping down. Here's a look at the entire Do_My_Draw_Menu() function from the MyMDEF example:

```
void  Do_My_Draw_Menu( MenuHandle the_menu, Rect *menu_rect_ptr )
{
   short    i;
   Rect     the_rect;
   Pattern  the_pat;
   short    item_height;

   item_height = MENU_PAT_HEIGHT + ( 2 * TOP_BOT_SPACE );

   the_rect.top = menu_rect_ptr->top + TOP_BOT_SPACE;
   the_rect.left = menu_rect_ptr->left + SIDE_SPACE;
   the_rect.bottom = the_rect.top + MENU_PAT_HEIGHT;
   the_rect.right = the_rect.left + MENU_PAT_WIDTH;

   for ( i = 1; i <= NUM_MENU_ITEMS; i++ )
   {
      GetIndPattern( &the_pat, sysPatListID,
                  SYS_PAT_LIST_OFFSET + i );
      FillRect( &the_rect, &the_pat );
      FrameRect( &the_rect );

      the_rect.top += item_height;
      the_rect.bottom = the_rect.top + MENU_PAT_HEIGHT;
   }
}
```

Handling an mChooseMsg Message

As the user drags the cursor over the items of the dropped menu, the Menu Manager will send the menu definition procedure mChooseMsg messages. In response to an mChooseMsg message, the main() function should invoke a routine that handles the highlighting and unhighlighting of items in the menu. This function, named Do_My_Choose_Item() in the MyMDEF example, is responsible for nothing more than inverting menu items as the cursor sweeps across them.

There are two primary scenarios that `Do_My_Choose_Item()` will look for and handle. The first is the case where the cursor has moved from one point in the dropped menu to another point in the menu. The second is the case where the cursor has moved from one point in the dropped menu to a point outside the menu. Keep in mind that when the user drags the mouse such that the cursor moves out of a dropped menu, that menu does not disappear. Instead, the menu stays dropped, and whatever item was previously highlighted becomes unhighlighted. Figure 1.16 shows this situation.

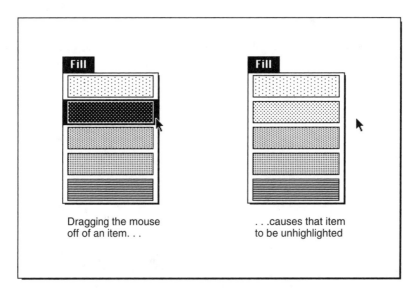

Dragging the mouse off of an item. . .

. . .causes that item to be unhighlighted

FIGURE 1.16 DRAGGING THE CURSOR OFF A DROPPED MENU UNHIGHLIGHTS THE PREVIOUSLY SELECTED ITEM.

While you may consider the display of a nonstandard menu the primary purpose of your menu definition procedure, another important task of the menu definition procedure is to mimic the normal behavior of standard menus. That means properly responding to the movement of the mouse over one of your menus.

I will first examine the case of the cursor moving from one point to another within the menu. To handle this scenario, Do_My_Choose_Item( ) will require three parameters that the Menu Manager passes to main( ). With that in mind, here's the declaration for Do_My_Choose_Item( ):

```
void  Do_My_Choose_Item( Rect   *menu_rect_ptr,
                         Point  hit_point,
                         short  *which_item_ptr )
```

Do_My_Choose_Item( ) will use three local variables, which are as follows. The first, selected_item, will be used to hold the item number of the item the cursor is currently over. The old_item variable will be used to hold the item number of whatever item the cursor was previously over. The last variable, item_height, will be used to hold the height of a single menu item.

```
short  selected_item;
short  old_item;
short  item_height;
```

Before determining where the cursor is currently located, I'll take care of a couple of preliminary assignments. First, item_height is assigned the pixel height of a single menu item:

```
item_height = MENU_PAT_HEIGHT + ( 2 * TOP_BOT_SPACE );
```

NOTE
You may have noticed that this is the second routine that declares and calculates item_height. **This is necessary because the MDEF can't have global variables. An application finds its global variables by looking to the value held in the A5 register of the CPU. Because a code resource isn't part of the application that is currently running, it can't make the assumption that the A5 register is set up with the proper value at the time a call is made to the code in the code resource. This inability to reference the A5 world is the reason a code resource can't contain traditional global variables. It is possible for a code resource to set up the A4**

register and then make use of variables global to the code resource, but that's usually not necessary.

Next, I'll set the old_item variable to the number of the menu item that was previously highlighted. The which_item_ptr parameter, originally passed in to main(), points to a value the represents this item. If no item was previously highlighted, the value that which_item_ptr points to will be 0.

```
old_item = *which_item_ptr;
```

Now it's time to handle the scenario of the cursor that has been moved from one point to another within the menu. Here is the snippet that takes care of this case:

```
if ( PtInRect( hit_point, menu_rect_ptr ) )
{
   selected_item = ((hit_point.v - menu_rect_ptr->top)/item_height)+1;

   if ( ( old_item > 0 ) && ( old_item != selected_item ) )
      Invert_My_Item( old_item, menu_rect_ptr );

   if ( selected_item != old_item )
   {
      Invert_My_Item( selected_item, menu_rect_ptr );
      *which_item_ptr = selected_item;
   }
}
```

PtInRect() is a Toolbox function that accepts two parameters and returns a Boolean value. If the Point parameter hit_point lies in the Rect pointed to by the menu_rect_ptr, PtInRect() returns a value of true. If the point lies outside the Rect parameter, PtInRect() returns false. If the result is in fact true, it's time to handle the highlighting of the menu items.

The first order of business is to determine the value of selected_item—the item that the cursor is currently over. The following line of code takes care of that task:

```
selected_item = ((hit_point.v - menu_rect_ptr->top)/item_height)+1;
```

Figure 1.17 substitutes some numerical values for the variables to show just what's taking place in this assignment statement. In the figure it's assumed that the mChooseMsg message was sent when the cursor was 55 pixels down from the top of the screen. As you study the figure keep in mind that both menu_rect_ptr->top and hit_point.v are in global coordinates. Also take note of the fact that because the short variable selected_item is an integral variable type—not a floating-point type—the fractional portion of the division result will always be dropped.

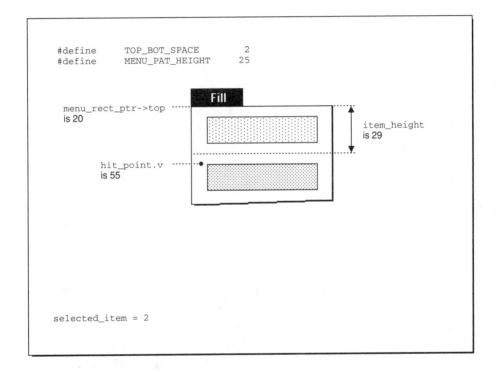

FIGURE 1.17 DETERMINING IN WHICH MENU ITEM THE CURSOR IS CURRENTLY LOCATED.

With the value of selected_item determined, the function checks to see if the previously highlighted menu should be inverted back to its unhighlighted state.

This will happen only if two conditions are true. First, an item must previously have been selected (old_item > 0). Second, the newly selected item must be different from the previously selected item. If the cursor has moved from one point in an item to another point in that same item, the values of selected_item and old_item will be the same and there is no need to change the highlighting. If both of these conditions apply, the utility routine Invert_My_Item( ) is called to change the state of the previously highlighted item:

```
if ( ( old_item > 0 ) && ( old_item != selected_item ) )
   Invert_My_Item( old_item, menu_rect_ptr );
```

Next, a check is made to see if the currently selected menu item should be inverted. If this current item is different than the previous item, it should be inverted, or selected. If the new item does indeed get highlighted, the which_item_ptr variable is set to point to this item. The Menu Manager keeps track of this variable, so setting its value to the new menu item number lets the Menu Manager in on the change. The next time the Menu Manager calls the main( ) routine of the menu definition procedure, it will pass in this changed value.

```
if ( selected_item != old_item )
{
   Invert_My_Item( selected_item, menu_rect_ptr );
   *which_item_ptr = selected_item;
}
```

Together, the previous two if statements have the effect of unhighlighting the old item and highlighting the new item, if applicable. Next, Do_My_Choose_Item( ) must handle the case of a cursor that moves out of the menu. That scenario is handled in an else-if section:

```
if ( PtInRect( hit_point, menu_rect_ptr ) )
{
   // handle highlighting when cursor is in the menu
}
else if ( old_item > 0 )
{
   Invert_My_Item( old_item, menu_rect_ptr );
   *which_item_ptr = 0;
}
```

If the value of hit_point doesn't lie within the boundaries of the menu, the code reaches the else-if statement. There, a check is made to see if a menu item was previously selected (old_item > 0). If it was selected, that item should be unhighlighted to reflect the fact that the cursor is no longer over that item. A call to Invert_My_Item() takes care of that. Again, the Menu Manager must be notified that the item number of the selected item has changed. This time no item is currently selected, so which_item_ptr is set to point to a value of 0.

Now, here is a look at the completed version of the Do_My_Choose_Item() routine:

```
void  Do_My_Choose_Item( Rect    *menu_rect_ptr,
                         Point   hit_point,
                         short   *which_item_ptr )
{
   short   selected_item;
   short   old_item;
   short   item_height;

   item_height = MENU_PAT_HEIGHT + ( 2 * TOP_BOT_SPACE );

   old_item = *which_item_ptr;

   if ( PtInRect( hit_point, menu_rect_ptr ) )
   {
      selected_item = ((hit_point.v - menu_rect_ptr->top)/
                      item_height)+1;

      if ( ( old_item > 0 ) && ( old_item != selected_item ) )
         Invert_My_Item( old_item, menu_rect_ptr );

      if ( selected_item != old_item )
      {
         Invert_My_Item( selected_item, menu_rect_ptr );
         *which_item_ptr = selected_item;
      }
   }

   else if ( old_item > 0 )
   {
      Invert_My_Item( old_item, menu_rect_ptr );
      *which_item_ptr = 0;
   }
}
```

`Do_My_Choose_Item()` has three conditions in which a menu item must be inverted. Rather than repeat the code that inverts a menu item, I have written a short utility routine to handle that one task. `Invert_My_Item()` sets up a `Rect` variable the size of the entire menu. Then it adjusts the top and bottom of that rectangle to the coordinates of the menu item that is to be inverted. A call to the Toolbox routine `InvertRect()` then does the actual inverting.

```
void  Invert_My_Item( short  item_number,
                      Rect  *menu_rect_ptr )
{
   Rect    the_rect;
   short   item_height;

   item_height = MENU_PAT_HEIGHT + ( 2 * TOP_BOT_SPACE );

   the_rect = *menu_rect_ptr;

   the_rect.top += ( ( item_number - 1 ) * item_height );
   the_rect.bottom = the_rect.top + item_height;

   InvertRect( &the_rect );
}
```

The MyMDEF Source Code Listing

I will end this section with the complete listing for MyMDEF. The listing consists of just four functions—each of which has been described in detail on the preceding pages.

```
//_____
//                                      function prototypes

void   Do_My_Size_Of_Menu( MenuHandle );
void   Do_My_Draw_Menu( MenuHandle, Rect * );
void   Do_My_Choose_Item( Rect *, Point, short * );
void   Invert_My_Item( short, Rect * );


//_____
//                                      #define directives
```

```
#define        TOP_BOT_SPACE          2
#define        SIDE_SPACE             5
#define        MENU_PAT_WIDTH       100
#define        MENU_PAT_HEIGHT       25
#define        NUM_MENU_ITEMS         5
#define        SYS_PAT_LIST_OFFSET   20


//_____
//                                  entry point to the code

pascal void  main( short        message,
                   MenuHandle  the_menu,
                   Rect        *menu_rect_ptr,
                   Point        hit_point,
                   short       *which_item_ptr )
{
   switch ( message )
   {
      case mSizeMsg:
         Do_My_Size_Of_Menu( the_menu );
         break;

      case mDrawMsg:
         Do_My_Draw_Menu( the_menu, menu_rect_ptr );
         break;

      case mChooseMsg:
         Do_My_Choose_Item( menu_rect_ptr, hit_point, which_item_ptr );
         break;
   }
}


//_____
//                                  set the size of the entire menu

void  Do_My_Size_Of_Menu( MenuHandle the_menu )
{
   (**the_menu).menuWidth  = MENU_PAT_WIDTH + (2 * SIDE_SPACE);
   (**the_menu).menuHeight = NUM_MENU_ITEMS *
                        (MENU_PAT_HEIGHT + (2 * TOP_BOT_SPACE));
}


//_____
//                                  draw the menu items
```

```
void  Do_My_Draw_Menu( MenuHandle the_menu, Rect *menu_rect_ptr )
{
    short    i;
    Rect     the_rect;
    Pattern  the_pat;
    short    item_height;

    item_height = MENU_PAT_HEIGHT + ( 2 * TOP_BOT_SPACE );

    the_rect.top = menu_rect_ptr->top + TOP_BOT_SPACE;
    the_rect.left = menu_rect_ptr->left + SIDE_SPACE;
    the_rect.bottom = the_rect.top + MENU_PAT_HEIGHT;
    the_rect.right = the_rect.left + MENU_PAT_WIDTH;

    for ( i = 1; i <= NUM_MENU_ITEMS; i++ )
    {
        GetIndPattern( &the_pat, sysPatListID,
                       SYS_PAT_LIST_OFFSET + i );
        FillRect( &the_rect, &the_pat );
        FrameRect( &the_rect );

        the_rect.top += item_height;
        the_rect.bottom = the_rect.top + MENU_PAT_HEIGHT;
    }
}


//_____
//                         handle cursor movement over menu items

void  Do_My_Choose_Item( Rect    *menu_rect_ptr,
                         Point    hit_point,
                         short   *which_item_ptr )
{
    short  selected_item;
    short  old_item;
    short  item_height;

    item_height = MENU_PAT_HEIGHT + ( 2 * TOP_BOT_SPACE );

    old_item = *which_item_ptr;

    if ( PtInRect( hit_point, menu_rect_ptr ) )
    {
        selected_item = ((hit_point.v - menu_rect_ptr->top)/item_height)+1;

        if ( ( old_item > 0 ) && ( old_item != selected_item ) )
            Invert_My_Item( old_item, menu_rect_ptr );
```

```
   if ( selected_item != old_item )
   {
      Invert_My_Item( selected_item, menu_rect_ptr );
      *which_item_ptr = selected_item;
   }
}

else if ( old_item > 0 )
{
   Invert_My_Item( old_item, menu_rect_ptr );
   *which_item_ptr = 0;
}
}


//_____
//                            invert a single menu item

void  Invert_My_Item( short  item_number,
                      Rect   *menu_rect_ptr )
{
   Rect    the_rect;
   short   item_height;

   item_height = MENU_PAT_HEIGHT + ( 2 * TOP_BOT_SPACE );

   the_rect = *menu_rect_ptr;

   the_rect.top += ( ( item_number - 1 ) * item_height );
   the_rect.bottom = the_rect.top + item_height;

   InvertRect( &the_rect );
}
```

BUILDING THE MDEF CODE RESOURCE

To create an MDEF resource you'll first create a project file, just as you would for an application. Next, you'll add the MDEF source code file to the project, along with the appropriate libraries. Then, turning the source code into an MDEF resource is simply a matter of telling your development environment that you want it to generate a code resource rather than an application. Your compiler will then create an MDEF resource and place it in its own resource file. Figure 1.18 shows the MyMDEF code resource in a resource file named MyMDEF.rsrc.

Your compiler will let you specify whether the resource file should be one that gets launched by Apple's ResEdit resource editor or Mathemaesthetics Resorcerer resource editor. A file type of rsrc and a creator of RSED tells the compiler to place the MDEF in a ResEdit file. If you instead specify a file type of RSRC and a creator of Doug, the MDEF will end up in a Resorcerer file. Use the file type and creator that match the resource editor you use.

The resource file serves as a storage area for the MDEF resource. To use this code resource you'll copy the MDEF from this file and paste it into the resource fork of any application that needs to use it. This chapter concludes by describing how to create a simple application to test the MDEF resource.

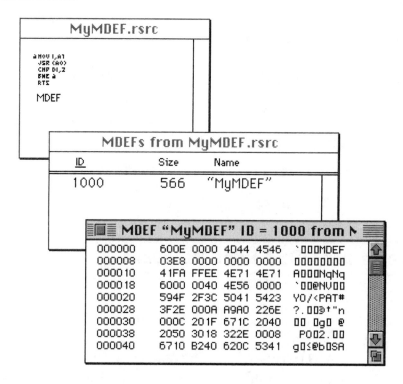

FIGURE 1.18 AN MDEF CODE RESOURCE GETS SAVED TO A RESOURCE FILE.

You will find the project file and source code file for this chapter's example on the included disk. As with all of the code presented in this book, the disk holds two versions of the example—one for CodeWarrior users and another for Symantec users. The preference settings of each project file are set according to the following descriptions.

Building with CodeWarrior

If you use CodeWarrior, launch the Metrowerks C/C++ 68K compiler and create a new project. Give the project a descriptive name such as MyMDEF.µ. Then add the MyMDEF.c source code file, along with the MacOS.lib library. Figure 1.19 shows what your project file will look like.

File	Code	Data		
▽ **Sources**	0	0		▾
MyMDEF.c	0	0	•	▸
MacOS.lib	0	0		▸
2 file(s)	0	0		

FIGURE 1.19 THE PROJECT WINDOW FOR A METROWERKS CODEWARRIOR MDEF CODE RESOURCE.

 If you're compiling with the Metrowerks PowerPC compiler, use the three standard PPC libraries—MWCRuntime.Lib, MathLib, and InterfaceLib—in place of the MacOS.lib library.

NOTE

Before compiling, you'll want to tell the compiler to generate a code resource rather than an application. Select **Preferences** from the Edit menu and click on the Project icon to display the Project panel. Use the pop-up menu to set the Project Type to Code Resource, as I've done in Figure 1.20. Then fill in the edit boxes as shown in Figure 1.20.

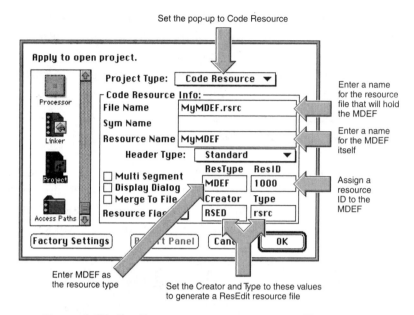

Set the pop-up to Code Resource

Enter a name
for the resource
file that will hold
the MDEF

Enter a name
for the MDEF
itself

Assign a
resource
ID to the
MDEF

Enter MDEF as
the resource type

Set the Creator and Type to these values
to generate a ResEdit resource file

FIGURE 1.20 THE PROJECT PANEL SETTINGS FOR A METROWERKS
CODEWARRIOR MDEF CODE RESOURCE.

Next, click on the Processor icon to display the Processor Info panel. Use
the Code Model pop-up menu to select the Small code model. The other
options in this menu are Smart and Large. For all code resources, you'll
use the Small code model.

Dismiss the Preferences dialog box by clicking in its **OK** button. Then
select **Make** from the Project menu. After just a couple of seconds, the
build will complete, and you'll have a new resource file in the folder that
holds the MyMDEF.µ project.

Building with Symantec C++/THINK C

If you work with Symantec C++ or THINK, launch the THINK Project
Manager and create a new project. Give the project a name that associ-
ates it with your source code, such as MyMDEF.π. Next, add the
MyMDEF.c source code file and the MacTraps library to the project.
Figure 1.21 shows the project window for a Symantec project.

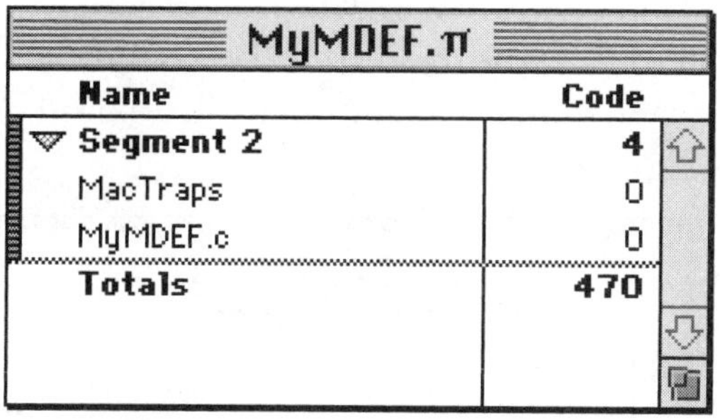

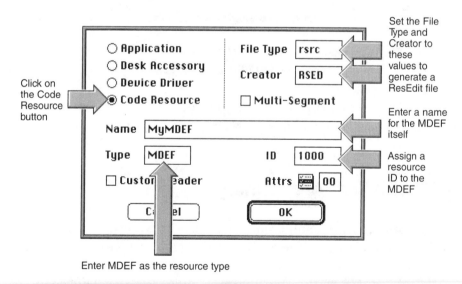

FIGURE 1.21 THE PROJECT WINDOW FOR A SYMANTEC **MDEF** CODE RESOURCE.

Before you compile the MyMDEF code you'll want to tell the THINK Project Manager to generate a code resource rather than an application. Select **Set Project Type** from the Project menu. Click on the **Code Resource** radio button in the dialog box that appears. Then fill in the edit boxes as I've done in Figure 1.22.

FIGURE 1.22 THE SET PROJECT TYPE SETTINGS FOR A SYMANTEC **MDEF** CODE RESOURCE.

Dismiss the dialog box by clicking in its **OK** button. Then choose **Build Code Resource** from the Project menu. The THINK Project Manager will compile the MDEF.c code. Then it will present a dialog box that allows you to enter a name for the resource file to which the MDEF code resource will be saved. Enter a name that will remind you that this is a resource file (see Figure 1.23).

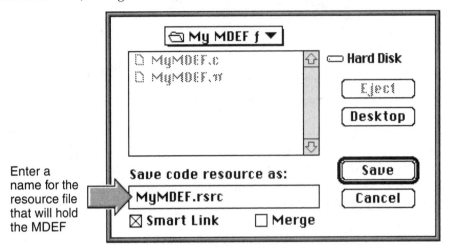

Enter a name for the resource file that will hold the MDEF

FIGURE 1.23 THE SYMANTEC DIALOG BOX FOR NAMING THE RESOURCE FILE THAT WILL HOLD THE **MDEF** CODE RESOURCE.

After clicking the dialog box **Save** button, you'll have a new resource file in the same folder that contains the MyMDEF.π project.

THE **MDEF** TEST APPLICATION

A code resource isn't stand-alone code, that is, you can't double-click a code resource to execute it. Instead, a code resource such as an MDEF is used by an application. So to test a code resource you'll need a simple Mac application that uses that resource. This chapters ends with just such a program. Because the code will look similar to the code for other simple Macintosh programs you've seen in the past, I'll keep the walk-through of it to a minimum. Instead, I'll concentrate on how the test application makes use of the MDEF code resource.

What the Test Application Does

This chapter, and the next few chapters that follow, include a test application named MyTestApp. This chapter's version of MyTestApp displays four menus, but only one will be of interest. The Fill menu will be used to test the MyMDEF menu definition procedure. When a user clicks on the Fill menu, the MDEF developed in this chapter will control the menu, not the system MDEF.

MyTestApp begins by displaying a window with a framed rectangle drawn in it. A click on the Fill menu displays a menu with five patterns in it. Selecting any one pattern has the effect of filling the framed rectangle with that pattern. Figure 1.24 shows how the program looks as a Fill menu selection is being made, and after.

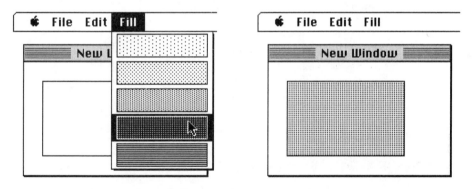

FIGURE 1.24 THE TEST APPLICATION RESPONDS TO A MENU SELECTION IN THE MENU CONTROLLED BY THE MYMDEF CODE RESOURCE.

The Test Application Resources

You know all about the few resources that are in every Macintosh program, so you may be tempted to skim or skip this section. Don't! You'll want to do a few nontraditional things to the MyTestApp project resource file to ensure that the Fill menu works correctly.

First, create four MENU resources. The File menu will be used to quit the application, and the Fill menu will be used to test the MDEF. The MyTestApp application won't be concerned with the Apple menu and the Edit menu. Figure 1.25 shows the four MENU resources.

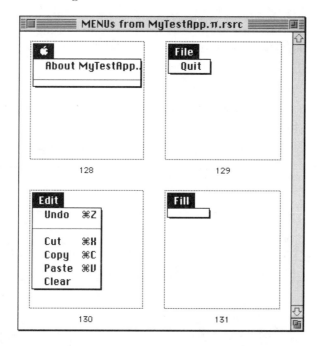

FIGURE 1.25 THE MENU RESOURCES FOR THE TEST APPLICATION PROJECT.

Before moving on to other resources, double-click on MENU 131—the Fill menu. When you do, you'll see the MENU editor shown in Figure 1.26.

When you open a MENU resource you'll see that ResEdit has added a new menu to its menu bar—a menu titled MENU. Select **Edit Menu & MDEF ID** from that menu. Now, perform the very important step of changing the MDEF ID value from 0 to 1000. This MDEF ID value must match the value of the MDEF resource that you'll be copying into the compiled MyTestApp application. I gave the MyMDEF MDEF code resource an ID of 1000, so that's the value I need to enter for this MENU resource's MDEF ID. Figure 1.27 emphasizes this point.

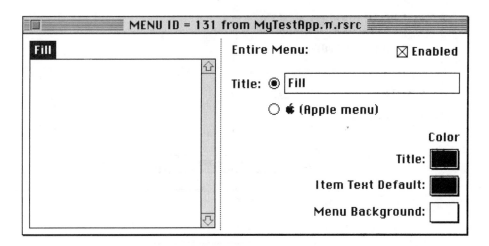

FIGURE 1.26 THE **MENU** RESOURCE FOR THE MENU THAT WILL BE CONTROLLED BY THE **MYMDEF** CODE RESOURCE.

If you forget to perform this step, the Fill menu will not work in the MyTestApp application!

T I P

The MDEF ID values of the other three menus should each keep the value of 0 that ResEdit assigned them. Only the Fill menu will be using the custom MDEF.

Next, create an MBAR resource and add the four MENU resource IDs to it. Make sure the order of the IDs matches the order I've used in Figure 1.28.

Finally, add a WIND resource. This resource will define the window that holds the patterned rectangle that gets drawn by the Fill menu. The size and type of window that you define by the WIND resource isn't critical.

Please enter the Menu ID and the resource ID of the MDEF to be used below.
Menu ID: 131
MDEF ID: 1000
Cancel
OK
MyMDEF.rsrc
MDEF
IDEFs from MyMDEF.rsrc
Size
Name
1000
566
"MyMDEF"

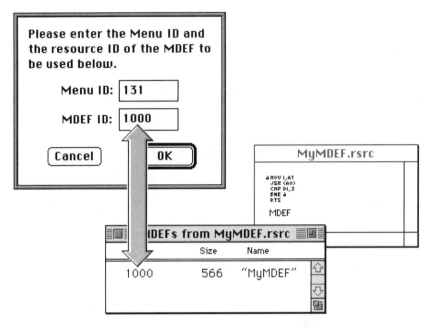

FIGURE 1.27 THE MDEF ID MUST BE SET TO THE ID OF THE MDEF CODE RESOURCE.

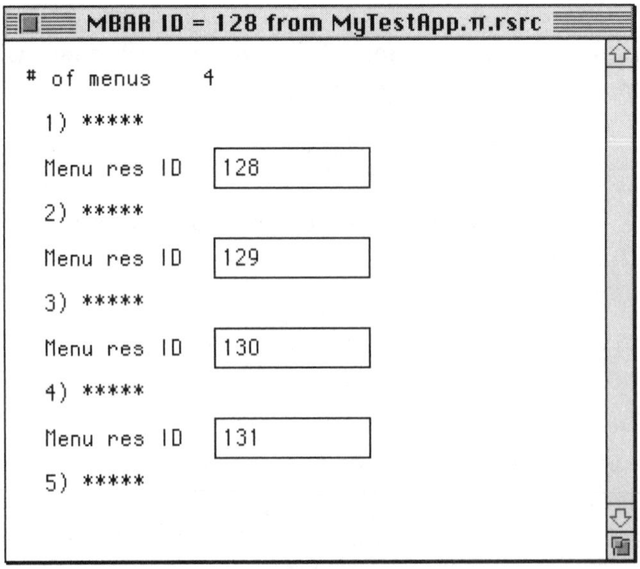

MBAR ID = 128 from MyTestApp.π.rsrc
# of menus 4
1) *****
Menu res ID 128
2) *****
Menu res ID 129
3) *****
Menu res ID 130
4) *****
Menu res ID 131
5) *****

FIGURE 1.28 THE MBAR RESOURCE FOR THE TEST APPLICATION PROJECT.

The Test Application Source Code

As mentioned, there's nothing fancy about the MyTestApp source code. A look at the function prototypes and the #define directives will provide a good preview of what's in store.

```
//_____
//                                              function prototypes

void   Initialize_Toolbox( void );
void   Set_Up_Menu_Bar( void );
void   Open_Window( void );
void   Handle_One_Event( void );
void   Handle_Mouse_Down( EventRecord * );
void   Handle_Menu_Choice( long );
void   Handle_Apple_Choice( short );
void   Handle_File_Choice( short );
void   Handle_Fill_Choice( short );
void   Update_Window( WindowPtr );


//_____
//                                              #define directives

#define      MENU_BAR_ID          128
#define      APPLE_MENU_ID        128
#define         SHOW_ABOUT_ITEM     1
#define      FILE_MENU_ID         129
#define         QUIT_ITEM           1
#define      EDIT_MENU_ID         130
#define      FILL_MENU_ID         131

#define      WIND_ID             128

#define      SYS_PAT_LIST_OFFSET  20
```

MyTestApp uses three global variables. All_Done signals that the program should quit. Pattern_Index holds an index into the system pattern list and is used to keep track of the pattern that is currently being used to draw and update the rectangle in the program's window. Pat_Rect defines the coordinates of the rectangle that gets filled with a pattern.

```
//_____
//                                     global variables

Boolean   All_Done = false;
short     Pattern_Index;
Rect      Pat_Rect;
```

The main() function performs standard initializations, displays the menu bar, opens a window, then loops until the program terminates.

```
//_____
//                                            main()

void  main( void )
{
   Initialize_Toolbox();
   Set_Up_Menu_Bar();
   Open_Window();

   while ( All_Done == false )
      Handle_One_Event();
}
```

Initialize_Toolbox() and Set_Up_Menu_Bar() take care of setting up the application. Both functions should look familar to Mac programmers.

```
//_____
//                                     initialize the Mac

void  Initialize_Toolbox( void )
{
   InitGraf( &qd.thePort );
   InitFonts();
   InitWindows();
   InitMenus();
   TEInit();
   InitDialogs( 0L );
   FlushEvents( everyEvent, 0L );
   InitCursor();
}
```

```
//_____
//                               set up menu bar and menus

void  Set_Up_Menu_Bar( void )
```

```
{
   Handle      menu_bar_handle;
   MenuHandle  apple_menu;

   menu_bar_handle = GetNewMBar( MENU_BAR_ID );

   SetMenuBar( menu_bar_handle );
   DisposHandle( menu_bar_handle );

   apple_menu = GetMHandle( APPLE_MENU_ID );
   AddResMenu( apple_menu, 'DRVR' );

   DrawMenuBar();
}
```

The Open_Window( ) function does just what its name says. It also sets up the coordinates for the rectangle that will be drawn to the window and gives Pattern_Index an initial value. SYS_PAT_LIST_OFFSET is a #define that is set to a value of 20. That means the pattern that is initially used will be the twentieth in the system pattern list. Pattern twenty happens to be a solid white pattern. When the rectangle is initially drawn (a little later), it will be filled with white. As you'll see a little later, the value of Pattern_Index changes when a selection is made from the Fill menu.

```
//_____
//                                     open a display window
void  Open_Window( void )
{
   WindowPtr  the_window;

   the_window = GetNewWindow( WIND_ID, 0L, (WindowPtr)-1L );
   ShowWindow( the_window );
   SetPort( the_window );

   SetRect( &Pat_Rect, 20, 20, 150, 100 );
   Pattern_Index = SYS_PAT_LIST_OFFSET;
}
```

Handle_One_Event( ) is called repeatedly from main( ). It uses a call to WaitNextEvent( ) to retrieve information about the most current event. A switch statement then calls the proper function to handle the event.

```
//_____
//                                    handle single event

void  Handle_One_Event( void )
{
   EventRecord  the_event;

   WaitNextEvent( everyEvent, &the_event, 15L, 0L );

   switch ( the_event.what )
   {
      case mouseDown:
         Handle_Mouse_Down( &the_event );
         break;

      case updateEvt:
         Update_Window( (WindowPtr)the_event.message );
         break;
   }
}
```

A mouseDown event is handled in the standard fashion by the
Handle_Mouse_Down( ) function.

```
//_____
//                                    handle a click of the mouse

void  Handle_Mouse_Down( EventRecord *the_event )
{
   WindowPtr    window;
   short        the_part;
   long         menu_choice;

   the_part = FindWindow ( the_event->where, &window );

   switch ( the_part )
   {
      case inMenuBar:
         menu_choice = MenuSelect( the_event->where );
         Handle_Menu_Choice( menu_choice );
         break;

      case inSysWindow:
         SystemClick ( the_event, window );
         break;

      case inDrag:
```

```
        DragWindow( window, the_event->where,
                    &qd.screenBits.bounds );
        break;
    }
}
```

A mouse click in the menu bar sends the program to Handle_Menu_ Choice(). This routine relies on three subroutines to do the actual handling of a click on either the Apple, File, or Fill menus. A click on the Edit menu will drop down the Edit menu, but any menu selections will be ignored.

```
//_____
//                              handle a click on a menu
void  Handle_Menu_Choice( long  menu_choice )
{
    short  the_menu;
    short  the_menu_item;

    if ( menu_choice != 0 )
    {
        the_menu = HiWord( menu_choice );
        the_menu_item = LoWord( menu_choice );

        switch ( the_menu )
        {
            case APPLE_MENU_ID:
                Handle_Apple_Choice( the_menu_item );
                break;

            case FILE_MENU_ID:
                Handle_File_Choice( the_menu_item );
                break;

            case EDIT_MENU_ID:
                break;

            case FILL_MENU_ID:
                Handle_Fill_Choice( the_menu_item );
        }
        HiliteMenu(0);
    }
}
```

The handling of menu selections from the Apple menu and the File menu is done in the same way that you've seen done in numerous Mac applications.

```
//_____
//                                  handle a click in the Apple menu

void  Handle_Apple_Choice( short the_item )
{
    Str255      desk_acc_name;
    int         desk_acc_number;
    MenuHandle  apple_menu;

    switch ( the_item )
    {
        case SHOW_ABOUT_ITEM:
            SysBeep( 5 );
            break;

        default:
            apple_menu = GetMHandle( APPLE_MENU_ID );
            GetItem( apple_menu, the_item, desk_acc_name );
            desk_acc_number = OpenDeskAcc( desk_acc_name );
            break;
    }
}


//_____
//                                  handle a click in the File menu

void  Handle_File_Choice( short the_item )
{
    switch ( the_item )
    {
        case QUIT_ITEM:
            All_Done = true;
            break;
    }
}
```

In response to a menu selection from the Fill menu, MyTestApp ends up at Handle_Fill_Choice(). The menu definition procedure code that appears in the MyMDEF MDEF takes care of the display of the Fill menu and the highlighting of its menu items. But it doesn't actually perform any tasks once a menu selection is made; that is up to your application. For this test program I've decided that a selection from the Fill menu will result in the filling of a rectangle with the same pattern that is pictured in the Fill menu item.

Handle_Fill_Choice() is aware of which menu item was selected—the item number is in the variable named item. I will use that value, and the SYS_PAT_LIST_OFFSET to set the value of the global variable Pattern_Index to the proper index into the system pattern list. Then, a call to EraseRect() clears the window and a call to InvalRect() marks the window's port rectangle as invalid. That tells the Window Manager that the window needs updating. The system then generates an updateEvt.

```
//_____
//                              handle a click in the Fill menu

void  Handle_Fill_Choice( short item )
{
   WindowPtr  window;

   window = FrontWindow();

   Pattern_Index = SYS_PAT_LIST_OFFSET + item;

   EraseRect( &window->portRect );
   InvalRect( &window->portRect );
}
```

What happens when the system generates the updateEvt? The next call to WaitNextEvent() will send the program to the Update_Window() function. This routine gets the proper pattern from the system pattern list and then uses this pattern to fill the rectangle defined by the global variable Pat_Rect.

```
//_____
//                              update the window in response to updateEvt


void  Update_Window( WindowPtr window )
```

```
{
    Pattern  the_pat;

    BeginUpdate( window );
        GetIndPattern( &the_pat, sysPatListID, Pattern_Index );
        FillRect( &Pat_Rect, &the_pat );
        FrameRect( &Pat_Rect );
    EndUpdate( window );
}
```

That is it for the test application source code. You can see that most of the code supports the basic functioning of Mac program. Very little new code is needed to actually test the MDEF itself.

With the source code entered, the next step is to build the stand-alone application. After that, I'll quit my development environment and return to the desktop.

The last thing I'll want to do is copy the MDEF code resource from its own resource file and paste it into the MyTestApp application. I'll launch a resource editor and open both the MDEF code resource file and the MyTestApp application. Note that I'm opening the application itself, not the MyTestApp.π.rsrc file. Then I'll perform the **Copy** and **Paste**. When complete, the screen looks like Figure 1.29.

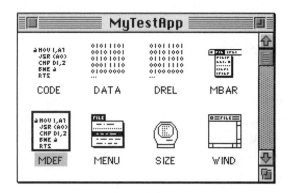

FIGURE 1.29 THE RESULT OF PASTING THE MDEF CODE RESOURC
INTO THE APPLICATION'S RESOURCE FORK.

Some of the resources in your MyTestApp program may differ from those shown in Figure 1.29. That's because the Symantec compiler and the CodeWarrior compiler each add

N O T E   **one or two different resources during their build processes.**

There's nothing more to do to get the MDEF to work—just launch the MyTestApp application, move the mouse over the Fill menu, and click!

CHAPTER SUMMARY

The look and behavior of all Macintosh menus is provided by MDEF resources. Unless instructed to do otherwise, the Menu Manager uses the system 0 MDEF. To give a menu its own unique look you can write menu definition procedure code. You'll then use your development environment to compile that source code and save it in a resource file as an MDEF code resource.

Besides providing a menu that has a look and functionality not normally supported by a Mac application, an MDEF resource provides the added benefit of being reusable. You can paste a copy of an MDEF resource into any number of applications to provide each program with the use of the MDEF code.

Chapter

2

CUSTOM CONTROLS AND THE CDEF

The Macintosh Toolbox, along with a graphical resource editor, makes the creation, display, and handling of standard controls such as push buttons, radio buttons, and check boxes an easy task for Mac programmers. While these standard controls suffice for most purposes, they don't provide the slick look that both programmers and users have come to expect from the computer that set the standards for how a graphical user interface should look. The Mac applications that look the most professional and are the most compelling to use usually have controls that have the look of dials, three-dimensional buttons, and sliders. Most Mac programmers are surprised—and disappointed—when they learn that these types of controls are not readily supported by the Macintosh Toolbox.

While fancy controls of the types just mentioned can't be created as readily as standard controls, they can be created and brought to life with just a little extra programming effort. And once you know the technique for creating one new type of control, you'll find that it becomes relatively easy to create all sorts of fancy, unique controls that will give your applications a custom look.

Chapter 1 introduced you to code resources—in the form of the MDEF resource. In this chapter you'll learn about a second type of code resource—the CDEF resource. Your understanding of the MDEF code resource, the menu definition procedure, and how the MENU resource specifies an MDEF resource will be important as you read this chapter. That's because each of these menu-related concepts has an analogous control-related concept.

In this chapter you'll see how a CDEF can be used to create custom controls that use pictures as buttons. The techniques discussed in this chapter will apply not only to picture buttons, but to sliders—the topics covered in Chapter 3.

THE CDEF AND CONTROL DEFINITION FUNCTION

Mac programmers are familiar with the look of standard controls such as check boxes, radio buttons, and push buttons—they're shown in Figure 2.1. With the introduction of System 7 came a few changes to the Mac graphical user interface—there's more and better shading in windows, for instance. Controls such as buttons and check boxes, however, were not changed from System 6 to System 7.

Just as standard menus are given their look and feel by an MDEF code resource found in the System file, so too are standard controls given their properties by resource code found in the System file. For standard controls such as push buttons, check boxes, and radio buttons, this code is supplied in a *control definition function* that's kept in a System file CDEF with a resource ID of 0.

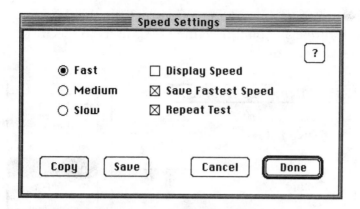

FIGURE 2.1 A DIALOG BOX WITH STANDARD CONTROLS IN IT.

Setting the CDEF ID of a CNTL Resource

In Chapter 1, you saw that a MENU resource specifies which MDEF code resource will control the menu defined by the MENU resource. Controls follow this same organization. When you create standard controls in a DITL resource by using the floating palette that accompanies the DITL—as in Figure 2.2—your resource editor will specify that each of those controls be handled by the system's CDEF.

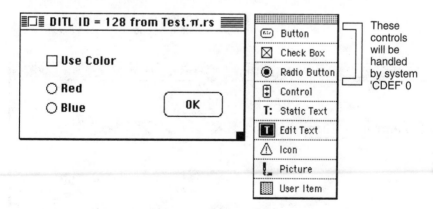

FIGURE 2.2 STANDARD CONTROLS CAN BE ADDED TO A DIALOG BOX USING A **DITL** RESOURCE.

If you create a control by adding a Control from the floating palette—as shown in Figure 2.3—you'll have the opportunity to specify which CDEF should handle that control.

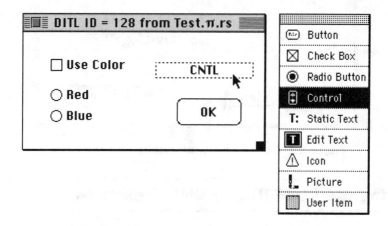

FIGURE 2.3 ADDING WHAT WILL BE A CUSTOM CONTROL TO A DITL.

In ResEdit, double-clicking on the newly added control will open a window like the one shown in Figure 2.4. In this window, the ID of a CNTL resource that holds information about the new control can be entered.

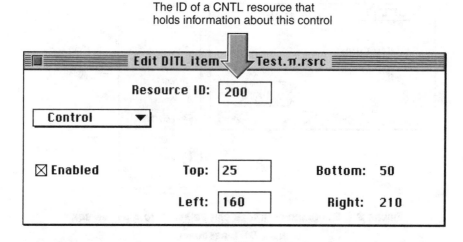

FIGURE 2.4 A CUSTOM CONTROL SPECIFIES THE ID OF THE CNTL RESOURCE IT USES.

One of the key pieces of information that is held in a CNTL resource is the ID of the CDEF that will handle controls based on the CNTL resource. Figure 2.5 shows the trail from a Control DITL item to the CNTL resource item and then to the CDEF item.

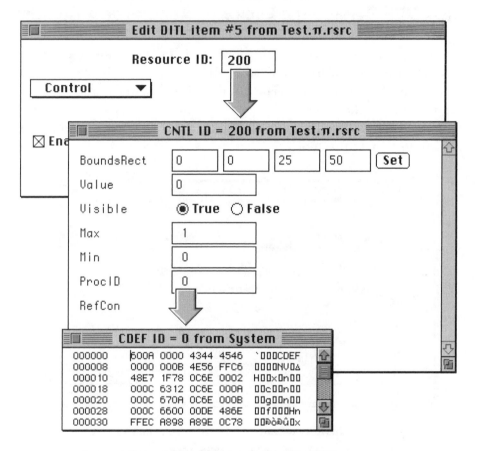

FIGURE 2.5 A CUSTOM CONTROL SPECIFIES A CNTL RESOURCE,
WHICH IN TURN SPECIFIES A CDEF RESOURCE.

To create a custom control you'll first write a control definition function and use your compiler to save that code to a CDEF code resource. Then, in the resource file of an application project, you'll create a CNTL resource with a ProcID that includes the resource ID of your CDEF. Finally, as you add items to a DITL resource in the resource file of the application project, you'll make one of those items a Control item defined by your CNTL resource.

THE CDEF DEFINES THE LOOK AND ACTIONS OF A CONTROL

A developer creates a custom control when he or she is not satisfied with the look or actions of the standard controls that are available as part of the Macintosh user interface. For instance, if you want to give the interface to your programs a more three dimensional look, you can begin by defining your own types of controls. Figure 2.6 shows how your own controls could achieve this look.

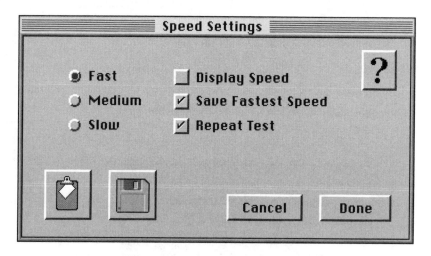

FIGURE 2.6 CUSTOM CONTROLS ALLOW AN APPLICATION TO GIVE ITS DIALOG BOXES A UNIQUE LOOK.

Dials and sliders offer a range of settings rather than the on/off settings of buttons. Sliders are the controls that add the most graphical look to a Mac program—yet they are a type of control that are seldom, if ever, used by the average programmer. That's because aside from the scroll bar, sliders don't exist as a predefined control type—as buttons and check boxes do. Figure 2.7 provides a representative sample of the types of sliders you'll be able to add to your Mac programs after reading this chapter and Chapter 3.

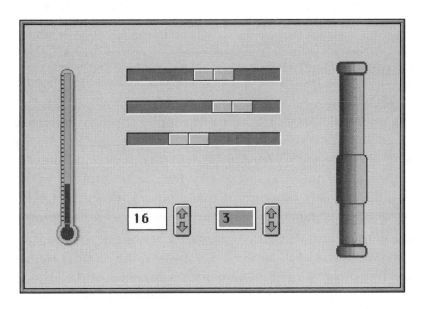

FIGURE 2.7 TYPICAL CUSTOM SLIDERS THAT CAN BE CREATED USING CDEF CODE RESOURCES.

In this chapter and the next I'll develop two controls—a new type of button and a slider—using CDEF resources. And, as I did for the MDEF, after creating the CDEF resources I can easily copy them into more than one program.

THE CDEF SOURCE CODE

In this section I'll develop a CDEF that consists of a control definition function that uses pictures in place of standard buttons. The pictures that define what a button looks like won't actually be a part of the CDEF. Instead, the CDEF will rely on PICT resources that are in the application's resource fork. That keeps the CDEF generic enough for it to be usable by any application.

The CDEF code won't place any limits on the size or color level of the pictures. That means I can use a graphics program to draw a set of pictures and, after pasting the pictures into the resource file of an application project, use those pictures as a button.

The Control Definition Function Entry Point

Mouse clicks on a control tell the Control Manager to execute the code definition function associated with that control. If you've defined a control based on a CNTL resource with a `ProcID` other than 0, the Control Manager won't use the system control definition function. Instead, it will look in the application's resource fork for the appropriate CDEF and execute the `main()` function of that code resource. As it is for the MDEF, the `main()` function is the entry point into a CDEF resource.

The entry point to a CDEF is a callback routine, so its header needs to begin with the `pascal` keyword. For a CDEF, the `main()` routine has a return type of `long` and four parameters—as shown in this example:

```
pascal long  main( short          var_code,
                   ControlHandle  the_control,
                   short          message,
                   long           msg_param )
```

As it was for the MDEF, the CDEF `message` parameter is a constant that tells `main()` what type of action needs to be handled. The `message` parameter can take on any one of the 11 Apple-defined constants listed here.

drawCntl	Draw the control to a dialog box or window
testCntl	Test to see if cursor is over control
calcRgns	Calculate control's region (24-bit systems)
initCntl	Initialize the control
dispCntl	Dispose the control
posCntl	Position control's indicator, update settings
thumbCntl	Calculate dragging indicator parameters

`dragCntl`	Handle dragging of control or indicator
`autoTrack`	Invoke control's action procedure
`calcCntlRgn`	Calculate control's region (32-bit systems)
`calcThumbRgn`	Calculate indicator's region

The body of a CDEF `main()` routine is similar to that of an MDEF `main()`: it examines the value of the `message` parameter and invokes a routine that specifically handles the action. Here's the shell of a CDEF `main()` for a control definition function that could be made to handle each of the possible `message` values:

```
pascal long  main( short         var_code,
                   ControlHandle the_control,
                   short         message,
                   long          msg_param )

{
   long  return_val = 0L;

   switch( message )
   {
      case drawCntl:
         // each case would invoke a routine
         // to handle one type of message
         break;
      case testCntl:
         break;
      case calcCRgns:
         break;
      case initCntl:
         break;
      case dispCntl:
         break;
      case posCntl:
         break;
      case thumbCntl:
         break;
      case dragCntl:
         break;
      case autoTrack:
         break;
      case calcCntlRgn:
         break;
```

```
        case calcThumbRgn:
            break;
        default:
            break;
    }
    return ( return_val );
}
```

Fortunately, controls defined by most CDEF code resources won't need to
respond to each type of message. You can see by the description of the
message constants that many of the messages make sense only for controls
that act as dials or sliders. For instance, this section's MyButtonCDEF
example control definition function, which works with buttons, will only
need to handle two types of messages: testCtl and drawCtl. Here's a
look at the main() function for MyButtonCDEF:

```
pascal long  main( short          var_code,
                   ControlHandle  the_control,
                   short          message,
                   long           msg_param )

{
    long   return_val = 0L;

    switch( message )
    {
        case testCntl:
            return_val = Test_Control( the_control, msg_param );
            break;

        case drawCntl:
            Draw_Control( the_control );
            break;

        default:
            break;
    }

    return ( return_val );
}
```

The first parameter to main(), var_code, is used only for CDEF
resources that support multiple variations of a single control. This para-

meter will be ignored in the MyButtonCDEF, but will be used in Chapter 3 in an example that supports control variations.

The second parameter to `main()`, `the_control`, is a handle to the control record of the control receiving the action. Various routines in the CDEF will examine fields of the control record before operating on the control.

The final `main()` parameter, `msg-param`, is a `short` that holds additional information about the message sent to `main()`. The exact meaning of `msg_param` is dependent on the type of message sent to `main()`.

Taking Care of the Preliminaries

The MyButtonCDEF source code has a single `#include` directive used to bring the GestaltEqu.h header file into the source code:

```
#include <GestaltEqu.h>
```

The CDEF code will use two of four pictures in the display of a single button. If the Macintosh using the CDEF is a color system, one pair of pictures will be used. If the Mac is monochrome (or color, but set to display only black and white), the CDEF will use a different pair of pictures. Because a call to `Gestalt()` will be used in determining the color level, or bit depth, of the Mac, I'll need to include the GestaltEqu.h header file.

Since I've brought up the topic of using multiple pictures for a single button, now is as good a time as any to elaborate. A button control has two states: its normal state and a depressed state. When the cursor is not over a control, or when it is over a control but the mouse button is not pressed, the control is in its normal state. When the mouse button is pressed while the cursor is over a control, the control is in its depressed state—it appears to be pressed down. For a standard button, the depressed state inverts the button. Figure 2.8 shows a button in both states.

If MyButtonCDEF only worked with black and white buttons, only two pictures would be needed for a single control—one for each of the control's two states. Since MyButtonCDEF is much more user-friendly than that—it supports both color and monochrome systems—it requires four pictures for each control. One pair will be used if the CDEF detects a color system, and the second pair will be used for a monochrome system.

MyButtonCDEF uses two constants to aid in determining which picture the CDEF should display:

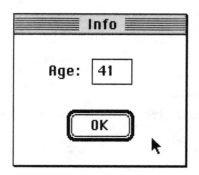 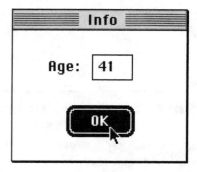

FIGURE 2.8 BUTTONS HAVE TWO STATES: ON THE LEFT IS THE NORMAL STATE, ON THE RIGHT IS THE DEPRESSED, OR DOWN, STATE.

```
#define      DOWN_OFFSET      1
#define      BW_OFFSET        2
```

Figure 2.9 shows the four pictures that have been drawn for a typical button. You'll want to refer to this figure as you read the following discussion. The CDEF considers the picture that will be used for a button in the normal, or up, state on a color system as the base picture. Whatever its ID is, the color picture representing a depressed, or down, button should have an ID one greater. The constant DOWN_OFFSET represents this difference. The picture that will be used as the up button on a monochrome system should have an ID two greater than the base picture ID. The BW_OFFSET constant is used to represent this value. Finally, the monochrome down picture should have an ID three greater than the base picture. That means it will have a value one greater than the monochrome up picture. Again, DOWN_OFFSET will be used for specifying this picture.

Button up, color
(base picture)

Button up, black and white
(base picture + 2)

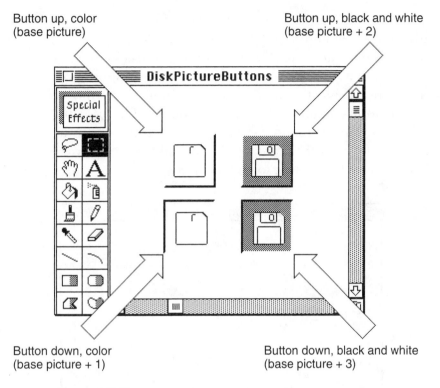

Button down, color
(base picture + 1)

Button down, black and white
(base picture + 3)

FIGURE 2.9 FOUR PICTURES WILL BE USED FOR ANY ONE BUTTON.

To create pictures that are usable by the CDEF, the four drawn buttons should be individually copied from the graphics program in which they were rendered and pasted into an application project's resource file. Assuming that I'll be using the pictures in an application named Test, I'd paste the pictures in the Test.π.rsrc file. Figure 2.10 shows how four typically numbered PICT resources would look. While the selection of an ID for the base PICT is not important, the consecutive numbering of the four PICT resources is crucial.

MyButtonCDEF has three additional constants that it defines:

```
#define       CNTRL_INACTIVE        255
#define       CNTRL_INVISIBLE         0
#define       SYS_GRAY_PAT_INDEX      4
```

To mark a control as inactive the `contrlHilite` field of the control's control record should be set to a value of 255. That tells the Control Manager to dim the control and ignore mouse clicks over that control. Since the MyButtonCDEF will be responsible for drawing and handling a picture button control, it will also be responsible for graying out the button and ignoring mouse clicks to it. The constant `CNTRL_INACTIVE` will be used for these purposes. If a picture button is inactive, the `SYS_GRAY_PAT_INDEX` constant will be used to superimpose a gray pattern over the picture button to give it a dim appearance.

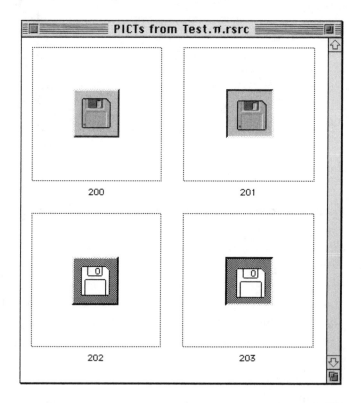

FIGURE 2.10 THE FOUR PICTURES WILL BECOME PICT RESOURCES.

A control can be set to visible or invisible by altering the value of the control's `contrlVis` field. A value of 0 tells the Control Manager to completely cover the control with the background pattern of the window or dialog box in which the control resides. The `CNTRL_INVISIBLE` constant will be used to determine if a picture button is visible.

The MyButtonCDEF consists of just four functions—their prototypes are shown below. `Draw_Control()` does the actual drawing of the control and `Test_Control()` checks to see if a mouse click occurred in the control. `Color_Is_On()` is a utility routine that determines if the user's machine has a color monitor, and `Dim_Item()` is a second utility routine that handles the dimming of a picture button.

```
void     Draw_Control( ControlHandle );
long     Test_Control( ControlHandle, long );
Boolean  Color_Is_On( Rect );
void     Dim_Item( Rect );
```

Handling a testCntl Message

When a mouse click may affect a control, the Control Manager will send a `testCntl` message to the `main()` function of the CDEF code. For a `testCntl` message, the value of the `msg_param` variable becomes important because it holds the local coordinates of the cursor. The `main()` function should send this information, along with the handle to the control, to a routine that determines if the cursor is over a control governed by the CDEF code. For MyButtonCDEF, that routine is named `Test_Control()`. Here's the call to `Test_Control()`, as made from the `main()` function of the CDEF:

```
case testCntl:
   return_val = Test_Control( the_control, msg_param );
   break;
```

Here's the header for `Test_Control()`:

```
long  Test_Control( ControlHandle control, long mouse_loc )
```

`Test_Control()` receives the `msg_param` as a `long` variable, not as a `Point`. The function begins by extracting the coordinates of the mouse location from this `long` variable:

```
Point   the_point;

the_point.v = HiWord( mouse_loc );
the_point.h = LoWord( mouse_loc );
```

Next, Test_Control() sets a local variable to the size of the control rectangle. That information is found in the contrlRect field of the control record:

```
Rect    the_rect;

the_rect = (**control).contrlRect;
```

Then it's a simple matter of comparing the coordinates of the cursor with the coordinates of the rectangle that bounds the control. If the point representing the cursor position is in the rectangle, the cursor is over the picture button control:

```
if ( PtInRect( the_point, &the_rect ) )
   return ( inButton );
else
   return ( 0 );
```

If the PtInRect() test passes, Test_Control() returns a value of inButton to main(). This Apple-defined constant is a part code that designates that the mouse is pressed while over a button. Let's jump back to the body of main() to see what's going on. After Test_Control() executes, return_val will have a value of inButton if the mouse was pressed in the control, or a value of 0 if it wasn't. The main() function ends by returning this value to the Control Manager. The Control Manager will see to it that this value ends up in the contrlHilite field of the picture button's control record:

```
long   return_val = OL;

switch( message )
{
   case drawCntl:
      Draw_Control( the_control );
```

```
      break;

   case testCntl:
      return_val = Test_Control( the_control, msg_param );
      break;

   default:
      break;
}

return ( return_val );
```

Once the value of `return_val` has been stored in the button's control record, the button can be properly updated (drawn), or, if the value is 0, the button will be left as is. If the button is to be updated, the Control Manager will again execute the CDEF—this time passing a `drawCntl` message.

Below is the listing for `Test_Control()`. Notice that before the `PtInRect()` test is made `Test_Control()` checks to see if the control is invisible or inactive. If the control is in either of these states, `Test_Control()` properly concludes that it doesn't matter if the mouse is pressed when the cursor is over the control.

```
long  Test_Control( ControlHandle control, long mouse_loc )
{
   Rect    the_rect;
   Point   the_point;

   if ( (**control).contrlVis == 0 )
      return ( 0 );

   if ( (**control).contrlHilite == 255 )
      return ( 0 );

   the_point.v = HiWord( mouse_loc );
   the_point.h = LoWord( mouse_loc );

   the_rect = (**control).contrlRect;

   if ( PtInRect( the_point, &the_rect ) )
      return ( inButton );
   else
      return ( 0 );
}
```

**Yes, you caught me. I could just as easily combine the intro-
ductory** if **logic in** Test_Control() **into one** if **statement. But I thought that using separate tests would be easier to follow than a single combined statement like this:**

N O T E

```
if ((((**control).contrlVis == CNTRL_INVISIBLE ) ||
     ((**control).contrlHilite == CNTRL_INACTIVE ))
   return ( 0 );
```

Handling a drawCntl Message

The CDEF main() routine receives a drawCntl message anytime the
mouse button is depressed and the user's dragging of the mouse may
affect the state of a control that the CDEF handles. A change in the highlighting of the control will also result in main() receiving a drawCntl
message. In either case, the CDEF will respond by calling its own drawing
routine. For MyButtonCDEF, that routine is named Draw_Control():

```
case drawCntl:
   Draw_Control( the_control );
   break;
```

In order to operate on the proper control, Draw_Control() needs to
receive a handle to the control record of the affected control:

```
void  Draw_Control( ControlHandle control )
```

The first thing the control-drawing function should do is check to see if
the control is visible. A hidden control should not respond to mouse
clicks, and of course should not be drawn. The contrlVis field of the
control holds a value in the range of 0 to 255. A value of 0, or
CNTRL_INVISIBLE, means the control is invisible. If that's the case,
there's no work to be done, and Draw_Control() should terminate:

```
if ( (**control).contrlVis == CNTRL_INVISIBLE )
   return;
```

If the test of `contrlVis` results in the identification of a visible control, `Draw_Control()` should handle the drawing. Before drawing can take place, `Draw_Control()` needs to determine which of the four pictures should be used. To do that, a call to the Toolbox routine `GetControlReference()` is made to get the ID of the base picture:

```
short  pict_ID;
pict_ID = GetControlReference( control );
```

Pass `GetControlReference()` a handle to a control record, and the Toolbox will return the `contrlRfCon` field of that control record. A control record has more than a dozen fields, many of which are filled by a CNTL resource. Earlier in this chapter you saw that when you want a control to be handled by one of your own CDEF code resources, you create a CNTL resource to describe that control. The `RefCon` field of that CNTL resource corresponds to the `contrlRfCon` field of the control record. When loaded into memory, the information in the CNTL resource will be used in filling the control record. The CNTL `RefCon` field can be used by an application for any purpose. I've decided to use it as a holder for the PICT ID of the control's base picture. Figure 2.11 illustrates how this might work.

Once `Draw_Control()` has the ID of the base picture, the routine sets out to determine which of the four pictures should be used. First, the control's boundary rectangle is obtained by examining the `contrlRect` field of the control record:

```
Rect        control_rect;

control_rect = (**control).contrlRect;
```

Next, that rectangle is passed to the utility routine `Color_Is_On()` to determine if the rectangle lies within a monitor that has color turned on. The `Color_Is_On()` function is covered a little later in this section If the rectangle is located in a color monitor, `Color_Is_On()` will return a value of `true`; otherwise it returns a value of `false`. If the monitor is color, I'll leave the value of `pict_ID` alone—it's already set to the base picture ID, which is a color picture. If the monitor is monochrome, I'll add BW_OFFSET to pict_ID to come up with the ID of the first black-and-white picture:

```
if ( Color_Is_On( control_rect ) == false )
   pict_ID += BW_OFFSET;
```

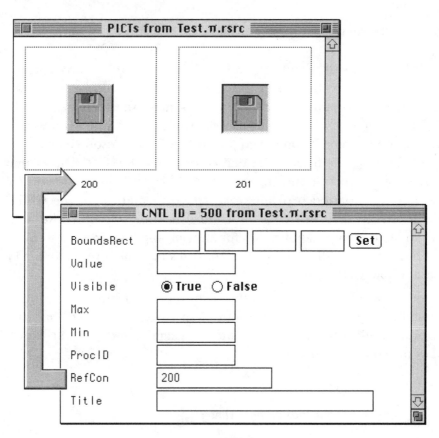

FIGURE 2.11 THE REFCON FIELD OF A CUSTOM CONTROL'S **CNTL** RESOURCE SPECIFIES
THE BASE PICTURE FOR THAT CONTROL.

Now pict_ID holds the ID of either the first color picture or the first black-and-white picture. If the button hasn't been clicked on, I've got the correct picture. If, however, the user has clicked the mouse button and the cursor is over the button, I'll need to add the offset that gives the ID of the down, or depressed, picture. The contrlHilite field of the control record provides this information. You know that if this field has a value of 255, the control is inactive, but this field also provides other information. If it has a value that corresponds to the Apple-defined constant inButton, then the control is active and is currently receiving a mouse press within its boundaries. If that's the case, I'll add DOWN_OFFSET to the value of pict_ID to arrive at the correct picture to use:

```
if ( (**control).contrlHilite == inButton )
   pict_ID += DOWN_OFFSET;
```

A draw routine must handle each of the four conditions for which a picture exists. Figures 2.12 and 2.13 show how Draw_Control() handles two of these four conditions.

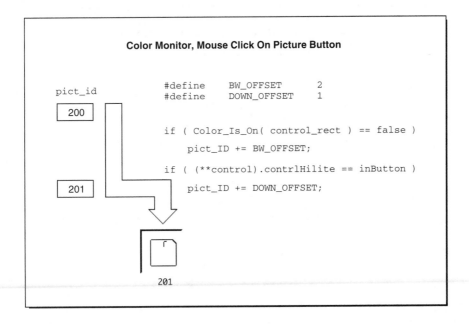

FIGURE 2.12 DRAW_CONTROL() HANDLING A MOUSE CLICK ON A COLOR SYSTEM.

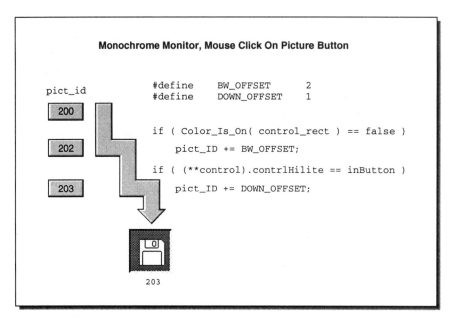

Monochrome Monitor, Mouse Click On Picture Button

```
pict_id                  #define    BW_OFFSET      2
                         #define    DOWN_OFFSET    1

 [ 200 ]
                         if ( Color_Is_On( control_rect ) == false )
 [ 202 ]                     pict_ID += BW_OFFSET;

                         if ( (**control).contrlHilite == inButton )
 [ 203 ]                     pict_ID += DOWN_OFFSET;



                                203
```

**FIGURE 2.13 DRAW_CONTROL() HANDLING A MOUSE CLICK
ON A BLACK-AND-WHITE SYSTEM.**

Once it has been determined which picture should be used, it's a simple matter of calling the Toolbox routine GetResource() to load the correct picture into memory and receive a handle to it. Then a call to the Toolbox function DrawPicture() draws the picture to the rectangle occupied by the control:

```
PicHandle  pict_handle;

pict_handle = (PicHandle)GetResource( 'PICT', pict_ID );

DrawPicture( pict_handle, &control_rect );
```

There's one last check that Draw_Control() must make. If the contrlHilite field of the control record has a value of 255, or CNTRL_INACTIVE, the control is said to be inactive. If this is the case, the call to DrawPicture() will have properly drawn the picture that shows the control in the up state. Now it's time to superimpose a gray pattern over the picture to provide the effect of a dimmed item. A call to the utility routine Dim_Item( ), which is discussed later in this section, takes care of that task:

```
if ( (**control).contrlHilite == CNTRL_INACTIVE )
   Dim_Item( control_rect );
```

Here's a look at the source code for the entire Draw_Control( ) function.

```
void  Draw_Control( ControlHandle control )
{
   GrafPtr     saved_port;
   Rect        control_rect;
   short       pict_ID;
   PicHandle   pict_handle;

   if ( (**control).contrlVis == CNTRL_INVISIBLE )
      return;

   GetPort( &saved_port );

   pict_ID = GetControlReference( control );

   control_rect = (**control).contrlRect;

   if ( Color_Is_On( control_rect ) == false )
      pict_ID += BW_OFFSET;

   if ( (**control).contrlHilite == inButton )
      pict_ID += DOWN_OFFSET;

   pict_handle = (PicHandle)GetResource( 'PICT', pict_ID );

   if ( pict_handle == nil )
      ExitToShell();

   DrawPicture( pict_handle, &control_rect );

   if ( (**control).contrlHilite == CNTRL_INACTIVE )
      Dim_Item( control_rect );

   SetPort( saved_port );
}
```

Before walking through the only other message routine that
MyButtonCDEF uses, I'll finish this section with a look at the two utility
routines used by Draw_Control(). The first is Color_Is_On().
Here's the source code for that function:

```
Boolean  Color_Is_On( Rect the_rect )
{
   OSErr         error;
   long          response;
   GDHandle      current_device;
   PixMapHandle  the_pix_map;

   error = Gestalt( gestaltQuickdrawVersion, &response );

   if ( error != noErr )
      ExitToShell();
   else if ( response == gestaltOriginalQD )
      return ( false );
   else
   {
      LocalToGlobal( (Point*) &the_rect );
      LocalToGlobal( 1 + (Point*) &the_rect );
      current_device = GetMaxDevice( &the_rect );
      the_pix_map = (**current_device).gdPMap;
      if ( (**the_pix_map).pixelSize > 1 )
         return ( true );
      else
         return ( false );
   }
}
```

N O T E **Determining which monitor holds a given rectangle, and determining the pixel depth—or color level—of that monitor, involves
knowledge of graphics devices. As you read the explanation of
Color_Is_On(), you may find that this topic seems a little
deep. If that is the case, you can accept at face value that the
Color_Is_On() function works. Or, you can spend a couple of
hours reading all about devices in the "Graphics Devices" chapter of *Inside Macintosh: Imaging With QuickDraw*.**

Color_Is_On() begins with a call to Gestalt(). Gestalt() is a
Toolbox function that returns information about the machine on which

a program is running. The first parameter—the *selector code*—tells Gestalt() what information I want. When the call is complete, the second parameter—the *response*—will hold that information. By passing the Apple-defined constant gestaltQuickdrawVersion, I'm telling Gestalt() to determine which version of QuickDraw is in the Macintosh. If it's gestaltOriginalQD—the original, older QuickDraw—the machine can only display black and white. If that's the case, Color_Is_On() has found the information it was looking for, and it can return a value of false to the calling function.

Any version of QuickDraw other than gestaltOriginalQD means the Mac is capable of displaying color—though the user may have set the monitor to black and white. The code in the else section determines whether color is on or off. The Rect variable the_rect, which was passed to Color_Is_On(), holds the coordinates of the rectangle that bounds the control that is to be drawn. These coordinates are local to the window or dialog box in which the control appears. The following lines convert these coordinates to global values—coordinates that are in terms of the desktop area:

```
LocalToGlobal( (Point *) &the_rect );
LocalToGlobal( 1 + (Point *) &the_rect );
```

A rectangle can be expressed as four integers or two points. The Toolbox routine LocalToGlobal() is expecting the address of a Point as its parameter, so the first call to LocalToGlobal() casts the_rect to a pointer to a Point. So the first call to LocalToGlobal() converts the first of the two points that define the_rect to global coordinates. By again casting the_rect to a pointer to a Point, and then adding one to the address, the parameter to the second call to LocalToGlobal() becomes the address of the second Point that defines the_rect.

I agree, it is confusing. Keep in mind that the first Point of a rectangle defines the upper-left corner of the rectangle, while the second Point **defines the lower-right corner.** N O T E **Each call to** LocalToGlobal() **isolates one of these** Points **and converts it to global coordinates. The result is**

> **a rectangle of the same size as the original rectangle, but in global coordinates.**

Once the rectangle is converted to global coordinates, a call to `GetMaxDevice()` is made. When passed a rectangle (in global coordinates), the Toolbox routine `GetMaxDevice()` determines in which video device the rectangle lies. This is necessary to handle the case of a user running a system with two monitors, each set to a different color level.

```
GDHandle  current_device;

current_device = GetMaxDevice( &the_rect );
```

`GetMaxDevice()` returns a handle to the graphics device that holds the control. Dereferencing this handle twice leads to a `GDevice` structure. One of the fields of the `GDevice` structure is `gdPMap`—a `PixMapHandle`. A `PixMapHandle` is a pixel map of the screen—in this case, the screen of the monitor that holds the control to draw. The last step is to double dereference the `PixMapHandle` to get to the pixel depth of the screen. If `pixelSize` is 1, the screen is set to monochrome; if it's greater than 1, color is turned on.

```
PixMapHandle  the_pix_map;

the_pix_map = (**current_device).gdPMap;
if ( (**the_pix_map).pixelSize > 1 )
   return ( true );
else
   return ( false );
```

The second utility routine used by `Draw_Control()` is `Dim_Item()`—shown here:

```
void  Dim_Item( Rect dim_rect )
{
```

```
    PenState    saved_pen_state;
    Pattern     gray_pattern;

    GetPenState( &saved_pen_state );
    PenNormal();
    GetIndPattern( &gray_pattern, sysPatListID, SYS_GRAY_PAT_INDEX );
    PenPat( &gray_pattern );
    PenMode( patBic );
    PaintRect( &dim_rect );
    SetPenState( &saved_pen_state );
}
```

Dim_Item() begins by saving the state of the graphics pen with a call to GetPenState() and ends by restoring the pen to its initial condition with a call to SetPenState(). In between these Toolbox calls, Dim_Item() sets the graphics pen such that a painted rectangle will superimpose a light gray pattern over the picture button.

Keep in mind that the code that makes up a code resource is not part of an application. As such, the application is not aware of exactly when the code resource will execute. Thus the application can't be responsible for saving any graphics pen characteristics that it might want to retain. Instead, it's up to the code resource to save and restore these attributes.

T I P

Overlaying a light gray pattern over the existing button picture is accomplished by first getting a gray pattern from the system pattern list. Chapter 1 described how a call to GetIndPattern() works. Next, the pen pattern is set to this gray pattern. Then the pen transfer mode is set to patBic. By setting the mode to this constant, the painting of a pattern over the button picture won't wipe out the entire picture. Instead, parts of the picture will show through. This will give the effect of a dimmed picture, as shown in Figure 2.14.

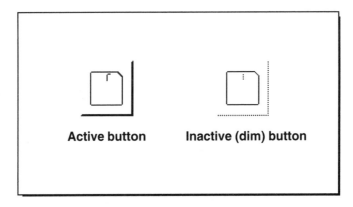

Active button   **Inactive (dim) button**

FIGURE 2.14 DRAWING A GRAY PATTERN OVER A BUTTON PICTURE
GIVES IT A DIM, OR INACTIVE, LOOK.

THE MYBUTTONCDEF SOURCE CODE LISTING

Aside from main( ), the MyButtonCDEF code contains just four functions, two of which are short utility routines. Here's the complete source code listing for this chapter's CDEF code resource:

```
//_____
//                                            #include directives
#include <GestaltEqu.h>


//_____
//                                            function prototypes

void      Draw_Control( ControlHandle );
long      Test_Control( ControlHandle, long );
Boolean   Color_Is_On( Rect );
void      Dim_Item( Rect );


//_____
//                                            #define directives

#define      DOWN_OFFSET      1
#define      BW_OFFSET        2
```

```
#define         CNTRL_INACTIVE      255
#define         CNTRL_INVISIBLE       0
#define         SYS_GRAY_PAT_INDEX    4

//_____
//                                        entry point to the code

pascal long  main( short        var_code,
                   ControlHandle the_control,
                   short         message,
                   long          msg_param )

{
   long  return_val = 0L;

   switch( message )
   {
      case drawCntl:
         Draw_Control( the_control );
         break;

      case testCntl:
         return_val = Test_Control( the_control, msg_param );
         break;

      default:
         break;
   }

   return ( return_val );
}


//_____
//                                        draw the control

void  Draw_Control( ControlHandle control )
{
   GrafPtr     saved_port;
   Rect        control_rect;
   short       pict_ID;
   PicHandle   pict_handle;

   if ( (**control).contrlVis == CNTRL_INVISIBLE )
      return;

   GetPort( &saved_port );
```

```
   pict_ID = GetControlReference( control );

   control_rect = (**control).contrlRect;

   if ( Color_Is_On( control_rect ) == false )
      pict_ID += BW_OFFSET;

   if ( (**control).contrlHilite == inButton )
      pict_ID += DOWN_OFFSET;

   pict_handle = (PicHandle)GetResource( 'PICT', pict_ID );

   if ( pict_handle == nil )
      ExitToShell();

   DrawPicture( pict_handle, &control_rect );

   if ( (**control).contrlHilite == CNTRL_INACTIVE )
      Dim_Item( control_rect );

   SetPort( saved_port );
}


//_____
//                           test for mouse clicks in the control

long  Test_Control( ControlHandle control, long mouse_loc )
{
   Rect    the_rect;
   Point   the_point;

   if ( (**control).contrlVis == CNTRL_INVISIBLE )
      return ( 0 );

   if ( (**control).contrlHilite == CNTRL_INACTIVE )
      return ( 0 );

   the_point.v = HiWord( mouse_loc );
   the_point.h = LoWord( mouse_loc );

   the_rect = (**control).contrlRect;

   if ( PtInRect( the_point, &the_rect ) )
      return ( inButton );
   else
```

```
      return ( 0 );
}



//_____
//                         is color available, and turned on?

Boolean  Color_Is_On( Rect the_rect )
{
   OSErr         error;
   long          response;
   GDHandle      current_device;
   PixMapHandle  the_pix_map;

   error = Gestalt( gestaltQuickdrawVersion, &response );
   if ( error != noErr )
      ExitToShell();
   else if ( response == gestaltOriginalQD )
      return ( false );
   else
   {
      LocalToGlobal( (Point*) &the_rect );
      LocalToGlobal( 1 + (Point*) &the_rect );
      current_device = GetMaxDevice( &the_rect );
      the_pix_map = (**current_device).gdPMap;
      if ( (**the_pix_map).pixelSize > 1 )
         return ( true );
      else
         return ( false );
   }
}



//_____
//                dim an item by overlaying light gray pattern

void  Dim_Item( Rect dim_rect )
{
   PenState   saved_pen_state;
   Pattern    gray_pattern;

   GetPenState( &saved_pen_state );
   PenNormal();
   GetIndPattern( &gray_pattern, sysPatListID, SYS_GRAY_PAT_INDEX );
   PenPat( &gray_pattern );
   PenMode( patBic );
   PaintRect( &dim_rect );
   SetPenState( &saved_pen_state );
}
```

BUILDING THE CDEF CODE RESOURCE

The steps for building a CDEF are essentially the same as the steps for building an MDEF:

1. Create a new project.
2. Add the necessary library and code resource source code file to the project.
3. Tell the compiler to generate a code resource rather than an application.
4. Build the code resource.

The code resource will be saved to its own resource file. When an application requires the CDEF code, it's a simple matter to use a resource editor to copy the code resource from its resource file and paste it directly into the resource fork of an application.

Building with CodeWarrior

CodeWarrior users should launch their C/C++ compiler and create a new project. After adding the appropriate files, the project window will look like the one shown in Figure 2.15.

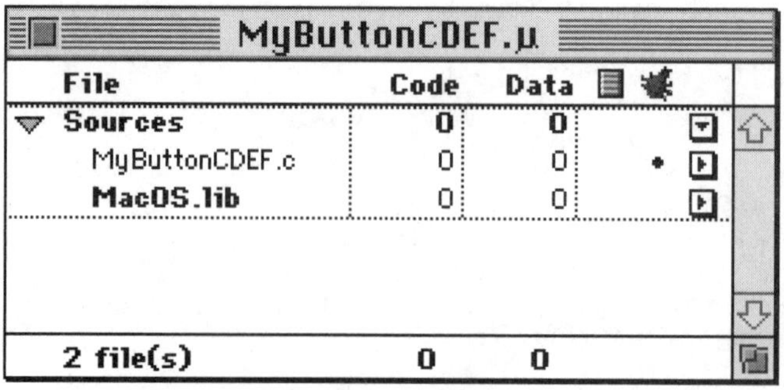

File	Code	Data	📄	🍁	
▽ **Sources**	0	0		▾	
MyButtonCDEF.c	0	0	•	▸	
MacOS.lib	0	0		▸	
2 file(s)	**0**	**0**			

MyButtonCDEF.μ

FIGURE 2.15 THE PROJECT WINDOW FOR A METROWERKS CODEWARRIOR CDEF CODE RESOURCE.

The **Preferences** menu item from the Edit menu allows the project to be marked as a code resource rather than an application. Figure 2.16 shows the preference settings in the Project panel of the Preferences dialog box. Note that all of the items that get filled in are the same as they are for an MDEF code resource. The only significant change is in the ResType, which should be CDEF rather than MDEF.

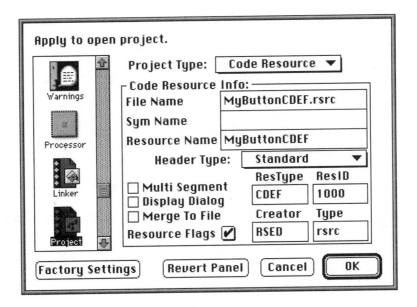

FIGURE 2.16 THE PROJECT PANEL SETTINGS FOR A METROWERKS
CODEWARRIOR CDEF CODE RESOURCE.

 As you saw in Chapter 1, Metrowerks code resource projects must use the Small code model. Click on the Processor icon to display the Processor Info panel. Then use the Code Model pop-up menu to select the Small code model.

N O T E

After dismissing the Preferences dialog box, it's time to build the code resource by selecting **Make** from the Project menu. The result will be a CDEF code resource in a file named MyButtonCDEF.rsrc.

Building with Symantec C++/THINK C

Symantec C++ and THINK C owners will begin by launching the THINK Project Manager and creating a new project. Adding the MacTraps library and the code resource source code file complete the project. It should look like the one in Figure 2.17.

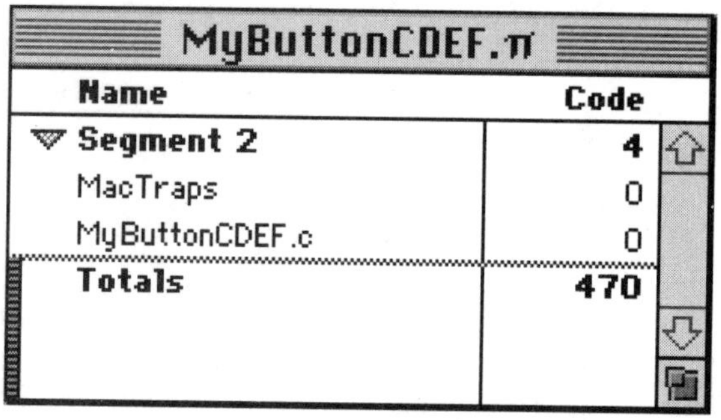

```
╔══════ MyButtonCDEF.π ══════╗
║ Name                    Code ║
║ ▽ Segment 2                4  ⇧║
║   MacTraps                 0  ║
║   MyButtonCDEF.c           0  ║
║   Totals                 470  ⇩║
║                              🗗║
╚══════════════════════════════╝
```

FIGURE 2.17 THE PROJECT WINDOW FOR A SYMANTEC CDEF CODE RESOURCE.

Selecting the **Set Project Type** item in the Project menu will display the dialog box shown in Figure 2.18. The various items that need to be filled in are the same as those that were filled in for the MDEF in Chapter 1. The only important change is the Type, which should now be CDEF.

After dismissing the dialog box, select **Build Code Resource** from the Project menu. Again, this is the same step you performed for the MDEF code resource. In the dialog box that opens, type in a name for the resource file that will be created to hold the CDEF resource—just as I've done in Figure 2.19. Make sure the **Merge** check box is not checked, then click **Save**.

The THINK Project Manager will compile the control definition function source code and build the CDEF code resource. The result will appear in a new resource file.

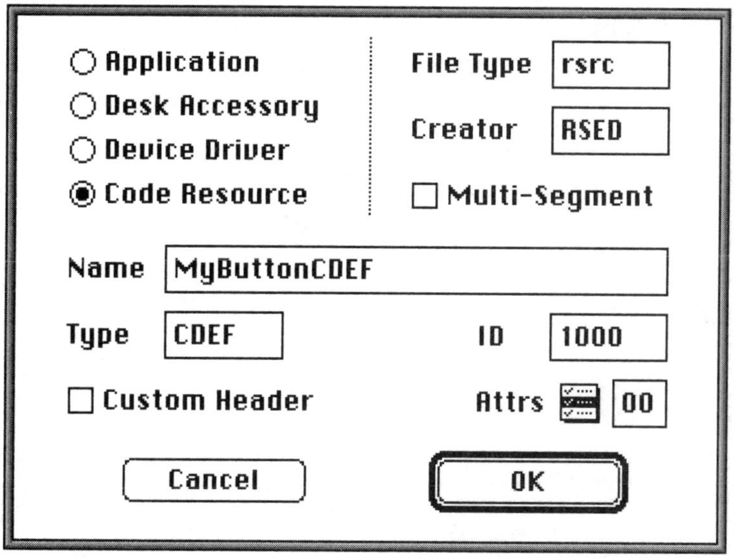

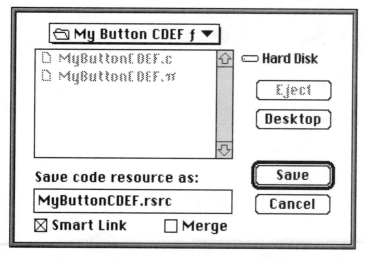

FIGURE 2.18 THE SET PROJECT TYPE SETTINGS FOR A SYMANTEC CDEF CODE RESOURCE.

FIGURE 2.19 THE SYMANTEC DIALOG BOX FOR NAMING THE RESOURCE FILE THAT WILL HOLD THE CDEF CODE RESOURCE.

The CDEF Test Application

As you learned in Chapter 1, a code resource is not stand-alone code and, as such, cannot be tested without the help of an application that uses the code. Since this chapter's test application has no menus or menu bar, you'll find that its source code listing is shorter than Chapter 1's listing.

What the Test Application Does

If you've migrated to Apple's System 7.5, you may have noticed a few changes in the Macintosh graphical user interface. While most dialog boxes and control panels still use the standard controls, a few interface components use a sleeker looking set of controls. Figure 2.20 shows the AppleCD Audio Player, with its polished-looking controls.

FIGURE 2.20 THE APPLECD AUDIO PLAYER.

Because I like the look of the AppleCD Audio Player, I'll have my test application display a button that looks similar to one found in the Apple program. I'll draw four pictures that will be used to mimic one button that has the look of the controls that appear in the bank of buttons to the left of the volume slider in the AppleCD Audio Player. Figure 2.21 shows the four pictures, still in the window of the graphics program in which I drew them. Each of the four pictures will become a PICT resource in a resource file—as discussed in the next section.

This chapter's version of MyTestApp simply displays a dialog box that holds four controls. Two of the controls are standard controls that will be handled by the Dialog Manager, and two are handled by the Control Manager and this chapter's MyButtonCDEF control definition function. Figure 2.22 shows what the MyTestApp dialog box looks like.

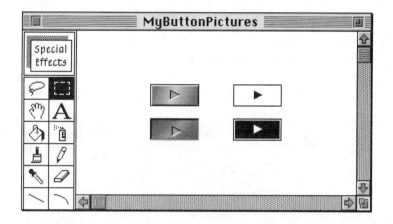

FIGURE 2.21. USING A GRAPHICS PROGRAM TO DRAW FOUR PICTURES FOR USE AS ONE BUTTON.

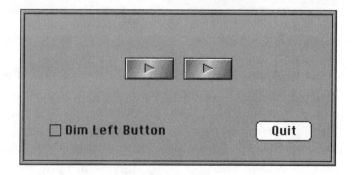

FIGURE 2.22 THE MYTESTAPP DIALOG BOX.

Actions in the check box and the **Quit** push button are taken care of by the Dialog Manager (which makes use of the Control Manager). A mouse click over either of the arrow buttons will be handled by the CDEF. The source code that makes up the test application, however, will make no distinction between controls that are handled by the MyButtonCDEF and the system CDEF. Instead, the distinction will be made in the resource file, where the CNTL resources that define the two arrow buttons will specify that the MyButtonCDEF code be used with the two picture buttons.

Figure 2.23 shows how the MyTestApp dialog box looks when a user clicks the mouse button while the cursor is over one of the arrow buttons. The figure shows that the MyButtonCDEF code takes over and draws a depressed button picture over the existing arrow button. When either arrow button is clicked, the test application will beep the Mac's speaker—one beep for a click on the left button, two beeps for a click on the right button.

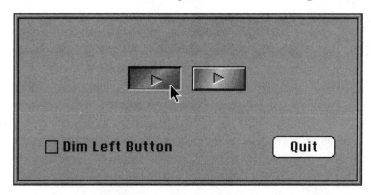

FIGURE 2.23 THE MYTESTAPP DIALOG BOX WITH ONE CUSTOM CONTROL DEPRESSED.

The MyButtonCDEF includes code that handles the case when a button is inactive. When the application source code marks a button handled by the CDEF as inactive, the Draw_Control() routine that is a part of MyButtonCDEF draws a gray pattern over the button and refuses to process mouse clicks in the button's rectangle. Figure 2.24 shows that when the **Dim Left Button** box is checked, the arrow button on the left becomes inactive. Once the button is dim, mouse clicks on it will not result in the display of the depressed arrow button picture. That provides verification that the CDEF is indeed ignoring mouse clicks. Additionally, when the button is dim, a mouse click on it will not result in a sounding of the Mac's speaker, verifying that mouse clicks on the inactive control are also ignored by the application.

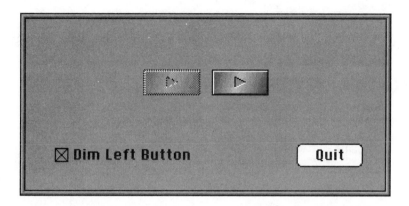

FIGURE 2.24 THE MYTESTAPP DIALOG BOX WITH ONE CUSTOM CONTROL INACTIVE.

THE TEST APPLICATION RESOURCES

The test application will display two picture buttons, but they will both be based on the same set of pictures. Figure 2.25 shows the four PICT resources that will be used for a button.

When you draw the four pictures that will represent a button, make them all the same size. While you're in your graphics program make a note of the pixel dimensions of one of the pictures. In Figure 2.26 you can see that I'm using an enlarged view mode to manually count the size of a picture. The size of any one picture in my example turns out to be 22 pixels high by 50 pixels wide.

I'll need a CNTL resource for each picture button that is to appear in the dialog box of the test application. Four of the CNTL fields are of significance:

BoundsRect	The local pixel coordinates of the control in the dialog box
Visible	Specifies that the control be visible
ProcID	Tells which CDEF handles the control
RefCon	Provides the PICT ID of the base picture for this control

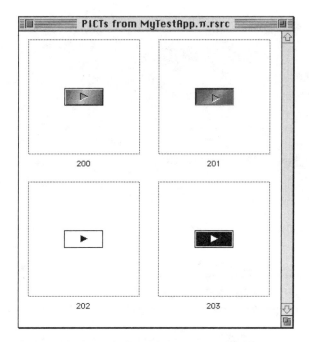

FIGURE 2.25 THE PICT RESOURCES FOR MYTESTAPP.

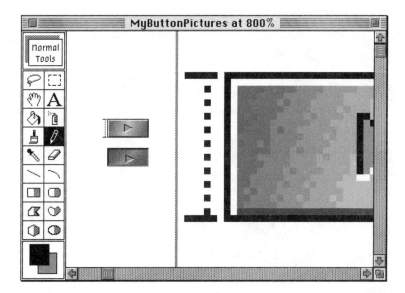

FIGURE 2.26 ENLARGING ONE BUTTON PICTURE TO DETERMINE ITS PIXEL DIMENSIONS.

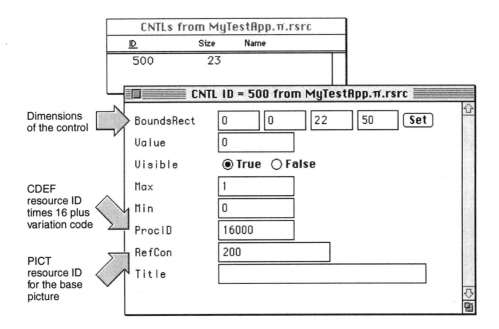

FIGURE 2.27 SHOWS THE VALUES IN THE **CNTL** RESOURCE
FOR A CONTROL WITH AN **ID** OF **500.**

The order of the BoundsRect fields is top, left, bottom, right. Notice that I set the boundaries so that they make up a rectangle 22 pixels high and 50 pixels wide—the same size as one of the PICT resources.

When I created the MyButtonCDEF, I gave it an ID of 1000. Yet the ProcID field of the CNTL resource shows I've entered a value of 16000. That's because the ProcID doesn't hold the ID of the CDEF—at least not directly. Instead, the ProcID follows this formula:

```
ProcID  = ( 'CDEF' ID * 16 ) + variation code
```

Variation codes are described in Chapter 3. For now, I'll just say that a single CDEF can be written such that it supports different variations of a control type. For example, the MyButtonCDEF uses a picture to display a button. A variation of that could be to use the same picture and to display a button title under the picture.

The MyButtonCDEF has no variations, so the variation code is 0. That makes the value of ProcID 16000:

```
ProcID = ( 'CDEF' ID * 16 ) + variation code
ProcID = (    1000    * 16 ) +   0
```

After defining the CNTL resource, I create the DITL resource that holds all of the items in the dialog. Figure 2.28 shows the four items in the DITL.

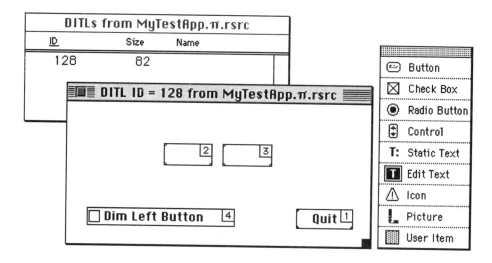

FIGURE 2.28 THE DITL RESOURCES FOR MYTESTAPP.

Items 2 and 3 are the two controls. They were each created by clicking on the control item in the floating palette and dragging the mouse over to the DITL editor. The default ID and size of a control item won't match the numbers I used in my CNTL resources, so I'll double-click on each item to edit that information. Figure 2.29 shows the result of double-clicking on item 2.

In Figure 2.29 you can see that I've entered a Resource ID of 500. That tells this control item to use the information found in the CNTL resource with an ID of 500. After entering the CNTL ID, I entered the Top and Left coordinates of the control. These numbers are the pixel coordinates that the control will have in the dialog box. After entering these values, ResEdit supplied the Height and Width values—I had no control over those values. Figure 2.30 shows both the CNTL resource and the DITL item 2 so that you can compare.

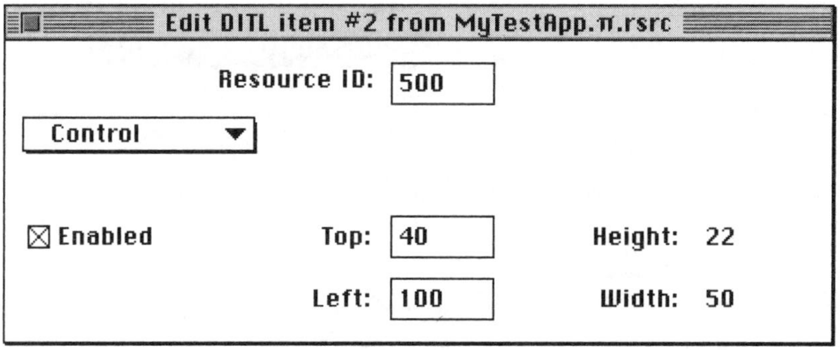

FIGURE 2.29 SETTING THE CONTROL'S LOCATION AND THE RESOURCE ID OF THE CNTL USED BY THE CUSTOM CONTROL.

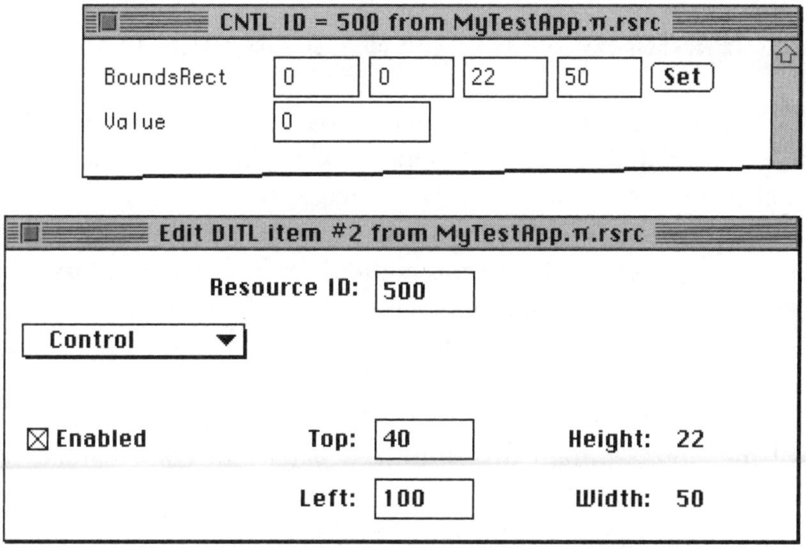

FIGURE 2.30 THE DITL ITEM SPECIFIES WHICH CNTL RESOURCE IS USED BY THE CUSTOM CONTROL.

If you're using ResEdit, your DITL item window may display the Bottom and Right dimensions rather than Height and Width. You can set ResEdit to display either pair using the Item menu (see Figure 2.31).

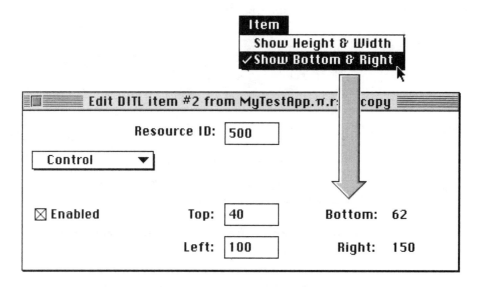

FIGURE 2.31 RESEDIT CAN DISPLAY EITHER A CONTROL'S DIMENSIONS OR ITS LOCATION.

A DITL is a dialog item list for a dialog box, so I need to add a DLOG resource to hold dialog box information. Figure 2.32 shows that DLOG. The background, or content area, of a dialog box is normally white. In Figure 2.32, you can see that the background of my dialog box is gray. To add color (or grayscale) to the content area of a dialog box, add a dctb resource to the resource file. This can easily be done from within the DLOG editor of ResEdit; Figure 2.33 shows the two steps. First, click on the **Custom** radio button. That displays a group of dialog box parts that can have color added to them. Clicking on the rectangle to the right of the word Content drops down a palette of color choices (see Figure 2.33).

After selecting a color from the palette, the alert pictured in Figure 2.34 appears. A dctb, or dialog color table, defines the colors that appear in a dialog box. Click **OK** to let ResEdit create and add the resource.

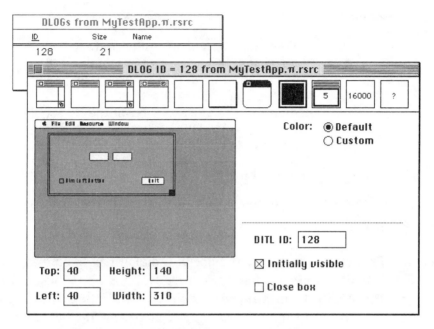

FIGURE 2.32 THE DLOG RESOURCE FOR MYTESTAPP.

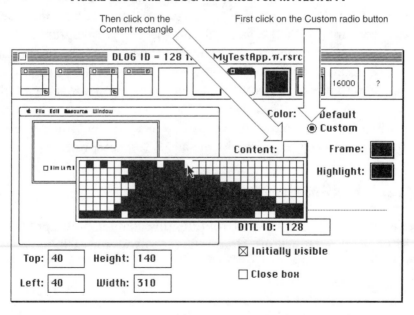

FIGURE 2.33 ADDING COLOR TO THE CONTENT AREA OF A DIALOG BOX.

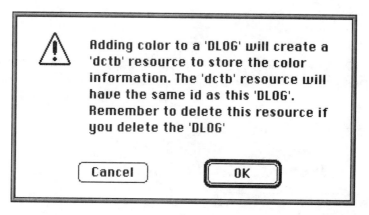

FIGURE **2.34** ADDING COLOR TO A DIALOG BOX CREATES A DCTB RESOURCE.

N O T E Providing a background color in a dialog box is safe regardless of the system the application will end up running on. In the MyTestApp source code I'll be loading the DLOG resource into memory using a call to the Toolbox routine GetNewDialog(). If the MyTestApp application is running on a color system, GetNewDialog() will search for a dctb resource with the same ID as the DLOG resource and use the information found within that resource. If the application is running on a monochrome system, GetNewDialog() will ignore any dctb resources in the application's resource fork.

Figure 2.35 shows the dctb resource, as well as all of the other resource types that make up the resource file for the MyTestApp project.

The Test Application Source Code

Aside from the required main() routine, this chapter's test application consists of just three functions. Here's the prototypes for each:

```
//_____
//                                  function prototypes

void    Initialize_Toolbox( void );
```

```
void    Open_Dialog( void );
short   Set_Check_Box( DialogPtr, short );
```

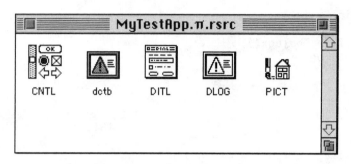

FIGURE 2.35 THE RESOURCE TYPES FOR MYTESTAPP.

The first five of the nine #define directives listed in the source code are resource-related. DLOG_ID is the resource ID of both the DLOG and DITL resource for the program's dialog box. The next four constants represent the item numbers of the four DITL items.

The CHECKBOX_OFF and CHECKBOX_ON constants are used when handling a click in the check box of the dialog box. The CNTRL_INACTIVE and CNTRL_ACTIVE constants are used in setting the highlight level of one of the two picture buttons.

```
//_____
//                                          #define directives

#define     DLOG_ID                 128
#define         DONE_BUTTON_ITEM     1
#define         ARROW_1_ITEM         2
#define         ARROW_2_ITEM         3
#define         DIM_ARROW_1_ITEM     4

#define     CHECKBOX_OFF            0
#define     CHECKBOX_ON             1
#define     CNTRL_INACTIVE          255
#define     CNTRL_ACTIVE            0
```

The main() function performs the standard Toolbox initializations, then calls a function named Open_Dialog() to display and handle the program's modal dialog box.

```
//_____
//                                          main()

void  main( void )
{
   Initialize_Toolbox();
   Open_Dialog();
}



//_____
//                              initialize the Mac

void  Initialize_Toolbox( void )
{
   InitGraf( &qd.thePort );
   InitFonts();
   InitWindows();
   InitMenus();
   TEInit();
   InitDialogs( 0L );
   FlushEvents( everyEvent, 0L );
   InitCursor();
}
```

Open_Dialog() displays the dialog box that is described in the "What
the Test Application Does" section. A call to GetNewDialog() loads the
dialog record, while calls to ShowWindow() and SetPort() make sure
the dialog box is visible and ready to receive graphics commands.
Open_Dialog() then enters a while loop that repeatedly calls
ModalDialog() to capture mouse clicks in active items in the dialog box.

A mouse click on either of the two arrow picture buttons will result in
the display of one of the PICT resources. Open_Dialog() needs no
special code to make this happen; it's all handled by the MyButtonCDEF
code that gets called by the Control Manager in response to a click on
either button. A mouse click on an arrow button also sounds the Mac's
speaker:

```
case ARROW_1_ITEM:
   SysBeep( 5 );
   break;
```

```
case ARROW_2_ITEM:
   SysBeep( 5 );
   SysBeep( 5 );
   break;
```

The handling of a mouse click on the check box relies on the utility routine `Set_Check_Box( )`. This function—described later—toggles the check box. It also returns a value of 0 (`CHECKBOX_OFF`) if the check box has been unchecked, or 1 (`CHECKBOX_ON`) if the check box is now checked. The returned value, held in `check_box_val`, is then tested. The Toolbox routine `HiliteControl( )` is then called to either activate or inactivate one of the picture buttons:

```
case DIM_ARROW_1_ITEM:
   check_box_val = Set_Check_Box( the_dialog, the_item );
   GetDItem( the_dialog, ARROW_1_ITEM,
             &the_type, &the_handle, &the_rect );
   if ( check_box_val == CHECKBOX_ON )
      HiliteControl( (ControlHandle)the_handle,
                     CNTRL_INACTIVE );
   else
      HiliteControl( (ControlHandle)the_handle,
                     CNTRL_ACTIVE );
   break;
```

Here's a look at the complete listing for `Open_Dialog( )`:

```
//_____
//                                    open a display dialog

void  Open_Dialog( void )
{
   DialogPtr   the_dialog;
   short       the_item;
   Boolean     all_done = false;
   short       check_box_val;
   short       the_type;
   Handle      the_handle;
   Rect        the_rect;

   the_dialog = GetNewDialog( DLOG_ID, nil, (WindowPtr)-1L );
   ShowWindow( the_dialog );
```

```
SetPort( the_dialog );

while ( all_done == false )
{
   ModalDialog( nil, &the_item );

   switch ( the_item )
   {
      case ARROW_1_ITEM:
         SysBeep( 5 );
         break;

      case ARROW_2_ITEM:
         SysBeep( 5 );
         SysBeep( 5 );
         break;

      case DIM_ARROW_1_ITEM:
         check_box_val = Set_Check_Box( the_dialog, the_item );
         GetDItem( the_dialog, ARROW_1_ITEM,
                  &the_type, &the_handle, &the_rect );
         if ( check_box_val == CHECKBOX_ON )
            HiliteControl( (ControlHandle)the_handle,
                           CNTRL_INACTIVE );
         else
            HiliteControl( (ControlHandle)the_handle,
                           CNTRL_ACTIVE );
         break;

      case DONE_BUTTON_ITEM:
         all_done = true;
         break;
   }
}
DisposDialog( the_dialog );
}
```

The last function in MyTestApp is Set_Check_Box(). This short routine can be used—without modification—in any program that uses check boxes. Set_Check_Box() receives a pointer to the dialog box that received a mouse click and the item number of the clicked-on item as its two parameters. Set_Check_Box() begins with a call to GetDItem() to obtain a handle to the clicked-on check box. That handle is used in a call to GetCtlValue() to get the value of the check box. That value is then tested in an `if` statement. If the check box was on, a call to `SetCtlValue()` turns it off. If it was off, a different call to `SetCtlValue()` turns it on. In either case, `Set_Check_Box()` returns a short that will let the calling routine know the new state of the check box.

```
//_____
//                                    toggle checkbox to opposite state

short  Set_Check_Box( DialogPtr the_dialog, short the_item )
{
   short   the_type;
   Handle  the_handle;
   Rect    the_rect;
   int     old_value;

   GetDItem( the_dialog, the_item, &the_type,
             &the_handle, &the_rect );

   old_value = GetCtlValue( ( ControlHandle )the_handle );

   if ( old_value == CHECKBOX_ON )
   {
      SetCtlValue( ( ControlHandle )the_handle, CHECKBOX_OFF);
      return ( CHECKBOX_OFF );
   }
   else
   {
      SetCtlValue( ( ControlHandle )the_handle, CHECKBOX_ON );
      return ( CHECKBOX_ON );
   }
}
```

As with all of the examples in this book, you'll find separate Symantec and CodeWarrior versions of the source code for this new version of MyTestApp in folders on the included disk.

After compiling and building a stand-alone application, it is time to add the CDEF resource, just as the MDEF resource was added to Chapter 1's version of MyTestApp. To do this, open both the MyButtonCDEF.rsrc file and the MyTestApp application using a resource editor. Then copy the MyButtonCDEF CDEF from the MyButtonCDEF.rsrc file and paste it into the application. Figure 2.36 shows the results.

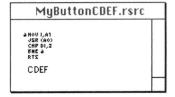

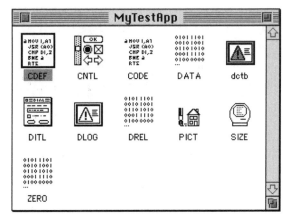

FIGURE 2.36 THE RESULT OF PASTING THE CDEF CODE RESOURCE
INTO THE APPLICATION'S RESOURCE FORK.

Now there's nothing left to do but give the program a test drive. Make sure the speaker volume of your Mac is on so you can hear the system alert sound that plays when a picture button is clicked on.

ADDING A SECOND BUTTON TO MYTESTAPP

Before jumping into a new CDEF, I'll cover Chapter 1's MyButtonCDEF. In this section you'll see how a couple of simple changes to the resource file of MyTestApp makes it possible to use MyButtonCDEF with any number of buttons.

Changing the MyTestApp Resource File

This chapter's version of MyTestApp displays a dialog box with two custom picture button controls in it. Because both controls in the MyTestApp program use the same set of PICT resources, they look identical. It would be a simple matter to instead have the program display two different looking picture controls. To do so, I need to add another set of four PICT resources (see Figure 2.37).

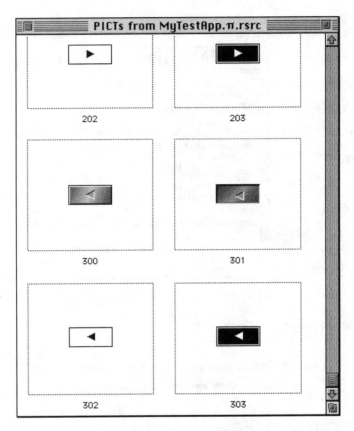

**FIGURE 2.37 ADDING A SECOND SET OF PICT RESOURCES TO THE
MYTESTAPP PROJECT'S RESOURCE FILE.**

After drawing the four pictures in my graphics program, I added each to the resource file of the MyTestApp project. Figure 2.37 shows that each of the four pictures has an arrow pointing to the left. I've kept the original four pictures (with arrows pointing to the right) in the resource file—you can see part of two of those PICT resources in Figure 2.37.

Next, I'll need to add a new CNTL resource so that one of the two custom controls will use the new pictures. In the new CNTL, which I've given an ID of 600, I'll change the RefCon field value. Recall that the RefCon field specifies the ID of the base PICT to be used as the button. Figure 2.38 shows how CNTL ID 600 would look.

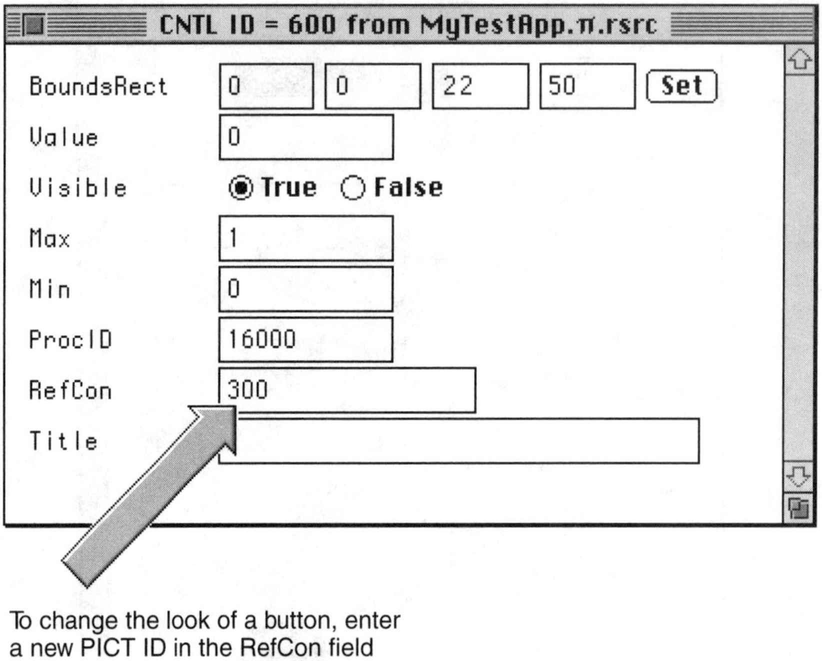

To change the look of a button, enter
a new PICT ID in the RefCon field

**FIGURE 2.38 ADDING A SECOND CNTL RESOURCE TO THE
MYTESTAPP PROJECT'S RESOURCE FILE.**

Next, I need to change the CNTL resource ID of one of the two custom control's in the DITL resource. Since I want the left button to display the new left arrow picture, I'll change the ID listed in the left control. Figure 2.39 shows this change.

Building a New MyTestApp Application

To make the changes that were made to the MyTestApp resource file go into effect, a new version of the MyTestApp application needs to be built. When I use my development environment to do that, the MyTestApp.c source code won't be recompiled. Instead, the build will just link the altered MyTestApp resource file to the existing MyTestApp object code to create a new application. After copying the existing CDEF resource from

MyButtonCDEF and pasting it into the new MyTestApp, launching the application would result in a dialog box like the one in Figure 2.40.

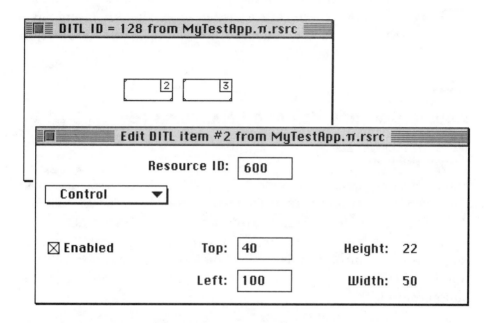

FIGURE 2.39 CHANGING THE RESOURCE ID OF A CONTROL DITL ITEM SO THAT THE ITEM USES THE NEW CNTL RESOURCE.

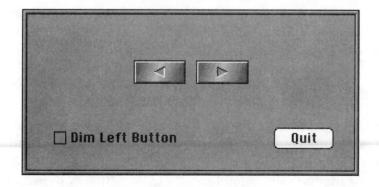

FIGURE 2.40 THE DIALOG BOX DISPLAYED BY THE NEW VERSION OF MYTESTAPP.

Notice that the MyButtonCDEF project was not changed in any way. The CDEF can be used as is to handle any number of picture buttons. To add more buttons or change the look of existing ones, change the PICT and CNTL resources in the resource file of the application project that uses the CDEF.

ADDING CONTROL VARIATION HANDLING TO MYBUTTONCDEF

Earlier in this chapter I mentioned that one CDEF can be made to handle different types of controls. That's what the system CDEF resource does. The System file CDEF with ID 0 handles push buttons, radio buttons, and check boxes. It can do this because it knows how to work with variations of a control. In this section you'll see how you can easily give your own CDEF the power to work with different variations of the picture button control.

Changing the MyTestApp Resource File

While the MyButtonCDEF allows a picture button to take on any look, it still supports only one type of control. Each button handled by MyButtonCDEF will simply be a PICT resource drawn to a dialog box or window. MyButtonCDEF could, however, be written in such a way that it would give a programmer options on how a button should look in an application. For instance, the MyButtonCDEF CDEF is written to allow the use of a picture as a button. This type of control would be considered the default control, and would have a variation value of 0. This same CDEF could also be written such that a picture button control could be drawn with a title beneath it. If the button was to have a title, the variation value would be 1. This situation is shown in Figure 2.41.

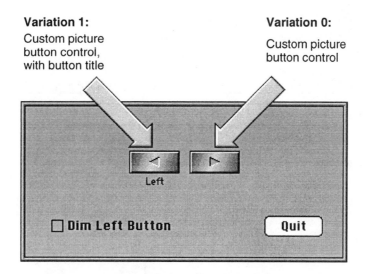

FIGURE 2.41 ONE TYPE OF CONTROL CAN HAVE DIFFERENT VARIATIONS.

The CNTL is the resource that provides the details of what a custom control looks like. The `ProcID` is the field of the CNTL that specifies which CDEF should handle the control. But if one CDEF is to support multiple variations of a control, how does one include this information in the CNTL? The answer lies in the formula for determining the value of the `ProcID`:

```
ProcID  = ( 'CDEF' ID * 16 ) + variation code
```

For a default control that simply displays a PICT resource, the variation code will be 0 and the `ProcID` will be 16000; you've seen that earlier in this chapter. If I want the custom control to display a picture and have a title underneath it, I'll include the variation code in my calculation of the `ProcID`. Since I said that my new version of MyButtonCDEF will have just one variation, the variation code will be 1:

```
ProcID  = ( 'CDEF' ID * 16 ) + variation code
ProcID  = ( 1000 * 16 ) + 1
ProcID  =   16001
```

Figure 2.42 shows how the CNTL resource would look for a custom control that is to display both a picture and a title.

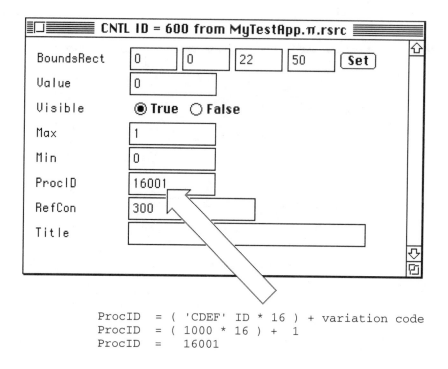

```
ProcID  = ( 'CDEF' ID * 16 ) + variation code
ProcID  = ( 1000 * 16 ) +  1
ProcID  =   16001
```

FIGURE 2.42 CHANGING THE CNTL PROCID SO THAT THE CUSTOM CONTROL WILL BE GOVERNED BY A CONTROL VARIATION.

For some control variations, this change may be the only resource modification needed. For my button title example, however, I need to make one other change: the addition of an STR resource.

If a custom control is to have a title, I'll include that title in an STR resource. To associate the title with a particular control, I'll give the STR resource the same ID as the PICT resource that holds the control's base picture. Since the ID of the left arrow picture is 300, I'll give the new STR resource an ID of 300 also (see Figure 2.43).

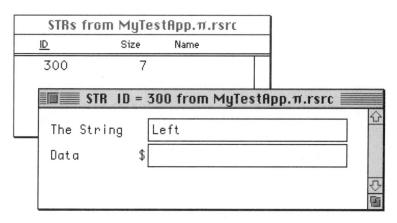

**FIGURE 2.43 CREATING THE STR RESOURCE THAT WILL HOLD
THE TITLE OF A BUTTON CUSTOM CONTROL.**

**Giving a PICT resource and STR resource the same ID
doesn't provide any actual connection or association
between the two in the resource file. That pairing will be
made later, in the CDEF source code.**

N O T E

Changing the variation of a custom control involves changing at least
one resource—the CNTL resource—in the application project's resource
file. It may also require other changes, such as the addition of an STR
resource as shown above. Of course, in order for these changes to be
meaningful, there will also have to be some changes made to the CDEF
source code.

The CDEF Source Code for Control Variations

You saw that the MyButtonCDEF source code didn't make use of the first
parameter to main()—the short parameter var_code. Here's a
reminder of what the declaration of main() looks like:

```
pascal long  main( short        var_code,
              ControlHandle the_control,
```

```
short        message,
long         msg_param )
```

If a CDEF is to support control variations, it will use `var_code` to draw the correct control. When the mouse button is clicked on a custom control, the Control Manager will use information from the control's CNTL resource to determine which variation code should be passed to the CDEF `main()` routine. Figure 2.44 shows that it's the CNTL `ProcID` that holds the variation code.

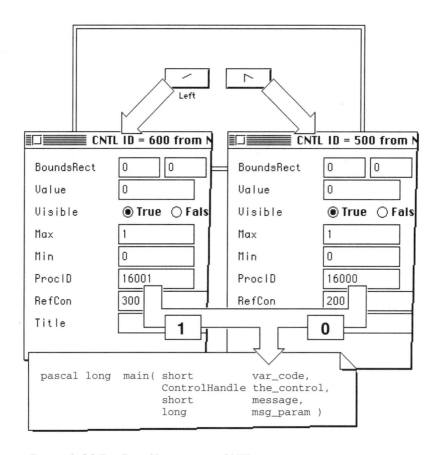

FIGURE 2.44 THE PROCID FIELD OF A CNTL RESOURCE DETERMINES WHICH CODE VARIATION GETS USED.

In the previous MyButtonCDEF example, a `drawCntl` message resulted in a call to `Draw_Control()`. In this example CDEF, MyButtonVarCDEF, a `drawCntl` message also results in a call to a drawing function. However, where the previous CDEF only passed a control handle to the drawing routine, this chapter's CDEF will pass both the control handle and the variation code. Here's the snippet from `main()` that makes the call:

```
case drawCntl:
   Draw_Control( the_control, var_code );
   break;
```

MyButtonVarCDEF is an adaptation of MyButtonCDEF. The changes that need to be made to MyButtonCDEF in order for it to support variation codes are minimal. You just saw the first change—`Draw_Control()` gets a second parameter passed to it. The other changes are to the `Draw_Control()` routine itself.

   `Draw_Control()` determines which of the four PICT resources to draw by first getting the resource ID of the base picture. That information is held in the `RefCon` field of the control's CNTL resource, and subsequently in the `contrlRfCon` field of the control record. As you saw earlier, a call to `GetControlReference()` returns this value:

```
pict_ID = GetControlReference( control );
```

In the MyButtonVarCDEF, a call to `GetControlReference()` will be followed by an assignment statement.

```
short   pict_ID;
short   string_ID;

pict_ID   = GetControlReference( control );
string_ID = pict_ID;
```

The assignment of `string_ID` **must be made just after the initial assignment of** `pict_ID`. **The call to** `GetControlReference()` **returns the ID of the control's base picture—and that's the ID of the control title STR ID.**

> **Later in** `Draw_Control()` `pict_ID` **may change (to** `pict_ID` **plus an offset). That new value won't be useful in obtaining the STR ID.**

There's one more addition I'll need to make to `Draw_Control()`. After drawing the correct picture, `Draw_Control()` should examine `var_code` to see if the control being drawn is a variant control. If `var_code` has a value other than 0, it is. If `var_code` has a value of 1, MyButtonVarCDEF will need to draw a title under the button picture:

```
switch ( var_code )
{
   case 1:
      Draw_Button_Title( saved_port, string_ID, control_rect );
      break;
}
```

I could have used an `if` **statement to handle this single variation:**

```
if ( var_code == 1 )
   Draw_Button_Title( saved_port, string_ID,
                      control_rect );
```

N O T E

Instead, I choose to use a `switch` **statement to show how several different variation codes would be handled by a CDEF.**

`Draw_Button_Title()` is the only routine that's been added to MyButtonCDEF to turn it into MyButtonVarCDEF. Before examining that function, here's a look at the new version of `Draw_Control()`. The few additions to MyButtonCDEF version have been printed in **boldface** type.

```
void  Draw_Control( ControlHandle control, short var_code )
{
   GrafPtr     saved_port;
   Rect        control_rect;
   short       pict_ID;
   PicHandle   pict_handle;
```

```
short        string_ID;

if ( (**control).contrlVis == CNTRL_INVISIBLE )
   return;

GetPort( &saved_port );

pict_ID   = GetControlReference( control );
string_ID = pict_ID;

control_rect = (**control).contrlRect;

if ( Color_Is_On( control_rect ) == false )
   pict_ID += BW_OFFSET;

if ( (**control).contrlHilite == inButton )
   pict_ID += DOWN_OFFSET;

pict_handle = (PicHandle)GetResource( 'PICT', pict_ID );

if ( pict_handle == nil )
   ExitToShell();

DrawPicture( pict_handle, &control_rect );

if ( (**control).contrlHilite == CNTRL_INACTIVE )
   Dim_Item( control_rect );

switch ( var_code )
{
   case 1:
      Draw_Button_Title( saved_port, string_ID, control_rect );
      break;
}

SetPort( saved_port );
}
```

If the clicked-on button has a variation code of 1, (Draw_Button_
Title()) will be called. Draw_Button_Title() has only one task: to
draw a title beneath a button's picture. Although it takes only a few lines
of code to perform this chore, Draw_Button_Title() consists of several local variables and 18 lines of code. Here's a look at why
Draw_Button_Title() needs this extra baggage:

```
void  Draw_Button_Title( GrafPtr the_port,
                         short    string_ID,
                         Rect     control_rect )
{
   Save the current state of the graphics pen
   Save the current font information
   Set the graphics pen to its default settings
   Set the font information to the desired values

   Get a handle to the title string
   Move the graphics pen such that the string will be centered
   Draw the string
   Release the string handle

   Return the font information to the saved values
   Return the graphics pen to its saved state
}
```

From the above comments you can see that much of the code in `Draw_Button_Title()` exists to ensure that when the function is completed, all drawing settings will be as they were when the function began. Again, this is a courtesy to the calling application. When a user clicks on a button, an application won't save the drawing information. So if my CDEF code is going to alter the state of the graphics pen or the current font, my CDEF should also restore all of this information when it is done.

`Draw_Button_Title()` uses a call to `GetPenState()` to preserve the state of the graphics pen. To save the current font information, `Draw_Button_Title()` looks at two fields of the current graphics port; that's why the one of the function parameters is a `GrafPtr`. After a call to `PenNormal()` sets the graphics pen to its default settings, calls to `TextFont()` and `TextSize()` set the font information for the text in which the title will appear. Here's the part of `Draw_Button_Title()` that takes care of these preliminary tasks:

```
PenState  saved_pen_state;
short     saved_font;
short     saved_size;

GetPenState( &saved_pen_state );
saved_font = the_port->txFont;
```

```
saved_size = the_port->txSize;
PenNormal();
TextFont( geneva );
TextSize( 9 );
```

Next comes the drawing of the title. First, `Draw_Button_Title()` makes a call to the Toolbox routine `GetString()` to obtain a handle to the title string. The value of the parameter to `GetString()`, `string_ID`, was found in `Draw_Control()` and passed to (`Draw-_Button_Title()`). Because Toolbox routines generally work with a `Str255` or `StringPtr`, the string handle is dereferenced and the resulting pointer is stored in the `StringPtr` variable `button_title`:

```
StringHandle   str_handle;
StringPtr      button_title;

str_handle = GetString( string_ID );
button_title = *str_handle;
```

`Draw_Button_Title()` now determines where to draw the string. First the width of the button is calculated using the control's boundary rectangle. Next, the center of the button is determined. Then, with the help of the Toolbox function `StringWidth()`, the point to which the graphics pen should be moved is figured, and the results are saved to the variables `x` and `y`:

```
short          button_width;
short          center;
short          x, y;

button_width = control_rect.right - control_rect.left;
center = control_rect.left + ( button_width / 2 );
x = center - ( StringWidth( button_title ) / 2 );
y = control_rect.bottom + 12;
```

After moving the graphics pen, the button title is drawn. Since `Draw_Button_Title()` declared and allocated memory for the string, `Draw_Button_Title()` will clean up by releasing this memory with a call to `ReleaseResource()`:

```
MoveTo( x, y );
DrawString( button_title );
ReleaseResource( (Handle)str_handle );
```

Finally, `Draw_Button_Title()` restores the graphics pen settings and the font information:

```
TextFont( saved_font );
TextSize( saved_size );
SetPenState( &saved_pen_state );
```

Here's an uninterrupted look at the `Draw_Button_Title()` function.

```
void  Draw_Button_Title( GrafPtr  the_port,
                         short    string_ID,
                         Rect     control_rect )
{
   PenState       saved_pen_state;
   StringHandle   str_handle;
   short          saved_font;
   short          saved_size;
   StringPtr      button_title;
   short          button_width;
   short          center;
   short          x, y;

   GetPenState( &saved_pen_state );
   saved_font = the_port->txFont;
   saved_size = the_port->txSize;
   PenNormal();
   TextFont( geneva );
   TextSize( 9 );

   str_handle = GetString( string_ID );
   button_title = *str_handle;
   button_width = control_rect.right - control_rect.left;
   center = control_rect.left + ( button_width / 2 );
   x = center - ( StringWidth( button_title ) / 2 );
   y = control_rect.bottom + 12;
   MoveTo( x, y );
   DrawString( button_title );
   ReleaseResource( (Handle)str_handle );

   TextFont( saved_font );
   TextSize( saved_size );
```

```
   SetPenState( &saved_pen_state );
}
```

MyButtonVarCDEF is derived from the MyButtonCDEF CDEF developed in this chapter. Aside from the addition of a new function—`Draw_Button_Title()`—the changes to MyButtonCDEF are minimal, and have all been covered here. If you'd like to examine the entire source code listing for the new CDEF, you'll find it in the MyButtonVarCDEF.c file on the included disk.

Adding More Control Variations to a CDEF

A CDEF can support any number of variations. For example, you might want to modify MyButtonVarCDEF so that it has separate variations for different title sizes. Variation 1 could draw the button title in 9-point Geneva—as it does now—while variation 2 could draw the title in 12-point Chicago (the system font). To handle this second variation you need to add another case label to the switch in `Draw_Control()`:

```
switch ( var_code )
{
   case 1:
      title_font = geneva;
      title_size = 9;
      Draw_Button_Title( saved_port, string_ID, control_rect,
                         title_font, title_size );
      break;

   case 2:
      title_font = systemFont;
      title_size = 12;
      Draw_Button_Title( saved_port, string_ID, control_rect );
                         title_font, title_size );
      break;
}
```

From the above snippet you can also see that the (`Draw_Button_Title()`) routine now has five parameters instead of three. By passing along the font information for the button title, (`Draw_Button_Title()`) becomes a more versatile function. Besides the addition of

the two new parameters, the only changes that would need to be made to
Draw_Button_Title() would be to the parameters to TextFont()
and TextSize():

```
void  Draw_Button_Title( GrafPtr the_port,
                         short   string_ID,
                         Rect    control_rect,
                         short   title_font,
                         short   title_size )
{
   // Local variables
   // Save pen and font information

   TextFont( title_font);
   TextSize( title_size  );

   // Draw title
   // Restore pen and font information
}
```

To make use of this new control variation, I would just have to modify the
CNTL resource for one of the custom controls in the resource file of the
MyTestApp project. If I gave CNTL 500 a ProcID of 16002, the
MyButtonVarCDEF would be used with a variation code of 2 for the right
arrow button. The dialog box posted by MyTestApp would then look like
the one in Figure 2.45.

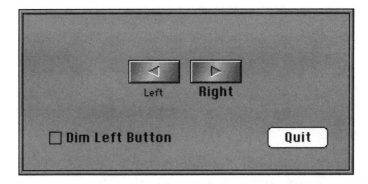

FIGURE 2.45 THE DIALOG BOX DISPLAYED BY THE NEW VERSION OF MYTESTAPP.

CHAPTER SUMMARY

While the Macintosh Toolbox makes it easy to create all of the standard controls, such as buttons and check boxes, it has no provisions for letting a programmer quickly and easily create fancier controls. Instead, a programmer must create a CDEF code resource to carry out this task. A CDEF consists of a control definition function that describes how a control should be drawn and how it should be handled.

Like an MDEF, a CDEF is code that exists outside and apart from the code of an application. With a CDEF, it is a mouse click on an application's custom control that causes this external code to execute. The Control Manager is responsible for invoking the CDEF code and for returning authority to the application after the control has been handled.

After writing the source code that will serve as the CDEF code resource, your developmental environment will turn that source code into a code resource. It will then be your job to copy this code resource and paste it into the resource fork of the application that uses the custom controls.

Chapter

3

More Mac Programming Techniques

MORE CUSTOM CONTROLS: SLIDERS

A control definition function, or CDEF, can be written such that it works with any kind of custom control, not just buttons. Sliders are a type of control that seems very "Mac-like," yet there is no resource type or tool-box functions that readily allow sliders to be added to programs. In this chapter you'll see how a CDEF can be written to support the use of slid-ers in any Mac application.

Because Chapter 2 supplied you with the foundation for developing control definition functions, the basics of how a slider control is created will be familiar to you. A slider, however, is more complex than the sim-ple picture buttons developed in Chapter 2, so there will be plenty of new topics to explore.

The CDEF and Slider Controls

The dragging of a slider's thumb, or indicator, can be accomplished in a number of ways. In this chapter you'll see a few different ways of implementing a horizontal slider like the one pictured in Figure 3.1.

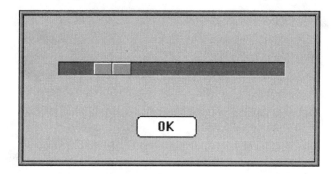

Figure 3.1 A typical slider control in a dialog box.

Drawing the Slider Control and Indicator

A slider consists of two separate parts. The indicator, or thumb, of the control is the part the user clicks on and drags. The control itself—the path on which the thumb travels—is the other slider part. As it is for all custom controls, it is the responsibility of the control definition function to draw the parts of a slider. When the `main()` function of a CDEF receives a `drawCtl` message, the CDEF can use a series of QuickDraw calls to draw the parts of the control, or, as I'll do in this chapter, the CDEF can display pictures that are stored in PICT resources.

Typically, a slider control that is drawn with the use of pictures will use two PICT resources—one for the control and one for the indicator. If a CDEF is to support drawing to both color and monochrome screens, four pictures should be available to the application. Depending on the color level of the monitor, the application will use one pair or the other from the four pictures. Figure 3.2 shows a set of four PICTs used to draw the control and slider in Figure 3.3. Figure 3.3 shows the same dialog box on both a color monitor and a monochrome monitor.

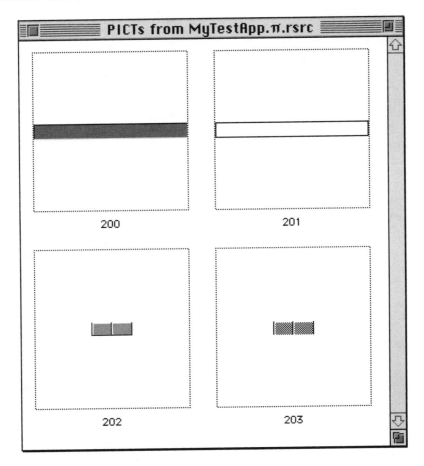

FIGURE 3.2 THE APPLICATION PROJECT'S RESOURCE FILE WILL HOLD A SET OF FOUR PICTURES FOR A SINGLE SLIDER.

When a control that is to be used as a slider is added to a DITL resource, its size will be determined by the CNTL resource referenced by the control DITL item. This is as it was for Chapter 2's picture button controls. The size of the control should be the size of the slider's path—the control picture. An example of this is in Figure 3.4.

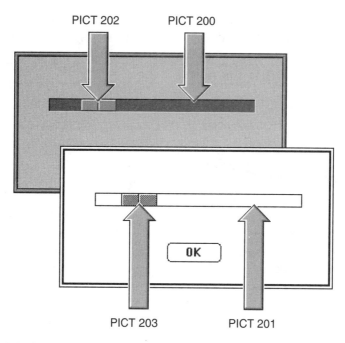

PICT 202   PICT 200

OK

PICT 203   PICT 201

FIGURE 3.3 TWO PICTURES WILL BE USED FOR A COLOR SLIDER, AND TWO DIFFERENT PICTURES WILL BE USED FOR A BLACK-AND-WHITE SLIDER.

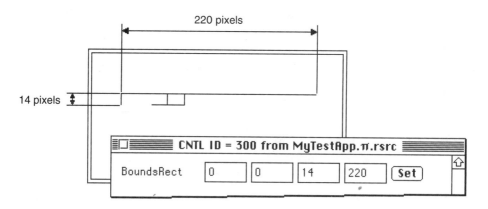

220 pixels

14 pixels

CNTL ID = 300 from MyTestApp.π.rsrc

BoundsRect   0   0   14   220   Set

FIGURE 3.4 THE **CNTL** RESOURCE ESTABLISHES THE SIZE OF A SLIDER.

The color control can be drawn in a graphics program and pasted it into a resource file. After that, the thumb should be drawn in the graphics program, right on top of the control. Figure 3.5 shows an enlarged view of a thumb drawn in a control.

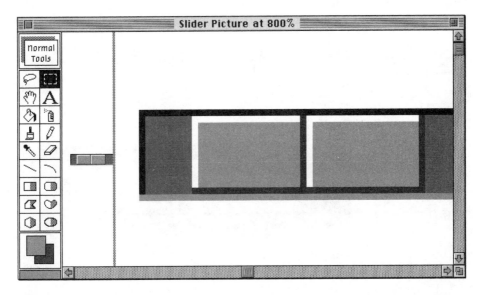

FIGURE 3.5 A GRAPHICS PROGRAM SHOULD BE USED TO DRAW THE SLIDER'S THUMB.

When the slider control's indicator picture is copied from the graphics program, the selection rectangle used should be just the size of the thumb. Figure 3.6 shows the thumb being selected. After pasting the indicator picture into the application project's resource file, the same steps should be taken to create and save two black-and-white pictures.

When it comes time to update the entire control, the CDEF will first use a call to `DrawPicture()` to draw the larger control picture, and "stamp" the thumb picture on top of the control picture using a second call to `DrawPicture()`.

The Slider Resources

A slider may or may not require PICT resources; it depends on how the programmer chooses to implement the drawing of the slider. But a slider will always need a control item in a DITL resource and a CNTL resource—as did the picture button controls in Chapter 2. Figure 3.7 shows a control item in a DITL. In the figure you can see that information about this DITL item can be found in the CNTL resource with an ID of 300.

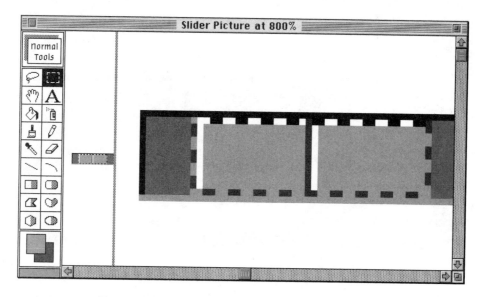

FIGURE 3.6 THE SELECTION OF THE THUMB SHOULD BE MADE JUST INSIDE
THE BOUNDARIES OF THE CONTROL.

You've already seen that the BoundsRect of a CNTL holds the size of a control item. For some controls, such as a slider, the Value, Max, and Min fields become important. Together, these three values determine the current location of the thumb within a slider control. The Min and Max fields hold the range of numbers that the Value field can have. In Figure 3.8 you can see that the thumb of the slider that uses CNTL 300 will have a range of 100 and is initially located at the dead center of the control.

The Value field of the CNTL resource provides the initial location of the thumb in the control. This value gets copied to the slider's control record. As the user drags the thumb of a slider, calls to SetControlValue() will update this value in the control record.

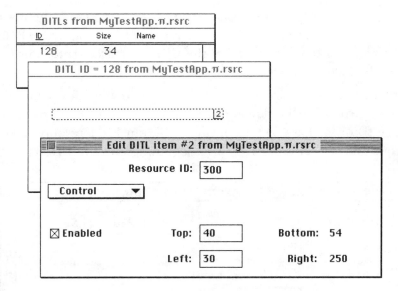

FIGURE 3.7 THE INFORMATION ABOUT A CONTROL ITEM IS STORED IN A **CNTL** RESOURCE—
RESOURCE **300** FOR THIS EXAMPLE.

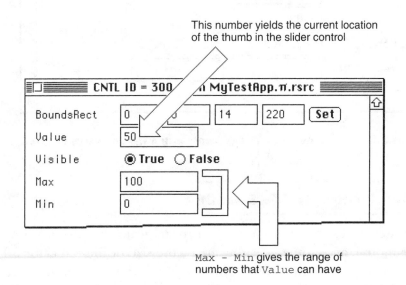

FIGURE 3.8 THE **CNTL** RESOURCE SUPPLIES INFORMATION ABOUT THE RANGE AND
PLACEMENT OF A CONTROL'S INDICATOR.

The `ProcID` of a slider's CNTL resource indirectly holds the resource ID of the CDEF code resource that governs the slider. In Figure 3.9 `ProcID` has a value of 8000, telling you that the CDEF resource ID for this CNTL must be 500 (8000 / 16 = 500).

The `RefCon` for a CNTL can be used to hold any information that a custom control will need. For the slider, I'll use the `RefCon` to hold the resource ID of the base picture of the set of four PICT resources. Figure 3.9 shows that this slider uses pictures beginning with PICT resource 200.

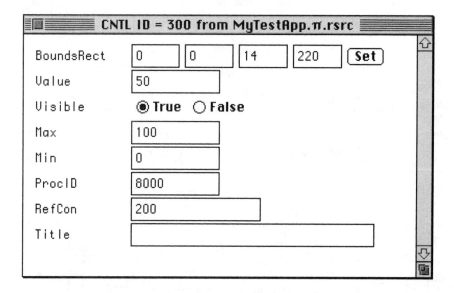

FIGURE 3.9 THE COMPLETED CNTL RESOURCE, WITH A REFCON VALUE OF 200.

SLIDER CONTROL SOURCE CODE

When a user clicks the mouse on a control indicator and begins dragging the mouse, an outline—or gray area—the size of the indicator follows the movement of the mouse. This is evidenced when you move the thumb of a scroll bar in a typical Macintosh application. Figure 3.10 shows what the scroll bar of a word processor document looks like as the thumb is being dragged.

Annual Report			
November	50.6	112.0	322.5
December	62.5	205.0	405.4
Total	587.4	1342.3	3455.1

FIGURE 3.10 TYPICALLY, AN INDICATOR THAT IS BEING DRAGGED WILL DISPLAY A GRAY OUTLINE OF THE THUMB.

In this section I'll develop the source code for a CDEF named MySlider GrayCDEF. It uses this style of dragging for horizontal sliders like the one pictured in Figure 3.11.

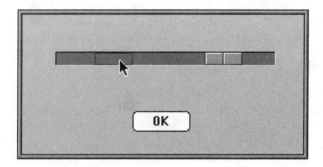

FIGURE 3.11 THE MYSLIDERGRAYCDEF SUPPORTS THE OUTLINED DRAGGING OF A THUMB.

The Slider CDEF Entry Point

All control definition functions can make use of the format of the main() routine discussed in Chapter 2—regardless of the type of custom control the definition is supporting. So this chapter's slider example will have a main() function that looks much like the other CDEF entry points you've seen:

```
pascal long  main( short         var_code,
                   ControlHandle the_control,
                   short         message,
                   long          msg_param )
{
   long           return_val = 0L;
   unsigned long  high_bit;
   unsigned long  strip_bit;

   switch ( message )
   {
      case testCntl:
         return_val = Test_Control( the_control, msg_param );
         break;

      case calcThumbRgn:
         Calc_Thumb_Region( the_control, (RgnHandle)msg_param );
         break;

      case calcCRgns:
         high_bit = (unsigned long)msg_param & 0x80000000;
         if ( high_bit == 0x80000000 )
         {
            strip_bit = (unsigned long)msg_param & 0x7FFFFFFF;
            Calc_Thumb_Region( the_control, (RgnHandle)strip_bit );
         }
         break;

      case thumbCntl:
         Calc_Thumb_Drag_Limits( the_control,
                                 (ThumbDragInfo *)msg_param );
         break;

      case posCntl:
         Position_Thumb( the_control, msg_param );
         break;

      case drawCntl:
         Draw_Control( the_control );
         break;
   }

   return ( return_val );
}
```

A slider control will need to respond to more message types than a button control because the slider has more parts: The slider has both a control and an indicator, while the button has just the picture that represents the button. While the above `main()` function handles six message types, it's not uncommon for a slider control to watch for other messages as well. Later in this chapter you'll see other slider control messages, including `dragCntl` and `calcCntlRgn`.

The six messages handled by the `main()` routine of MySliderGrayCDEF, and the functions each message invokes, are covered on the next pages. As an overview, I'll briefly describe each message here.

As was the case in the Chapter 2 examples, the Control Manager sends the CDEF a `testCntl` message when a mouse click needs to be tested to see if it occurred in the boundaries of a control. When the Control Manager sends this message, it will also send the coordinates of the mouse click in the `msg_param` parameter.

When a user clicks on the thumb of a slider control and drags the mouse, the CDEF will be called several times, with different message types. The `testCntl` message will be sent to see if the cursor was over the thumb. If it was, the region in which the thumb is currently located needs to be calculated. When dragging an indicator, the Control Manager works with a region rather than a rectangle. If the user's Mac has 24-bit addressing, the CDEF will be called with a `calcCRgns` message. If the Mac has 32-bit addressing turned on, the message will instead be a `calcThumbRgn`.

As the user drags the mouse, `thumbCntl` messages will be sent to the CDEF to draw an outline of the thumb. Only when the user releases the mouse will a `posCntl` message be sent to reposition the thumb. The routine that handles a `posCntl` message will calculate the new, final position of the thumb and will then send the CDEF a `drawCntl` message to do the actual drawing.

A message type of `drawCntl` is sent to the CDEF by the Control Manager when either the control or the thumb needs to be drawn—the `msg_param` value indicates which. If a `msg_param` value of 0 accompanies the `drawCntl` message, the control needs to be drawn. If `msg_param` has a value of 129, then the thumb should be drawn.

The six messages sent to the MySliderGrayCDEF CDEF are summarized in Figure 3.12.

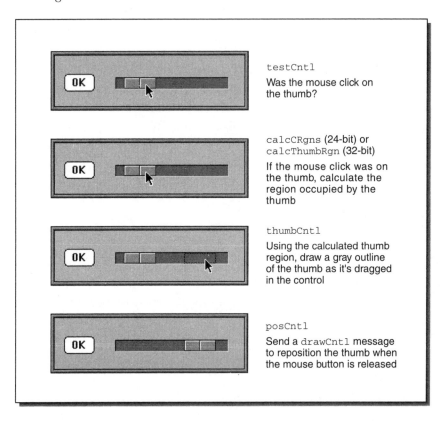

FIGURE 3.12 SEVERAL MESSAGE TYPES ARE INVOLVED IN THE DRAGGING OF AN INDICATOR.

Taking Care of the Preliminaries

MySliderGrayCDEF makes a call to `Gestalt()` to see if the system it's running on has a color monitor, so it includes the GestaltEqu.h header file:

```
#include <GestaltEqu.h>
```

MySliderGrayCDEF is the first CDEF example that declares its own data structure. The ThumbDragInfo struct will be used to hold information that tells the CDEF in what boundaries the user can drag the thumb:

```
typedef   struct
{
   Rect   limitRect;
   Rect   slopRect;
   short  axis;
} ThumbDragInfo;
```

This CDEF uses a PICT numbering scheme similar to the one used for picture buttons. The resource ID of the PICT used as the control on color systems is considered the base ID. The black-and-white version of that picture has an ID one greater than the base picture, while the color picture used for the thumb has an ID two greater than the base picture. The black-and-white version of the thumb picture has an ID one greater than the color version. That numbering sequence is summed up in three #define directives:

```
#define       CONTROL_BW_OFFSET        1
#define       THUMB_OFFSET             2
#define       THUMB_BW_OFFSET          1
```

MySliderGrayCDEF consists of main() and seven other functions. You've seen Color_Is_On() in Chapter 2, so it won't be discussed in this chapter.

```
void    Draw_Control( ControlHandle );
long    Test_Control( ControlHandle, long );
void    Calc_Thumb_Region( ControlHandle, RgnHandle );
void    Calc_Thumb_Drag_Limits( ControlHandle, ThumbDragInfo * );
void    Position_Thumb( ControlHandle, long );
Rect    Calc_Thumb_Rect( ControlHandle );
Boolean Color_Is_On( Rect );
```

Calculating the Thumb Rectangle

Many of the actions that take place in a slider are dependent on the size of the rectangle that encloses the control's indicator. In order to elimi-

nate redundant code, MySliderGrayCDEF has a utility routine named
`Calc_Thumb_Rect()`. You'll come to see that `Calc_Thumb_Rect()`
gets invoked by four of the functions in the CDEF.

`Calc_Thumb_Rect()` begins by determining the width of the
thumb. That's done by obtaining a handle to one of the thumb pictures
(they're both the same size) and examining the `picFrame` field of the
`Picture` data structure.

```
short       pict_ID;
PicHandle   pict_handle;
Rect        pict_rect;
short       thumb_width;

pict_ID = GetControlReference( control );
pict_ID += THUMB_OFFSET;
pict_handle = (PicHandle)GetResource( 'PICT', pict_ID );
if ( pict_handle == nil )
   ExitToShell();

pict_rect = (**pict_handle).picFrame;

thumb_width  = pict_rect.right - pict_rect.left;
```

The `thumb_width` variable will be used a little later in the function. Before
that time, the pixel width of the entire control is needed. That value can be
obtained from the `contrlRect` field of the control record. Figure 3.13 is a
reminder of where the pixel coordinates of the control originated.

```
Rect    control_rect;
short   control_pixel_width;

control_rect = (**control).contrlRect;
control_pixel_width = control_rect.right - control_rect.left;
```

The control uses the `contrlValue` member of the control record to
keep track of the location of the thumb. This number only has meaning
in the context of the range of values that the control can have. After
using the minimum and maximum control values to determine the
range, the current control value is used to see how far the thumb is offset
from the minimum value. Then a ratio is calculated. In Figure 3.14 you

can see that the initial position of the thumb is at the center of the control. This won't be the case for the duration of the CDEF execution—the `contrlValue` will be changing as the thumb moves.

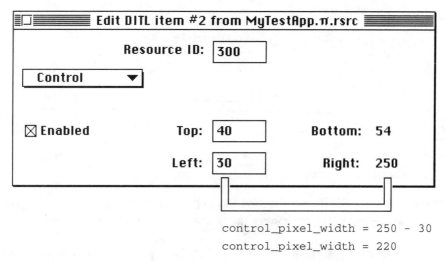

control_pixel_width = 250 - 30
control_pixel_width = 220

FIGURE 3.13 THE CONTROL ITEM IN THE **DITL** RESOURCE PROVIDE
THE ORIGINAL BOUNDARIES OF A CONTROL.

```
short   control_unit_width;
short   control_offset;
float   ratio;

control_unit_width = (**control).contrlMax -
                     (**control).contrlMin;
control_offset = (**control).contrlValue - (**control).contrlMin;
ratio = (float)control_offset / (float)control_unit_width;
```

`Calc_Thumb_Rect()` calculates a ratio because the control's value is relative to the control's minimum and maximum settings, not to any pixel numbering. The ratio can be used with pixel values to determine the pixel center of the thumb:

```
short       thumb_center;

thumb_center = control_rect.left + ( ratio * control_pixel_width );
```

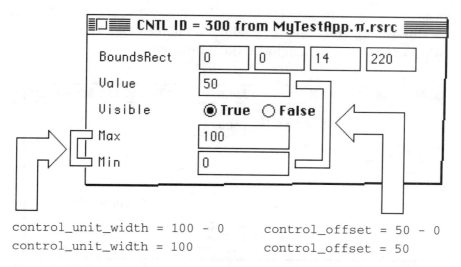

```
control_unit_width = 100 - 0        control_offset = 50 - 0
control_unit_width = 100            control_offset = 50
```

FIGURE 3.14 **THE CNTL MIN AND MAX FIELDS PROVIDE THE RANGE IN WHICH A THUMB CAN TRAVEL—THE VALUE FIELD GIVES THE THUMBS INITIAL PLACEMENT IN THAT RANGE.**

Carrying on with the numbers used in the example, the thumb's horizontal center is at pixel 140—midway between the control's left side at 30 pixels and its right side at 250 pixels. Figure 3.15 points this out.

```
thumb_center = control_rect.left + ( ratio * control_pixel_width )
thumb_center = 30 + ( 0.5 * 220 )
thumb_center = 140
```

After the horizontal midpoint of the thumb rectangle has been determined, it's a simple task to find the four rectangle boundaries. The previously calculated thumb_width is used to determine the left and right boundaries. Since I always create a thumb that rests in the control one pixel from the top and one pixel from the bottom, I'll use the control's rectangle to calculate the thumb rectangle's top and bottom coordinates.

```
Rect   thumb_rect;

thumb_rect.left   = thumb_center - ( thumb_width / 2 );
thumb_rect.right  = thumb_rect.left + thumb_width;
thumb_rect.top    = control_rect.top + 1;
thumb_rect.bottom = control_rect.bottom - 1;
```

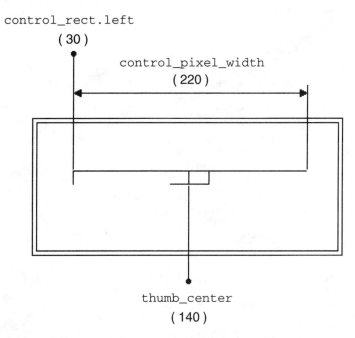

control_rect.left
(30)

control_pixel_width
(220)

thumb_center

(140)

FIGURE 3.15 THE THUMB'S PIXEL LOCATION IS CALCULATED BY CALC_THUMB_RECT().

You'll find that all six messages handled by MySliderGrayCDEF use
Calc_Thumb_Rect(); that's why I've elected to describe the routine in
such detail. Here's a look at the entire Calc_Thumb_Rect() listing.

```
Rect  Calc_Thumb_Rect( ControlHandle control )
{
   short       pict_ID;
   PicHandle   pict_handle;
   Rect        pict_rect;
   short       thumb_width;
   short       thumb_center;
   Rect        thumb_rect;
   Rect        control_rect;
   short       control_pixel_width;
   short       control_unit_width;
   short       control_offset;
   float       ratio;

   pict_ID = GetControlReference( control );
   pict_ID += THUMB_OFFSET;
   pict_handle = (PicHandle)GetResource( 'PICT', pict_ID );
```

143

```
if ( pict_handle == nil )
    ExitToShell();

pict_rect = (**pict_handle).picFrame;

thumb_width  = pict_rect.right - pict_rect.left;

control_rect = (**control).contrlRect;
control_pixel_width = control_rect.right - control_rect.left;

control_unit_width = (**control).contrlMax -
                       (**control).contrlMin;
control_offset = (**control).contrlValue -
                   (**control).contrlMin;
ratio = (float)control_offset / (float)control_unit_width;

thumb_center = control_rect.left + ( ratio *
                 control_pixel_width );

thumb_rect.left   = thumb_center - ( thumb_width / 2 );
thumb_rect.right  = thumb_rect.left + thumb_width;
thumb_rect.top    = control_rect.top + 1;
thumb_rect.bottom = control_rect.bottom - 1;

return ( thumb_rect );
}
```

Handling a testCntl Message

A click of the mouse requires that the CDEF compare the point of the mouse click with the current location of the control's thumb. You'll recall from Chapter 2 that a testCntl message sends the mouse click coordinates in the msg_param parameter. Calls to HiWord() and LoWord() extract these coordinates. After making a call to Calc_Thumb_Rect(), a call to PtInRect() should be made to compare the location of the mouse click to the coordinates of the thumb. If the click was in the thumb, a value of inThumb should be returned to main(). The Control Manager will see to it that this value is entered into the contrlHilite field of the slider's control record.

```
long  Test_Control( ControlHandle control, long mouse_loc )
{
```

```
    Point   the_point;
    Rect    thumb_rect;

    the_point.v = HiWord( mouse_loc );
    the_point.h = LoWord( mouse_loc );

    thumb_rect = Calc_Thumb_Rect( control );

    if ( PtInRect( the_point, &thumb_rect ) )
        return ( inThumb );
    else
        return ( 0 );
}
```

MySliderGrayCDEF assumes that the slider will always be visible and active. If you'd like to change these assumptions, add the tests of the control record contrlVis **and** contrlHilite **fields, as you saw in the** Test_Control() **routine of the Chapter 2 CDEF MyButtonCDEF.**

NOTE

Calculating the Thumb Region

After a call to Test_Control() confirms that a mouse click has occurred in the thumb of a slider, the Control Manager will again invoke the CDEF. This time the Control Manager will be interested in obtaining the region occupied by the thumb. As mentioned, the Control Manager likes to work with an indicator's region rather than its rectangle. Once the bounding rectangle of the thumb is known, calculating the region is easy. Passing a region handle and a rectangle to the Toolbox routine RectRgn() will take care of this task. RectRgn() will set up the region structure that the handle references such that it has the coordinates of the rectangle. In Calc_Thumb_Region() you see the first use of the Calc_Thumb_Rect() routine:

```
void  Calc_Thumb_Region( ControlHandle control,
                         RgnHandle     indicator_rgn )
{
    Rect  indicator_rect;

    indicator_rect = Calc_Thumb_Rect( control );
```

```
    RectRgn( indicator_rgn, &indicator_rect );
}
```

Converting a rectangle to a region is easy. Getting to the `Calc_Thumb_Region()` routine that accomplishes this takes a little bit of work, though. In the days prior to 32-bit addressing, some data structures and Toolbox routines used the high order bit of an address for special nonaddress purposes. Now that new Macintoshes require all 32-bits for use in addressing, these old scheme's don't work. Calculating the region of the thumb of a control is one such instance where this 24-bit/32-bit conflict has to be handled.

For a CDEF running on a Mac that has 32-bit addressing turned on, things are very simple. If the Control Manager needs the region of a control's thumb, it sends a `calcThumbRgn` message. The `msg_param` field will hold an address that can be typecast to a handle to a region. It will be the job of the CDEF to calculate the thumb's region boundaries and to place these values in the data structure that the region handle indirectly points to. For a `calcThumbRgn` message, the `main()` routine should simply call the region-calculating routine `Calc_Thumb_Region()`:

```
case calcThumbRgn:
   Calc_Thumb_Region( the_control, (RgnHandle)msg_param );
   break;
```

If the Control Manager instead needs the region of the entire control, it sends a `calcCntlRgn` message. In this case the `msg_param` again holds a handle to a region, but the region data structure should be filled with the boundaries of control. Since MySliderGrayCDEF never needs to calculate the region of the entire control, it doesn't handle a `calcCntlRgn` message.

Before 32-bit addressing, the Control Manager would send a `calcCRgns` message to a CDEF to indicate that it needed the region of either a control's thumb or of the control itself. The `calcCntlRgn` and `calcThumbRgn` that were added after the arrival of 32-bit systems would be ignored on older 24-bit systems. Because addresses only occupied 24 of the 32 bits of a `long` word, the Control Manager felt free to embed extra information in the unused upper bits of a long. For the `msg_param` parameter of a `calcCRgns` message, the Control Manager uses the upper bit to hold a flag that indicates whether the thumb region or the control region should be calculated. Figure 3.16 shows how the `msg_param` holds this information on a 24-bit system.

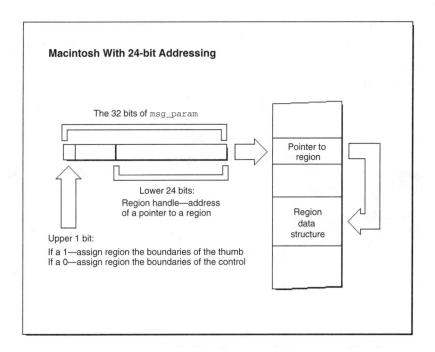

FIGURE 3.16 THE BIT VALUES OF THE LONG VARIABLE MSG_PARAM HOLD TWO KEY PIECES OF INFORMATION.

On a 24-bit system it is the responsibility of the CDEF to determine which region is to be calculated. The CDEF can do this by examining the value of only the high bit of the `msg_param` long word. That's done by masking out all of the lower 31 bits, as shown here:

```
unsigned long  high_bit;

high_bit = (unsigned long)msg_param & 0x80000000;
```

If the result of the masking operation is a `high_bit` value the same as the mask, the highest bit of `msg_param` is a one. That means the

Control Manager wants the region of the thumb. The CDEF can then calculate this region using the same routine that handles a `calcThumbRgn` on 32-bit systems—`Calc_Thumb_Region()`. Before making a call to this function, the highest bit—the flag—should be stripped off of `msg_param`. The resulting value is the address that will serve as the region handle.

If the original masking of the high bit results in a value other than the mask, the high bit is a zero. This reveals that the Control Manager is interested in the region of the entire control, not the region of the thumb. Again, MySliderGrayCDEF doesn't work with the region of the control, so this result is ignored. Here's how a `calcCRgns` message is handled in the `main()` routine of MySliderGrayCDEF:

```
unsigned long  high_bit;
unsigned long  strip_bit;

case calcCRgns:
   high_bit = (unsigned long)msg_param & 0x80000000;
   if ( high_bit == 0x80000000 )
   {
      strip_bit = (unsigned long)msg_param & 0x7FFFFFFF;
      Calc_Thumb_Region( the_control, (RgnHandle)strip_bit );
   }
   break;
```

Handling a thumbCntl Message

When a control's thumb has been clicked on, the Control Manager will send the control definition function a `dragCntl` message. If the CDEF handles this type of message, the CDEF gets the opportunity to perform thumb dragging in whatever way it sees fit. MySliderGrayCDEF doesn't support custom dragging, so this message will be ignored. Later in this chapter you'll see code for a CDEF that does perform custom dragging. If the CDEF ignores dragCntl messages, the Control Manager will use the Toolbox routine `TrackControl()` to handle thumb dragging. `TrackControl()` is the routine that draws the gray outline of an indicator as it's dragged about the control. This is how MySliderGrayCDEF handles thumb dragging.

To draw a properly sized outline of the thumb, `TrackControl()` needs to know the size of the indicator. To get this information, `TrackControl()` will issue a call to the CDEF, passing a `calcCRgns` or `calcThumbRgn` message.

Before beginning to track the cursor as the user drags the mouse, `TrackControl()` needs to know the rectangle to which dragging should be constrained. As the user moves the mouse within this rectangle, `TrackControl()` will continuously draw the outline of the thumb. Should the user move the mouse out of this rectangle, `TrackControl()` will know that the outline should not be drawn.

Your first thought might be to simply make the dragging rectangle the size of the control's rectangle. After all, that's the logical confines of the thumb. Unfortunately, things aren't quite that easy. As its point of reference, `TrackControl()` uses the mouse location at which the mouse click took place. If, for example, the left boundary of the dragging rectangle was the left boundary of the control, `TrackControl()` would allow dragging from the point of the mouse click up to the left edge of the control. As shown in Figure 3.17, the result would be that the thumb could be dragged past the left edge of the control.

To alleviate this potential problem, the Control Manager uses a data structure to hold more accurate information about the constraints it should apply to thumb dragging. The `struct` that it uses has the following three fields:

```
Rect    limitRect;
Rect    slopRect;
short   axis;
```

The `limitRect` field is the rectangle that holds the screen coordinates of the rectangle to which dragging will be confined. This rectangle will be the size of the control's boundary rectangle, inset some amount to prevent the situation shown in Figure 3.17.

The `slopRect` is a rectangle that can be a little larger than the `limitRect` rectangle. This rectangle can be used to add a little play, or slop, to the user's movement of the mouse. As a consideration to the user, the `slopRect` will let the user drag the mouse slightly past the edge of the control, but still constrain the display of the thumb to the control.

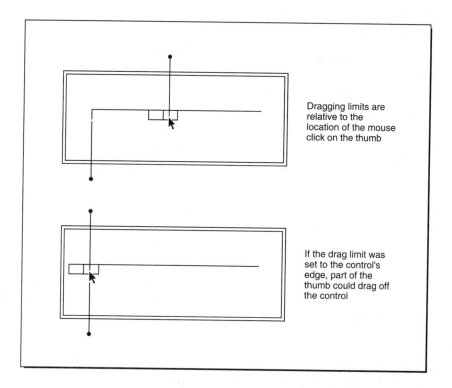

Dragging limits are relative to the location of the mouse click on the thumb

If the drag limit was set to the control's edge, part of the thumb could drag off the control

FIGURE 3.17 THE DRAGGING LIMITS OF A THUMB MUST BE INSET FROM THE CONTROL BOUNDARIES OR THE THUMB CAN BE DRAGGED OUTSIDE THE CONTROL.

The final `struct` member, `axis`, names the axis to which the user may drag the control. For a horizontal control like the one used in MySliderGrayCDEF, the thumb should be limited to horizontal motion. One of three Apple-defined constants can be used for this field: `noConstraint`, `hAxisOnly`, or `vAxisOnly`.

To get all of the information that's held in the `struct`, the Toolbox sends the CDEF a `thumbCntl` message before dragging begins. Along with this message, the Toolbox sends a pointer to a `struct` in the long parameter `msg_param`. It is the job of the control definition function to fill in the fields of the structure that this pointer points to. To do that,

MySliderGrayCDEF defines a data type that matches the format of the struct the Toolbox is looking to fill. While this struct can be given any name, it must have the three fields shown here:

```
typedef  struct
{
   Rect    limitRect;
   Rect    slopRect;
   short   axis;
} ThumbDragInfo;
```

When a thumbCntl message is received, the main() function of MySliderGrayCDEF calls a routine named Calc_Thumb_Drag_Limits(). The second parameter to this function is msg_param, typecast to point to a ThumbDragInfo struct:

```
case thumbCntl:
   Calc_Thumb_Drag_Limits( the_control,
                        (ThumbDragInfo *)msg_param );
   break;
```

Here's how Calc_Thumb_Drag_Limits() receives the parameters that are passed to it:

```
void  Calc_Thumb_Drag_Limits( ControlHandle control,
                        ThumbDragInfo *thumb_drag_struct )
```

It is the job of Calc_Thumb_Drag_Limits() to fill the three fields of the ThumbDragInfo struct. Before writing any values to these members, the routine first extracts one piece of information that the Control Manager has supplied in the struct. The first field, limitRect, holds the coordinates of the mouse click. Since the thumb will be constrained to horizontal motion, the routine is only interested in the horizontal location of the mouse click. Here's how that information is obtained:

```
short  mouse_click_h;

mouse_click_h = (*thumb_drag_struct).limitRect.left;
```

Calc_Thumb_Drag_Limits() will also need the pixel coordinates of the thumb and of the control:

```
Rect    control_rect;
Rect    thumb_rect;

thumb_rect  = Calc_Thumb_Rect( control );

control_rect = (**control).contrlRect;
```

Figure 3.18 shows the coordinates that are important to determining the dragging rectangle. I've included an arbitrary pixel value for each, after making the assumption that the control has a width of 220 pixels and that the thumb has a width of 40 pixels. I'll use those values in the remainder of this discussion.

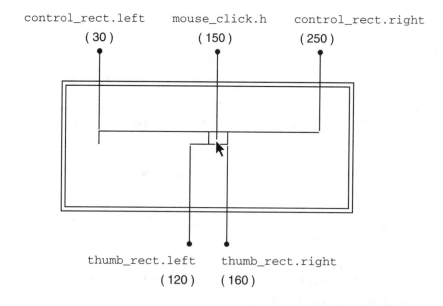

FIGURE 3.18 SEVERAL COORDINATES ARE IMPORTANT IN THE DETERMINATION OF THE DRAGGING RECTANGLE OF A THUMB.

The rectangle that serves as the boundary for thumb dragging will be close to the size of the control rectangle, but not as big. Its coordinates will be dependent on the location of the thumb and the cursor location over the thumb when the mouse was clicked. Here's how the left and right boundaries are found:

```
Rect   bounds_rect;

bounds_rect.left  = control_rect.left +
                    ( mouse_click_h - thumb_rect.left );
bounds_rect.right = control_rect.right -
                    ( thumb_rect.right - mouse_click_h );
```

Using the numbers from Figure 3.18, here's the values of the left and right edges of the bounding rectangle:

```
bounds_rect.left  =  30 + ( 150 - 120 ) =  60
bounds_rect.right = 250 - ( 160 - 150 ) = 240
```

Figure 3.19 shows that if the thumb is dragged to a location 60 pixels from the left of the dialog box, the thumb will end up all of the way to the left of the control—as hoped for. The figure also shows that dragging the thumb to bounds_rect.right places the thumb at the far right of the control. Note that these values only apply for this control and thumb when the mouse click occurs at a horizontal pixel value of 150, as was shown in Figure 3.18.

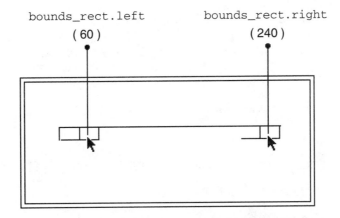

FIGURE 3.19 THE BOUNDS_RECT RECTANGLE PROPERLY CONSTRAINS THE MOVEMENT OF THE THUMB.

Because the thumb doesn't move in a vertical direction, the top and bottom coordinates of the boundary rectangle can be the same as those of the control rectangle:

```
bounds_rect.top    = control_rect.top;
bounds_rect.bottom = control_rect.bottom;
```

With the coordinates of the boundary rectangle set, an assignment to the limitRect member of the ThumbDragInfo structure can be made:

```
(*thumb_drag_struct).limitRect = bounds_rect;
```

To make things simple, I'll set the slopRect to the size of the limitRect. That means that I won't allow any slop, or play, in the user's dragging of the mouse. If the user drags past the left or right edges of the limitRect, the gray outline of the thumb will immediately disappear:

```
(*thumb_drag_struct).slopRect = bounds_rect;
```

Finally, I'll constrain movement of the thumb to the horizontal axis by setting the axis member to the constant hAxisOnly:

```
(*thumb_drag_struct).axis = hAxisOnly;
```

Here's the entire Calc_Thumb_Drag_Limits() routine:

```
void   Calc_Thumb_Drag_Limits( ControlHandle control,
                               ThumbDragInfo *thumb_drag_struct )
{
   Rect    control_rect;
   Rect    bounds_rect;
   Rect    thumb_rect;
   short   mouse_click_h;

   mouse_click_h = (*thumb_drag_struct).limitRect.left;

   thumb_rect  = Calc_Thumb_Rect( control );

   control_rect = (**control).contrlRect;

   bounds_rect.left  = control_rect.left +
                       ( mouse_click_h - thumb_rect.left );
   bounds_rect.right = control_rect.right -
                       ( thumb_rect.right - mouse_click_h );

   bounds_rect.top    = control_rect.top;
```

```
    bounds_rect.bottom = control_rect.bottom;

    (*thumb_drag_struct).limitRect = bounds_rect;
    (*thumb_drag_struct).slopRect = bounds_rect;
    (*thumb_drag_struct).axis = hAxisOnly;
}
```

Handling a posCntl Message

When the user clicks on a control's thumb and drags it across the control, only the outline of the thumb follows the cursor. It's not until the user releases the mouse that the thumb actually gets redrawn. It's at this mouseUp event that the Control Manager sends the CDEF a posCntl message. The main() function of MySliderGrayCDEF handles this message type with a call to Position_Thumb():

```
case posCntl:
    Position_Thumb( the_control, msg_param );
    break;
```

On the receiving end, Position_Thumb() looks like this:

```
void  Position_Thumb( ControlHandle control, long total_offset )
```

For a posCntl message, the msg_param parameter holds pixel values for the horizontal and vertical offsets from the point at which the mouse was clicked on the thumb to the final position at which the mouse was released. Consider the case of a user that clicks the mouse button on the thumb at the point (150, 45) and drags the mouse (and thumb outline) to the left and releases the mouse button at the point (80, 45). Embedded in msg_param would be a horizontal offset of –70 and a vertical offset of 0.

Position_Thumb() needs the horizontal component of this offset so that it can determine at what point on the screen the thumb should be redrawn. A call to LoWord() extracts this horizontal coordinate:

```
short  horiz_offset;

horiz_offset = LoWord( total_offset );
```

155

When the new thumb position is determined, its location will be stored in the `contrlValue` field of the control record. As you've seen, this field holds the position as a single value in the range of the control's minimum and maximum values, not as a pixel coordinate. So a few preliminary calculations are in order. The values of the variables `control_pixel_width` and `control_unit_width`, shown as follows, are found in this same manner as they were found in `Calc_Thumb_ Rect()`:

```
Rect    control_rect;
short   control_pixel_width;
short   control_unit_width;

control_rect = (**control).contrlRect;
control_pixel_width = control_rect.right - control_rect.left;
control_unit_width = (**control).contrlMax -
                     (**control).contrlMin;
```

Next, the number of units that the thumb moved is calculated:

```
float   pixels_per_unit;
short   units_moved;

pixels_per_unit = (float)control_pixel_width /
                  (float)control_unit_width;
units_moved = horiz_offset / pixels_per_unit;
```

As an example of the value that would be calculated for `units_moved`, consider the following scenario. A CNTL resource defines that a control have a minimum value of 0 and a maximum value of 100, and that the thumb initially be at a value of 50—at the center of the control. The entire control has a pixel width of 220 pixels. When the program in which the control appears is running, the user clicks on the thumb and drags it 55 pixels to the left before releasing the mouse button. Figure 3.20 illustrates this situation. The value of `pixels_per_unit` would be 2.2, and the value of units moved would be –25:

```
pixels_per_unit = control_pixel_width / control_unit_width
pixels_per_unit = 220 / 100
pixels_per_unit = 2.2
```

```
units_moved = horiz_offset / pixels_per_unit
units_moved = -55 / 2.2
units_moved = -25
```

If the thumb was moved 55 pixels to the left, it has moved one-fourth of the total pixel width of the control's 220 pixels. That means the thumb has also moved one-fourth of the total unit width, or 25 units, as well.

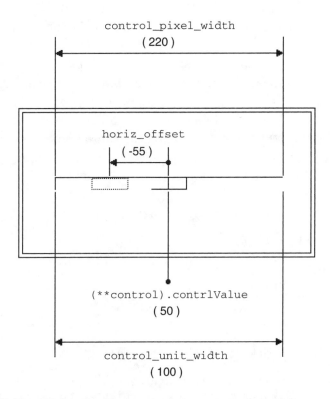

FIGURE 3.20 THE HORIZONTAL OFFSET OF THE THUMB IS THE NUMBER OF PIXELS THAT THE THUMB HAS MOVED FROM ITS ORIGINAL POSITION.

After determining the number of units moved, the `contrlValue` field of the control record needs to be updated to reflect the change. A call to `GetControlValue()` returns the value before the move. The number of units moved (-25) is then added to this value. The resulting total is then stored back in the control record with a call to `SetControl Value()`:

```
control_value = GetControlValue( control );
control_value += units_moved;
SetControlValue( control, control_value );
```

The call to `SetControlValue()` is the last line of code in `Position_Thumb()`. So it would appear that `Position_Thumb()` didn't complete its goal of redrawing the thumb at its final destination. But in fact it has. That's the interesting part of `Position_Thumb()`—the thumb will get drawn without the function drawing it and without an explicit call to the control definition's drawing routine, `Draw_Control()`. Here's why: a CDEF call to `SetControlValue()`, `SetControlMinimum()`, or `SetControlMaximum()` will automatically cause another message to be sent to the CDEF. The message type? A `drawCntl` message. So, as `Position_Thumb()` ends, `Draw_Control()` will begin.

```
void  Position_Thumb( ControlHandle control, long total_offset )
{
   short   horiz_offset;
   Rect    control_rect;
   short   control_pixel_width;
   short   control_unit_width;
   float   pixels_per_unit;
   short   units_moved;
   short   control_value;

   horiz_offset = LoWord( total_offset );

   control_rect = (**control).contrlRect;
   control_pixel_width = control_rect.right - control_rect.left;
   control_unit_width = (**control).contrlMax -
                        (**control).contrlMin;

   pixels_per_unit = (float)control_pixel_width /
                     (float)control_unit_width;
   units_moved = horiz_offset / pixels_per_unit;

   control_value = GetControlValue( control );
   control_value += units_moved;
   SetControlValue( control, control_value );
}
```

Handling a drawCntl Message

For MySliderGrayCDEF, the drawing of a control is done in much the same manner as it was for the Chapter 2 CDEF MyButtonCDEF. Using the ID of one of the PICT resources, a call to GetResource() returns a PicHandle to Draw_Control(). Then a call to DrawPicture() draws the control. For the control itself, the picture can be drawn to the control's rectangle:

```
Rect        control_rect;
short       pict_ID;
PicHandle   pict_handle;

control_rect = (**control).contrlRect;

pict_ID = GetControlReference( control );
if ( Color_Is_On( control_rect ) == false )
   pict_ID += CONTROL_BW_OFFSET;

pict_handle = (PicHandle)GetResource( 'PICT', pict_ID );
DrawPicture( pict_handle, &control_rect );
```

Drawing the control picture serves to obscure the old thumb picture. That's exactly what should happen. Remember, Draw_Control() will be called in response to the thumb being dragged and the mouse being released. The picture of the thumb at its original location—before the mouse click—is still present in the dialog box or window. The above call to DrawPicture() wipes it out.

After drawing the control picture, it's time to draw the thumb. The new location of the indicator is stored in the contrlValue field of the control record. A call to Calc_Thumb_Rect() retrieves that value and uses it to calculate and return the thumb's new pixel coordinates. After obtaining a handle to the proper picture, a call to DrawPicture() stamps the thumb over the control picture:

```
pict_ID = GetControlReference( control );
pict_ID += THUMB_OFFSET;
if ( Color_Is_On( control_rect ) == false )
   pict_ID += THUMB_BW_OFFSET;
```

159

```
thumb_rect = Calc_Thumb_Rect( control );

pict_handle = (PicHandle)GetResource( 'PICT', pict_ID );
DrawPicture( pict_handle, &thumb_rect );
```

Here's a look at Draw_Control().

 It's important to place the code that draws the control picture before the code that draws the thumb picture. Reversing the order of drawing would cause the thumb to immediately be NOTE **obscured by the control picture.**

```
void   Draw_Control( ControlHandle control )
{
   Rect        control_rect;
   Rect        thumb_rect;
   short       pict_ID;
   PicHandle   pict_handle;

   control_rect = (**control).contrlRect;

   pict_ID = GetControlReference( control );
   if ( Color_Is_On( control_rect ) == false )
      pict_ID += CONTROL_BW_OFFSET;

   pict_handle = (PicHandle)GetResource( 'PICT', pict_ID );
   DrawPicture( pict_handle, &control_rect );
   ReleaseResource( (Handle)pict_handle );


   pict_ID = GetControlReference( control );
   pict_ID += THUMB_OFFSET;
   if ( Color_Is_On( control_rect ) == false )
      pict_ID += THUMB_BW_OFFSET;

   thumb_rect = Calc_Thumb_Rect( control );

   pict_handle = (PicHandle)GetResource( 'PICT', pict_ID );
   DrawPicture( pict_handle, &thumb_rect );
   ReleaseResource( (Handle)pict_handle );
}
```

Building the CDEF Code Resource

The process of building the MyButtonCDEF in Chapter 2 should have given you all of the information and confidence you need to build any CDEF code resource. If you have forgotten how to set up a code resource project, refer back to Chapter 2. You can also take a look at the MySliderGrayCDEF project, which is located in the My Slider Gray CDEF ƒ folder.

If you use the Metrowerks compiler, select **Preferences** from the Edit menu. After clicking on the **Project** panel, make sure that the panel settings are correct. The Project Type should be set to Code Resource and CDEF should be entered in the ResType field. The ResID should be 500 so that the CNTL resources can work with this CDEF. When you're satisfied that everything's okay, dismiss the Preferences dialog box and select **Make** from the Project menu to build the code resource.

If you're a Symantec user, select **Set Project Type** from the Project menu and look at the dialog box settings. Verify that the **Code Resource** radio button is selected and that the Type field is filled out as CDEF. The ID field should be set to 500 so that the CNTL resources in the resource file will use the MySliderGrayCDEF. After dismissing the dialog box you can build the code resource by selecting **Build Code Resource** from the Project menu.

THE SLIDER TEST APPLICATION

This chapter's test application is one of the shortest Mac programs you'll ever write. MyTestApp simply displays the dialog box shown in Figure 3.21—the dialog box you've seen throughout this chapter.

Clicking on the control's thumb allows the outline of the thumb to be dragged back and forth across the control. A click on the **OK** button ends the program.

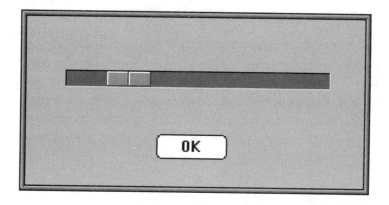

FIGURE 3.21 THE DIALOG BOX DISPLAYED BY MYTESTAPP.

The Test Application Resources

You've already seen the key resources used in this chapter's MyTestApp—they've been used in the figures that accompanied discussions of slider CDEFs earlier in this chapter. To save you a lot of page flipping, I've repeated them here. The MyTestApp resource file holds four PICT resources so that the application will be able to display both color and monochrome versions of the control and its thumb. These PICTs are shown in Figure 3.22.

The resource file's one DITL holds just two items—an OK push button and a Control item that will become the slider. As shown in Figure 3.23, the Control item relies on CNTL resource 300 for its information. Because I've given the MySliderGrayCDEF an ID of 500, the CNTL resource has a ProcID of 8000. Figure 3.24 shows the one CNTL resource used by MyTestApp.

```
ProcID  = ( 'CDEF' ID * 16 ) + variation code
ProcID  = (     500    * 16 ) +    0
ProcID  = 8000
```

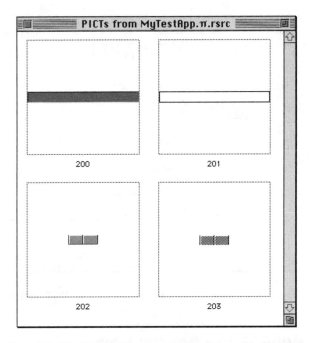

FIGURE 3.22 THE PICT RESOURCES USED BY MYTESTAPP.

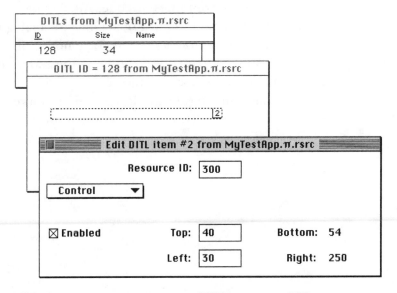

FIGURE 3.23 THE CONTROL ITEM RELIES ON CNTL RESOURCE 300 FOR ITS INFORMATION.

```
┌─────────────────────────────────────────────────────────┐
│ ▨▤▤▤▤▤    CNTL ID = 300 from MyTestApp.π.rsrc   ▤▤▤▤▤  │ ⬆
├─────────────────────────────────────────────────────────┤
│  BoundsRect    │ 0    │ │ 0    │ │ 14   │ │ 220  │ [ Set ] │
│                                                           │
│  Value         │ 50                       │              │
│                                                           │
│  Visible         ◉ True   ○ False                        │
│                                                           │
│  Max           │ 100                      │              │
│                                                           │
│  Min           │ 0                        │              │
│                                                           │
│  ProcID        │ 8000                     │              │
│                                                           │
│  RefCon        │ 200                          │          │
│                                                           │
│  Title         │                              │          │
│                                                        ⬇  │
└─────────────────────────────────────────────────────────┘
```

FIGURE 3.24 THE CNTL RESOURCE USED BY MYTESTAPP.

The Test Application Source Code

MyTestApp contains just a few dozen lines of code. After initializing the Toolbox, the program displays a modal dialog box. Once the dialog box is up, the code loops until the **OK** button is pressed. Take notice of the fact that the application needs no source code to support the slider control that was added in the application's resource file. The MySliderGrayCDEF will handle everything. After building the application, don't forget to use your resource editor to copy the CDEF from its own resource file and paste it into the application.

```
//_____
//                                          function prototypes

void   Initialize_Toolbox( void );
void   Display_Dialog( void );


//_____
//                                                    main()
main ( )
```

```
{
   Initialize_Toolbox();
   Display_Dialog();
}



//_____
//                           open and display a modal dialog box

void  Display_Dialog( void )
{
   DialogPtr   the_dialog;
   short       the_item;
   Boolean     all_done = false;

   the_dialog = GetNewDialog( 128, nil, (WindowPtr)-1L );
   ShowWindow( the_dialog );

   while ( all_done == false )
   {
      ModalDialog( nil, &the_item );

      switch ( the_item )
      {
         case ok:
            all_done = true;
            break;
      }
   }
   DisposDialog( the_dialog );
}



//_____
//                                      initialize the Mac

void  Initialize_Toolbox( void )
{
   InitGraf( &qd.thePort );
   InitFonts();
   InitWindows();
   InitMenus();
   TEInit();
   InitDialogs( 0L );
   FlushEvents( everyEvent, 0L );
   InitCursor();
}
```

SLIDERS AND CUSTOM DRAGGING

The MySliderGrayCDEF relied on the Control Manager to implement the dragging of the thumb of the slider. When the Control Manager handles indicator dragging, it does so in a standard manner: It displays the outline of the indicator and constantly updates that outline as the user drags the mouse. If you'd like your slider to have its indicator dragged in a different manner, you're free to do so. In this section you'll learn how to have a CDEF implement custom dragging.

The MySliderRoughCDEF will handle a horizontal slider—just as MySliderGrayCDEF does. The difference will be that MySliderRough CDEF won't display the outline of the thumb as it gets dragged by the user. Instead, it will move the thumb itself.

 As the thumb moves across the control, how smoothly will it appear to glide from one end to the other? The answer lies in the title of the CDEF! Don't worry, though, we'll improve

N O T E **upon things a little before the chapter ends.**

The CDEF Messages

MySliderRoughCDEF responds to only three types of messages: `testCntl`, `drawCntl`, and `dragCntl`. Because the CDEF will be performing the dragging of the thumb, it won't need to send region information back to the Toolbox—that's why it won't need to handle `calcThumbRgn` or `calcCRgns` messages. The CDEF also won't need to send back information about the drag boundaries or thumb position—so `thumbCntl` and `posCntl` messages won't be handled either.

While MySliderRoughCDEF handles fewer messages than MySliderGrayCDEF, it does handle one message type that the previous slider didn't watch for: the `dragCntl` message.

Before responding to the user's attempt to drag an indicator, the Control Manager sends a CDEF a `dragCntl` message. If the CDEF returns a 0, or doesn't handle a `dragCntl` message (as was the case for

MySliderGrayCDEF), the Control Manager will assume that it should drag the indicator in its standard fashion. If, on the other hand, the CDEF handles the `dragCntl` message, the Control Manager will not attempt to display the outlined indicator. Instead, it will relent control to the CDEF. It then becomes the responsibility of the control definition to invoke its own dragging routine. For MySliderRoughCDEF, this routine is named `Drag_Control()`:

```
pascal long  main( short          var_code,
                   ControlHandle the_control,
                   short          message,
                   long           msg_param )
{
   long  return_val = 0L;

   switch ( message )
   {
      case testCntl:
         return_val = Test_Control( the_control, msg_param );
         break;

      case dragCntl:
         return_val = Drag_Control( the_control );
         break;

      case drawCntl:
         Draw_Control( the_control );
         break;
   }

   return ( return_val );
}
```

If the Control Manager sends a msg_param value of 0 along with the `dragCntl` **message, then the entire control is to be dragged by the user. If, as is more likely, a nonzero** msg_param **value is sent, just the indicator is to be moved by the custom drag routine of the CDEF. You'll find information on dragging an entire control in** *Inside Macintosh: Macintosh Toolbox Essentials.*

Messages of the `testCntl` and `drawCntl` types will be handled exactly as they were for MySliderGrayCDEF, so there's no need to repeat that source code of `Test_Control()` and `Draw_Control()` here. That means there's only one new routine to cover—the `Drag_Control()` function that's called to handle a `dragCntl` message.

Handling a dragCntl Message

Once `testCntl` confirms that the mouse button has been clicked on the slider's thumb, it's up to `Drag_Control()` to handle the dragging of the indicator. Since this CDEF doesn't rely on the Control Manager to do any dragging calculations or dragging, it should make sense to you that the work done by `Drag_Control()` will be performed in a loop. As the user moves the mouse, `Drag_Control()` must constantly determine the change of position of the mouse and redraw the thumb as needed. Before examining the function's code, here's an overview of what `Drag_Control()` will be doing:

```
long  Drag_Control( ControlHandle control )
{
    Perform size calculations for the control and thumb
    Get the mouse location at point of mouse click

    Begin Loop
        Get the new mouse location as it is moved by user
        Determine pixel change from old mouse location to new
        location
        Translate pixel change to corresponding change in unit
        value
        Set the control's value field to the new value
        Update the control (redraw the thumb and control)
        Mark the new mouse location as the old mouse location
    End Loop
}
```

By the time `Drag_Control()` is called, the `Test_Control()` function has determined that there was a mouse click in the thumb of a slider. Before entering the loop that will trace the user's mouse movements and redraw the control, `Drag_Control()` will perform a few calculations that will be used within the loop body.

You've already seen how to determine the size of the control—in both pixel dimensions and unit dimensions:

```
Rect    control_rect;
short   control_pixel_width;
short   control_unit_width;

control_rect = (**control).contrlRect;

control_pixel_width = control_rect.right - control_rect.left;
control_unit_width  = (**control).contrlMax -
(**control).contrlMin;
```

A call to `Calc_Thumb_Rect()` will return the rectangle that holds the boundaries of the indicator. From this rectangle one other useful dimension will be determined—the width of the thumb:

```
short   thumb_width;
Rect    thumb_rect;

thumb_rect = Calc_Thumb_Rect( control );

thumb_width = thumb_rect.right - thumb_rect.left;
```

A call to `GetMouse()` returns the point of the cursor when the mouse is first clicked on the control's indicator:

```
Point   old_mouse_loc;

GetMouse( &old_mouse_loc );
```

Now it's time for the loop. As long as the mouse button is held down by the user, the loop will repeatedly execute—the call to the Toolbox routine `StillDown()` makes sure of this. Once in the loop body, a call to `GetMouse()` is made. The mouse location is saved in a different variable than the point taken just before the loop started:

```
Point   new_mouse_loc;

while ( StillDown() )
{
   GetMouse( &new_mouse_loc );

   // rest of loop body
}
```

The change in the horizontal mouse position from the time the mouse was pressed to the time it was moved is saved in a variable named `horiz_change`. Then a test is performed to see if there was any change in mouse position and to see if the cursor is still over the indicator:

```
short  horiz_change;

horiz_change = new_mouse_loc.h - old_mouse_loc.h;

if ( ( horiz_change != 0 ) &&
     ( PtInRect( new_mouse_loc, &control_rect ) ) )
{
   // move the thumb
}
```

If both tests pass, it's time to determine the new location to which the thumb should be moved. The left and right coordinates of the previously calculated `thumb_rect` are adjusted for the change in position of the mouse. Then the center of the thumb is located:

```
thumb_rect.left  += horiz_change;
thumb_rect.right += horiz_change;

thumb_center = thumb_rect.left + ( thumb_width / 2 );
```

The center of the thumb, which is in pixel coordinates, is now translated to a unit location. First it's determined how far (in pixels) the center of the thumb is from the left side of the control:

```
control_offset = thumb_center - control_rect.left;
```

This offset value is then used to calculate a ratio. What fraction of the entire control length was the thumb moved?

```
 ratio = (float)control_offset / (float)control_pixel_width;
```

Along with the minimum control value (as set in the CNTL resource) and the total number of units in the control, this ratio can then be used in the determination of the unit value at which the thumb should be placed:

170

```
control_value = (**control).contrlMin +
                ( control_unit_width * ratio );
```

Next, a call to `SetControlValue()` sets the `contrlValue` field of the control record to this new value:

```
SetControlValue( control, control_value );
```

Now the really important part. Recall from earlier discussions that a call to `SetControlValue()` automatically causes the Control Manager to send a `drawCntl` message to the CDEF. That means that at this point a call to `Draw_Control()` is made. The execution of `Draw_Control()` draws the entire control, thereby covering up the old thumb. It also draws the thumb in its new position.

Before the body of the loop ends, the value of `old_mouse_loc` is set to the value of `new_mouse_loc`:

```
old_mouse_loc = new_mouse_loc;
```

When the body of the loop again executes, `GetMouse()` will return a new mouse point and store it in `new_mouse_loc`. A comparison will then be made between this location and the location that was obtained in the last iteration of the loop.

Before looking at the entire `Drag_Control()` routine, there's one last snippet to discuss. After the pixel location of the thumb is determined in the loop body, two checks are made. `Drag_Control()` needs to verify that the user didn't move the mouse past either the left or right boundaries of the control. If that happens, the routine adjusts the thumb boundaries so that they stop a few pixels from the end of the control, regardless of how far past the edge the user has dragged the mouse.

```
if ( thumb_rect.left < ( control_rect.left + 3 ) )
{
   thumb_rect.left = control_rect.left + 3;
   thumb_rect.right = thumb_rect.left + thumb_width;
}
if ( thumb_rect.right > ( control_rect.right - 2 ) )
{
   thumb_rect.right = control_rect.right - 2;
```

```
      thumb_rect.left = thumb_rect.right - thumb_width;
}
```

Now, here's the complete source code listing for the Drag_Control() function.

```
long  Drag_Control( ControlHandle control )
{
   short   thumb_width;
   short   thumb_center;
   Rect    thumb_rect;
   Rect    control_rect;
   short   control_pixel_width;
   short   control_unit_width;
   short   control_offset;
   short   control_value;
   float   ratio;
   Point   new_mouse_loc;
   Point   old_mouse_loc;
   short   horiz_change;

   control_rect = (**control).contrlRect;

   control_pixel_width = control_rect.right - control_rect.left;
   control_unit_width  = (**control).contrlMax -
                         (**control).contrlMin;

   thumb_rect = Calc_Thumb_Rect( control );

   thumb_width = thumb_rect.right - thumb_rect.left;

   GetMouse( &old_mouse_loc );

   while ( StillDown() )
   {
      GetMouse( &new_mouse_loc );
      horiz_change = new_mouse_loc.h - old_mouse_loc.h;

      if ( ( horiz_change != 0 ) &&
           ( PtInRect( new_mouse_loc, &control_rect ) ) )
      {
         thumb_rect.left  += horiz_change;
         thumb_rect.right += horiz_change;

         if ( thumb_rect.left < ( control_rect.left + 3 ) )
         {
            thumb_rect.left = control_rect.left + 3;
            thumb_rect.right = thumb_rect.left + thumb_width;
```

```
   }
   if ( thumb_rect.right > ( control_rect.right - 2 ) )
   {
      thumb_rect.right = control_rect.right - 2;
      thumb_rect.left = thumb_rect.right - thumb_width;
   }

   thumb_center = thumb_rect.left + ( thumb_width / 2 );

   control_offset = thumb_center - control_rect.left;
   ratio = (float)control_offset /
           (float)control_pixel_width;

   control_value = (**control).contrlMin +
                    ( control_unit_width * ratio );
   SetControlValue( control, control_value );
   }

   old_mouse_loc = new_mouse_loc;
   }

   return ( 1L );
}
```

Remember, if the CDEF has a provision for handling a `dragCntl` **message, and it doesn't handle the dragging, it should return a value of 0 to the Control Manager. Since MySliderRoughCDEF does handle the dragging, it should be sure to make the Control Manager aware of this fact by returning a value other than 0. That's the purpose of the last statement in** `Drag_Control()`.

N O T E

Use your development environment to build a CDEF code resource with an ID of 500. Then copy it from its resource file and paste it into MyTestApp. Since it has the same ID as the MySliderGrayCDEF that's already in the test application, you'll be warned that you're about to replace an existing resource. Go ahead and do so. Then exit the resource editor and run MyTestApp. Click on the control's thumb and drag the mouse. As you do that, you'll see that the thumb follows the cursor, but the result is unacceptably jerky. In the next section you'll see what can be done to smooth things out a little.

SMOOTHER CUSTOM DRAGGING

MySliderRoughCDEF adequately demonstrates how the handling of a dragCntl message can be used to implement custom dragging of a control's indicator. The end result of that CDEF, however, was a thumb that flickered as it was dragged across the control. In this section you'll see how a few simple changes can greatly reduce flicker.

N O T E **If you're very familiar with off-screen drawing techniques, then you already know the best way to create smooth, flicker-free animated effects. You can use a series of** GWorlds **to smoothly move a thumb PICT over the control background. If you aren't familiar with** GWorlds**, this technique requires several lines of code and a correspondingly lengthy discussion. For that reason the use of off-screen** PixMaps**, or** GWorlds**, is considered beyond the scope of this book.**

Adding New PICT Resources

For the new version of the slider CDEF, which I'll call MySliderSmooth CDEF, changes will need to be made to the PICT resources. The first change is to an existing PICT—the picture that is used as the slider's thumb. I have launched my graphics program and opened the document that held the thumb graphics. Now, instead of selecting just the thumb, I've included two pixels of the control itself, as shown in Figure 3.25. Then I copied this picture and pasted it in the application project's resource file. I deleted the old PICT with ID 202 and changed the ID of the new PICT to 202.

Next, I copied a small part of the background pattern of the control itself. The size of this picture isn't too important—it will be changed by the CDEF before being drawn. I pasted this new picture into the application project's resource file and gave it an ID of 205.

To support monochrome monitors, I added black-and-white versions of the same two pictures that have just been discussed. Because the black-and-white version of the control has a white background, the change to the thumb picture won't be evident, and the new background picture won't be visible at all. Figure 3.26 shows the PICT resources of the MyTestApp project's resource file.

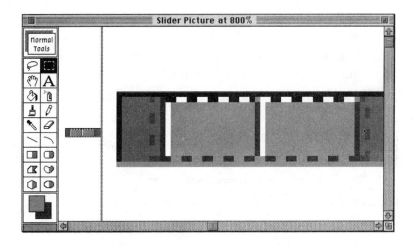

FIGURE 3.25 THE SELECTION OF THE NEW THUMB PICTURE SHOULD INCLUDE TWO PIXELS OF THE CONTROL ON BOTH THE LEFT AND RIGHT SIDES OF THE THUMB.

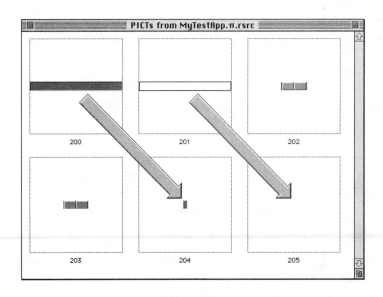

FIGURE 3.26 TWO NEW **PICT**S SHOULD BE ADDED TO THE APPLICATION PROJECT'S RESOURCE FILE—PICTURES **204** AND **205**.

Figure 3.27 shows why I've made the previous changes to the pictures. In that figure you can see how MySliderRoughCDEF handled the updating of the control's thumb as it was moved across the control. A drag of the mouse caused the control picture to be redrawn first, and the thumb picture to be redrawn second. The drawing of the entire control picture caused the thumb to completely disappear before it was redrawn, and was responsible for the flicker that's seen when the thumb is dragged.

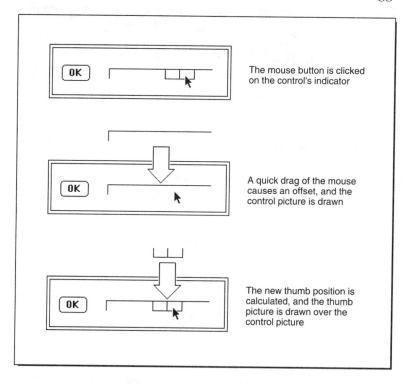

FIGURE 3.27 MySliderRoughCDEF HAD FLICKER BECAUSE THE ENTIRE CONTROL PICTURE WAS DRAWN OVER THE THUMB PICTURE.

Figure 3.28 shows how the new set of pictures will greatly reduce flicker. When the mouse is dragged on the thumb, the thumb picture will be drawn at the new location, without first drawing the control picture. Then the small control pattern picture will be drawn behind the new thumb to obscure what remains of the old thumb. The result will be a slight blurring of the thumb as its moved, but flicker will be eliminated.

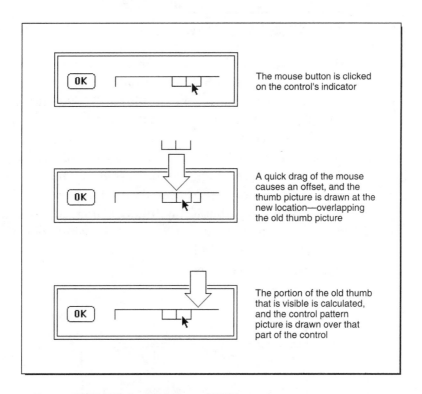

The mouse button is clicked on the control's indicator

A quick drag of the mouse causes an offset, and the thumb picture is drawn at the new location—overlapping the old thumb picture

The portion of the old thumb that is visible is calculated, and the control pattern picture is drawn over that part of the control

FIGURE 3.28 MySliderSmoothCDEF reduces flicker by avoiding the drawing of the control picture.

Taking Care of the Preliminaries

Because there have been new pictures added, the source code for MySliderSmoothCDEF will define a new constant. When CONTROL_PART_OFFSET is added to the ID of the base picture, the result will be the ID of the appropriate control background picture.

```
#define        CONTROL_BW_OFFSET        1
#define        THUMB_OFFSET             2
```

```
#define        THUMB_BW_OFFSET            1
#define        CONTROL_PART_OFFSET        4
```

Handling a dragCntl Message

MySliderSmoothCDEF uses the same custom dragging routine that MySliderRoughCDEF uses—but with a couple of important additions. First, an additional Rect variable has been added. At the end of the while loop in Drag_Control(), the old_thumb_rect will be assigned the rectangle coordinates of thumb_rect. At the next pass through the loop, the thumb will be drawn at its new location. Then both the new rectangle and the old rectangle will be passed to a function that draws the control's background pattern over the visible part of the old thumb picture. Figure 3.29 shows that if the thumb is dragged to the left, it will be the right coordinate of thumb_rect and the right coordinate of old_thumb_rect that will determine the boundaries of the rectangle to which the pattern should be drawn.

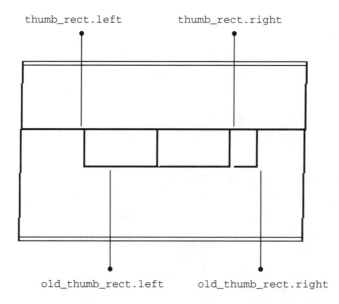

FIGURE 3.29 BOTH THE NEW AND OLD COORDINATES OF THE THUMB ARE USED TO DETERMINE WHERE TO DRAW THE CONTROL PATTERN PICTURE.

While there are only a few changes to `Drag_Control()`, they are important. So I've again supplied the entire listing of the routine. The changes from the MySliderRoughCDEF version appear in bold type.

```
long  Drag_Control( ControlHandle control )
{
    short        thumb_width;
    short        thumb_center;
    Rect         thumb_rect;
    Rect         control_rect;
    short        control_pixel_width;
    short        control_unit_width;
    short        control_offset;
    short        control_value;
    float        ratio;
    Point        new_mouse_loc;
    Point        old_mouse_loc;
    short        horiz_change;
    Rect         old_thumb_rect;

    control_rect = (**control).contrlRect;

    control_pixel_width = control_rect.right - control_rect.left;
    control_unit_width  = (**control).contrlMax -
                          (**control).contrlMin;

    thumb_rect = Calc_Thumb_Rect( control );
    old_thumb_rect = thumb_rect;

    thumb_width = thumb_rect.right - thumb_rect.left;

    GetMouse( &old_mouse_loc );

    while ( StillDown() )
    {
        GetMouse( &new_mouse_loc );
        horiz_change = new_mouse_loc.h - old_mouse_loc.h;

        if ( ( horiz_change != 0 ) &&
             ( PtInRect( new_mouse_loc, &control_rect ) ) )
        {
            thumb_rect.left  += horiz_change;
            thumb_rect.right += horiz_change;

            if ( thumb_rect.left < ( control_rect.left + 4 ) )
            {
```

```
            thumb_rect.left = control_rect.left + 4;
            thumb_rect.right = thumb_rect.left + thumb_width;
        }
        if ( thumb_rect.right > ( control_rect.right - 2 ) )
        {
            thumb_rect.right = control_rect.right - 2;
            thumb_rect.left = thumb_rect.right - thumb_width;
        }

        thumb_center = thumb_rect.left + ( thumb_width / 2 );

        control_offset = thumb_center - control_rect.left;
        ratio = (float)control_offset /
                (float)control_pixel_width;

        control_value = (**control).contrlMin +
                        ( control_unit_width * ratio );
        SetControlValue( control, control_value );

        Draw_Over_Old_Thumb( control, old_thumb_rect, thumb_rect );

        old_thumb_rect = thumb_rect;
    }

    old_mouse_loc = new_mouse_loc;
  }

  return ( 1L );
}
```

SetControlValue() is called near the end of the while loop. Recall that a call to this routine triggers a drawCntl message. When that happens, Draw_Control() will be called to draw the thumb in its new location. Then Draw_Over_Old_Thumb(), which will be discussed in just a bit, is called to obscure the remnants of the old thumb picture.

Handling a drawCntl Message

The previous version of Draw_Control() drew both the control picture and the thumb picture—that was the source of the flicker in MySliderRoughCDEF. This new version has the same code to draw each picture, but it now has some logic added so that it only draws one or the other. The dragging of the thumb never requires that the control picture be drawn—just the thumb and the control pattern. But there are times when the window or dialog box in which the control appears may need updating, so `Draw_Control()` needs to keep its ability to draw the entire control.

When the Control Manager sends CDEF a `drawCntl` message, it includes a part code in the `msg_param` parameter. If that part code is 0, the entire control should be drawn. If the part code is 129, the thumb should be drawn. In the previous version of `Draw_Control()`, this `msg_param` part code was ignored and both the control and thumb were drawn. In this new version, the part code will be examined:

```
case drawCntl:
   Draw_Control( the_control, msg_param );
   break;
```

When a control needs updating, perhaps because the dialog box in which it appears has been covered and then exposed, the Control Manager will send a `drawCntl` message with a `msg_param` value of 0. In that case, `Draw_Control()` will draw the control:

```
if ( part_code != 129 )
{
   pict_ID = GetControlReference( control );
   if ( Color_Is_On( control_rect ) == false )
      pict_ID += CONTROL_BW_OFFSET;

   pict_handle = (PicHandle)GetResource( 'PICT', pict_ID );
   DrawPicture( pict_handle, &control_rect );
}
```

If, on the other hand, a `drawCntl` message is sent as the result of a call to `SetControlValue()`, the Control Manager will include a `msg_param` value of 129. That means just the thumb should be drawn. Since the above code executes when `msg_param` is *not* 129, it will be skipped. The code for drawing the thumb, however, is always executed:

```
pict_ID = GetControlReference( control );
pict_ID += THUMB_OFFSET;
```

181

```
if ( Color_Is_On( control_rect ) == false )
   pict_ID += THUMB_BW_OFFSET;

thumb_rect = Calc_Thumb_Rect( control );

pict_handle = (PicHandle)GetResource( 'PICT', pict_ID );
DrawPicture( pict_handle, &thumb_rect );

ReleaseResource( (Handle)pict_handle );
```

The `Drag_Control()` routine that was discussed just a while back had
a call to `SetControlValue()`. It is that call that triggers the redrawing
of the thumb—but not the control. Here is a look at the new version of
`Draw_Control()`:

```
void  Draw_Control( ControlHandle control, long part_code )
{
   Rect        control_rect;
   Rect        thumb_rect;
   short       pict_ID;
   PicHandle   pict_handle;

   control_rect = (**control).contrlRect;

   // Draw the control
   // This code will be skipped if coming from Drag_Control()

   if ( part_code != 129 )
   {
      pict_ID = GetControlReference( control );
      if ( Color_Is_On( control_rect ) == false )
         pict_ID += CONTROL_BW_OFFSET;

      pict_handle = (PicHandle)GetResource( 'PICT', pict_ID );
      DrawPicture( pict_handle, &control_rect );
   }


   // Draw the thumb
   // This code will be executed in all cases

   pict_ID = GetControlReference( control );
   pict_ID += THUMB_OFFSET;
   if ( Color_Is_On( control_rect ) == false )
```

```
   pict_ID += THUMB_BW_OFFSET;

thumb_rect = Calc_Thumb_Rect( control );

pict_handle = (PicHandle)GetResource( 'PICT', pict_ID );
DrawPicture( pict_handle, &thumb_rect );

ReleaseResource( (Handle)pict_handle );
}
```

Covering the Old Thumb

There is just one routine left to cover in MySliderSmoothCDEF—
Draw_Over_Old_Thumb(). After SetControlValue() triggers the
execution of Draw_Control(), Draw_Over_Old_Thumb() is called
from within Drag_Control().

The first thing Draw_Over_Old_Thumb() does is get a handle to
the control background pattern picture. Then it calculates the size of the
rectangle to which this picture should be drawn. Because the picture is a
solid pattern, there's no need to be concerned with distortion as the size
of the picture changes.

```
Rect        control_rect;
short       pict_ID;
PicHandle   pict_handle;

pict_ID = GetControlReference( control );
pict_ID += CONTROL_PART_OFFSET;
if ( Color_Is_On( control_rect ) == false )
   pict_ID += CONTROL_BW_OFFSET;

pict_handle = (PicHandle)GetResource( 'PICT', pict_ID );
```

Next, the coordinates of the rectangle that is to provide the boundaries
for the background picture need to be calculated. The top and bottom
coordinates are easy to derive:

```
Rect  cover_rect;

cover_rect.top    = control_rect.top + 1;
cover_rect.bottom = control_rect.bottom - 1;
```

The right and left boundaries of cover_rect are dependent on the direction in which the thumb has moved. If it moved to the right, the covering rectangle must appear to the left of the new thumb picture. If the thumb moved to the left, the covering rectangle must appear to the right of the thumb picture:

```
if ( new_thumb_rect.left > old_thumb_rect.left )   // moving right
{
   cover_rect.left = old_thumb_rect.left - 1;
   cover_rect.right = new_thumb_rect.left;
}
else                                               // moving left
{
   cover_rect.left = new_thumb_rect.right - 2;
   cover_rect.right = old_thumb_rect.right + 1;
}
```

The last step is to draw the background picture:

```
DrawPicture( pict_handle, &cover_rect );
```

Listed as follows is the source code for the entire Draw_Over_Old_Thumb() routine.

```
void  Draw_Over_Old_Thumb( ControlHandle control,
                           Rect          old_thumb_rect,
                           Rect          new_thumb_rect )
{
   Rect       control_rect;
   short      pict_ID;
   PicHandle  pict_handle;
   Rect       cover_rect;

   control_rect = (**control).contrlRect;

   pict_ID = GetControlReference( control );
   pict_ID += CONTROL_PART_OFFSET;
   if ( Color_Is_On( control_rect ) == false )
      pict_ID += CONTROL_BW_OFFSET;

   pict_handle = (PicHandle)GetResource( 'PICT', pict_ID );
```

```
cover_rect.top    = control_rect.top + 1;
cover_rect.bottom = control_rect.bottom - 1;

if ( new_thumb_rect.left > old_thumb_rect.left )  // moving
                                                  // right
{
   cover_rect.left = old_thumb_rect.left - 1;
   cover_rect.right = new_thumb_rect.left;
}
else                                              // moving
                                                  // left
{
   cover_rect.left = new_thumb_rect.right - 2;
   cover_rect.right = old_thumb_rect.right + 1;
}

DrawPicture( pict_handle, &cover_rect );
ReleaseResource( (Handle)pict_handle );
}
```

As always, the project file and source code file for this section's example CDEF have been included on disk. After building a CDEF code resource, copy the resource and paste it into the same version of MyTestApp that you've been using in this chapter. Then build a new application. As a short cut, you can open the application itself and paste the CDEF into the application fork directly. Then run MyTestApp to see that the animation of the slider has indeed improved.

Adding a Label to the Control

As a final step to giving your sliders a clean look, you may want to add a label above or below the control. In Figure 3.30 I've added a new PICT resource to the resource file of the MyTestApp project.

Next, I added a Picture item to the DITL resource, as shown in Figure 3.31. After building a new application, the slider's dialog box looked like the one shown in Figure 3.32. Figure 3.33 shows a couple of other examples of how you might want to provide feedback to the user of your slider.

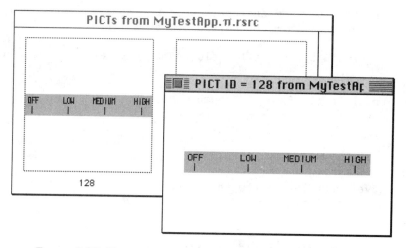

FIGURE 3.30 TO ADD A LABEL TO A SLIDER, FIRST ADD A PICT TO
THE APPLICATION PROJECT'S RESOURCE FILE.

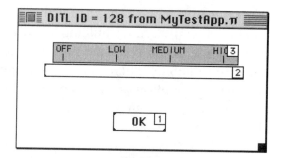

FIGURE 3.31 TO DISPLAY THE PICTURE, ADD A PICTURE ITEM TO THE DITL.

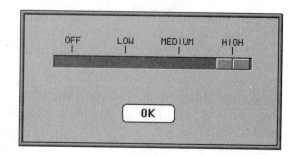

FIGURE 3.32 THE RESULT OF ADDING THE PICT RESOURCE.

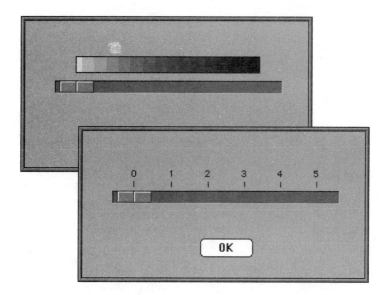

FIGURE 3.33 TWO EXAMPLES OF SLIDERS WITH LABELS.

CHAPTER SUMMARY

Sliders are a very "Mac-like" control, yet most programmers choose not to include them in their applications. That's because sliders are not supported by the Toolbox in the same way that standard push buttons, check boxes, and radio buttons are. Because a control definition function can be written so that it handles any style of control, you'll want to use a CDEF to add sliders to any of your Macintosh programs.

Just as last chapter's picture button CDEF watched for `testCntl` and `drawCntl` messages, so do this chapter's slider CDEF examples. By also responding to the `calcCRgns`, `calcThumbRgn`, `thumbCntl`, and `posCntl` messages, a CDEF can be written such that it displays the standard indicator outline as a thumb is dragged across a control.

To implement a less traditional means of dragging a control's thumb, use custom control dragging. To do that, your CDEF should handle `dragCntl` messages.

Chapter

4

More Mac Programming Techniques

Control Panels and cdevs

Control panels are small "programs" that enable a Macintosh user to easily change such features as the speaker volume, the desktop pattern, and the speed at which the cursor moves across the screen. In short, a control panel exists for the purpose of allowing the user to change a *systemwide* feature of the Macintosh. Unlike applications, control panels usually aren't used daily—the functions that a control panel performs are usually needed only occasionally.

A control panel is a special type of code resource that is used without the help of an application. Rather than requiring the presence of an application to load and execute it—as MDEF and CDEF resources do—a control panel code resource, or cdev, relies on the Finder. When a control panel is opened, it is the Finder that loads the code resource, interacts with it, and sends it messages.

Control panels don't clutter up the desktop. Instead, they're neatly tucked away in a folder that can be easily accessed from the Apple menu. So while control panels aren't accessed often, when the need to open one does arise, the control panel can easily be found. In this chapter, you'll see how to create your own Control Panel to add to the ones Apple supplies to each owner of a Macintosh.

CONTROL PANELS AND THE FINDER

The arrival of System 7 brought many changes to the way in which the Desktop looks and functions. One of these changes involves the way in which control panels are implemented.

Accessing Control Panels

In System 6, a single Control Panel desk accessory was used to make any and all system changes. That desk accessory is shown in Figure 4.1. In the figure, you can see that on the left of the Control Panel is a list of icons. Clicking on one of these icons changes the system features displayed on the right of the desk accessory.

The System 6 method of accessing systemwide features from a single desk accessory has a couple of significant drawbacks. First, only one set of features can be displayed at one time. Second, the display of features is always limited to the fixed size of the Control Panel desk accessory dialog box. To eliminate these hindrances, the manner in which systemwide features are accessed has changed with System 7.

Starting with System 7, the Control Panel desk accessory no longer exists as a single item. Instead, the one Control Panel has been replaced by individual control panels. Each control panel is created to control the function of a specific machine setting. Figure 4.2 shows the Mouse control panel, which is used to alter the mouse tracking speed and the speed at which mouse clicks are made.

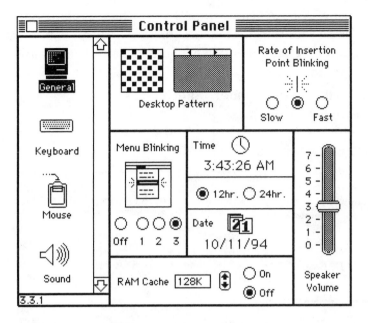

FIGURE 4.1 THE SYSTEM 6 CONTROL PANEL DESK ACCESSORY.

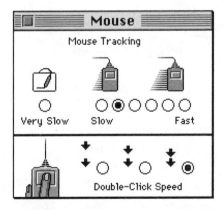

FIGURE 4.2 A TYPICAL SYSTEM 7 CONTROL PANEL.

In System 7, a single **Control Panels** menu item can be found in the Apple menu. Instead of opening a Control Panel desk accessory, however, selecting this menu item opens a Control Panels folder. This folder holds the icons for each individual control panel found on the Mac. Double-clicking on an icon launches that one control panel. Figure 4.3 shows the **Control Panels** menu item and the Control Panels folder.

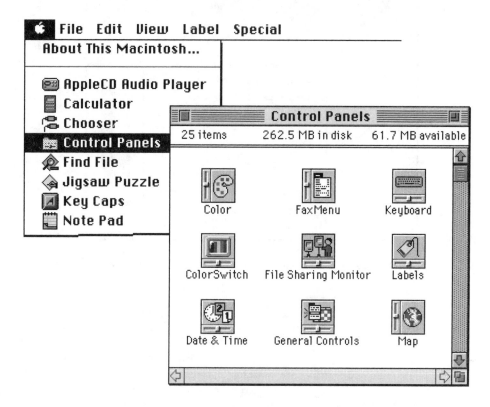

FIGURE 4.3 ACCESSING CONTROL PANELS FROM THE APPLE MENU ON A MAC RUNNING SYSTEM 7.

For System 7.5, accessing control panels has become even easier. Instead of opening a folder, a **Control Panels** menu item selection displays a hierarchical menu that lists all of the control panels available for that Macintosh. Sliding the cursor over to any item in the list opens that control panel. Figure 4.4 shows the System 7.5 implementation of control panels.

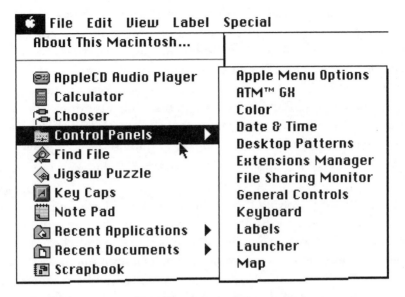

FIGURE 4.4 ACCESSING CONTROL PANELS FROM THE APPLE MENU ON
A MAC RUNNING SYSTEM 7.5.

A Control Panel or an Application?

If you have an idea for a small, simple program that could be used to vary
a system feature, you may be tempted to turn that idea into an application. After all, you already know how to develop Macintosh applications.
While that temptation is great, you'll want to overcome it and instead
develop a control panel. Here's why:

■   If your utility alters systemwide features, users will naturally assume
    that it can be found by selecting the **Control Panels** menu item.

■   A control panel may actually be easier to develop than an applica-
    tion.

That second point merits some discussion. A control panel is a file that
consists of several resources. Among these resources is a cdev code

resource. The cdev consists of the code for a *control device function*, or *cdev function*. Like the code for a menu definition procedure or a control definition function, the code for a control device function does not look like the code for a standalone application. There is no main event loop, no call to `WaitNextEvent()`, and no code to support the moving of a modeless dialog box. For MDEF and CDEF code resources, these elements are all found in the application that uses the MDEF or CDEF. For a cdev code resource, all of these things are handled by the Finder.

In this book's MDEF and CDEF chapters, a few different test applications were written. If a dialog box was to be opened, the test application was responsible for supplying the DLOG resource and calls to the Toolbox routines that opened and displayed the dialog box. Had any of these test applications worked with a modeless dialog box, the test application would have been responsible for supporting the movement of the dialog box and its interaction with other windows on the screen. For a cdev code resource, the Finder handles all of these tasks—no driving application needs to be developed in order for a control panel to function.

 Because of this, a control panel is double-clickable. Double-clicking on a control panel causes the Finder to load the control panel in memory and open and display the Modeless dialog box that houses the control panel's items.

N O T E

When shouldn't you develop a control panel? When the implementation of your feature-setting code requires placing menus in the menu bar or the display of multiple dialog boxes. Control panels are meant to be clean and simple. If your code is more complex, develop an application rather than a control panel.

CONTROL PANEL RESOURCES

A control panel consists of both required and optional resources. To create a control panel, you must add these resources to a resource file. Next, you'll write the control device function source code that your programming environment will turn into a cdev code resource. Your compiler will then link this cdev resource with the resources in the resource file. The result will be a *control panel file*—known simply as a *control panel* to Mac users.

In this section, you'll see the resources necessary to develop a control panel named MySetSound. In the next section, you'll see the corresponding control device function source code for the same control panel.

About the MySetSound Control Panel

Varying the sound level of the Mac's speaker is a task just about all Mac users have performed. Apple's Sound control panel, shown in Figure 4.5, makes this task simple to carry out. The MySetSound control panel performs just one of the many tasks that Apple's Sound control panel handles—it allows the user to set the speaker volume to high, or to turn it off. Figure 4.6 shows the MySetSound control panel.

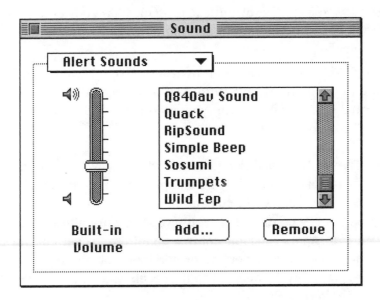

FIGURE 4.5 APPLE'S SOUND CONTROL PANEL.

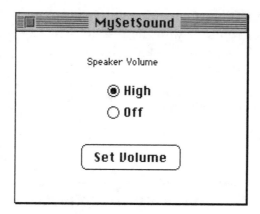

FIGURE 4.6 THIS BOOK'S MYSETSOUND CONTROL PANEL.

To change the Mac's speaker volume using MySetSound, a user clicks on either radio button, then clicks the **Set Volume** push button. If the **High** radio button is on, the speaker will beep once at the highest speaker volume. If the **Off** radio button is on, the Mac will flash the menu bar. Once the volume is set, the Mac's speaker volume will remain at the selected level until it is again changed, either through the MySetSound, the Sound control panel, or any other sound-setting control panel.

If you have Apple's Sound control panel open when you make a sound level change in MySetSound, you'll see the slider in the Sound control panel jump to the appropriate end of the scale. Figure 4.7 shows both sound control panels.

N O T E

The MySetSound is a good introductory example of a control panel because it is very simple. It's not an example of a practical real-world control panel, however, because it duplicates the control of a systemwide feature already controlled by an Apple-supplied control panel. Your own control panel should provide a service or services not already handled by Apple control panels. You'll see an example that does this later in this chapter.

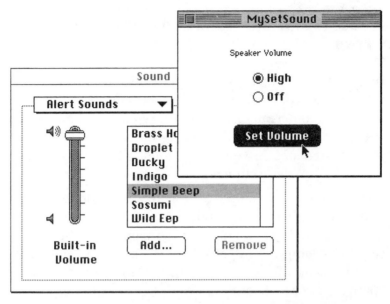

FIGURE 4.7 WHEN THE SYSTEM SPEAKER VOLUME IS CHANGED IN MYSETSOUND, THE CHANGE WILL BE REFLECTED IN APPLE'S SOUND CONTROL PANEL.

From the previous figures, you can see that the MySetSound control panel doesn't present much of a threat to Apple's Sound control panel. That's alright because the MySetSound isn't meant to compete with Apple's handy control panel. Instead, it's meant to demonstrate how easy it is to develop a control panel. In creating the MySetSound, you'll discover all of the following:

- Which resources a control panel requires
- What the function of each required resource is
- What the source code of a typical control panel looks like
- How a systemwide feature can be set by a control panel
- How the Finder interacts with a control panel
- How a single control panel can be compatible with both System 6 and System 7

MySetSound and the Required Control Panel Resources

A control panel, more correctly referred to as a *control panel file*, consists of several resource types. All but one of the resources will originate in a resource file that you create using a resource editor. The final resource, of type cdev, will be linked to this resource file to form the control panel file. The cdev is created by your programming environment and holds the compiled control device function code.

Figure 4.8 shows the resource file for the MySetSound control panel project. In keeping with the naming convention of the other code resources in this book, I've ended the file name with the type of code resource that is being developed—here it's a cdev resource. When it comes time to name the control panel itself, I'll drop the cdev ending and simply name it MySetSound.

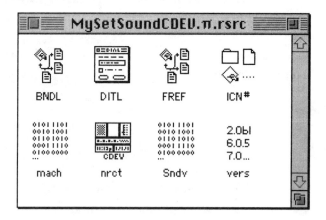

FIGURE 4.8 THE MYSETSOUND RESOURCE FILE, WITH THE RESOURCES REQUIRED OF A CONTROL PANEL.

While a control panel file can contain any number of resources and resource types, the ones shown in Figure 4.8 are the types that are required for any control panel.

The file in Figure 4.8 doesn't contain a cdev resource because it is the resource file for the control panel project, not for the control panel itself.

Most of the resource types shown in Figure 4.8 should look familiar to you. The BNDL resource group is used to create a family of icons for the control panel. As a by-product of creating a BNDL resource, your resource editor will add an ICN#, FREF, and signature resource to the resource file. For the MySetSound example, the signature is Sndv, so the signature resource file is Sndv. The ICN# resource holds the black-and-white icon drawn in the BNDL icon editor. The FREF is a file reference resource that associates the ICN# resource with this control panel.

The other two resources that you'll recognize are the DITL and the vers resources. The DITL resource holds all of the items that will appear in the control panel's dialog box. There's no DLOG resource because the Finder will be responsible for creating the dialog box itself. The vers resource, while not strictly required, is recommended for all System 7 code. The vers resource holds version information about the control panel.

The MySetSound resource file holds only two resource types that you won't find in application resource files. Control panels often use two-pixel-wide lines to divide the control panel into separate areas. The nrct resource lists the number and size of the rectangles that will be in the control panel's dialog box. Finally, the mach resource specifies which types of Macintosh the control panel will run on. Figure 4.9 summarizes the resource types that are to appear in a control panel's resource file.

MySetSound and the Familiar Resource Types

MySetSound has several resource types that you're already familiar with. I'll briefly cover each of them here. After that, I'll spend a few extra pages on the two new types: the nrct and the mach resources.

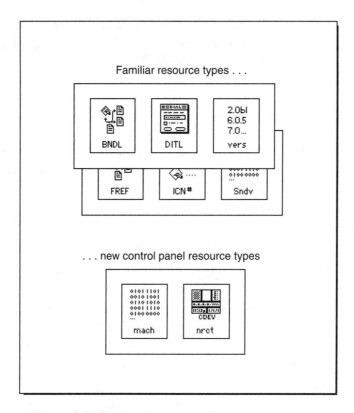

FIGURE 4.9 THE RESOURCE TYPES THAT MUST APPEAR IN A
CONTROL PANEL'S RESOURCE FILE.

Before looking at the resources, a few words about resource ID numbering are in order. A control panel is serviced and controlled by the Finder.
That means that a control panel's required resources will be accessed by
the Finder. Because of this, there are restrictions on the resource IDs you
can give to control panel resources. When a user selects a control panel
from the Apple menu, for instance, the Finder will open a Modeless dialog box and look to the control panel's resource fork for a DITL
resource with an ID of -4064. When it finds a DITL with that ID, the
Finder will use Dialog Manager and Control Manager routines to display
the items listed in that DITL. If the control panel does not contain a
DITL with an ID of -4064, the loading of the control panel will fail.

The DITL, BNDL, mach, and nrct resources each must have a resource ID of -4064. The FREF and ICN# resources that are automatically generated by the creation of the BNDL resource will (and must) also have IDs of -4064. The signature resource that is also created along with a BNDL will have an ID of 0. The vers resource, which is not technically a required control panel resource, should have an ID of 1.

N O T E

MySetSound has a DITL with four items, as shown in Figure 4.10. The control device function code (covered later) will be responsible for handling mouse clicks in the radio button and push button items. Note that the DITL has been given an ID of -4064, as required.

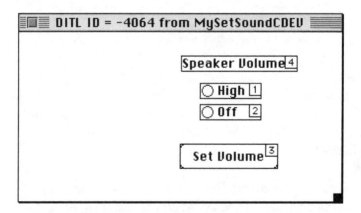

FIGURE 4.10 THE DITL RESOURCE FOR MYSETSOUND.

The reasoning behind the off-centered placement of the DITL items will be discussed when the nrct resource is covered.

N O T E

As required, the MySetSound has a BNDL resource with an ID of -4064, which is shown in Figure 4.11. A control panel can have any four-character signature. I have picked Sndv to give an indication that this control panel is a "sound device."

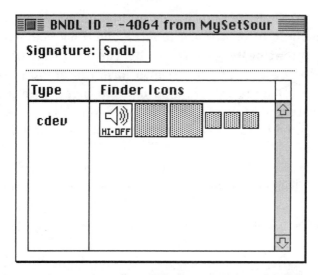

FIGURE 4.11 THE BNDL RESOURCE FOR MYSETSOUND.

Double-clicking on the row of gray patterned rectangles in the BNDL resource opens the ResEdit icon editor. Using this editor, I created a simple black-and-white icon for the MySetSound control panel, which is shown in Figure 4.12. I opened Apple's Sound control panel in ResEdit to get an idea of how to draw a small speaker.

 Before performing this blatant theft of an Apple icon, I of course verified that no Apple employees were looking over my shoulder!

N O T E

To better support users with color monitors, you might want to also add color icons to the control panel resource file. For MySetSound, I've kept things simple by sticking to black and white. The example cdev that follows MySetSound uses color icons and small icons.

I've added a vers resource to the MySetSound resource file so that the MySetSound displays version information in the Finder's Get Info window. This resource, which should have an ID of 1, is shown in Figure 4.13.

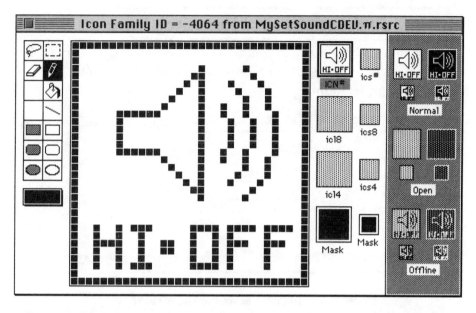

FIGURE 4.12 THE ICON EDITOR AND THE BLACK-AND-WHITE ICON FOR MYSETSOUND.

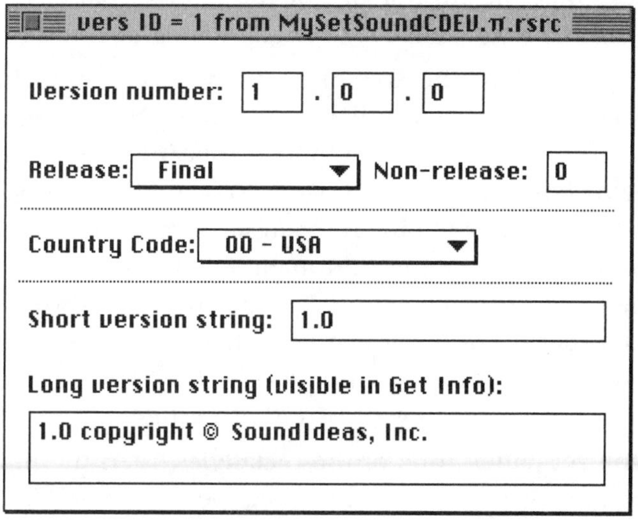

FIGURE 4.13 THE VERS RESOURCE FOR MYSETSOUND.

MySetSound and the nrct Resource Type

Control panels contain two resource types that aren't found in applications: the nrct and the mach resources. Figure 4.14 shows the nrct resource for MySetSound.

```
▧▧▨ nrct ID = -4064 from MySetSoundCDEU.π.rsrc ▨▨▨
NumOfRects    1

  1) *****

  Rectangle    │ -1 │  │ 87 │  │ 169 │  │ 322 │  ( Set )

  2) *****
```

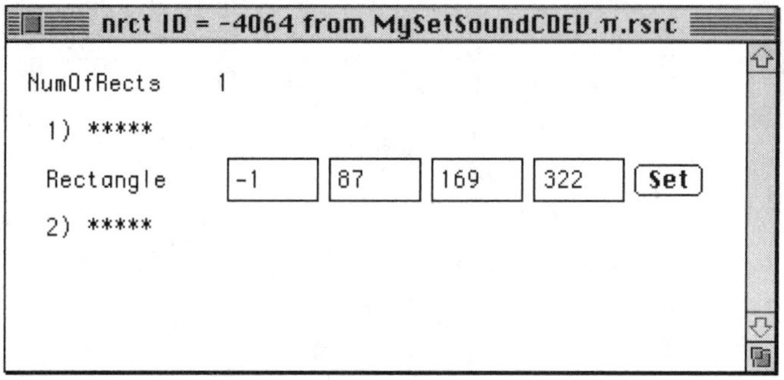

FIGURE 4.14 THE NRCT RESOURCE FOR MYSETSOUND.

The nrct resource, which must have an ID of -4064, serves two purposes. First, it determines the overall size of the control panel's dialog box. Second, the nrct divides the control panel's dialog box into rectangles.

For an application, the size of a dialog box is held in a DLOG resource. A control panel, you'll recall, has no DLOG resource—the Finder is responsible for opening and displaying the control panel's Modeless dialog box. So the Finder needs to be told how large the dialog box should be. It is the combined dimensions of all of a control panel's nrct rectangles that provide this information. Since MySetSound only has one rectangle, that one rectangle is the control panel's size. In the nrct resource, the ordering of the four rectangle dimensions is (T, L, B, R). Figure 4.15 shows that MySetSound rectangle (-1, 87, 169, 322) results in a dialog box that is 235 pixels wide by 170 pixels high.

For all control panels, one of the rectangles listed the nrct resource must have a top coordinate of -1 and a left coordinate of 87. If your control panel will be System 6 compatible, it will appear in the single Control Panel desk accessory that is used to display all control panels. As shown in Figure 4.16, the point (87, -1) represents the upper-left corner of the control panel display area.

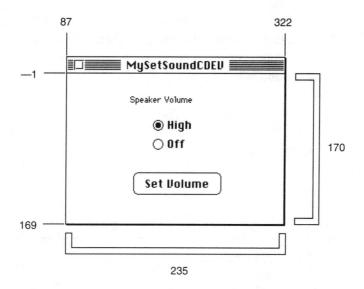

FIGURE 4.15 THE COORDINATES OF THE RECTANGLE IN WHICH
THE MYSETSOUND CONTROL PANEL WILL APPEAR.

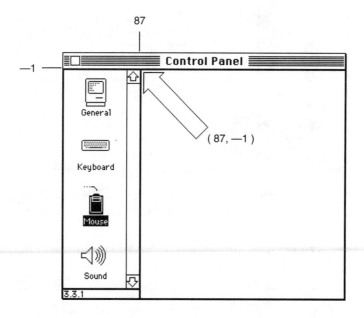

FIGURE 4.16 THE REFERENCE FOR THE PLACEMENT OF THE CONTROL PANEL ITEMS IN A
CONTROL PANEL APPEARING IN THE SYSTEM 6 CONTROL PANEL DESK ACCESSORY.

Even if your Control Panel will not be backwards compatible with System 6 and the Control Panel desk accessory, it *must* contain a nrct resource with a rectangle that has (87, -1) as its upper-left corner.

T   I   P

When you place a control panel's dialog items in the control panel's DITL resource, the 87-pixel offset must be considered. Earlier you saw the DITL for MySetSound. Recall that the four items in that DITL appeared to have been placed too far to the right in the DITL. Figure 4.17 shows why this was done.

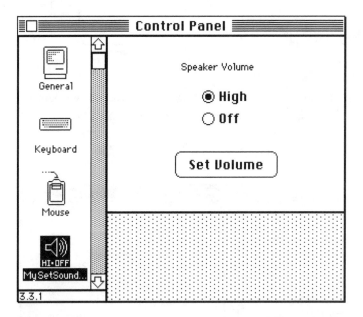

FIGURE 4.17 THE 87-PIXEL OFFSET ALLOWS A CONTROL PANEL TO FIT INSIDE THE DISPLAY AREA OF THE SYSTEM 6 CONTROL PANEL DESK ACCESSORY.

When a cdev is opened under System 6, the DITL items will be placed in the Control Panel dialog box (see Figure 4.17). In Figure 4.18, I've overlaid the MySetSound DITL over the Control Panel to emphasize just why you need to place DITL items off-center.

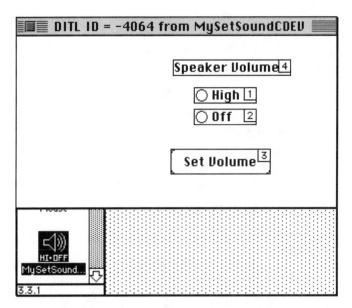

FIGURE 4.18 THE **DITL** ITEMS ARE OFFSET SO THAT THEY WILL APPEAR CENTERED IN THE SYSTEM 6 CONTROL PANEL DESK ACCESSORY'S DISPLAY AREA.

What happens if the Control Panel is opened while running on a Mac with System 7? The Finder knows enough to shift all of the items 87 pixels to the left before placing them in the dialog box that it opens.

Setting the size of the control panel's dialog box is one purpose of the nrct resource. The second purpose of the nrct is to divide the control panel's dialog box into rectangles. The MySetSound control panel has a single rectangle. Figure 4.19 shows an example that uses two rectangles.

Control panel rectangles exist for aesthetic purposes only. They're used to separate or group logically related items in a control panel. The Finder simply uses the values in the nrct

N O T E **to determine where to draw dividing lines in the control panel's dialog box. The Finder will not distinguish between mouse clicks that occur in one rectangle or another.**

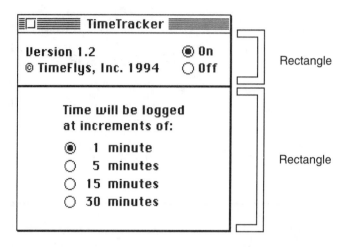

FIGURE 4.19 THE NRCT RESOURCES DIVIDE A CONTROL PANEL INTO SEPARATE AREAS.

If the combined area of the rectangles that make up an nrct resource doesn't cover a single rectangle, the Finder will fill any empty space with a gray pattern. Figure 4.20 shows an nrct resource that defines two rectangles. Figure 4.21 shows how the two rectangles would be placed in a System 7 control panel.

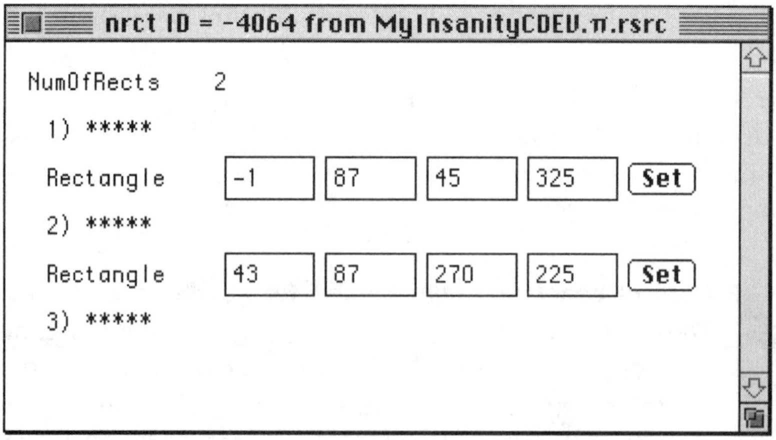

```
┌──────────────────────────────────────────────────────┐
│ ▓▓ ▓▓▓▓  nrct ID = -4064 from MyInsanityCDEV.π.rsrc ▓▓▓ │ ⬆
│                                                         │
│  NumOfRects    2                                        │
│    1) *****                                             │
│   Rectangle  ┌──┐ ┌──┐ ┌──┐ ┌───┐  ┌─────┐             │
│              │-1│ │87│ │45│ │325│  │ Set │             │
│              └──┘ └──┘ └──┘ └───┘  └─────┘             │
│    2) *****                                             │
│   Rectangle  ┌──┐ ┌──┐ ┌───┐ ┌───┐ ┌─────┐            │
│              │43│ │87│ │270│ │225│ │ Set │             │
│              └──┘ └──┘ └───┘ └───┘ └─────┘            │
│    3) *****                                             │
│                                                      ⬇  │
└──────────────────────────────────────────────────────┘
```

FIGURE 4.20 TWO NRCT RESOURCES DEFINE TWO SEPARATE DISPLAY AREAS.

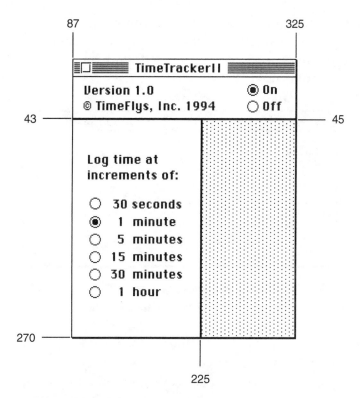

FIGURE 4.21 THE AREA OF A CONTROL PANEL DIALOG BOX
THAT IS NOT COVERED BY NRCT RECTANGLES WILL APPEAR GRAY.

MySetSound and the mach Resource Type

Because control panels usually make systemwide changes, all control panels cannot run on all Macintosh models and all versions of the system software. For example, if a control panel you're developing adjusts a color level, it might make no sense to have the control panel run on a black-and-white Macintosh like an old MacPlus. The mach resource is used to let the Finder know whether or not your control panel runs on all Macintosh models.

If a mach resource (which must have an ID of -4064) has a value of FFFF 0000, then the Finder assumes the control panel runs on all

Macintosh models, and it will open the control panel regardless of the Mac on which it resides. Figure 4.22 shows the mach resource for MySetSound. Because MySetSound will run on any Mac, its mach resource has a value of FFFF 0000.

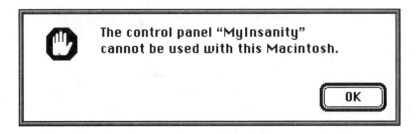

mach ID = -4064 from MySetSound

```
000000    FFFF 0000              0000
000008
000010
000018
000020
000028
000030
000038
000040
000048
```

FIGURE 4.22 THE MACH RESOURCE FOR A CONTROL PANEL
THAT IS TO RUN ON ANY MACINTOSH.

If a mach resource instead has a value of 0000 FFFF, the Finder will not make the assumption that the control panel can be opened. Instead, it will invoke the control panel's cdev code and send a message requesting that the control device function determine if the control panel works on the current machine. It is up to the control device function code to then perform any necessary tests to see if the control panel will work on the machine. If the control panel can't run on the Mac, the Finder will display an alert like the one shown in Figure 4.23.

The control panel "MyInsanity" cannot be used with this Macintosh.

OK

FIGURE 4.23 THE FINDER WILL DISPLAY AN ALERT IF A CONTROL PANEL
CANNOT RUN ON THE HOST MACHINE.

The MyInsanity control panel that appears later in this chapter works this way. It makes a call to Gestalt() to see if the Mac has color QuickDraw. If it does, the control panel will load. If it doesn't, the control panel will not appear, and the alert shown in Figure 4.23 will be posted.

N O T E

CONTROL PANEL SOURCE CODE

A control panel, or cdev, code resource has many similarities to the other types of code resources you've worked with. It also has some important differences. Key among them is the control panel's need for a private storage area in which to hold data.

Control Panels and Private Data Storage

When a user selects a control panel from the Apple menu, the Finder executes the cdev code. For as long as the control panel is open, this cdev code will be executed repeatedly. Whenever the user performs an action that involves the control panel (such as clicking on an item in it), the Finder must call the cdev code to handle that action. Even when no user action is taking place in the control panel, the Finder will still be executing the cdev code, sending null events to it periodically. If a control panel needs to retain any information between these calls, it needs some means of storing values.

Because a control panel has dialog box items in it, it usually needs to store information for the duration of its life on the screen. Since a control panel is only one of several pieces of code that the Finder works with, a control panel needs some means of storing values between these calls. The MySetSound control panel, for instance, keeps track of which of its two radio buttons is currently on. That way, when the user clicks on a radio button in the control panel, MySetSound knows which button to turn off. If the user clicks on the desktop while MySetSound is open, the control panel will move to the background. If the user then clicks on the control panel, the Finder will again make the control panel active and again call the cdev code. Between those calls the control panel must retain its data—the item number of the radio button that is currently on.

To hold data, a control panel allocates memory for a data structure and obtains a handle to that memory. This handle should be created when the control panel is opened. During the execution of the cdev, the control device function can work with the data that the handle references. Then, when the current call to the cdev code is complete, the cdev should pass the handle back to the Finder. The next time the Finder calls the control panel, it will pass the handle back to the control panel. When the control panel is inactive, the handle to its data is safely kept track of by the Finder. The handle is created only once while the control panel is open. The passing of the handle between the control panel and the Finder, however, occurs every time the cdev code is invoked. Figure 4.24 summarizes how a control panel maintains its private data.

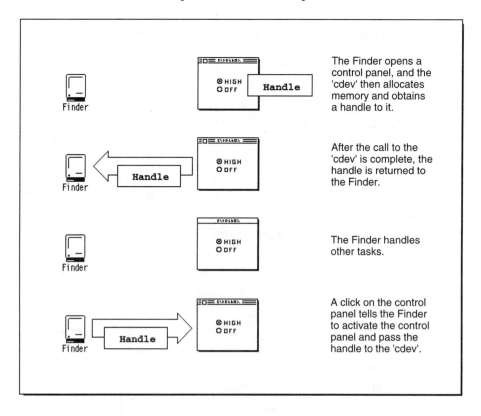

FIGURE 4.24 A CONTROL PANEL MAINTAINS A DATA STRUCTURE
FOR ITS OWN PRIVATE DATA.

The MySetSound control panel defines a data structure that holds two members. The first field keeps track of the item number of the radio button that is currently on. The second field holds the current system volume. The handle to this struct, CDEVHandle, is the handle that will be passed between the control panel and the Finder.

```
typedef  struct
{
   short  current_button_sys_vol;
   short  current_sys_vol;
} CDEVRecord, *CDEVPtr, **CDEVHandle;
```

The Control Device Function Entry Point

A cdev is a code resource, so, like MDEF and CDEF code resources, it requires an entry point by which application code can access it. For a cdev, that application is the Finder.

The entry point for a cdev begins with the pascal keyword. The return type should be the handle type defined by the cdev. For MySetSound, that type is CDEVHandle. After the return type comes main and the seven function parameters. Here is the entry point for MySetSound:

```
pascal  CDEVHandle  main( short      message,
                          short      item,
                          short      num_items,
                          short      control_panel_ID,
                          EventRecord *the_event,
                          CDEVHandle  cdev_storage,
                          DialogPtr   the_dialog )
```

As it has been for other code resource types you've seen, the message parameter indicates the type of action that is to be handled by the control device function.

initDev	Perform initializations when Control Panel opens
hitDev	Handle a mouse click on an enabled dialog box item
macDev	Determine if the Control Panel can run on this Macintosh
nulDev	Perform background processing chores during null event

updateDev	Update text or items not updated by the Dialog Manager
activDev	Handle Control Panel becoming active
deActivDev	Handle Control panel becoming inactive
keyEvtDev	Handle a keystroke
closeDev	Perform any clean up before Control Panel quits

The second parameter to main() is applicable only when an enabled item in the control panel has been clicked on, that is, only if message has a value of hitDev. The item parameter holds the item number of the clicked-on item.

The third parameter, num_items, is used when the cdev is running under System 6. It holds the number of items in the scrolling list of items in the Control Panel desk accessory. For a control panel running under System 7, this parameter has a value of 0.

The fourth parameter to main(), control_panel_ID, holds a private value used by the Finder and control panel to access the control panel's resources. Your control panel source code will never need to reference this parameter.

The the_event parameter holds the EventRecord for the event that caused the invocation of the cdev.

The sixth parameter to main(), cdev_storage, is the handle to the control panel's private data. After the control panel opens, it will return this handle to the Finder. From that point on, the Finder will pass this handle back to the cdev every time it calls it.

The last parameter to main() is the_dialog. This parameter is a pointer to the control panel's dialog record.

The control device function's main() routine should handle a message by determining which type of message was sent by the Finder, and then responding to that message. If the message is a hitDev type, then main() should determine which dialog item was clicked on. Here is a look at the format of a cdev that handles initDev and hitDev messages:

```
switch ( message )
{
```

```
case initDev:
   // control panel opened, perform any initializations

case hitDev:
   // enabled item clicked on, handle appropriately:
   switch ( item )
   {
      case 1:
         // handle click on 'DITL' item #1
      case 2:
         // handle click on 'DITL' item #2
      // case label for each item
   }
}
```

Taking Care of the Preliminaries

The MySetSound control panel changes the system sound volume by
making a call to the Toolbox routine SetSoundVol(). This routine is
defined in the Sound.h universal header file, so the Sound.h file should
be included at the top of the source code:

```
#include <Sound.h>
```

The resource file for MySetSound has a DITL resource with three
enabled items. The MySetSound source code defines a constant for each
of the items:

```
#define      HIGH_SYS_VOL_ITEM      1
#define      OFF_SYS_VOL_ITEM       2
#define      SET_SYS_VOL_ITEM       3
```

As mentioned, MySetSound will adjust the speaker volume by making a
call to the Toolbox routine SetSoundVol(). As its only parameter,
SetSoundVol() accepts a short integer in the range of 0 to 7. A 0 turns
the volume off, while a 7 sets the volume to its highest level:

```
#define      SYS_VOL_OFF      0
#define      SYS_VOL_HIGH     7
```

Handling an initDev Message

When a control panel opens, the Finder sends it an initDev message. This gives the control panel an opportunity to perform any one-time initializations. Because the Dialog Manager will handle the drawing of dialog box items, your initialization code won't have to. What it should do is allocate memory for the data structure that will be saved in the control panel's private storage area, and then assign initial values to the members.

MySetSound defines a `struct` named `CDEVRecord` to hold its data. Below is another look at the `CDEVRecord` structure. Following the `struct` definition is the line of code that allocates storage for one structure and returns a handle to that memory. Recall that the `cdev_storage` variable is passed in as one of the parameters to `main()` and initially does not point to any valid data.

```
typedef  struct
{
   short   current_button_sys_vol;
   short   current_sys_vol;
} CDEVRecord, *CDEVPtr, **CDEVHandle;

cdev_storage = (CDEVHandle)NewHandle( sizeof( CDEVRecord ) );
```

The `current_button_sys_vol` member will hold the DITL item number of the radio button that is currently on. I've arbitrarily decided to open the control panel with the **High** radio button on, so I'll assign a value of 1 (HIGH_SYS_VOL_ITEM) to this `struct` member. To make the assignment, I'll need to dereference the handle twice:

```
(**cdev_storage).current_button_sys_vol = HIGH_SYS_VOL_ITEM;
```

If the **High** radio button is on, then the system speaker volume should be set to its highest level. I'll assign the `current_sys_vol` member a value of 7 (HIGH_SYS_VOL_ITEM). This assignment only stores the system volume level in the structure—it doesn't make the actual change to the speaker volume:

```
(**cdev_storage).current_sys_vol = SYS_VOL_HIGH;
```

MySetSound has a function named `Set_Radio_Buttons` that's used to set the control panel's radio buttons. In response to a click on a radio button, `Set_Radio_Buttons()` turns the old button off and the newly clicked-on button on. The control panel uses two local variables—`new_radio` and `old_radio`—to hold the DITL item numbers of these two buttons. This is the snippet that adjusts the radio buttons to their initial settings:

```
new_radio = (**cdev_storage).current_button_sys_vol;
old_radio = OFF_SYS_VOL_ITEM;
Set_Radio_Buttons( the_dialog, old_radio, new_radio, num_items );
```

Here's a look at the complete section of code that handles an `initDev` message.

```
case initDev:
   cdev_storage = (CDEVHandle)NewHandle( sizeof( CDEVRecord ) );

   (**cdev_storage).current_button_sys_vol = HIGH_SYS_VOL_ITEM;
   (**cdev_storage).current_sys_vol = SYS_VOL_HIGH;

   new_radio = (**cdev_storage).current_button_sys_vol;
   old_radio = OFF_SYS_VOL_ITEM;
   Set_Radio_Buttons( the_dialog, old_radio, new_radio, num_items );
   break;
```

Setting the Radio Buttons

`Set_Radio_Buttons()` is a simple utility function that would normally deserve very little mention. For use in a control panel, however, it warrants some discussion.

The purpose of `Set_Radio_Buttons()` is to turn off one radio button and on another one. The first parameter to the function is a `DialogPtr` that points to the control panel's `DialogRecord`. The second parameter is the DITL item number of the button to turn off, while the third parameter is the DITL item number of the button to turn on.

The fourth parameter is the number of items in the control panel, excluding the DITL items. This last parameter is the one that deserves a closer look. First, a look at the function definition:

```
void Set_Radio_Buttons( DialogPtr  dlog,
                        short      old_radio,
                        short      new_radio,
                        short      num_items )
```

To turn off a radio button, you'd normally use a call to `GetDialog Item()` to get a handle to the DITL item, then make a call to `SetControlValue()` to turn off the button. The handle needs to be typecast to a `ControlHandle`, and the value should be set to 0 to turn off the control. Assuming that `old_radio` is the DITL item number of the radio button to turn off, the following snippet would do the trick:

```
Handle  handle;
short   type;
Rect    box;

GetDialogItem( dlog, old_radio, &type, &handle, &box );
SetControlValue( (ControlHandle)handle, 0 );
```

For a control panel, you'll want to make one significant change. If your cdev is to be backwards compatible to System 6, you'll have to take into consideration that the Control Panel desk accessory has a few DITL items of its own. The Control Panel maintains an item list that holds the items that appear in the Control Panel's scrolling list. Each icon is an item. When an icon is clicked on in the System 6 Control Panel, the items in the clicked-on Control Panel are appended to the Control Panel's list. Figure 4.25 shows that if MySetSound is running under System 6, the Control Panel with four icons considers the three MySetSound items to be items numbered 5, 6, and 7, respectively.

In order to access any one of the MySetSound items under System 6, the cdev code must refer to the item by the item number the Control Panel uses, not by its MySetSound DITL value.

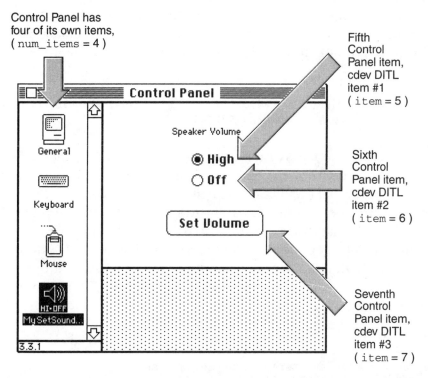

FIGURE 4.25 WHEN RUNNING UNDER SYSTEM 6, A CONTROL PANEL'S DITL ITEMS ARE APPENDED TO THE ITEM LIST OF THE CONTROL PANEL DESK ACCESSORY.

The workings of the System 6 Control Panel explain why the Finder passes the control device function the `num_items` parameter. This variable holds the number of icons in the Control Panel's scrolling list. It is this value that must be added to the control panel DITL item value in a call to `GetDialogItem()`. In that way, a handle to the correct item is obtained. Here's how a radio button is turned off in a control panel:

```
Handle   handle;
short    type;
Rect     box;

GetDialogItem( dlog, old_radio + num_items, &type, &handle, &box );
SetControlValue( (ControlHandle)handle, 0 );
```

To turn a radio button on—the second task that Set_Radio_ Buttons() performs—the same two Toolbox functions are used. This time a value of 255 is passed to SetControlValue() to signal that the control is to be turned on:

```
GetDialogItem( dlog, new_radio + num_items, &type, &handle, &box );
SetControlValue( (ControlHandle)handle, 255 );
```

If Set_Radio_Buttons() adds the number of control panel items to new_radio and old_radio, then it is important that these values be passed in as the DITL values of the items, not as the combined value of control panel items and cdev item number. You can see from the initDev code that this is exactly what MySetSound does. First, the data structure member current_button_sys_vol is set to 1—the DITL item of the **High** radio button. Then new_radio is assigned this same value. Next, old_radio is assigned a value of 2—the DITL item number of the **Off** radio button:

```
(**cdev_storage).current_button_sys_vol = HIGH_SYS_VOL_ITEM;

new_radio = (**cdev_storage).current_button_sys_vol;
old_radio = OFF_SYS_VOL_ITEM;
```

Finally, a call to Set_Radio_Buttons() is made:

```
Set_Radio_Buttons( the_dialog, old_radio, new_radio, num_items );
```

What about a cdev that's running under System 7? In System 7, each control panel is self-contained. There's no reliance on a Control Panel desk accessory, and thus no need to include the number of icon items in the System 6 Control Panel in determining item numbers. Fortunately, the Finder is smart enough to realize this. When your control panel is opened on a Mac with System 7, the Finder will give num_items a value of 0 and pass that value to your control panel. That means you can use the very same System 6 code. Any time num_items appears in the code as an offset, it will in effect be ignored.

Even if you're sure your control panel will only be used under System 7, you should still consider using num_items **in your cdev code. Since its value of 0 will be ignored, there's no harm done. And should you ever change your mind and decide to make your control panel backwards compatible, you'll be all set.**

NOTE

You'll see Set_Radio_Buttons() (exactly as it's shown below) in each of the three control panel examples in this chapter.

```
void Set_Radio_Buttons( DialogPtr  dlog,
                        short      old_radio,
                        short      new_radio,
                        short      num_items )
{
   Handle  handle;
   short   type;
   Rect    box;

   GetDialogItem( dlog, old_radio + num_items, &type, &handle,
                &box );
   SetControlValue( (ControlHandle)handle, 0 );

   GetDialogItem( dlog, new_radio + num_items, &type, &handle,
                &box );
   SetControlValue( (ControlHandle)handle, 1 );
}
```

Handling a hitDev Message

When the user clicks on an enabled control panel item, the Finder sends the control device function a hitDev message. Along with the message, the item number will be sent in the item parameter and, as always, the number of control panel items will be sent in the num_items parameter. If the control panel is running under System 6, item will have a value that includes the number of Control Panel icon items—as shown in Figure 4.25.

Consider a System 6 control panel with four icons in its scrolling list and the three enabled MySetSound items. The num_items parameter will have a value of 4. If the user clicks on the **High** radio button (DITL item number 1), item will have a value of 5.

The first thing to do in response to a hitDev message is to subtract num_items from item. That will give the DITL item number of the clicked-on item. Since a control panel running under System 7 will always have a num_items value of 0, this operation will have no adverse effect on the item parameter. Next, a switch that runs the appropriate code for that item is entered:

```
case hitDev:
   item = item - num_items;

   switch ( item )
   {
      case HIGH_SYS_VOL_ITEM:          // HIGH_SYS_VOL_ITEM = 1
         // handle radio button

      case OFF_SYS_VOL_ITEM:           // OFF_SYS_VOL_ITEM  = 2
         // handle radio button

      case SET_SYS_VOL_ITEM:           // SET_SYS_VOL_ITEM  = 3
         // handle push button
   }
   break;
```

The reason for subtracting num_items from item is so that the code can freely use the #define directives for the control panel items, without concern for any offset and without trying to factor in the number of control panel items. When I created my control panel DITL in ResEdit, I defined the **High** radio button to be item number 1. That's how I intuitively think of this button—item number 1. I don't want to consider the control panel offset each time I think of a DITL item.

When should I be concerned about the item offset that's used in the System 6 Control Panel? Only in my utility routine or routines that access items. The Set_Radio_Buttons() is an example.

MySetSound handles a click on a radio button by determining which button should be considered the new button and which should be the old button. The new button will of course be the one that was clicked on. The old button will be whatever button was stored in the current_ button_sys_vol field of the control panel's private storage area. For a click on the **High** radio button, this snippet would suffice:

```
old_radio = (**cdev_storage).current_button_sys_vol;
new_radio = HIGH_SYS_VOL_ITEM;
```

Next, a call to Set_Radio_Buttons() is made to turn off the old button and to turn on the new button:

```
Set_Radio_Buttons( the_dialog, old_radio, new_radio, num_items );
```

After setting the radio buttons, the current_button_sys_vol member of the storage structure must be updated to hold the DITL item number of the clicked-on button.

```
(**cdev_storage).current_button_sys_vol = new_radio;
```

The speaker volume is based on the current radio button, so now is the time to store that value. If the **High** radio button was clicked, the number 7 (SYS_VOL_HIGH, the highest volume value) should be stored in the other member of the control panel's data structure:

```
(**cdev_storage).current_sys_vol = SYS_VOL_HIGH;
```

Below is the complete code for handling a click on the **High** radio button. A click on the **Off** radio button is handled in a similar fashion.

```
case HIGH_SYS_VOL_ITEM:
   old_radio = (**cdev_storage).current_button_sys_vol;
   new_radio = HIGH_SYS_VOL_ITEM;
   Set_Radio_Buttons( the_dialog, old_radio, new_radio, num_items );
   (**cdev_storage).current_button_sys_vol = new_radio;
   (**cdev_storage).current_sys_vol = SYS_VOL_HIGH;
   break;
```

The two MySetSound radio buttons can be clicked on and off by the user as often as desired—without a change of the system volume going into effect. It's not until the user clicks on the **Set Volume** push button that this change happens. A call to the Toolbox function SetSoundVol()

takes care of that. SetSoundVol() accepts a short integer in the range of 0 to 7 and then sets the system speaker volume based on that value. The value to pass to SetSoundVol() is held in the current_sys_vol field of the Control Panel's data structure. It holds a value of either SYS_VOL_HIGH or SYS_VOL_OFF; it depends on which radio button is currently on.

   After setting the speaker volume, a call to SysBeep() sounds the system alert to give the user some audio feedback.

```
case SET_SYS_VOL_ITEM:
   SetSoundVol( (**cdev_storage).current_sys_vol );
   SysBeep( 1 );
```

Here is a look at the code that MySetSound uses to handle a hitDev message:

```
case hitDev:
   item = item - num_items;

   switch ( item )
   {
      case HIGH_SYS_VOL_ITEM:
         old_radio = (**cdev_storage).current_button_sys_vol;
         new_radio = HIGH_SYS_VOL_ITEM;
         Set_Radio_Buttons( the_dialog, old_radio, new_radio,
num_items );
         (**cdev_storage).current_button_sys_vol = new_radio;
         (**cdev_storage).current_sys_vol = SYS_VOL_HIGH;
         break;

      case OFF_SYS_VOL_ITEM:
         old_radio = (**cdev_storage).current_button_sys_vol;
         new_radio = OFF_SYS_VOL_ITEM;
         Set_Radio_Buttons( the_dialog, old_radio, new_radio,
num_items );
         (**cdev_storage).current_button_sys_vol = new_radio;
         (**cdev_storage).current_sys_vol = SYS_VOL_OFF;
         break;

      case SET_SYS_VOL_ITEM:
         SetSoundVol( (**cdev_storage).current_sys_vol );
         SysBeep( 1 );
```

```
   }
   break;
```

The MySetSound Source Code Listing

Now it's time to look at the complete source code listing for the MySetSound control panel. As always, you'll find the source code, project, and resource files for this example on the included disk.

```
//_____
//                                    #include directives

#include <Sound.h>


//_____
//                                    function prototypes

void  Set_Radio_Buttons( DialogPtr, short, short, short );


//_____
//                                    #define directives

#define       HIGH_SYS_VOL_ITEM      1
#define       OFF_SYS_VOL_ITEM       2
#define       SET_SYS_VOL_ITEM       3

#define       SYS_VOL_OFF            0
#define       SYS_VOL_HIGH           7


//_____
//                                    define data structures

typedef   struct
{
   short   current_button_sys_vol;
   short   current_sys_vol;
} CDEVRecord, *CDEVPtr, **CDEVHandle;


//_____
//                                    entry point to the code
```

225

```
pascal  CDEVHandle  main( short        message,
                         short        item,
                         short        num_items,
                         short        control_panel_ID,
                         EventRecord  *the_event,
                         CDEVHandle   cdev_storage,
                         DialogPtr    the_dialog )
{
   short  old_radio;
   short  new_radio;

   switch ( message )
   {
      case initDev:
         cdev_storage = (CDEVHandle)NewHandle(sizeof(CDEVRecord ) );

         (**cdev_storage).current_button_sys_vol =
                        HIGH_SYS_VOL_ITEM;
         (**cdev_storage).current_sys_vol = SYS_VOL_HIGH;

         new_radio = (**cdev_storage).current_button_sys_vol;
         old_radio = OFF_SYS_VOL_ITEM;
         Set_Radio_Buttons(the_dialog, old_radio, new_radio,
                        num_items);
         break;

      case hitDev:
         item = item - num_items;

         switch ( item )
         {
            case HIGH_SYS_VOL_ITEM:
               old_radio =
               (**cdev_storage).current_button_sys_vol;
               new_radio = HIGH_SYS_VOL_ITEM;
               Set_Radio_Buttons( the_dialog, old_radio,
                              new_radio, num_items );
               (**cdev_storage).current_button_sys_vol =
               new_radio;
               (**cdev_storage).current_sys_vol = SYS_VOL_HIGH;
               break;

            case OFF_SYS_VOL_ITEM:
               old_radio =
               (**cdev_storage).current_button_sys_vol;
               new_radio = OFF_SYS_VOL_ITEM;
```

```
            Set_Radio_Buttons( the_dialog, old_radio,
                               new_radio, num_items );
            (**cdev_storage).current_button_sys_vol =
            new_radio;
            (**cdev_storage).current_sys_vol = SYS_VOL_OFF;
            break;

        case SET_SYS_VOL_ITEM:
            SetSoundVol( (**cdev_storage).current_sys_vol );
            SysBeep( 1 );
        }
        break;
    }
    return ( cdev_storage );
}


//_____
//                                            set radio buttons

void Set_Radio_Buttons( DialogPtr   dlog,
                        short       old_radio,
                        short       new_radio,
                        short       num_items )
{
    Handle   handle;
    short    type;
    Rect     box;

    GetDialogItem( dlog, old_radio + num_items, &type, &handle,
               &box );
    SetControlValue( (ControlHandle)handle, 0 );

    GetDialogItem( dlog, new_radio + num_items, &type, &handle,
               &box );
    SetControlValue( (ControlHandle)handle, 1 );
}
```

BUILDING THE CDEV CODE RESOURCE

In the first three chapters of this book, you built a few different types of
code resources. For a cdev, things are a little different. A control panel
file is self-contained code. Besides the cdev resource, a control panel file

holds all of the other resources you created in the control panel's project resource file—resources such as the DITL, nrct, and mach. After building the code resource, you'll find that instead of having a resource file with a code resource in it, you'll have a new control panel, with an icon like the one pictured in Figure 4.26.

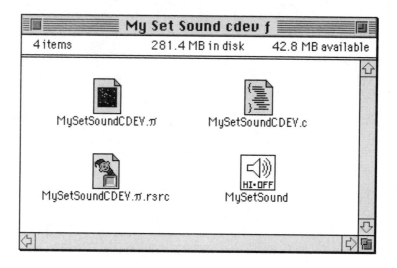

**FIGURE 4.26 BUILDING A CDEV CODE RESOURCE RESULTS IN
THE CREATION OF A NEW CONTROL PANEL.**

Because a control panel file is self-contained, you won't need an application to test it out. Instead, drop the control panel into your System folder. If you're using System 7, MySetSound will appear in the Control Panels folder in the Apple menu. Under System 6, the MySetSound icon will appear in the icon list of the Control Panel desk accessory.

If you're using System 7, you can simply double-click on a control panel file to execute its code. There's no need to place it in your System folder during testing. After you're satisfied with the results, then drop it in the System folder so that you can access it from the Apple menu.

N O T E

Building with CodeWarrior

If you're using the Metrowerks CodeWarrior compiler, create a new project and add the two files shown in Figure 4.27.

File	Code	Data		
▽ Segment 1	0	0		▽
MySetSoundCDEV.c	0	0	•	▷
MacOS.lib	0	0		▷
2 file(s)	0	0		

MySetSoundCDEV.µ

FIGURE 4.27 THE METROWERKS PROJECT WINDOW FOR THE MYSETSOUND CONTROL PANEL.

Before building the control panel, select Preferences from the Edit menu. Click the **Project** icon to bring up the Project panel, as shown in Figure 4.28. Make sure that all of the items in this panel are filled in correctly. The Project Type should be set to **Code Resource**, and a name should be entered in the **File Name** edit box. Unlike the other code resources you've created, the cdev will not be placed in its own resource file, so the name shouldn't include a reference to "resource." Instead of giving it a name like MySetSoundCDEV.rsrc, simply name it MySetSound.

For a control panel, the resource type must be cdev, and the resource ID must be -4064. The Type field should be cdev and the Creator field can be any four characters. Figure 4.28 shows that Sndv was picked to indicate that this is a sound control device.

Don't forget that Metrowerks code resource projects must use the Small code model. Click on the Processor icon to display the Processor Info panel. Use the Code Model pop-up menu to select the Small code model.

T I P

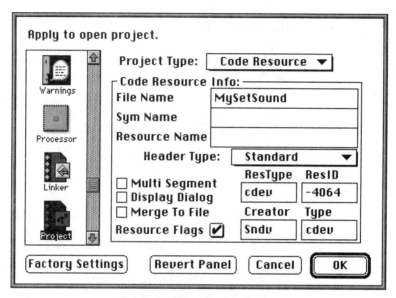

FIGURE 4.28 THE METROWERKS PREFERENCES DIALOG BOX FOR THE MYSETSOUND CONTROL PANEL.

To build the code resource, select **Make** from the Project menu. When the build completes, you'll have a new control panel, with an icon like the one shown in Figure 4.26.

Building with Symantec C++/THINK C

If you're working with a Symantec compiler, launch the THINK Project Manager and create a new project. Add the MacTraps library and MySetSoundCDEV.c source code file to the project, as shown in Figure 4.29.

Select Set Project Type from the Project menu. Click the **Code Resource** radio button to set the project type. Enter a name for the cdev resource, then fill in the Type field with cdev. The **File Type** should be cdev, and the Creator can be any four characters. Figure 4.30 shows a **Creator** of Sndv for the MySetSound sound control device. Finally, enter a resource ID of -4064 for the cdev. This is the ID a control panel code resource *must* have.

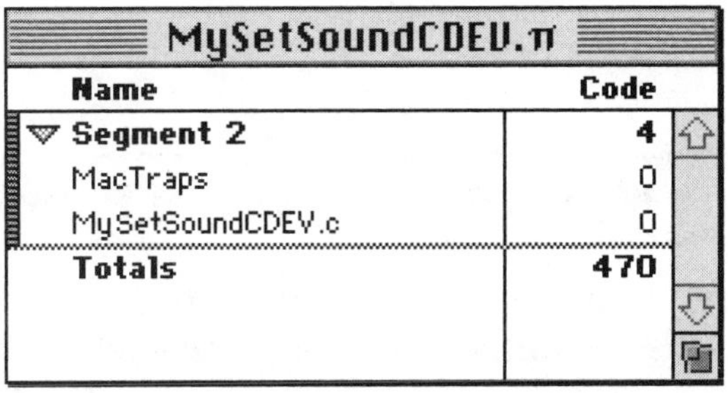

FIGURE 4.29 THE SYMANTEC PROJECT WINDOW FOR THE MYSETSOUND CONTROL PANEL.

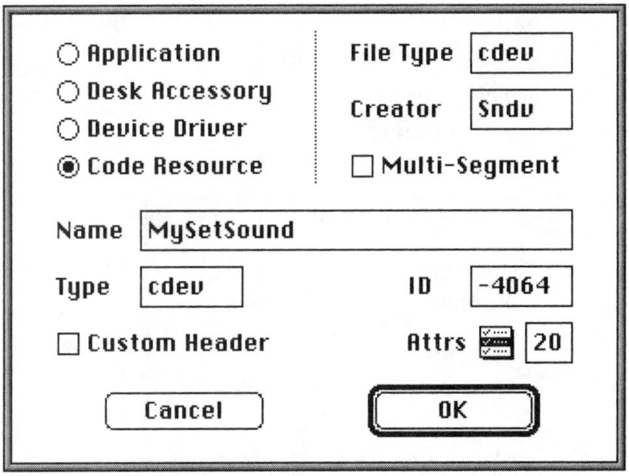

**FIGURE 4.30 THE SYMANTEC PROJECT TYPE WINDOW FOR
THE MYSETSOUND CONTROL PANEL.**

After clicking the **OK** button, create the control panel file by selecting
`Build Code Resource` from the Project menu. Here you'll get the
opportunity to name the code resource. In the past you may have given a
code resource a name that ended in .rsrc to make it obvious that the generated file was a resource file. For a control panel, this isn't necessary.
The cdev resource that's created during the build won't be placed in its
own resource file. Instead, the THINK Project Manager will merge the
cdev resource with the resources in the control panel's project resource

file to create a control panel file. For that reason, a name such as MySetSound is appropriate.

Enhancing the MySetSound Control Panel

MySetSound is a good first example of a control panel—it's as simple as they come. The MySetSoundPlus control panel shows how to add a few more resources to a control panel—resources found in just about every control panel. It also demonstrates how easy it is to expand the capabilities of a control panel.

Figure 4.31 shows the MySetSoundPlus control panel. On its left side are items to set the system speaker volume—the same controls found in MySetSound. On the right side are a new set of controls that are used to set the volume of the system alert.

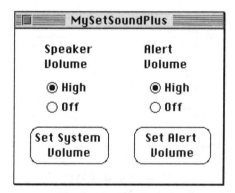

FIGURE 4.31 THE MYSETSOUNDPLUS CONTROL PANEL.

Starting with version 3.0 of the Sound Manager, it is possible to independently vary the volume that the system alert plays at and the volume that other sounds play at. The Toolbox routine SetSoundVol() controls the level of the system speaker volume. The new Sound Manager routine SetSysBeepVolume() controls the volume that the system alert plays at. Consider a program that calls SetSoundVol(7) and SetSysBeep Volume(1). If that program plays an snd resource, it will play it at the loudest volume. If that same program displays an alert that beeps, or calls SysBeep(), the volume of that sound will be low.

Before allowing the user to adjust the alert volume, the MySetSoundPlus control panel will have to first check to see if the machine it's running on contains version 3 of the Sound Manager. Not all Macs have the new Sound Manager. If the host machine has an earlier version, the SetSysBeepVolume() call will not be available, and the control panel will dim those items that control the alert volume, as shown in Figure 4.32.

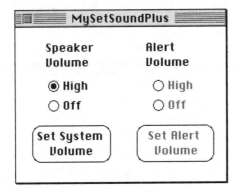

FIGURE 4.32 THE MYSETSOUNDPLUS CONTROL PANEL WHEN
SOUND MANAGER 3.0 IS NOT AVAILABLE.

Earlier in this chapter, I stated that your own control panels should not duplicate the efforts of Apple programmers. The MySetSoundPlus comes closer to this recommendation than MySetSound did. While this new control panel still allows for the adjustment of the speaker volume level—as Apple's Sound control panel does—it also allows the user to adjust the alert volume. That's something that the Apple Sound control panel doesn't do. An even better MySetSoundPlus could omit the speaker volume setting and just have sound-related settings for features not covered by the Sound control panel. It could also use a slider CDEF for each control.

Creating an Icon Family

The contents of the resource file for MySetSoundPlus have increased quite a bit from that of MySetSound. If you look closely at Figure 4.33, however, you'll see that of the seven new resource types, all but two of them are icon related. The icl4, icl8, ics#, ics4, and ics8 are all icons. The finf and snd are the only other additions; they'll be covered a few pages ahead.

MySetSound had only one icon—a black-and-white ICN# resource. To better support users with color monitors, MySetSoundPlus adds several color icons. Figure 4.34 shows what the BNDL resource looks like for the new control panel.

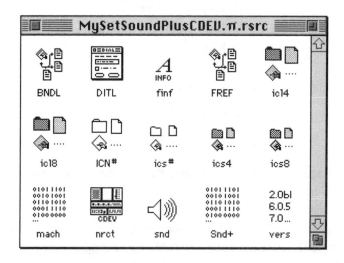

FIGURE 4.33 THE RESOURCE FILE FOR THE MYSETSOUNDPLUS PROJECT.

In Figure 4.35 you can see the icl8 icon being drawn in the icon editor. This icon will be used on machines that are set to display eight or more bits of color. Once again I used my resource editor to peek at Apple's Sound control panel icl8 icon to get an idea of how to add shading to my own icon.

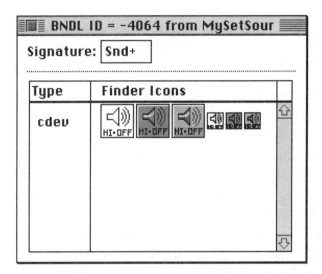

FIGURE 4.34 THE BNDL RESOURCE FOR THE MYSETSOUNDPLUS PROJECT.

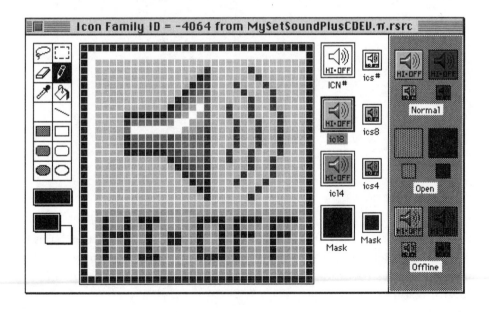

FIGURE 4.35 THE ICON EDITOR AND THE ICL8 ICON FOR THE MYSETSOUNDPLUS PROJECT.

Changing the Control Panel's Display Font

You may have noticed that the MySetSound control panel didn't use the system font, which is 12-point Chicago, to display its static text item. Instead, it used 9-point Geneva. A control panel will always use this font, unless instructed to do otherwise. The finf, or font information, resource is the means for doing this.

A finf resource holds the ID, style, and size of a font. When the control panel that uses this resource opens, the Finder reads this information and uses it in the display of static text items. For a control panel, the finf must have an ID of -4049 (see Figure 4.36).

To set the font ID, enter the ID of the font to use in the Font Number box of the finf resource. To get the ID of many of the commonly used fonts, refer to the constants listed in the Fonts.h universal header file:

```
systemFont     =    0
applFont       =    1
newYork        =    2
geneva         =    3
monaco         =    4
venice         =    5
london         =    6
athens         =    7
sanFran        =    8
toronto        =    9
cairo          =   11
losAngeles     =   12
times          =   20
helvetica      =   21
courier        =   22
symbol         =   23
mobile         =   24
```

To set the style of the font, use one of the constants found in the Types.h universal header file. To use more than one style, add the values of the individual styles together. Enter the value in the **Font Style** edit box of the finf resource.

```
normal         =    0
bold           =    1
italic         =    2
underline      =    4
outline        =    8
```

Finally, enter the font size in points in the **Font Size** edit box. In Figure 4.36, I've set the finf resource to use the system font (Chicago) in a plain style and in 12-point size.

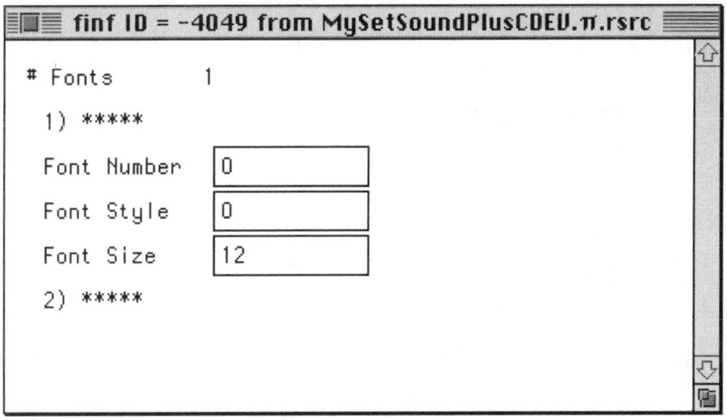

FIGURE 4.36 THE FINF RESOURCE FOR THE MYSETSOUNDPLUS PROJECT.

The information in a finf resource should be in hexadecimal format. You can, however, enter the values in decimal, as I've done in Figure 4.36. Don't be alarmed when you reopen a finf resource, as I've done in Figure 4.37. You'll find that the Resource editor now displays the information in hex.

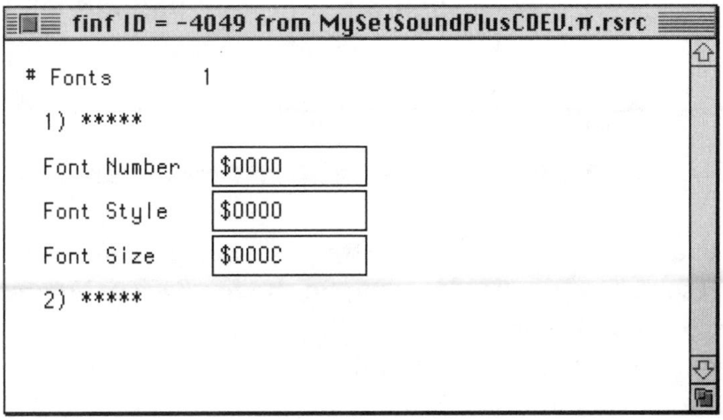

FIGURE 4.37 THE FINF RESOURCE FOR THE MYSETSOUNDPLUS PROJECT, AFTER IT IS REOPENED.

Additional Resources

The MySetSoundPlus control panel has the required DITL with an ID of -4064, as shown in Figure 4.38. In the source code file, you'll find a constant defined for each of the enabled items in the DITL:

```
#define     HIGH_SYS_VOL_ITEM       1
#define     OFF_SYS_VOL_ITEM        2
#define     SET_SYS_VOL_ITEM        3

#define     HIGH_ALRT_VOL_ITEM      5
#define     OFF_ALRT_VOL_ITEM       6
#define     SET_ALRT_VOL_ITEM       7
```

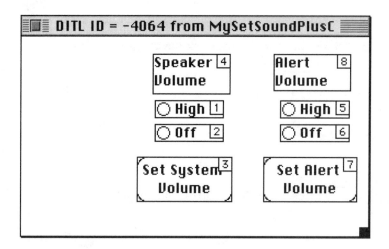

FIGURE 4.38 THE DITL RESOURCE FOR THE MYSETSOUNDPLUS PROJECT.

Control Panels may contain any resource types, not just the required ones. In response to the user clicking on the **Set System Volume** button, the MySetSoundPlus control panel will play a short sound. That sound comes from an snd resource stored in the control panel. Figure 4.39 shows this sound resource.

```
≣▣≣ snds from MySetSoundPlusCDEV.π.rsrc ≣▣≣
   ID        Size      Name
  9000      13558    "Glass breaking"                  ⇧


                                                        ⇩
                                                        ▣
```

FIGURE 4.39 THE SND RESOURCE FOR THE MYSETSOUNDPLUS PROJECT.

Additions to the Source Code

MySetSoundPlus works very much like the first example control panel, MySetSound. There are, however, a few differences worth noting.

Because MySetSoundPlus uses two sets of radio buttons (with two buttons per set), its private data storage needs to keep track of the current information for each radio button set. The CDEVRecord struct has the same two members used to keep track of the system speaker volume in MySetSound—current_button_sys_vol and current_sys_vol. But it also has two new members. The field current_button_alert_vol keeps track of which of the two buttons on the right side of the control panel is currently on. Member current_alert_vol holds the current volume setting, either 0 or 7, to be used for the system alert volume.

```
typedef   struct
{
   short   current_button_sys_vol;
   short   current_sys_vol;
   short   current_button_alert_vol;
   short   current_alert_vol;
} CDEVRecord, *CDEVPtr, **CDEVHandle;
```

Because MySetSoundPlus contains items that must be made active or inactive, depending on the availability of Sound Manager 3.0, the handling of an initDev message has become more complex. Checking for a particular version of the Sound Manager is a three-step process. First, a check is made to see if the SoundDispatch trap is available.

```
Boolean  snd_dispatch;

snd_dispatch = ( NGetTrapAddress( _SoundDispatch, ToolTrap ) !=
                 NGetTrapAddress( _Unimplemented, ToolTrap ) );
```

Using NGetTrapAddress() to compare a trap to the unimplemented trap will determine the presence or absence of the trap. If the Sound Dispatch trap exists on the host machine, snd_dispatch will be assigned a value of true.

```
Boolean     snd_dispatch;

snd_dispatch = ( NGetTrapAddress( _SoundDispatch, ToolTrap ) !=
                 NGetTrapAddress( _Unimplemented, ToolTrap ) );
```

Traps, the unimplemented trap, and NGetTrapAddress() **are discussed at length in another M&T book,** *Macintosh Programming Techniques.*

N O T E

If the SoundDispatch trap is present, you can safely assume that the Toolbox routine SndSoundManagerVersion() is also present. A call to this routine will fill snd_mgr_ver—a variable of type NumVersion—with version information about the Sound Manger.

```
NumVersion  snd_mgr_ver;

snd_mgr_ver.majorRev = 0;
if ( snd_dispatch == true )
   snd_mgr_ver = SndSoundManagerVersion();
```

If the SoundDispatch trap isn't present, the majorRev field of the snd_mgr_ver variable will retain its initial value of 0. If the Sound Dispatch trap is present, SndSoundManagerVersion() gets called and the `majorRev` field of `snd_mgr_ver` will hold the major version number of the Sound Manager. If the version is at least 3, the right bank of dialog items can be kept active. If the version is less than 3, the items will be made inactive. Since the Toolbox function that sets the alert volume isn't available in preversion 3 releases of the Sound Manager, this is a necessary step.

```
if ( snd_mgr_ver.majorRev >= 3 )
{
   (**cdev_storage).current_button_alert_vol =
HIGH_ALRT_VOL_ITEM;
   (**cdev_storage).current_alert_vol = kFullVolume;

   new_radio = (**cdev_storage).current_button_alert_vol;
   old_radio = OFF_ALRT_VOL_ITEM;
   Set_Radio_Buttons( the_dialog, old_radio, new_radio, num_items );
}
else
{
   Dim_Dialog_Item( the_dialog, HIGH_ALRT_VOL_ITEM, num_items );
   Dim_Dialog_Item( the_dialog, OFF_ALRT_VOL_ITEM, num_items );
   Dim_Dialog_Item( the_dialog, SET_ALRT_VOL_ITEM, num_items );
}
```

`Dim_Dialog_Item()` is the application-defined routine that dims one dialog item. Like `Set_Radio_Buttons()`, `Dim_Dialog_Item()` adds the value of `num_items` to the DITL item to dim. That allows the control panel to be compatible with System 6. A call to `HiliteControl()`, with a value of 255 marks the control item as inactive and draws it in a dim state.

```
void  Dim_Dialog_Item( DialogPtr  dlog,
                       short      item,
                       short      num_items )
{
   Handle  handle;
   short   type;
   Rect    box;

   GetDialogItem( dlog, item + num_items, &type, &handle, &box );
   HiliteControl( (ControlHandle)handle, 255 );
}
```

The MySetSoundPlus Source Code Listing

The complete listing for the MySetSoundPlus control panel follows. There are many similarities between it and the MySetSound code listing that was given earlier in this chapter. Because the `Set_Radio_Buttons()` function is unchanged from its previous incarnation, its code has been omitted from this listing.

```
//_____
//                                              #include directives

#include <Sound.h>


//_____
//                                              function prototypes

void   Set_Radio_Buttons( DialogPtr, short, short, short );
void   Dim_Dialog_Item( DialogPtr, short, short );


//_____
//                                              #define directives

#define     HIGH_SYS_VOL_ITEM       1
#define     OFF_SYS_VOL_ITEM        2
#define     SET_SYS_VOL_ITEM        3

#define     HIGH_ALRT_VOL_ITEM      5
#define     OFF_ALRT_VOL_ITEM       6
#define     SET_ALRT_VOL_ITEM       7

#define     SYS_VOL_OFF             0
#define     SYS_VOL_HIGH            7

#define     SND_GLASS_ID            9000


//_____
//                                              define data structures

typedef   struct
{
```

```
      short   current_button_sys_vol;
      short   current_sys_vol;
      short   current_button_alert_vol;
      short   current_alert_vol;
   } CDEVRecord, *CDEVPtr, **CDEVHandle;


   //_____
   //                                         entry point to the code

   pascal  CDEVHandle  main( short        message,
                            short        item,
                            short        num_items,
                            short        control_panel_ID,
                            EventRecord  *the_event,
                            CDEVHandle   cdev_storage,
                            DialogPtr    the_dialog )
   {
      short       old_radio;
      short       new_radio;
      Handle      snd_handle;
      NumVersion  snd_mgr_ver;
      Boolean     snd_dispatch;

      switch ( message )
      {
         case initDev:
            cdev_storage = (CDEVHandle)NewHandle(sizeof(CDEVRecord ) );

            (**cdev_storage).current_button_sys_vol =
   HIGH_SYS_VOL_ITEM;
            (**cdev_storage).current_sys_vol = SYS_VOL_HIGH;

            new_radio = (**cdev_storage).current_button_sys_vol;
            old_radio = OFF_SYS_VOL_ITEM;
            Set_Radio_Buttons( the_dialog, old_radio, new_radio,
                            num_items );

            snd_dispatch = ( NGetTrapAddress( _SoundDispatch,
                            ToolTrap ) !=
                            NGetTrapAddress( _Unimplemented,
                            ToolTrap ) );

            snd_mgr_ver.majorRev = 0;
            if ( snd_dispatch == true )
               snd_mgr_ver = SndSoundManagerVersion();

            if ( snd_mgr_ver.majorRev >= 3 )
```

```
      {
         (**cdev_storage).current_button_alert_vol =
         HIGH_ALRT_VOL_ITEM;
         (**cdev_storage).current_alert_vol = kFullVolume;

         new_radio =
         (**cdev_storage).current_button_alert_vol;
         old_radio = OFF_ALRT_VOL_ITEM;
         Set_Radio_Buttons( the_dialog, old_radio,
                            new_radio, num_items );
      }
      else
      {
         Dim_Dialog_Item( the_dialog, HIGH_ALRT_VOL_ITEM,
                          num_items );
         Dim_Dialog_Item( the_dialog, OFF_ALRT_VOL_ITEM,
                          num_items );
         Dim_Dialog_Item( the_dialog, SET_ALRT_VOL_ITEM,
                          num_items );
      }
      break;

   case hitDev:
      item = item - num_items;

      switch ( item )
      {
         case HIGH_SYS_VOL_ITEM:
            old_radio =
            (**cdev_storage).current_button_sys_vol;
            new_radio = HIGH_SYS_VOL_ITEM;
            Set_Radio_Buttons( the_dialog, old_radio,
                               new_radio, num_items );
            (**cdev_storage).current_button_sys_vol  =
            new_radio;
            (**cdev_storage).current_sys_vol = SYS_VOL_HIGH;
            break;

         case OFF_SYS_VOL_ITEM:
            old_radio =
            (**cdev_storage).current_button_sys_vol;
            new_radio = OFF_SYS_VOL_ITEM;
            Set_Radio_Buttons( the_dialog, old_radio,
                               new_radio, num_items );
            (**cdev_storage).current_button_sys_vol  =
            new_radio;
            (**cdev_storage).current_sys_vol = SYS_VOL_OFF;
```

```
                    break;

            case SET_SYS_VOL_ITEM:
                SetSoundVol( (**cdev_storage).current_sys_vol );
                snd_handle = GetResource( 'snd ', SND_GLASS_ID );
                SndPlay( nil, snd_handle, true );
                break;

            case HIGH_ALRT_VOL_ITEM:
                old_radio =
                (**cdev_storage).current_button_alert_vol;
                new_radio = HIGH_ALRT_VOL_ITEM;
                Set_Radio_Buttons( the_dialog, old_radio,
                                   new_radio, num_items );
                (**cdev_storage).current_button_alert_vol  =
                new_radio;
                (**cdev_storage).current_alert_vol = kFullVolume;
                break;

            case OFF_ALRT_VOL_ITEM:
                old_radio =
                (**cdev_storage).current_button_alert_vol;
                new_radio = OFF_ALRT_VOL_ITEM;
                Set_Radio_Buttons( the_dialog, old_radio,
                                   new_radio, num_items );
                (**cdev_storage).current_button_alert_vol  =
                new_radio;
                (**cdev_storage).current_alert_vol = kNoVolume;
                break;

            case SET_ALRT_VOL_ITEM:
                SetSysBeepVolume(
                (**cdev_storage).current_alert_vol );
                SysBeep( 1 );
                break;
            }
          break;
    }
    return ( cdev_storage );
}


//_____
//                                        set radio buttons
void  Dim_Dialog_Item( DialogPtr  dlog,
                       short      item,
                       short      num_items )
```

```
{
    Handle  handle;
    short   type;
    Rect    box;

    GetDialogItem( dlog, item + num_items, &type, &handle, &box );
    HiliteControl( (ControlHandle)handle, 255 );
}
```

THE MYINSANITY CONTROL PANEL

When running, this chapter's last example, the MyInsanity control panel, draws a tiny black rectangle at the center of its dialog box. The rectangle rapidly grows outward until it gets close to the edge of the dialog box. Then it disappears, only to immediately appear and to begin growing once again. Figure 4.40 shows the rectangle as it's growing.

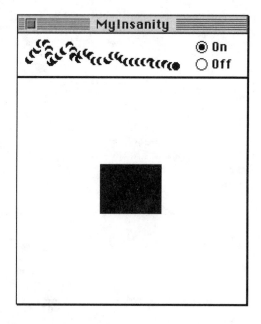

FIGURE 4.40 THE MYINSANITY CONTROL PANEL.

MyInsanity exists more as a diversion than as a control panel that works with systemwide features. But there's a lot to be learned from this seemingly trivial exercise in repetitive drawing. It has been mentioned several times in this chapter that the Finder is in constant communication with an open control panel. MyInsanity offers proof of this. Even when the control panel is delegated to the background, the panel's black rectangle will continue its endless cycle of growing and disappearing (see Figure 4.41).

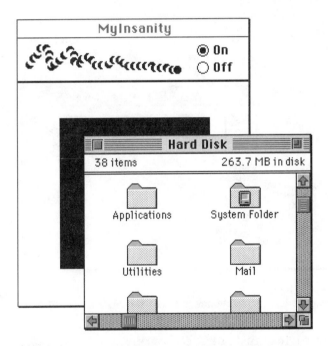

FIGURE 4.41 THE MYINSANITY CONTROL PANEL EXECUTE EVEN WHEN IT IS IN THE BACKGROUND.

MyInsanity also demonstrates how easy it is to include graphics in a control panel—that's something this chapter's first two examples didn't do. The control panel's dialog box is divided into rectangles, compliments of two nrct resources. A PICT resource is displayed in the top rectangle. In the bottom rectangle, the simple growing rectangle animation appears.

Finally, the MyInsanity control panel shows how a control panel can be written so that it executes only on certain types of machines and gracefully exists when the host machine doesn't meet the control panel's criteria. While backwards compatibility with System 6 is always welcomed by users, there are times when it just isn't feasible.

The MyInsanity Resources

Figure 4.42 shows the resource file for MyInsanity. Each of the resource types should now look familiar to you.

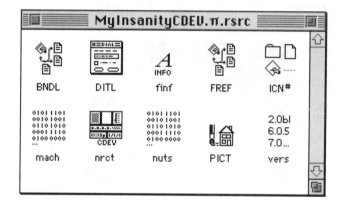

FIGURE 4.42 THE RESOURCE FILE FOR THE MYINSANITY PROJECT.

For simplicity, MyInsanity only defines one icon—the black-and-white ICN# resource. Since the control panel is all about animation, its icon tries to imply the idea of motion. The path of a bouncing ball is shown in the control panel's BNDL resource in Figure 4.43 and in the icon editor in Figure 4.44.

MyInsanity is the first example of a control panel that uses two nrct resources. Figure 4.45 shows the nrct resources.

Two nrct resources have been created to divide the control panel into two sections. Each nrct has the same left and right coordinates, 87 and 325, respectively. When the Finder opens the control panel's dialog box, it will draw a horizontal line on the boundaries of the two nrct resources. Figure 4.46 shows the MyInsanity control panel, without its dialog items.

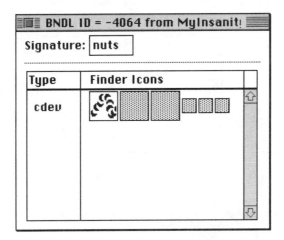

FIGURE 4.43 THE BNDL RESOURCE FOR THE MYINSANITY PROJECT.

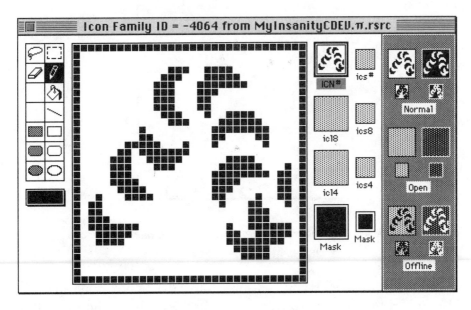

FIGURE 4.44 THE ICON EDITOR AND THE BLACK-AND-WHITE ICON FOR THE MYINSANITY PROJECT.

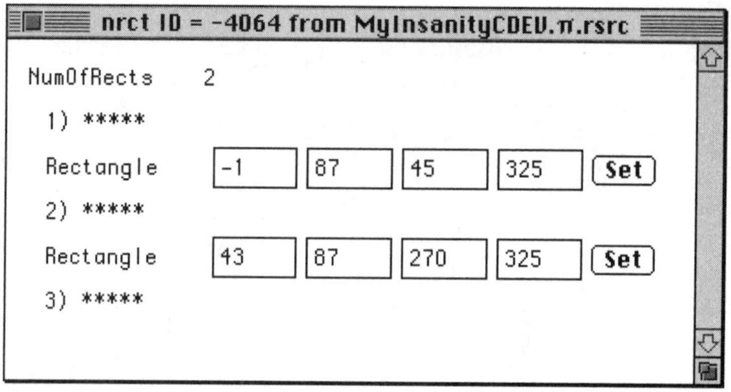

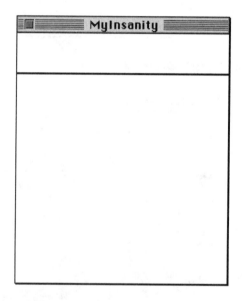

FIGURE 4.45 THE NRCT RESOURCE FOR THE MYINSANITY PROJECT.

FIGURE 4.46 THE TWO RECTANGLES FORMED BY THE NRCT RESOURCES
IN THE MYINSANITY PROJECT.

Because a control panel is always displayed in a dialog box, you can easily add graphics to any cdev you create. Figure 4.47 shows the one PICT resource MyInsanity uses.

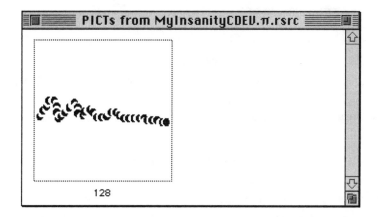

FIGURE 4.47 THE PICT RESOURCE FOR THE MYINSANITY PROJECT.

MyInsanity requires just three DITL items (see Figure 4.48). The first two are radio buttons, and the third is a picture item. You'll see constants for the first two items defined in the MyInsanity source code:

```
#define     ON_ITEM       1
#define     OFF_ITEM      2
```

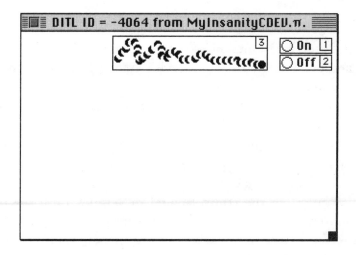

FIGURE 4.48 THE DITL RESOURCE FOR THE MYINSANITY PROJECT.

Handling a nulDev Message

This chapter's first two control panels responded to `initDev` and `hitDev` messages, as do almost all Control Panels. The MyInsanity Control Panel handles these two message types and two others: the nulDev and the macDev. The `nulDev` message is described here, while the `macDev` is discussed just ahead.

Once opened, the MyInsanity control panel repeatedly draws a growing square. Even when the cdev is inactive, it keeps executing its code. This isn't just the case for MyInsanity, it's true for any control panel. But because most control panels don't include a case label for the nulDev message, the Finder's `nulDev` message is ignored by the control panel and control is immediately returned to the Finder.

When MyInsanity receives a `nulDev` message, it responds by checking to see if the **On** radio button is set. If it is, it calls an application-defined routine to draw the growing square.

```
case nulDev:
   if ( (**cdev_storage).current_button_animate == ON_ITEM )
      Grow_Square();
   break;
```

The `Grow_Square()` function begins by drawing a rectangle zero pixels in width and height. After that, a loop is entered. Each pass through the loop draws the square one pixel larger in each direction. The effect, of course, is that the square is growing. After the loop has completed, the black square is erased by a call to `EraseRect()`.

One execution of `Grow_Square()` has the effect of drawing a dot in the center of the control panel and expanding it outward to the edge of the panel. Then `Grow_Square()` whites out this panel-filling square. As you watch the control panel in action, you'll see that this drawing and erasing occurs very quickly. That's the speed at which the Finder is sending null events to the control panel, whether the cdev is active or not.

```
void  Grow_Square( void )
{
   Pattern  the_pat;
   Rect     the_rect;
   int      i;

   SetRect( &the_rect, 205, 155, 205, 155 );

   for ( i = 0; i < 100; i++ )
   {
      InsetRect( &the_rect, -1, -1 );
      FrameRect( &the_rect );
   }

   EraseRect( &the_rect );
}
```

N O T E

Code resources don't have access to the qd **variables like the patterns white, black, etc. If your control panel needs to use patterns, use a call to** GetIndPattern() **to obtain one of the system patterns. By using a call to** EraseRect()**, MyInsanity gets by without needing the white pattern. Here's a second way that a white square could be drawn over the black square. Keep in mind that of the 38 system patterns, pattern 20 is solid white.**

```
Rect     the_rect;
Pattern  the_pat;

// use set SetRect() to set rectangle boundaries here

GetIndPattern( &the_pat, sysPatListID, 20 );
FillRect( &the_rect, &the_pat );
```

Grow_Square() is a simple routine that could be modified to draw much more complex and interesting graphics, including graphics that use color. If you do make this type of change, however, you'll want to make sure that the host computer is capable of displaying color. That type of check is the topic of the next section.

Selective Execution: The mach Resource and the macDev Message

If a control panel occupies more space than the System 6 Control Panel occupies, it isn't System 6 compatible. If a control panel uses certain Toolbox functions that aren't available on machines running under System 6, it too is unable to run on that machine. Additionally, your control panel may require that certain hardware features be present on the host Macintosh in order for it to properly execute. For these reasons, you'll want to know how to tell the Finder that your control panel won't run on every Macintosh model and under every system version. You'll also want to know how to make that control panel user-friendly in that it won't crash if a user does attempt to run it on an incompatible machine.

The control panel's mach resource is where the Finder initially determines if a control panel can run on the host machine. If a control panel has a mach resource with a value of FFFF 0000, as the chapter's MySetSound control panel does, the Finder will assume that the control panel is able to run on all Mac models, and on either System 6 or System 7. If, on the other hand, a control panel has a mach resource with a value of 0000 FFFF, as the MyInsanity control panel does—the Finder won't make this assumption. For your comparison, Figure 4.49 shows both the MySetSound mach resource and the MyInsanity mach resource.

If the Finder encounters a mach resource with a value of 0000 FFFF, the Finder will send as the control panel a macDev message. This message is sent as the very first message and is sent to the control panel only one time during the execution of the control panel. When a control panel receives a macDev message, it should perform the test or tests that are necessary to determine if the Macintosh meets whatever criteria the control panel requires of a host machine.

If the machine passes the tests that the control device function performs, it is capable of running the control panel, and the control device function should return a value of 1 to the Finder. When the Finder receives this value, it will open the control panel. If the Mac *isn't* able to run the control panel, a value of 0 should be returned. If the Finder receives a value of 0, it will not attempt to open the control panel. Instead, it will post the alert pictured in Figure 4.50.

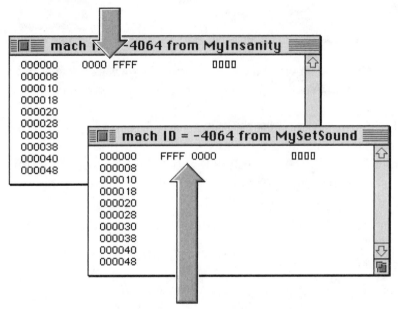

FIGURE **4.49** THE ORDERING OF THE HEX VALUES IN A MACH RESOURCE IS IMPORTANT.

MyInsanity performs only black-and-white drawing. To get prepared for its upgrade to a color version, though, it includes a test to see if the Macintosh it's running on has color QuickDraw. A call to Gestalt( ), with a selector of gestaltQuickdrawVersion, returns a response that holds the version of QuickDraw that resides on the Mac. If that version is the original "colorless" QuickDraw, a value of 0 is returned to the

Finder and the control panel isn't opened. Any other QuickDraw version supports color, so a 1 is returned and the Finder opens the cdev.

The control panel "MyInsanity" cannot be used with this Macintosh.

OK

FIGURE 4.50 THE ALERT DISPLAYED BY THE FINDER WHEN A USER ATTEMPTS TO USE THE MYINSANITY CONTROL PANEL ON A MONOCHROME MACINTOSH.

The MyInsanity code for handling a `macDev` message is shown as follows. Notice that because the control device function's `main()` routine returns a `CDEVHandle`, the values 0 and 1 must be typecast to this data type before being returned. The Finder will still interpret these returned values as simply the numbers 0 and 1.

```
case macDev:
   error = Gestalt( gestaltQuickdrawVersion, &response );
   if ( error != noErr )
      ExitToShell();
   else if ( response == gestaltOriginalQD )
      return ( (CDEVHandle)0 );
   else
      return ( (CDEVHandle)1 );
   break;
```

NOTE A more comprehensive test would also check the bit level of the Macintosh to see if it not only has color, but that it also has color turned on. You can refer back to the `Color_ Is_On()` routine in Chapter 2 to get an idea of how that test is made.

The MyInsanity Source Code Listing

This chapter ends with the complete listing for the MyInsanity control panel. Once you get the project up and running, you might want to try your hand at modifying the source code so that color is added to the animated graphics that MyInsanity draws.

```
//_____
//                                        #include directives

   #include <GestaltEqu.h>


//_____
//                                        function prototypes

void   Grow_Square( void );
void   Set_Radio_Buttons( DialogPtr, short, short, short );


//_____
//                                        #define directives

#define        ON_ITEM                 1
#define        OFF_ITEM                2

#define        SYS_PAT_LIST_OFFSET    20


//_____
//                                        define data structures

typedef   struct
{
   short   current_button_animate;
} CDEVRecord, *CDEVPtr, **CDEVHandle;


//_____
//                                        entry point to the code

pascal  CDEVHandle  main( short          message,
```

```
                           short       item,
                           short       num_items,
                           short       control_panel_ID,
                           EventRecord *the_event,
                           CDEVHandle  cdev_storage,
                           DialogPtr   the_dialog )
{
   short  old_radio;
   short  new_radio;
   OSErr  error;
   long   response;

   switch ( message )
   {
      case macDev:
         error = Gestalt( gestaltQuickdrawVersion, &response );
         if ( error != noErr )
            ExitToShell();
         else if ( response == gestaltOriginalQD )
            return ( (CDEVHandle)0 );
         else
            return ( (CDEVHandle)1 );
         break;

      case initDev:
         cdev_storage = (CDEVHandle)NewHandle(sizeof(CDEVRecord ) );

         (**cdev_storage).current_button_animate = ON_ITEM;

         new_radio = (**cdev_storage).current_button_animate;
         old_radio = OFF_ITEM;
         Set_Radio_Buttons( the_dialog, old_radio, new_radio );
         break;

      case hitDev:
         item = item = num_items;

         switch ( item )
         {
            case ON_ITEM:
               old_radio = (**cdev_storage).current_button_animate;
               new_radio = ON_ITEM;
               Set_Radio_Buttons( the_dialog, old_radio,
               new_radio );
               (**cdev_storage).current_button_animate  =
```

```
                new_radio;
                break;

            case OFF_ITEM:
                old_radio = (**cdev_storage).current_button_animate;
                new_radio = OFF_ITEM;
                Set_Radio_Buttons( the_dialog, old_radio,
                new_radio );
                (**cdev_storage).current_button_animate  =
                new_radio;
                break;
        }
        break;

    case nulDev:
        if ( (**cdev_storage).current_button_animate == ON_ITEM
)
            Grow_Square();
        break;

    }
    return ( cdev_storage );
}


//_____
//                              Grow square, then wipe it out

void  Grow_Square( void )
{
    Pattern   the_pat;
    Rect      the_rect;
    int       i;

    SetRect( &the_rect, 205, 155, 205, 155 );

    for ( i = 0; i < 100; i++ )
    {
        InsetRect( &the_rect, -1, -1 );
        FrameRect( &the_rect );
    }

    EraseRect( &the_rect );
}
```

CHAPTER SUMMARY

A control panel file is made up of several resources, the most significant of which is the cdev code resource. A cdev holds the compiled code for a control device function. The cdev control device function, like the MDEF menu definition procedure and the CDEF control definition function, is the code that performs the actions of the code resource.

Under System 6, all control panels appeared as icons in a single desk accessory—the Control Panel desk accessory. Under System 7, each control panel is its own independent entity. System 7 control panels are accessed from within the Control Panels folder under the Apple menu.

All control panel files consist of several required resources. A control panel needs a DITL resource to hold the items that will appear in the control panel's dialog box. The control panel doesn't, however, need a DLOG resource to define the dialog box itself—that's supplied by the Finder when the control panel is opened. Another required resource is the nrct. This resource defines the size of the control panel itself. The mach resource tells the Finder whether it should open the control panel without question or if it should first ask the control panel to perform tests to determine if the host computer is of a configuration capable of running the cdev. Other required resource types are the BNDL, FREF, and ICN#. These resources perform the same functions as they do for an application.

Chapter

More Mac Programming Techniques

5

RESOURCES

Resources hold information that defines what your application looks like—from every item in each menu to the buttons in each dialog box. Resources can also be used to store information about your program—a preferences file is nothing more than a resource file. The Toolbox routines that are a part of the Resource Manager make it possible for your programs to work with resources.

One interesting way to work with resources is to define several dialog box item lists that can be used in a single dialog box. In this chapter, you'll see how to use two or more DITL resources with a single DLOG resource. By displaying different items at different times, a dialog box in your application becomes very flexible. As the user selects different menu items, or clicks on different buttons, the look of the dialog box can change accordingly.

Resource editors allow you to use any of dozens of different types of resources. But even this wide variety may not be enough for your programming needs. If that's the case, you can create your own resource type. When you do, you'll use a hex editor to add and modify items in the resource. Because working in hex is too confusing, a resource editor allows you to create a template resource that can be used in conjunction with your own custom resource. The template allows a more graphic edit of the custom resource to be done, and it allows numbers and text to be added without using hexadecimal.

ABOUT RESOURCES

Any Macintosh file, whether a document file or application file, can consist of both a resource fork and a data fork. In many cases, both forks may be present, but one will be empty. For a 680x0 application, the data fork is usually empty. For a PowerPC application, it isn't. The resource fork of an application holds resources that define the application's menus, windows, controls, dialog boxes, and icons. Additionally, 680x0 applications store the code that makes up the application in CODE resources in the resource fork. PowerPC applications, however, keep the application code in the data fork. Though the resource fork of an application is just a part of the application file, programmers typically call the resource fork a resource file. This interchanging of terms is an acceptable practice, because from the programmer's perspective, the resource fork can and is accessed as if it were its own file.

Typically, an application's resources are created using a resource editor such as Apple's ResEdit or Mathemaesthetics Resorcerer. In Figure 5.1, ResEdit is being used to add a WIND resource to a new resource file.

Resources can also be created directly by your application. The routines that make up the Resource Manager allow you to give your application the ability to alter its own resources or to create an entirely new resource file with new resources. As you'll see in Chapter 6, this last task is done when an application requires a preferences file.

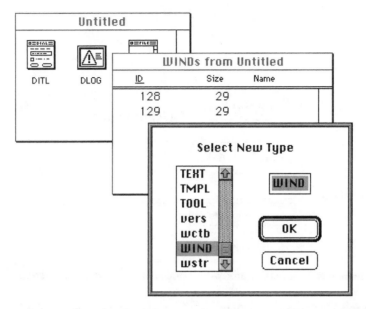

FIGURE 5.1 ADDING A WIND RESOURCE USING THE RESOURCE EDITOR RESEDIT.

USING MULTIPLE DITL RESOURCES IN ONE DIALOG BOX

One of the most interesting aspects of dialog boxes is that dialog box items can be added and removed as the program runs. That is, dialog box items can change dynamically. As an application runs, a dialog box can adapt itself to different conditions in the program by adding or taking away some or all of its items.

About Dynamic Dialog Box Items

Figure 5.2 is a dialog box with five dialog box items in it. To the left are two push buttons, labeled **Beep Once** and **Beep Twice**. At the top right are two radio buttons, and at the lower right is another push button. In this dialog box, only the three items on the right—the radio buttons and the **OK** button—are permanent parts of the dialog box. The two push buttons on the left will only be present when the **Play Beeps** radio button is on.

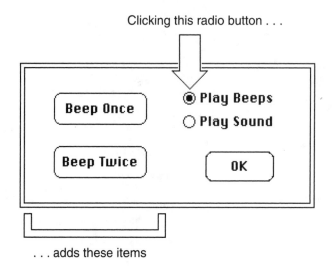

Clicking this radio button . . .

Beep Once

Beep Twice

Play Beeps
Play Sound

OK

. . . adds these items

FIGURE 5.2 A DIALOG BOX WITH DYNAMICALLY ADDED PUSH BUTTONS.

Figure 5.3 shows the same dialog box as pictured in Figure 5.2. In Figure 5.3, the two push button items that were on the left of the dialog box have been replaced by a single, larger push button.

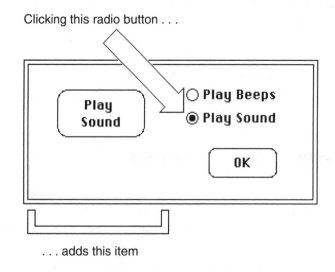

Clicking this radio button . . .

Play Sound

Play Beeps
Play Sound

OK

. . . adds this item

FIGURE 5.3 THE SAME DIALOG BOX AS PICTURED IN FIGURE 5.2, WITH DIFFERENT BUTTONS.

Changing dialog box items "on the fly" is a feature that is very useful for displaying only the items that pertain to a certain radio button, check box, or menu selection. The previous example uses radio buttons to change the dialog box items. You could just as easily have the displayed items be dependent on a pop-up menu selection rather than a button choice. And, with dynamic dialog box items, you don't have to limit the displayed items to only two sets, as this example does.

The example presented here is from a program that will be developed over the next several pages—it's named MultipleDITLs. You can see from the previous figures that this example is short on real-world usefulness. As usual, I've selected simplicity over complexity so that I can place the emphasis on technique. Once you understand the MultipleDITLs example, you'll be able to apply the program's concepts to more complex examples, like the one pictured in Figure 5.4.

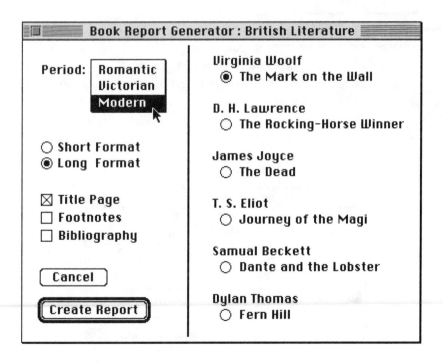

FIGURE 5.4 A MORE COMPLEX EXAMPLE USING DYNAMIC DIALOG BOX ITEMS.

Figure 5.4 shows the dialog box for a program that is the bane of all English teachers—an automated book report generator. In this example, all of the items on the left side of the dialog box's vertical line are permanent items. These items include the pop-up menu, the format radio buttons, the three check boxes, and the two push buttons. All of the items on the right side of the vertical line are *overlay* items. When a menu selection is made from the pop-up menu, these items would all change and a set of items would be added to the existing *base* items. As the user makes different menu selections, one overlay set is removed and a different one is added in its place. In this example, four DITL resources would be used: one for the base items, and one for each of the three sets of overlay items. Only one set of overlay items would be used at any one time, and the decision of which set to use would be based on the current selection in the pop-up menu.

The MulitpleDITLs Resources

To create a dialog box that is capable of displaying a variable number of items, begin as you would with any dialog box; that is, create a DLOG resource and a DITL resource. Determine which dialog box items will always be available in the dialog box and include them in the DITL resource. This will become the base DITL for the dialog box. Figure 5.5 shows the base DITL for the MulitpleDITLs program.

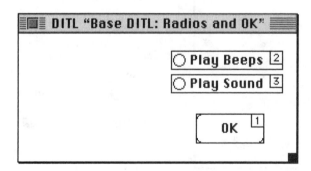

FIGURE 5.5 THE BASE DITL RESOURCE FOR THE MULTIPLEDITLS PROJECT.

The DLOG used in the MultipleDITLs program is shown in Figure 5.6. It has been given an ID of 128, which is the same ID as the base DITL resource.

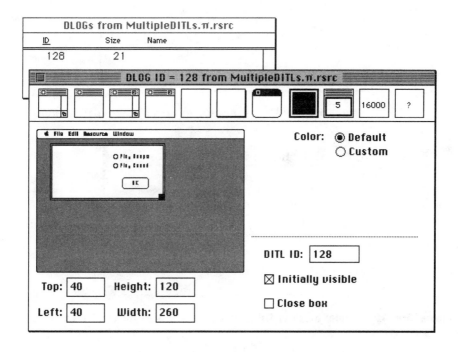

FIGURE 5.6 THE DLOG RESOURCE FOR THE MULTIPLEDITLS PROJECT.

For each set of items that will be added to the dialog box, a separate overlay DITL is created. Because the MultipleDITLs dialog box will use two separate sets of items (one for each radio button selection), it has two overlay DITL resources. Figure 5.7 shows the DITL used when the **Play Beeps** radio button is selected. Figure 5.8 shows the DITL that's used when the **Play Sound** radio button is clicked on.

When completed, the MultipleDITLs resource file will hold three DITL resources, which are shown in Figure 5.9. Only the ID of the base DITL is significant—it must match the resource ID given in the DLOG resource.

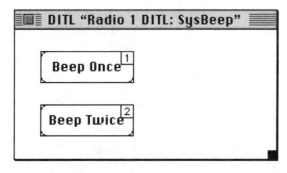

FIGURE 5.7 THE FIRST OVERLAY DITL RESOURCE FOR THE MULTIPLEDITLS PROJECT.

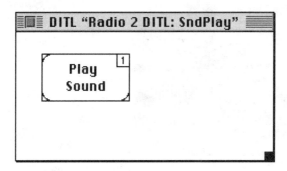

FIGURE 5.8 THE SECOND OVERLAY DITL RESOURCE FOR THE MULTIPLEDITLS PROJECT.

ID	Size	Name
128	62	"Base DITL: Radios and OK"
201	50	"Radio 1 DITL: SysBeep"
202	26	"Radio 2 DITL: SndPlay"

DITLs from MultipleDITLs.π.rsrc

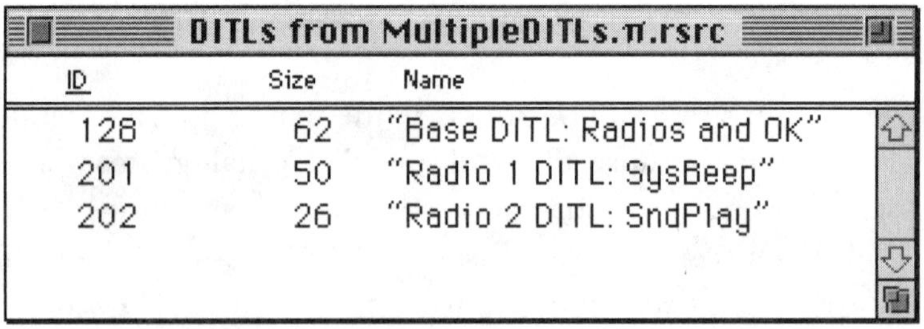

FIGURE 5.9 THE ID NUMBERS OF THE THREE DITL RESOURCES
FOR THE MULTIPLEDITLS PROJECT.

When a user of the MultipleDITLs program clicks on the **Play Sound**
radio button, the MultipleDITLs program will append the item in DITL
202 to the items in base DITL 128. Then, in response to a click on the

Play Beeps radio button, the program will remove the DITL 202 item and in its place append the items in DITL 201 to the base items. Figure 5.10 shows DITL 201 being overlaid onto DITL 128, with their upper-left corners about to be lined up.

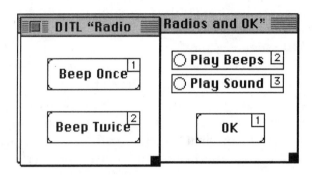

FIGURE 5.10 CONCEPTUALIZATION OF HOW AN OVERLAY DITL WORKS WITH A BASE DITL.

Figure 5.10 shows that the positioning you give to the items in an overlay DITL will determine where the items end up when appended to the items in the base DITL. The result of the combination of overlay DITL 201 and base DITL 128, as seen when the MultipleDITLs program is running, is shown in Figure 5.11.

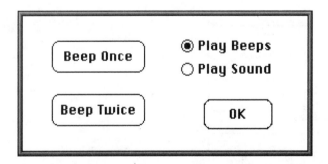

FIGURE 5.11 THE DIALOG BOX THAT RESULTS FROM USING THE BASE DITL AND ONE OVERLAY DITL.

Looking back at Figure 5.10 brings up one important question. When the items in two DITL resources are combined, how is the problem of

DITL numbering resolved? In Figure 5.10, you can see that there are two number 1 items and two number 2 items. This resolution is handled in the record that is maintained for the dialog box that holds the base DITL.

Each dialog box has a record, represented by the `DialogRecord` data structure, which holds information about the dialog box. One of the `DialogRecord` members, the `items` field, keeps track of the items in the dialog box. The `items` member is a handle to a list of items. When the dialog box opens, this list holds the items from the base DITL. When items are appended to the dialog box, they are appended to this list. Items that are appended to this list are numbered sequentially from the last item that was in the original list. Figure 5.12 shows how this works for the MultipleDITLs program when you use one of the overlays.

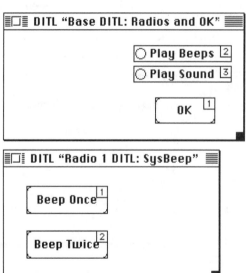

Item list

Item	Item Number
OK	1
○ Play Beeps	2
○ Play Sound	3
Beep Once	4
Beep Twice	5

FIGURE 5.12 THE DIALOGRECORD ITEM LIST HOLDS THE DITL ITEMS AND A NUMBER FOR EACH ITEM.

When referencing items in your source code, you'll use the item numbers as they appear in the DialogRecord item list—not as they exist in the DITL resources that hold the items. For base DITL items, these numbers are the same, but as you can see from Figure 5.12, for appended items, the item list numbers differ from the DITL items.

Yes, more than one overlay DITL can be used at any given time. Both DITL resources 201 and 202 could be appended to DITL 128. Then the single item in DITL 202, the Play Sound push button, would have an item list number of 6. Adding more than one DITL at a time makes things needlessly complex, however. It's much better to include all of the items that are to be added in a single DITL and then overlay that one DITL onto the base DITL.

N O T E

The AppendDITL() and ShortenDITL() Routines

To dynamically add items to a dialog box, you'll rely on the Toolbox function AppendDITL(). AppendDITL() requires three parameters: a pointer to the dialog that will hold the items, a handle to the items, and a constant that tells where the items should be added. Here's a call to AppendDITL():

```
DialogPtr   the_dialog;
Handle      item_list_handle;

AppendDITL( the_dialog, item_list_handle, overlayDITL );
```

The first parameter is the DialogPtr variable returned by the GetNewDialog() call that loaded the dialog box into memory. The second parameter is obtained from a call to Get1Resource(). The third parameter, overlayDITL, is an Apple-defined constant used to specify that the upper-left corner of the overlay DITL should line up with the upper-left corner of the base DITL, as shown in Figure 5.10. The following is a snippet that makes use of all three of these parameters.

```
DialogPtr   the_dialog;
Handle      item_list_handle;

the_dialog = GetNewDialog( 128, nil, (WindowPtr)-1L );

item_list_handle = Get1Resource( 'DITL', 201 );
AppendDITL( the_dialog, item_list_handle, overlayDITL );
```

This code uses a call to `GetNewDialog()` to open a dialog box using a DLOG resource with an ID of 128. Any items in the DITL associated with this DLOG will of course be displayed at this time. Next, a call to `Get1Resource()` is made to acquire a handle to the overlay DITL that has an ID of 201. The pointer to the dialog box and the handle to the DITL are then used to append the overlay items onto the dialog box.

You should follow a call to `AppendDITL()` with a call to the Toolbox routine `ReleaseResource()`, passing the item list handle as the only parameter:

```
ReleaseResource( item_list_handle );
```

If your dialog box no longer needs the appended items, make a call to the Toolbox routine `ShortenDITL()`. This function requires two parameters: a pointer to the dialog box that's to have items removed, and the number of items to remove. `ShortenDITL()` always removes the items from the end of a dialog box's item list. That makes it a convenient compliment to the `AppendDITL()` routine, which adds items to the end of the item list.

To determine how many items to remove, make a call to the Toolbox function `CountDITL()`. When passed, a `DialogPtr`, `CountDITL()` returns the number of items in that dialog box. The following snippet shows how the items in overlay DITL 201 could be removed from a dialog box. Recall that DITL 201 has two items and the base DITL has three items, for a total of five items currently in the dialog box.

```
#define   NUM_BASE_ITEMS   3

short  total_items;
```

```
total_items = CountDITL( the_dialog );
ShortenDITL( the_dialog, total_items - NUM_BASE_ITEMS  );
```

Keeping Track of DITL Items

With the Toolbox functions `AppendDITL()` and `ShortenDITL()`, adding and removing dialog box items becomes an easy task. But if these operations are to take place at the whim of the user, you'll need to keep track of which items are in the dialog box at any given time.

The following fragment outlines the logic used by the MultipleDITLs program. After a call to `ModalDialog()` returns the item number of a clicked-on item, a `switch` statement is used to take the appropriate action. The first three items are from the base DITL, and as such they will always be in the dialog box. The fourth and fifth items, however, must be handled differently. If DITL 201 is the overlay, then its two push buttons will be items 4 and 5. If DITL 202 is the overlay, then its one push button will be item 4.

```
do
{
   ModalDialog( nil, &the_item );

   switch ( the_item )
   {
      case 2:
         // handle click on 1st radio button, base 'DITL' item
         break;

      case 3:
         // handle click on 2nd radio button, base 'DITL' item
         break;

      case 4:
         // handle click on button from overlay 'DITL' 201 or...
         // handle click on button from overlay 'DITL' 202
         break;

      case 5:
         // handle click on button from overlay 'DITL' 201
         break;
   }

} while ( the_item != 1 );  // OK button, base 'DITL' item
```

From the above code, you can see that a `case` label is needed for each of the items that might possibly appear in the dialog box, even though it is only guaranteed that the base DITL items will be present.

The case label for the fourth item is unique in that it has to be able to handle two scenarios. If the **Play Beeps** radio button is on, DITL 201 is appended and the fourth item in the item list is the **Beep Once** push button. If, on the other hand, the second radio button is on, DITL 202 is appended in place of DITL 201 and the fourth item in the item list is the **Play Sound** push button. Figure 5.13 shows how the `DialogRecord` item list varies depending on which radio button is on.

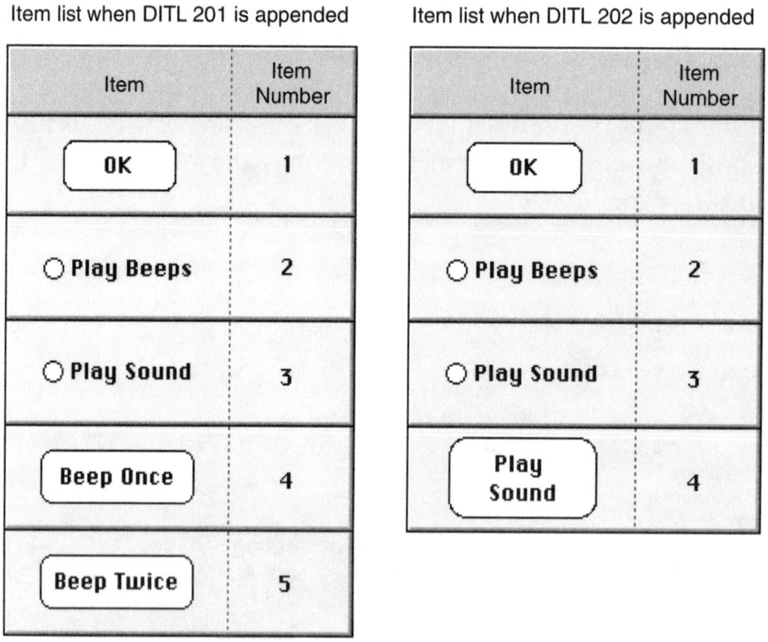

Item list when DITL 201 is appended

Item	Item Number
OK	1
○ Play Beeps	2
○ Play Sound	3
Beep Once	4
Beep Twice	5

Item list when DITL 202 is appended

Item	Item Number
OK	1
○ Play Beeps	2
○ Play Sound	3
Play Sound	4

FIGURE 5.13 THE DIALOGRECORD ITEM LIST AS IT WOULD APPEAR WHEN USING DITL 201, THEN DITL 202, AS THE OVERLAY.

To handle both possible situations, the case label for the fourth item will need to include its own `switch` statement. Whatever variable is being used to keep track of the current appended DITL will be used in the `switch`. Here's the format for handling this type of item:

```
case 4:
   switch ( overlay tracking variable )
   {
      case overlay 201:
         // beep speaker once

      case overlay 202:
         // play a sound from a 'snd ' resource
   }
   break;
```

Since DITL 201 adds a fifth item to the `DialogRecord` item list and DITL 202 doesn't, the case for item 5 only has to handle a click on the **Beep Twice** button that will be present when DITL 201 is the appended DITL:

```
case 5:
   // handle click on button from overlay 'DITL' 201
   break;
```

The next section presents the complete source code listing for the MultipleDITLs program. Before looking it over, you might want to look at how its primary function, `Open_Dialog()`, works. You've seen much of it piecemeal here, so it should look familiar to you.

```
void  Open_Dialog( void )
{
   // Open the dialog box
   // Set one of the two radio buttons
   // Append the appropriate 'DITL', based on the radio
   // button that is set
   // Set a variable to keep track of which overlay is current

   do
   {
      ModalDialog( nil, &the_item );

      switch ( the_item )
      {
         case 2:
            // Set radio buttons
            // Remove items from other overlay, 'DITL' 202
            // Add items from this overlay, 'DITL' 201
```

```
                // Set a variable to keep track of current overlay

          case 3:
              // Set radio buttons
              // Remove items from other overlay, 'DITL' 201
              // Add items from this overlay, 'DITL' 202
              // Set a variable to keep track of current overlay

          case 4:
              switch ( overlay tracking variable )
              {
                 case overlay 201:
                     // Beep speaker once

                 case overlay 202:
                     // Play a sound from a 'snd ' resource
              }
              break;

          case 5:
              // Beep speaker twice
              break;
      }

   } while ( the_item != 1 );

   // Dispose of the dialog
}
```

The MultipleDITLs Source Code Listing

There's only one part of the MultipleDITLs code that you won't recognize—these lines from main( ):

```
OSErr   error;
long    response;

error = Gestalt( gestaltDITLExtAttr, &response );
if ( response == gestaltDITLExtPresent )
  ExitToShell();
```

The AppendDITL( ) and ShortenDITL( ) routines aren't available in System 6. This means that you'll need to perform one of two checks before calling these functions. If you're forcing users to run your program on a machine with System 7, verify that this system is present when your program starts up. Or, if your program is backwards compatible with System 6, check for the presence of the DITL routines before using them. That's what the above snippet of code does.

NOTE

If you're making your program backwards compatible, you might want to use two different schemes for displaying DITL information. For System 7, you can use the multiple DITL technique presented here. For System 6 users, you'd have to instead use ShowDialogItem() **and** HideDialogItem(), **or else have separate dialog boxes for different options.**

Now here's the entire listing. As always, look on the included disk for all of the files needed to build your own version of the program.

```
//_____
//                                    #include directives

#include <GestaltEqu.h>
#include <Sound.h>


//_____
//                                    function prototypes

void    Initialize_Toolbox( void );
void    Open_Dialog( void );
void    Set_Radio_Buttons( DialogPtr, short *, short );


//_____
//                                    #define directives

#define       DLOG_ID           128
#define       OK_ITEM             1
#define       RADIO_1_ITEM        2
#define       RADIO_2_ITEM        3
#define       NUM_BASE_ITEMS      3

#define       RADIO_1_DITL      201
#define       RADIO_2_DITL      202
```

```
#define        SND_GLASS_ID        9000


//_____
//                                                      main()

void  main( void )
{
   OSErr  error;
   long   response;

   error = Gestalt( gestaltDITLExtAttr, &response );
   if ( response == gestaltDITLExtPresent )
     ExitToShell();

   Initialize_Toolbox();

   Open_Dialog();
}



//_____
//                                            initialize the Mac

void  Initialize_Toolbox( void )
{
   InitGraf( &qd.thePort );
   InitFonts();
   InitWindows();
   InitMenus();
   TEInit();
   InitDialogs( 0L );
   FlushEvents( everyEvent, 0L );
   InitCursor();
}



//_____
//                                        open a display dialog

void  Open_Dialog( void )
{
   DialogPtr  the_dialog;
   short      the_item;
   short      new_radio;
```

```
short      old_radio;
Handle     item_list_handle;
short      total_items;
short      append_type;
Handle     snd_handle;

the_dialog = GetNewDialog( DLOG_ID, nil, (WindowPtr)-1L );

old_radio = RADIO_2_ITEM;
new_radio = RADIO_1_ITEM;
Set_Radio_Buttons( the_dialog, &old_radio, new_radio );

item_list_handle = Get1Resource( 'DITL', RADIO_1_DITL );
AppendDITL( the_dialog, item_list_handle, overlayDITL );
ReleaseResource( item_list_handle );

append_type = RADIO_1_DITL;

ShowWindow( the_dialog );
SetPort( the_dialog );

do
{
   ModalDialog( nil, &the_item );

   switch ( the_item )
   {
      case RADIO_1_ITEM:
         new_radio = RADIO_1_ITEM;
         Set_Radio_Buttons( the_dialog, &old_radio, new_radio );

         total_items = CountDITL( the_dialog );
         ShortenDITL( the_dialog, total_items - NUM_BASE_ITEMS );

         item_list_handle = Get1Resource( 'DITL', RADIO_1_DITL );
         AppendDITL( the_dialog, item_list_handle, overlayDITL );
         ReleaseResource( item_list_handle );

         append_type = RADIO_1_DITL;
         break;

      case RADIO_2_ITEM:
         new_radio = RADIO_2_ITEM;
         Set_Radio_Buttons( the_dialog, &old_radio, new_radio );
```

```
            total_items = CountDITL( the_dialog );
            ShortenDITL( the_dialog, total_items - NUM_BASE_ITEMS );

            item_list_handle = Get1Resource( 'DITL', RADIO_2_DITL );
            AppendDITL( the_dialog, item_list_handle, overlayDITL );
            ReleaseResource( item_list_handle );

            append_type = RADIO_2_DITL;
            break;

        case 4:
            switch ( append_type )
            {
               case RADIO_1_DITL:
                  SysBeep( 1 );
                  break;

               case RADIO_2_DITL:
                  snd_handle = Get1Resource( 'snd ', SND_GLASS_ID );
                  SndPlay( nil, snd_handle, true );
                  break;
            }
            break;

        case 5:
            SysBeep( 1 );
            SysBeep( 1 );
            break;
      }

   } while ( the_item != OK_ITEM );

   DisposDialog( the_dialog );
}


//_____
//                                    set radio buttons

void Set_Radio_Buttons( DialogPtr  dlog,
                        short     *old_radio,
                        short      new_radio )
{
```

```
Handle   hand;
short    type;
Rect     box;

GetDItem( dlog, *old_radio, &type, &hand, &box );
SetCtlValue( (ControlHandle)hand, 0 );

GetDItem( dlog, new_radio, &type, &hand, &box );
SetCtlValue( (ControlHandle)hand, 1 );

*old_radio = new_radio;
}
```

The Toolbox routines that allow multiple DITL resources to work are `AppendDITL()` **and** `ShortenDITL()`. **These routines do** *not* **support ictb resources. An ictb, or item color table, is a resource that adds color to individual items in a dialog box. This shouldn't be a problem for most developers because Apple doesn't recommend adding nonstandard colors to dialog box items.**

Building the MultipleDITLs Program

From here on, building the example programs listed in this book will be an elementary task, regardless of the compiler you're using. After this point, I won't cover application building for the examples. You'll find that for each project, you need only follow the simple steps listed here.

Symantec users will create a new project and add the MacTraps library and the one source code file. Then select **Run** or **Build Application** from the Project menu. For a look at any of the projects or files, refer to the Symantec examples folder included on the disk.

Metrowerks users should create a new project and add the MacOS.lib library and the one source code file. Then choose **Run** or **Make** from the Project menu. To see the details of a project, resource, or source code file, look at the Metrowerks examples folder provided on the disk.

USING CUSTOM RESOURCE TEMPLATES

A graphical resource editor like ResEdit depends on *templates* to make resource editing easy. A template displays the value or values in a single resource of a single resource type. For example, you use the STR# template to edit the strings in a STR# resource. Figure 5.14 shows the STR# template. The template, which is built into ResEdit, displays the strings in a manner that is easy to read and easy to edit.

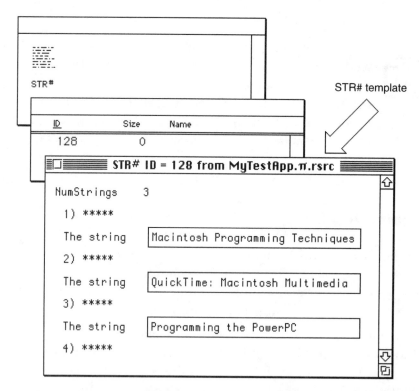

FIGURE 5.14 A RESOURCE EDITOR TEMPLATE DISPLAYS RESOURCE ITEMS IN A WAY THAT MAKES EDITING THE RESOURCE EASIER.

You don't have to use the built in STR# template when viewing a STR# resource. If you chose **Open Using Hex Editor** from the Resource menu, you'd see the same three strings in a window like the one shown in Figure 5.15. After looking at this window, you'll surely come to the conclusion that a template makes things much clearer.

```
STR# ID = 128 from MyTestApp.π.rsrc
000000    0003 204D 6163 696E    ▮▮ Macin
000008    746F 7368 2050 726F    tosh Pro
000010    6772 616D 6D69 6E67    gramming
000018    2054 6563 686E 6971     Techniq
000020    7565 731F 5175 6963    ues▮Quic
000028    6B54 696D 653A 204D    kTime: M
000030    6163 696E 746F 7368    acintosh
000038    204D 756C 7469 6D65     Multime
000040    6469 6117 5072 6F67    dia▮Prog
000048    7261 6D6D 696E 6720    ramming
000050    7468 6520 506F 7765    the Powe
000058    7250 43               rPC
000060
000068
000070
```

FIGURE 5.15 WITHOUT A TEMPLATE, EDITING A RESOURCE BECOMES MUCH MORE DIFFICULT.

ResEdit supplies templates for about 60 of the commonly used resource types, including the ALRT, DITL, and DLOG resources. For most of your programming needs, these built-in templates are all that you'll ever need. If you want to store your own data structures in a resource file, however, you'll want to create your own template so that you can view and edit your data. Fortunately, ResEdit makes it easy to add your own templates to a resource file.

A common task performed by a Macintosh program is to obtain information that's held in a resource. A call to `GetNewWindow()`, for example, acquires WIND resource data used to load a window into memory. The window example uses a predefined resource type and a Toolbox routine. It's also possible to store your own data in a resource of your own design and to access it from source code using the `Get1Resource()` Toolbox routine.

In this section, you'll see how to create your own resource type. Then you'll create a template to make data stored in your resource easy to work with. You'll also see how to access this same data from within a program. In Chapter 6, you'll see a very practical example that makes use of these tasks—the creation and use of a preferences file.

The TemplateUser Program

The disk that accompanies this book includes a project named TemplateUser. In the project's resource file is a TSTD resource type. This isn't a standard resource type, I've created it just for use by the TemplateUser program. There's no real significance to the four-character resource name. I chose the letters TSTD to stand for "test data," but I could have used any four characters.

The TSTD resource holds four pieces of data: a `short`, a `long`, a `Boolean`, and a string. Figure 5.16 shows how a resource of the TSTD type might look when opened with ResEdit's hex editor.

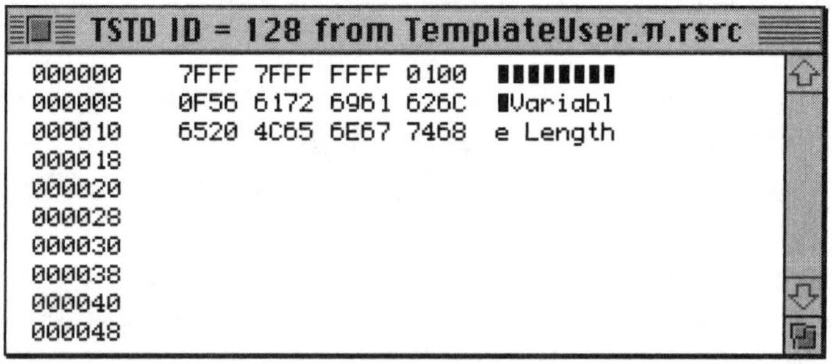

```
▤▥ TSTD ID = 128 from TemplateUser.π.rsrc ▤
 000000    7FFF 7FFF FFFF 0100   ▊▊▊▊▊▊▊▊
 000008    0F56 6172 6961 626C   ▊Variabl
 000010    6520 4C65 6E67 7468   e Length
 000018
 000020
 000028
 000030
 000038
 000040
 000048
```

FIGURE 5.16 A CUSTOM RESOURCE TYPE NAMED TSTD.

Since it's very difficult to determine what values are held in the TSTD resource and equally difficult to modify its data, I've added a template to the resource file. The template makes working with TSTD resources easy. The template addition is shown on the next pages.

Data are stored in a resource in an application so that it's available for use by that application. To demonstrate how this is done, the TemplateUser program loads the data from one TSTD resource and displays it in a window (see Figure 5.17).

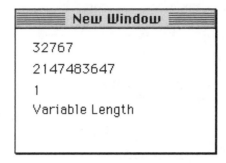

FIGURE 5.17 THE RESULT OF RUNNING THE TEMPLATEUSER PROGRAM.

Creating a New Resource Type and Template

Using ResEdit, a new resource of any type is added to a resource file by selecting **Create New Resource** from the Resource menu. If you're going to add a resource of a standard type, such as an ALRT or DITL resource, you'll find the resource name in the scrolling list in the Select New Type dialog box. If you want to add a resource of your own type, you obviously won't see its name in the list. Instead, just click in the Edit text box and type in whatever four character name you've settled on. Figure 5.18 shows a new TSTD resource about to be added to the resource file.

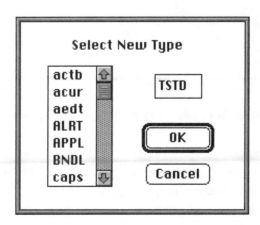

FIGURE 5.18 CREATING A NEW RESOURCE TYPE IN RESEDIT.

After clicking **OK**, a new resource icon will appear in the type picker window, and two new windows will open. The first holds a list of all of the TSTD resources in the file. Since this resource type was just created, there'll be only one resource listed here. ResEdit will give this first resource an ID of 128. The second window that opens is the ResEdit hex editor window. The new resource opens without any data in it (see Figure 5.19).

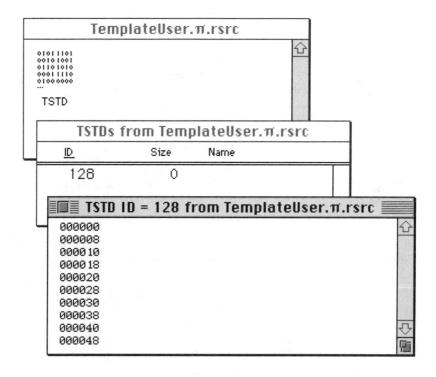

FIGURE 5.19 THE NEW, EMPTY TSTD RESOURCE-EDITING WINDOW.

Unlike a standard resource type, like a STR#, there is no template in ResEdit to define how data entered into a TSTD resource should be formatted. If you start typing, the hex equivalent to the keys you press will be displayed in the hex editor. If you wanted to enter the values **32767**, **2147483647**, **true**, and **Variable Length**, you'd have to enter the values as shown in Figure 5.20.

```
        TSTDs from TemplateUser.π.rsrc
   ID            Size       Name

   128            24
```

```
═▣≡  TSTD ID = 128 from TemplateUser.π.rsrc ≡
   000000    7FFF 7FFF FFFF 0100   ▮▮▮▮▮▮▮▮
   000008    0F56 6172 6961 626C   ▮Variabl
   000010    6520 4C65 6E67 7468   e Length
   000018
   000020
   000028
   000030
   000038
   000040
   000048
```

FIGURE 5.20 THE TSTD RESOURCE WITH DATA ENTERED.

Unless you can do decimal-to-hex conversions and alphanumeric-to-hex conversions in your head, this is way too much work! The solution, of course, is to create a template. To do this, you'll again select **Create New Resource** from the Resource menu. Templates are a standard resource type, so scrolling through the resource type list will eventually reveal the TMPL resource name in the list. A click on the name will place it in the Edit box. Figure 5.21 shows the Select New Type dialog box as it looks just before **OK** is clicked.

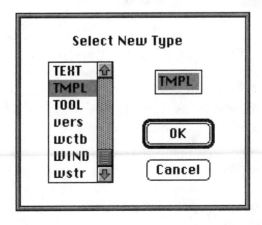

FIGURE 5.21 CREATING A TEMPLATE RESOURCE IN RESEDIT.

After clicking **OK**, the windows shown in Figure 5.22 will open. There will be one new TMPL resource, with ID 128. The template editor will open, and you can begin to edit the template.

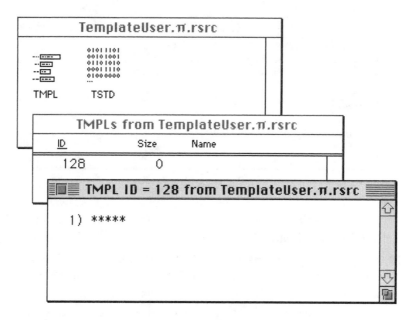

FIGURE 5.22 THE NEW, EMPTY 'TMPL RESOURCE-EDITING WINDOW.

When ResEdit created the TSTD resource and the template that will be used to edit this resource, it gave each an ID of 128. That's the ID that ResEdit gives the first resource of any type. The fact that both the TSTD resource and the TMPL resource have the same ID is not what binds them together. Instead, it's the TMPL name that associates it with the TSTD resource. To give the TMPL resource a name, first click on the resource to highlight it, as done in Figure 5.23. Then select **Get Resource Info** from the Resource menu.

In the dialog box that opens, type in **TSTD** (see Figure 5.24). Now that the template has the same name as the resource type it is to be used with, the association is made. Just to show that the ID of the template doesn't have to be the same as the resource it's to be used with, I've changed the TMPL ID to 200.

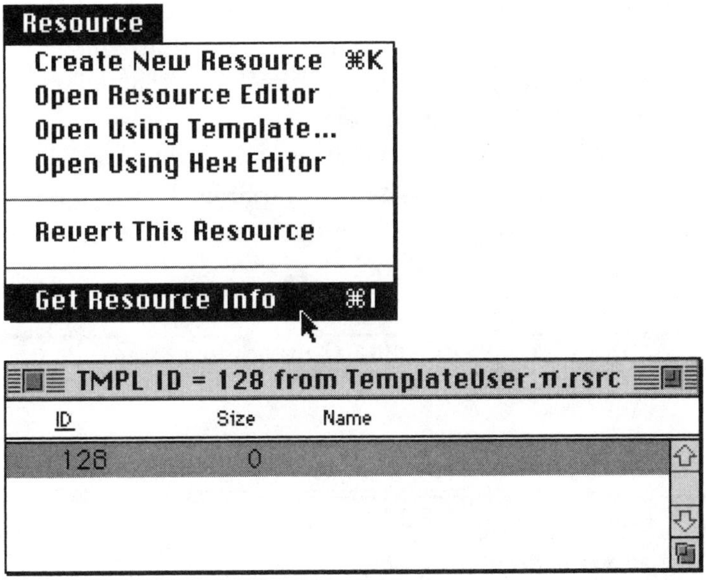

FIGURE 5.23 SELECTING GET RESOURCE INFO FOR THE TEMPLATE RESOURCE.

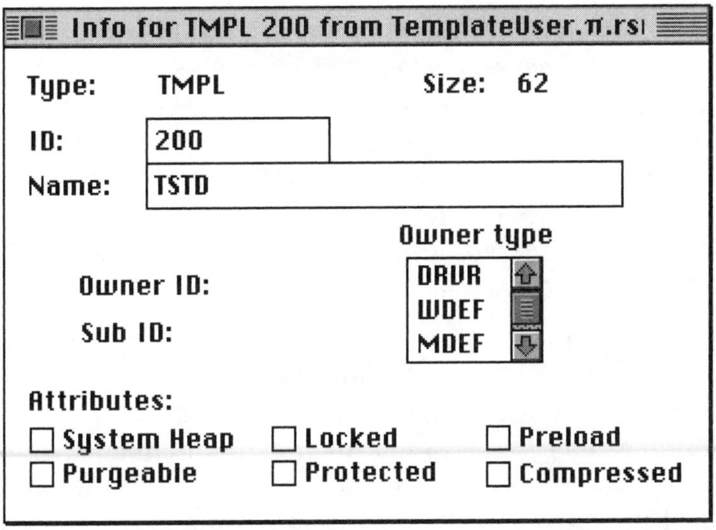

FIGURE 5.24 CHANGING THE RESOURCE ID AND THE RESOURCE
NAME OF THE TEMPLATE RESOURCE.

After closing the Get Info window, it's time to edit the template. The template will have an item for each data element that will be in a TSTD resource. The template item will give a label to the data element and will specify the type of data that the element is. Imagine that the TSTD resource will hold just a single data element, and that it will be a two-byte number. In C, that would be a `short` variable. In the template, there should be a single item that corresponds to this one data element. Figure 5.25 shows what this item would look like.

```
┌─────────────────────────────────────────────────┐
│▤▤▤  TMPL "TSTD" ID = 200 from Template.π.rsrc ▤▤▤│
├─────────────────────────────────────────────┬───┤
│                                             │ ⇧ │
│  1) *****                                    │   │
│                                             │   │
│  Label        │ short data              │   │   │
│                                         │   │   │
│  Type         │ DWRD      │             │   │   │
│                                             │   │
│  2) *****                                    │   │
│                                             │ ⇩ │
│                                             │ ▤ │
└─────────────────────────────────────────────┴───┘
```

**FIGURE 5.25 A TEMPLATE RESOURCE THAT DEFINES
ONE DATA FIELD—A TWO-BYTE NUMBER.**

A template item can have any label, but it should be descriptive of what the data element is or what it will be used for. I choose "short data" for the label. The item has to have a type, and it must be one of the types that ResEdit recognizes. For a two-byte value, or short, enter **DWRD** as the type. DWRD stands for decimal word.

As a test, close the template resource and double-click on the TSTD resource to open it. Now, instead of the hex editor opening, the template will open. You'll see the label in the left of the window and an Edit box to the right of the label (see Figure 5.26). To enter a number, just click in the Edit box and type it in. Since the template specified that this data element would be in decimal, you can type in a number as you normally would—there's no need to convert it to hex. Figure 5.26 shows the TSTD resource with the number 18 entered.

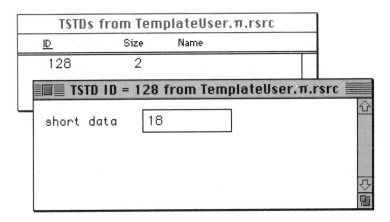

FIGURE 5.26 How the **TSTD** resource would look when using the **TMPL** resource.

Now let's go back to the template to complete it. The TemplateUser program is going to use four data elements, and it expects to find them in its resource fork—in a TSTD resource. The program will be looking for a short, a long, a Boolean, and a string. Figure 5.27 shows what the TSTD template should look like in order to meet these specifications. You can use the **Insert New Field(s)** menu item from the Resource menu to add each new item.

After closing the template, double-click on the TSTD resource to open it again. This time, the TSTD editor will look like the one pictured in Figure 5.28. Now the TSTD data can be edited in the same graphical manner that resources of standard types are edited. In Figure 5.28, I've entered a value for each of the four fields.

ResEdit allows you to specify that a template item represents just about any kind of data. Table 5.1 shows many of the four-character names you can use in your TMPL resources.

Now that some data is stored in a resource, what can be done with it? That depends on the requirements of the application that will use the data. The TemplateUser program will simply read in this data and display it in a window. To do that, a WIND resource needs to be added to the resource file. Figure 5.29 shows the WIND that TemplateUser works with.

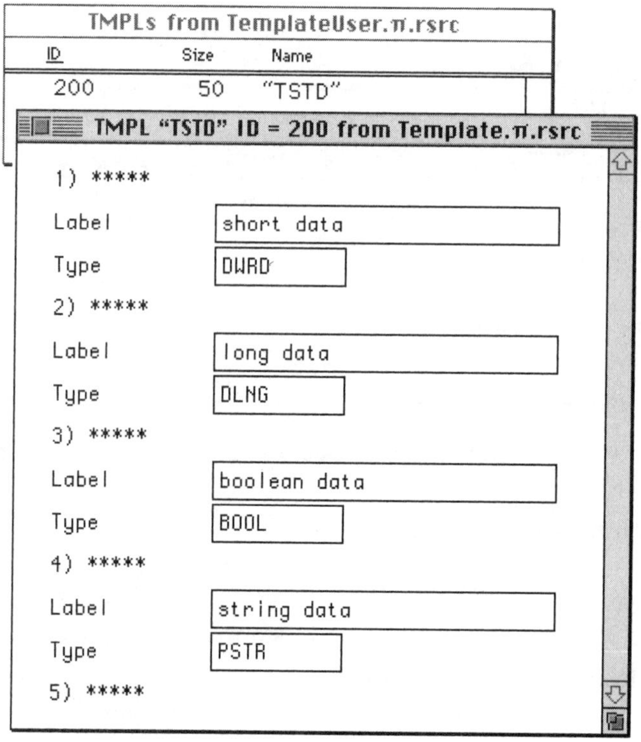

TMPLs from TemplateUser.π.rsrc

ID	Size	Name
200	50	"TSTD"

TMPL "TSTD" ID = 200 from Template.π.rsrc

1) *****

Label   short data

Type   DWRD

2) *****

Label   long data

Type   DLNG

3) *****

Label   boolean data

Type   BOOL

4) *****

Label   string data

Type   PSTR

5) *****

FIGURE 5.27 THE COMPLETED **TMPL** RESOURCE.

TSTDs from TemplateUser.π.rsrc

ID	Size	Name
128	24	

TSTD ID = 128 from TemplateUser.π.rsrc

short data   32767

long data   2147483647

boolean data   ● True   ○ False

string data   Variable Length

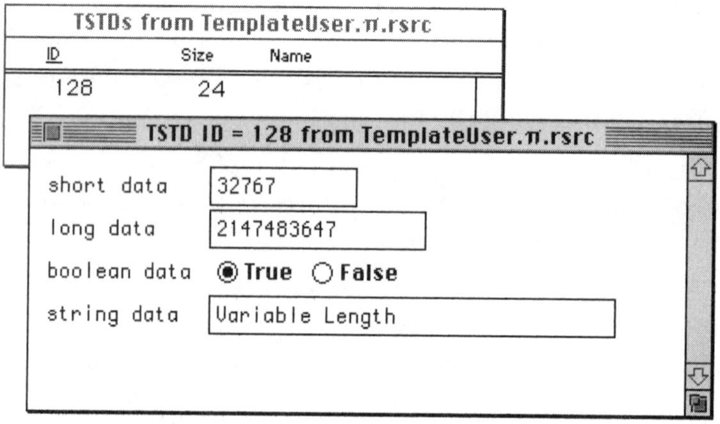

FIGURE 5.28 HOW THE **TSTD** RESOURCE WOULD LOOK
WHEN USING THE COMPLETED **TMPL** RESOURCE.

ResEdit Type	Description
DBYT	1–byte decimal field Maximum value for data of this type: 255
DWRD	2–byte decimal field Maximum value for data of this type: 32,767
DLNG	4–byte decimal field Maximum value for data of this type: 2,147,483,647
PSTR	Pascal string field Enter the text without leading or trailing characters (no "\p" or "\0")
CHAR	1-byte character field
BOOL	Boolean field Displayed as a pair of radio buttons
RECT	Rectangle field Displayed as four edit boxes, each used to enter one coordinate of the rectangle. Order of entry is: (top, left, bottom, right)

TABLE 5.1 SOME OF THE FOUR-CHARACTER NAMES THAT CAN BE USED IN A TEMPLATE RESOURCE.

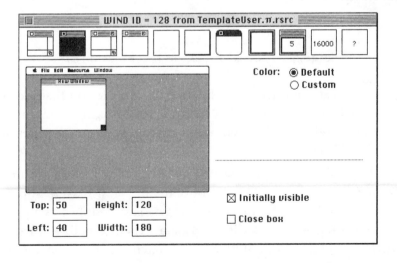

FIGURE 5.29 THE WIND RESOURCE USED BY THE TEMPLATEUSER PROJECT.

Figure 5.30 shows the complete resource file for the TemplateUser project. In the upcoming pages, you'll see how to read the TSTD data into TemplateUser. In Chapter 6, you'll see how this technique of storing and reading resource data is used to save a program's preference settings.

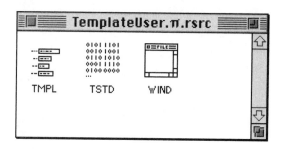

FIGURE 5.30 THE RESOURCE TYPES FOUND IN THE TEMPLATEUSER RESOURCE FILE.

Using Resource Data In an Application

When a Mac application makes a call to `GetNewWindow()`, the Toolbox loads information from a WIND resource into a `WindowRecord` data structure. It then supplies the program with a pointer to that data. This pointer is a `WindowPtr`:

```
WindowPtr  the_window;

the_window = GetNewWindow( WIND_ID, nil, (WindowPtr)-1L );
```

Your program can then use the `WindowPtr` variable to obtain information stored in the `WindowRecord`. That's possible because the `WindowRecord` data type is defined in the universal header files and is known to the Toolbox.

When you want an application that you're writing to access information from a resource type that you've defined, you'll have to supply the application with the format in which the data is stored. Just as a program needs to recognize a `WindowRecord` data structure before it can work with a WIND resource, your application will need to have a data structure defined for any programmer-defined resource type.

As you've seen, TemplateUser defines a resource type named TSTD. Any resource of that type contains a `short`, a `long`, a `Boolean`, and a Pascal string—in that order. That means the TemplateUser application needs to define a data structure that matches this format. Here's that structure:

```
typedef  struct
{
   short     short_val;
   long      long_val;
   Boolean  bool_val;
   Str255    str_val;
} TemplateRecord, *TemplatePtr, **TemplateHandle;
```

> **NOTE**
> **This technique is similar to one you encountered in Chapter 3. In that chapter, you saw that whenever the Control Manager sends a `thumbCntl` message to a cdev, it also sends a pointer to a data structure. That data structure holds information about the dragging limits, or boundaries, of a control. In Chapter 3, you saw that it was up to you to define a matching structure in the cdev source code so that you could read in the data that this pointer referenced.**

Now, when TemplateUser needs to access information from the TSTD resource, it makes a call to the Toolbox routine `Get1Resource()` to load the resource data into memory and to return a handle to the data:

```
Handle  data_handle;

data_handle = Get1Resource( 'TSTD', 128 );
```

`Get1Resource()` can be used to load one resource of any type into memory. The first parameter is the resource type, and the second is the ID of the particular resource to load.

> **NOTE**
> **Recall that the TemplateUser resource file defines a TMPL resource with an ID of 200 and a TSTD resource with an ID of 128. It's the TSTD resource being loaded here. The template resource is only used within ResEdit to make resource editing easier.**

295

Once the TSTD resource data is loaded into memory, it can be accessed by the TemplateUser application, but not until the application is told the format of the data. Until then, it appears as just a stream of information in memory. Type casting the generic `data_handle` variable to a `TemplateHandle` is the way to tell the application how the data formatted. To gain access to one piece of data, the `TemplateHandle` is dereferenced twice. Here's how a `short` variable would be assigned the value of the first piece of data in the TSTD resource:

```
#define    TSTD_RES_TYPE      'TSTD'
#define    TSTD_RES_ID         128

short    my_short;
Handle   data_handle;

data_handle = Get1Resource( TSTD_RES_TYPE, TSTD_RES_ID );

my_short  = (**(TemplateHandle)data_handle).short_val;
```

Henceforth, the `my_short` variable can be used, and the first member of the TSTD data in memory can be ignored. This applies to each of the four TSTD data members; once variables are assigned the values held in the resource, you don't have to use the handle. The following snippet loads the TSTD data into memory and extracts all of the data from that resource by assigning four variables its data:

```
short      my_short;
long       my_long;
Boolean    my_boolean;
Str255     my_str;
Handle     data_handle;
StringPtr  source_str;
Size       byte_count;

data_handle = Get1Resource( TSTD_RES_TYPE, TSTD_RES_ID );

my_short   = (**(TemplateHandle)data_handle).short_val;
my_long    = (**(TemplateHandle)data_handle).long_val;
my_boolean = (**(TemplateHandle)data_handle).bool_val;
```

```
source_str = (**(TemplateHandle)data_handle).str_val;
byte_count = (**(TemplateHandle)data_handle).str_val[0] + 1;
BlockMoveData( source_str, my_str, byte_count );
```

After obtaining a handle, the first three assignments are straightforward: cast the handle, then dereference it twice to get at a struct member. Assigning a value to the Str255 variable requires a little extra work. A string variable is an array of characters, and in C one array cannot be assigned the value of another array, so an assignment like this will result in an error during compilation:

```
my_str = (**(TemplateHandle)data_handle).str_val;  // not legal!
```

Instead of a direct assignment to a Str255 variable, make the assignment to a pointer:

```
StringPtr  source_str;
```

```
source_str = (**(TemplateHandle)data_handle).str_val;
```

Next, get the length of the string—it can be found in the first element of the array that holds the string. Add one byte to account for this first length byte. Then use the Toolbox routine BlockMoveData() to copy the string to the Str255 variable.

```
StringPtr  source_str;
Size       byte_count;
```

```
source_str = (**(TemplateHandle)data_handle).str_val;
byte_count = (**(TemplateHandle)data_handle).str_val[0] + 1;
BlockMoveData( source_str, my_str, byte_count );
```

Once a program has the resource data stored in variables, the information can be used just as data in any variable is used:

```
my_short *= my_short;      // square the value in my_short

MoveTo( 20, 80 );
DrawString( my_str );      // draw my_str to a window
```

The TemplateUser Source Code Listing

TemplateUser opens a window, loads data from a TSTD resource, then writes that data to the window. When you run the program, you'll see a window like the one shown in Figure 5.31. If you want to test out both the template resource and the program, try opening the project's resource file and double-clicking on the TSTD resource. Edit any or all of the four fields in that resource. Then save the resource and recompile the program. When it runs, TemplateUser should display the new values you've entered into the TSTD resource.

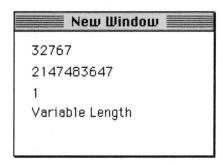

FIGURE 5.31 **THE RESULT OF RUNNING THE TEMPLATEUSER PROGRAM.**

The following is the listing for TemplateUser. To keep things simple, there's no real event loop—a click of the mouse button ends things. And to save a little paper, the listing for `Initialize_Toolbox()` has been omitted. You will, however, find it in the source code file on disk.

```
//_____
//                                                  function prototypes

void   Initialize_Toolbox( void );
void   Get_Template_Resource_Values( void );


//_____
//                                                  #define directives

#define        WIND_ID                      128
```

```
#define        TSTD_RES_TYPE        'TSTD'
#define        TSTD_RES_ID          128


//_____
//                                       define data structures

typedef   struct
{
   short    short_val;
   long     long_val;
   Boolean  bool_val;
   Str255   str_val;
} TemplateRecord, *TemplatePtr, **TemplateHandle;


//_____
//                                                       main()

void  main( void )
{
   WindowPtr   the_window;

   Initialize_Toolbox();

   the_window = GetNewWindow( WIND_ID, nil, (WindowPtr)-1L );
   SetPort( the_window );

   Get_Template_Resource_Values();

   while ( !Button() )
      ;
}


//_____
//                            retrieve data from 'TSTD' resource

void  Get_Template_Resource_Values( void )
{
   short       my_short;
   long        my_long;
   Boolean     my_boolean;
   Str255      my_str;
   Handle      data_handle;
   StringPtr   source_str;
   Size        byte_count;
   Str255      temp_str;
```

```
   data_handle = Get1Resource( TSTD_RES_TYPE, TSTD_RES_ID );

   my_short   = (**(TemplateHandle)data_handle).short_val;
   my_long    = (**(TemplateHandle)data_handle).long_val;
   my_boolean = (**(TemplateHandle)data_handle).bool_val;

   source_str = (**(TemplateHandle)data_handle).str_val;
   byte_count = (**(TemplateHandle)data_handle).str_val[0] + 1;
   BlockMoveData( source_str, my_str, byte_count );

   MoveTo( 20, 20 );
   NumToString( (long)my_short, temp_str );
   DrawString( temp_str );

   MoveTo( 20, 40 );
   NumToString( my_long, temp_str );
   DrawString( temp_str );

   MoveTo( 20, 60 );
   NumToString( (long)my_boolean, temp_str );
   DrawString( temp_str );

   MoveTo( 20, 80 );
   DrawString( my_str );
}
```

CHAPTER SUMMARY

Resources contain information that a program uses "on demand." When a program is to open a window, for example, it loads a WIND resource to get the characteristics of the window. Though resources generally hold information about the graphical interface parts of a program, such as descriptions of menus, windows, and dialog boxes, this isn't always the case. A resource can be created to hold any type of data. When you create your own custom resource, a resource editor will open a window that allows you to edit that resource in hexadecimal. Since this type of editing is quite a chore, resource editors also allow you to create a template resource that is used every time the custom resource is opened in the resource editor. This TMPL resource defines labels and fields that make the editing of custom resources simple.

When you define your own resource type, you'll also need to define a structure in your source code that corresponds to the format in which the resource data is held. When you load a custom resource into memory with a call to `Get1Resource()`, the Toolbox returns a handle to the memory location at which the resource data has been placed. Unless a structure is defined, to the program this resource information will appear to be just one continous stream of data. The structure can be used to view the data as individual members of a `struct` variable.

One useful programming trick that involves resources is to define several dialog box item lists that will be used by one dialog box. To do this, first define a base DITL with the same ID as the one specified in a DLOG resource. Then define as many different overlay DITL resources as needed. In your source code, use the `AppendDITL()` and `ShortenDITL()` Toolbox functions to add and remove these overlay DITL resources as needed. Generally, it will be some user action that triggers the changing of the DITL.

Chapter

6

More Mac Programming Techniques

RESOURCE FILES

When source code gets compiled and linked to form a standalone application, a single resource file is usually merged with the object code to become an integral part of the application. The resources that were in this file (along with the application code in a 680×0 application) then become the application's resource fork. As a program executes it uses the resources in its resource fork. An application can, however, use resources that are located in any resource file, not just resources in its own fork.

By having your program use different resource files, you can divide application-used information into logical groupings, much as you would divide a book's information into separate chapters. The advantage to this approach is that as information needs to be changed or updated, it can easily be altered by opening the proper resource file from outside the application. In this chapter, you'll see how to write a program that makes use of multiple resource files.

Resource files don't necessarily have to be created before an application runs—the application itself is capable of creating a new file. An application can also copy resources from its own resource fork or any other fork and add them to the new, empty resource file. You'll see how to tackle both of these tasks in this chapter.

Some application retain certain values between executions. These values hold information such as the user's choice of font and the dialog box settings that the user has selected. To preserve this information, an application uses a preferences file. This file is a resource file that can have its contents viewed or edited using any resource editor. This chapter discusses preferences files at length so that you can include a preferences file with any of your Mac applications.

WORKING WITH MULTIPLE RESOURCE FILES

An application's resources are generally found in the resource fork of the application—they're placed there by the development environment that was used to build the application. But an application can also make use of resources found outside its own resource fork. Any Mac program can be written such that it is capable of opening a resource file and accessing the resources found within that file.

The greatest advantage to using separate resource files—reduced application size—applies to large applications that hold an abundance of resources. An example might be an educational program that holds dozens or hundreds of PICT resources. Since so much of the disk space occupied by an application of this type consists of resources, the application's size is greatly reduced by placing most of its resources in separate files. While the overall disk space of the application and its resource files remains the same as an application that is self-contained, there is still a plus to this scheme. If an application is going to be revised frequently, it may be possible to make changes to just the application and not the resources. If the application revisions are distributed electronically, end users will need to download only the small application, and not a monolithic one that contains hundreds or perhaps thousands of kilobytes of resources. If the application is distributed by disk, the revised version can usually be shipped on one disk rather than multiple disks. Figure 6.1 shows an application that uses the resources found in ten resource files. The application itself is just 49 K in size, while the resources occupy over two and a half megabytes of disk space.

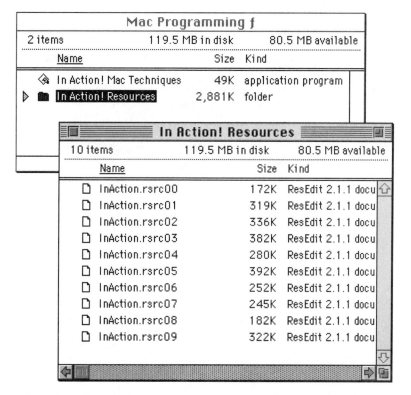

FIGURE 6.1 AN APPLICATION THAT USES THE RESOURCES HELD IN TEN RESOURCE FILES.

The MultipleRsrcFiles source code presented in this section is an example of an application that uses a resource located in an external file. MultipleRsrcFiles opens a dialog box and displays a picture in it(see Figure 6.2).

FIGURE 6.2 THE RESULT OF RUNNING THE **MULTIPLERSRCFILES** PROGRAM.

Figure 6.3 shows the folder that holds the project, source code, and project resource file for the MultipleRsrcFiles project; they're the three files at the left of the figure. These three files are used to build the application, shown at the center of the figure. On the right side of the figure is the resource file that MultipleRsrcFiles uses. If the MultipleRsrcFiles application is to be distributed to users, the MyRsrcFile resource file must accompany it.

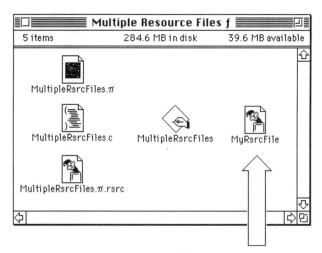

This file is used by the application

FIGURE 6.3 THE **MULTIPLERSRCFILES** APPLICATION USES THE RESOURCE
FOUND IN THE **MYRSRCFILE** RESOURCE FILE.

N O T E

In order for the MultipleRsrcFiles program to use the MyRsrcFile resource file, the application and the resource file must be in the same folder. If you'd like to nest resource files in a different folder, so that they're hidden from the user, see the information on file pathnames in Chapter 7.

The MultipleRsrcFiles Resources

The MultipleRsrcFiles program begins by opening a dialog box. The DITL and DLOG resources for the dialog box are found in the application's resource fork. That means these resources started out in the project's resource file. Figure 6.4 shows the DLOG resource. From this figure, you can see that the DITL has just a single dialog box item in it—an **OK** button.

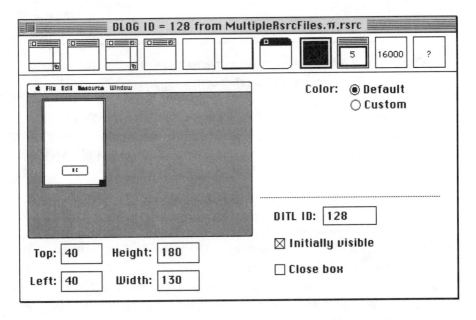

FIGURE 6.4 THE DLOG RESOURCE USED BY THE MULTIPLERSRCFILES PROGRAM.

Besides the DLOG and DITL resource there's a third resource in the project's resource file: a STR# resource that holds a single string. The string is the name of the external resource file that the MultipleRsrcFiles program uses. This resource is pictured in Figure 6.5.

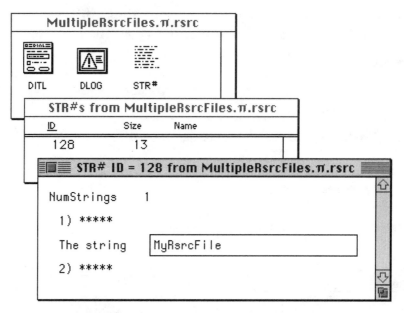

FIGURE 6.5 A STR# RESOURCE HOLDS THE NAME OF THE RESOURCE FILE USED BY THE MULTIPLERSRCFILES PROGRAM.

The resource file that MultipleRsrcFiles uses is named MyRsrcFile. It contains a single PICT resource. It is this picture that MultipleRsrcFiles will display in its dialog box. Figure 6.6 shows the contents of the MyRsrcFile resource file.

Resource File Reference Numbers

A file can have a data fork, resource fork, or both. That means that any file is capable of holding resources in a resource fork. A program, which is an application file, holds resources just as a resource file does—they each have a resource fork. Because an application can use resources in external files as well as use its own resources, confusion could arise if two open resource forks each contained a resource of the same type and same ID. To circumvent this problem, the File Manager assigns a reference number to each resource fork that opens. Only one resource fork can be the current fork, and it is the current fork from which resources are loaded.

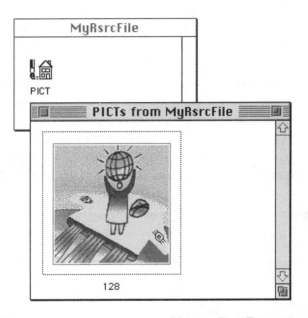

FIGURE 6.6 THE RESOURCE FILE USED BY THE MULTIPLERSRCFILES PROGRAM HOLDS A SINGLE **PICT** RESOURCE.

If an application relies on multiple resource forks, a call to the Toolbox routine UseResFile() should be made before accessing a resource. Just as SetPort() designates one of possibly many graphics ports to be the current port, UseResFile() designates that one particular resource fork be the current fork. UseResFile() requires only one parameter—a short that holds the reference number of the resource fork to use.

As an example, imagine that both an application and a resource file contain a snd resource. Each of the two snd resources has an ID of 8500, but they hold different sounds. To play the snd that resides in the application's resource fork, UseResFile() would first be called, with the application's resource fork reference number as the parameter:

```
short  Appl_Rsrc_Fork_Ref_Num;
short  File_Rsrc_Fork_Ref_Num;

// Get reference number of application's resource fork
// Get reference number of open resource file's resource fork
```

309

```
UseResFile( Appl_Rsrc_Fork_Ref_Num );

// play the sound
```

When an application is launched, the system opens the application's resource fork and makes it available for the application's use. This fork will remain open for the duration of the program's execution. You can get a reference number to the fork by calling the Toolbox routine CurResFile(). If you do this at application startup, you can be assured that the application's resource fork is the current resource fork:

```
short   Appl_Rsrc_Fork_Ref_Num;

Initialize_Toolbox();

Appl_Rsrc_Fork_Ref_Num = CurResFile();
```

A resource fork's reference number will be valid for the entire period that the fork is open. So once you've saved the reference number of an application's resource fork, you won't have to call CurResFile() again. And if you save the reference number to a global variable, you'll be able to make the application's resource fork current at any time.

Opening and Closing a Resource File Source Code

Opening a resource file consists of calling the Toolbox routine FSpOpenResFile(). The leading FSp in the function name tells you that it's one of the many file specification routines, and as such it will require an FSSpec as a parameter. You can make a call to FSMakeFSSpec() to request that the File Manager fill an FSSpec variable with information about the file of interest. Before calling FSMakeFSSpec(), you'll need to know the file's name and its location. The name is stored in the first (and only) string in the application's STR# resource. If the resource file exists in the same directory as the application, then its volume reference number and directory ID are both 0. The following snippet returns a file system specification record:

```
#define        RSRC_STR_ID                    128
#define        MY_FIRST_RES_FILE_INDEX          1

short    File_Rsrc_Fork_Ref_Num;

Str255   rsrc_file_name;
short    vol_ref;
long     dir_ID;
FSSpec   rsrc_FSSpec;

GetIndString( rsrc_file_name, RSRC_STR_ID,
              MY_FIRST_RES_FILE_INDEX );

vol_ref = 0;
dir_ID  = 0;

FSMakeFSSpec( vol_ref, dir_ID, rsrc_file_name, &rsrc_FSSpec );
```

Now the call to FSpOpenResFile() can be made. The first parameter
to this routine is a pointer to the FSSpec and the second is a file permission constant. Using the fsCurPerm constant means that the file will be
opened with whatever access is available—usually read and write permission. After FSpOpenResFile() opens the resource fork of a file, it
returns a file reference number. If the attempt to open the specified file
fails, a value of -1 will be returned as the reference number. If you save
this reference number to a global variable, you'll always be able to make
this file the current file with a call to UseResFile():

```
File_Rsrc_Fork_Ref_Num = FSpOpenResFile( &rsrc_FSSpec, fsCurPerm );

UseResFile( File_Rsrc_Fork_Ref_Num );
```

The File Manager treats an application's resource fork and a resource
file's resource fork in the same manner. After making sure that the correct fork is current, you can access a resource in any fork just as you have
in the past. If, for instance, a resource file contains a PICT with an ID of
128, you can draw that picture to the current port as follows:

```
PicHandle    pict_handle;

UseResFile( File_Rsrc_Fork_Ref_Num );
```

```
pict_handle = GetPicture( pict_id );

// Set up the rectangle to draw to

DrawPicture( pict_handle, &pict_rect );

ReleaseResource( (Handle)pict_handle );
```

When you're through with a resource fork, call the Toolbox routine
`CloseResFile()` to close it. After that, you can optionally set the global
reference number variable to 0. Then, if your application ever wants to
check to see if a nonapplication resource fork is open, it can do so. If a
check of this variable's value reveals that it is nonzero, then a resource
file resource fork is open. After closing the file, make a call to
`UseResFile()` to guarantee that the application's resource fork
becomes current.

```
CloseResFile( File_Rsrc_Fork_Ref_Num );

File_Rsrc_Fork_Ref_Num  = 0;

UseResFile( Appl_Rsrc_Fork_Ref_Num );
```

The MultipleRsrcFiles Source Code Listing

This section has described the code used by MultipleRsrcFiles. You'll
notice that MultipleRsrcFiles bundles the code that opens and closes a
resource fork into two functions: `Open_Resource_File()` and
`Close_Resource_File()`. To enable these routines to work with any
resource fork, they both require that information about the a file be
passed in.

Open_Resource_File() uses a call to GetIndString() to
obtain the name of the file to open. So `Open_Resource_File()`
expects the STR# resource ID and the index to the string as parameters:

```
void  Open_Resource_File( short rsrc_str_ID_num, short str_index )
```

After closing a resource fork, `Close_Resource_File()` sets the file reference number to 0 to indicate that no file is open. Pass `Close_Resource_File()` a pointer to this file number variable so that this assignment will hold after the function has ended:

```
void  Close_Resource_File( short *file_ref_num )
```

Now, here's the complete listing for the MultipleRsrcFiles program. You'll find that this short program does all of the following:

- Uses the DITL and DLOG resources from the application's resource fork to open a dialog box
- Opens a resource file's resource fork
- Loads a PICT resource from the external file
- Draws the picture using the PICT resource
- Closes the resource fork of the external file

```
//_____
//                                        function prototypes

void  Initialize_Toolbox( void );
void  Open_Dialog( void );
void  Open_Resource_File( short, short );
void  Close_Resource_File( short * );
void  Draw_One_Picture( short );


//_____
//                                        #define directives

#define      DLOG_ID                      128
#define      OK_ITEM                        1

#define      RSRC_STR_ID                  128
#define      MY_FIRST_RES_FILE_INDEX        1
#define      eWORLD_PICT_ID               128


//_____
//                                        declare global variables

short  Appl_Rsrc_Fork_Ref_Num;
```

```
short  File_Rsrc_Fork_Ref_Num = 0;


//_____
//                                                 main()

void  main( void )
{
   Initialize_Toolbox();

   Appl_Rsrc_Fork_Ref_Num = CurResFile();

   Open_Dialog();
}



//_____
//                                     open a display dialog

void  Open_Dialog( void )
{
   DialogPtr  the_dialog;
   Boolean    done = false;
   short      the_item;

   the_dialog = GetNewDialog( DLOG_ID, nil, (WindowPtr)-1L );

   ShowWindow( the_dialog );
   SetPort( the_dialog );

   Open_Resource_File( RSRC_STR_ID, MY_FIRST_RES_FILE_INDEX );

   Draw_One_Picture( eWORLD_PICT_ID );

   Close_Resource_File( &File_Rsrc_Fork_Ref_Num );

   while ( done == false )
   {
      ModalDialog( nil, &the_item );

      switch ( the_item )
      {
         case OK_ITEM:
            done = true;
            break;
      }
   }
```

```
   DisposDialog( the_dialog );
}


//_____
//                               open a resource file

void  Open_Resource_File( short rsrc_str_ID_num, short str_index )
{
   Str255  rsrc_file_name;
   short   vol_ref;
   long    dir_ID;
   FSSpec  rsrc_FSSpec;

   GetIndString( rsrc_file_name, rsrc_str_ID_num, str_index );

   vol_ref = 0;
   dir_ID  = 0;

   FSMakeFSSpec( vol_ref, dir_ID, rsrc_file_name, &rsrc_FSSpec );

   File_Rsrc_Fork_Ref_Num = FSpOpenResFile( &rsrc_FSSpec,
                                             fsCurPerm );

   if ( File_Rsrc_Fork_Ref_Num == -1 )
      ExitToShell();

   UseResFile( File_Rsrc_Fork_Ref_Num );
}


//_____
//                               close a resource file

void  Close_Resource_File( short *file_ref_num )
{
   CloseResFile( *file_ref_num );

   *file_ref_num = 0;

   UseResFile( Appl_Rsrc_Fork_Ref_Num );
}


//_____
//             get picture from 'PICT' resource, draw it
```

```
void  Draw_One_Picture( short pict_id )
{
   PicHandle   pict_handle;
   Rect        pict_rect;
   short       pict_width;
   short       pict_height;

   pict_handle = GetPicture( pict_id );
   if ( pict_handle == nil )
      ExitToShell();

   pict_rect = (**pict_handle).picFrame;

   pict_width  = pict_rect.right - pict_rect.left;
   pict_height = pict_rect.bottom - pict_rect.top;

   SetRect( &pict_rect, 0, 0, pict_width, pict_height );

   DrawPicture( pict_handle, &pict_rect );

   ReleaseResource( (Handle)pict_handle );
}
```

DYNAMICALLY CREATING A NEW RESOURCE FILE

A resource file is typically created not by your own application, but by a resource editor such as ResEdit or Resorcerer. Any application can, however, create a resource file. The most common need for this task comes when working with preferences files. A preferences file is usually a resource file stored in the Preferences folder in the System folder. If your program relies on a preferences file, it may not be safe to assume that the user hasn't inadvertently discarded or moved it. If that has happened, your application will need to replace the preferences file by creating a new resource file. This section's example program, CreateRsrcFile, does just that.

When launched, CreateRsrcFile attempts to create a new resource file named MyNewRsrcFile. If its attempt is successful, you'll see an alert box like the one on the left of Figure 6.7. If the attempt isn't successful, the alert box pictured on the right will appear.

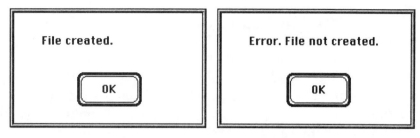

FIGURE 6.7 THE TWO MESSAGES THAT THE CREATERSRCFILE PROGRAM CAN DISPLAY.

After dismissing the alert box, the CreateRsrcFile program will exit. In the Create Resource File ƒ folder, you'll see a new, empty resource file—complete with the ResEdit file icon. Figure 6.8 shows the contents of this folder.

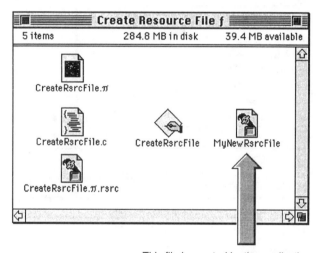

This file is created by the application

FIGURE 6.8 THE CREATERSRCFILE APPLICATION CREATES A NEW, EMPTY RESOURCE FILE NAMED MYNEWRSRCFILE.

N O T E

If you don't rename or delete the resource file between executions of the CreateRsrcFile program, the error message will be displayed in the alert. If you step through the program using the debugger, you'll see that the error variable gets a value of -48, which is a dupFNErr—a duplicate file name error.

The CreateRsrcFile Resources

The CreateRsrcFile program doesn't require any resources of its own for the task of creating a new resource file. The only two resources contained in the project's resource file—an ALRT and a DITL resource—exist to give the user a little feedback. If CreateRsrcFile didn't display an alert box, it would appear that the program simply launches and then quits without doing anything.

CreateRsrcFile uses a single alert box to display either of two messages. To do this, the DITL resource contains a static text item with the characters ^0 in it (see Figure 6.9).

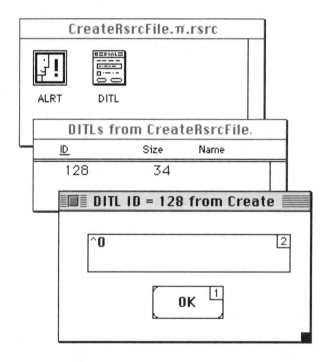

FIGURE 6.9 THE DITL RESOURCE USED BY THE CREATERSRCFILE PROGRAM.

The text to be displayed in the alert will be determined as the program runs. Before displaying the alert, a call to the Toolbox routine ParamText() will be made to set the static text item string to the proper text.

Resource File Creation Code

Creation of a resource file is achieved through a call to the File Manager routine `FSpCreateResFile()`. As was the case for opening a resource fork, you'll need to have an `FSSpec` handy before calling this routine. A call to `FSMakeFSSpec()`, as defined in the previous section, takes care of this. The CreateRsrcFile program will create a file that resides in the same folder as the application, so the volume reference number and the directory ID can both be 0. The program defines the new file's name in the source code—you might choose to list the name in a STR# resource in the application's resource fork, as done in the past.

```
Str255  prefF_file_name = "\pMyNewRsrcFile";
short   vol_ref;
long    dir_ID;
FSSpec  pref_FSSpec;

vol_ref = 0;
dir_ID  = 0;

FSMakeFSSpec( vol_ref, dir_ID, pref_file_name, &pref_FSSpec );
```

With the `FSSpec` created, it's time to call `FSpCreateResFile()`. This routine requires four parameters. You've seen the first one—a pointer to an `FSSpec`. The second parameter is an application signature. If you want the file to be owned by your application, you'll give it the same four-character creator name you're using for your application. In the Symantec THINK Project Manager, you set the creator using the **Set Project Type** menu item from the Project menu. The resulting Symantec dialog box is shown in Figure 6.10. If you're a CodeWarrior user, you use the Project panel in the Preferences dialog box to edit the creator (see Figure 6.11). In both environments, the default creator is ????.

The third parameter to `FSpCreateResFile()` is the file's type. If the resource file is owned by your application, you can use any four characters that are meaningful to your program.

The last parameter to `FSpCreateResFile()` is a script code. A file's script code identifies how the Finder will display the file's name. Here you can use the Apple-defined constant `smSystemScript`.

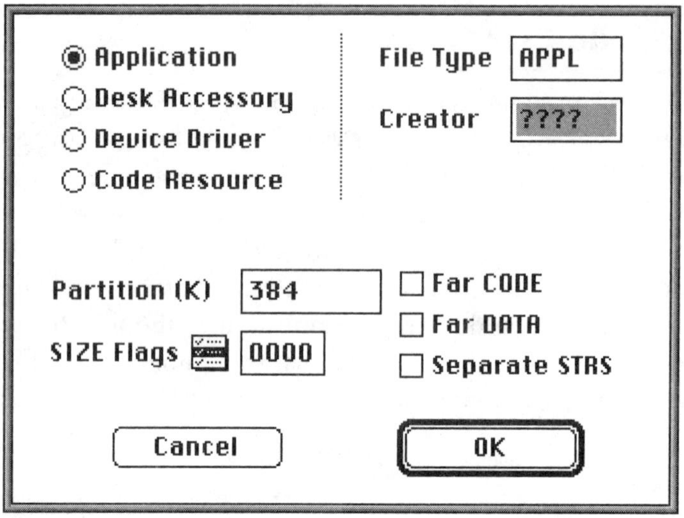

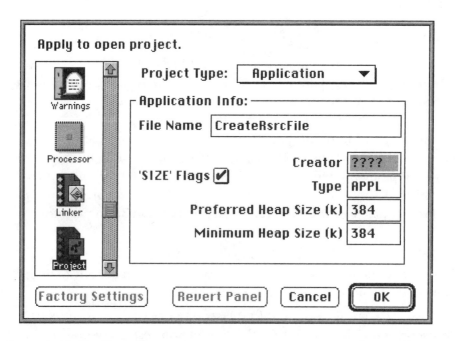

FIGURE 6.10 **THE SYMANTEC DIALOG BOX USED TO SET THE APPLICATION'S CREATOR.**

FIGURE 6.11 **THE METROWERKS DIALOG BOX USED TO SET THE APPLICATION'S CREATOR.**

Assuming I've given my application a creator of CrRF (for "create resource file"), and I've settled on this resource file having a file type of myRF (for "my resource file"), a call to `FSpCreateResFile()` would look like this:

```
FSpCreateResFile( &pref_FSSpec, 'CrRF', 'myRF', smSystemScript);
```

A call to `FSpCreateResFile()` results in the creation of a resource file—regardless of the creator and file type names you choose. If you launch your resource editor and choose **Open** from the File menu, you'll see the name of the new resource file in the list of files. And if you open it, you'll be able to add resources to it as you would any other resource file. What you won't be able to do is double-click on the file's icon from the Finder to launch your resource editor and open the file. That's because the Finder won't associate this file with any particular resource editor. If you want to give your resource file the same icon as your resource editor would assign a new file, and also make it double-clickable, use your resource editor's creator and file type in the call to `FSpCreateResFile()`. For ResEdit, that would result in a call that looked like this:

```
FSpCreateResFile( &pref_FSSpec, 'RSED', 'rsrc', smSystemScript);
```

If you use the resource editor Resorcerer, or feel that the majority of your program's users will, you can set up the call to `FSpCreateResFile()` as follows:

```
FSpCreateResFile( &pref_FSSpec, 'Doug', 'RSRC', smSystemScript);
```

You can verify the success of a call to a Resource Manager routine by calling the Toolbox function `ResError()`. `ResError()` returns an error code descriptive of any problem that the Resource Manager may have encountered. A result of `noErr` means the call succeeded. CreateRsrcFile uses this technique to determine if the resource file was created. If it was, it sets the alert box string to "File created." A failed attempt to create a new file will set the alert box string to "Error. File not created." In either case, the alert box is displayed with a call to `Alert()`.

If you aren't familiar with the `ParamText()` function, Figure 6.12 summarizes how it's used to assign up to four strings for display in static text items.

```
short   error;

FSpCreateResFile( &pref_FSSpec, 'RSED', 'rsrc', smSystemScript);

error = ResError();
if ( error == noErr )
   ParamText( "\pFile created.", "\p", "\p", "\p" );
else
   ParamText( "\pError. File not created.", "\p", "\p", "\p" );

Alert( ALERT_ID, nil );
```

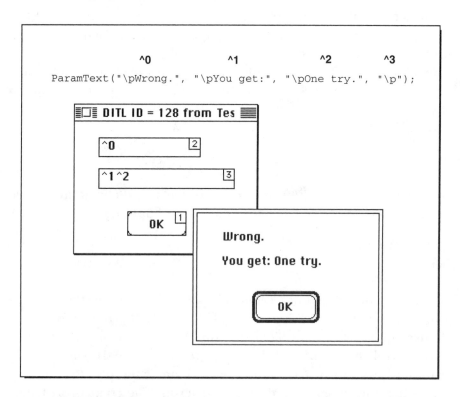

FIGURE 6.12 THE PARAMTEXT() FUNCTION IS USED TO CHANGE THE TEXT OF UP TO FOUR STRINGS THAT APPEAR IN A DIALOG BOX.

The CreateRsrcFile Source Code Listing

This very short program creates a new resource file named MyNewRsrcFile. If you open the file with a resource editor, you'll find that it is empty. You can remedy this situation by reading the next section of this book, which discusses how to write a program that is capable of copying resources from one file to another.

```
//_____
//                                          function prototypes

void  Initialize_Toolbox( void );
void  Create_New_Rsrc_File( void );


//_____
//                                          #define directives

#define       ALERT_ID       128


//_____
//                                                    main()

void  main( void )
{
   Initialize_Toolbox();

   Create_New_Rsrc_File();
}


//_____
//                                          initialize the Mac

void  Initialize_Toolbox( void )
{
   InitGraf( &qd.thePort );
   InitFonts();
   InitWindows();
   InitMenus();
   TEInit();
   InitDialogs( 0L );
   FlushEvents( everyEvent, 0L );
```

```
    InitCursor();
}


//_____
//                    create preference file if none exists
void  Create_New_Rsrc_File( void )
{
    Str255  pref_file_name = "\pMyNewRsrcFile";
    short   vol_ref;
    long    dir_ID;
    FSSpec  pref_FSSpec;
    short   error;

    vol_ref = 0;
    dir_ID  = 0;

    FSMakeFSSpec( vol_ref, dir_ID, pref_file_name, &pref_FSSpec );

    FSpCreateResFile( &pref_FSSpec, 'RSED', 'rsrc', smSystemScript );

    error = ResError();
    if ( error == noErr )
       ParamText( "\pFile created.", "\p", "\p", "\p" );
    else
       ParamText( "\pError. File not created.", "\p", "\p", "\p" );

    Alert( ALERT_ID, nil );
}
```

DYNAMICALLY COPYING A RESOURCE TO ANOTHER FILE

If your program creates a new, empty resource file, you'll most likely also want your program to add resources to it. The RsrcCopier program that's developed over the next several pages copies a single PICT resource from the resource fork of the RsrcCopier application and places it in an existing, empty resource file named MyAddToRsrcFile.

Like last section's CreateRsrcFile program, RsrcCopier uses a single alert box to provide feedback to the user. If the program successfully copies the PICT resource to the resource file, the alert message on the left side of Figure 6.13 is displayed. If the attempt to copy the resource fails, the message on the right side of the figure is posted.

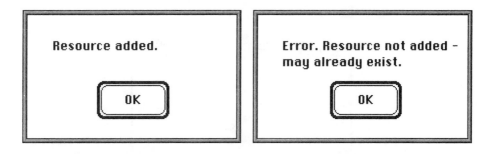

FIGURE 6.13 THE TWO MESSAGES THAT THE RSRCCOPIER PROGRAM CAN DISPLAY.

After running RsrcCopier, use your resource editor to open the MyAddToRsrcFile resource file. The previously empty resource file will now hold the one picture that is shown in Figure 6.14. Either delete or renumber its one PICT resource. If you don't, RsrcCopier will attempt to add a second PICT 128 to this same file, which should not be done. If this happens, and RsrcCopier will post the error message alert shown on the right side of Figure 6.13.

N O T E

The RsrcCopier Resources

The resource file for the RsrcCopier project holds the same DITL and ALRT resources found in this chapter's CreateRsrcFile program. As you can see from Figure 6.15, RsrcCopier also uses PICT and STR# resources.

This resource file will be empty before
RsrcCopier runs, but will contain one
PICT resource after it executes

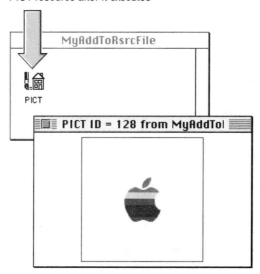

FIGURE 6.14 THE RSRCCOPIER PROGRAM ADDS ONE PICT RESOURCE TO THE EXISTING
MYADDTORSRCFILE RESOURCE FILE.

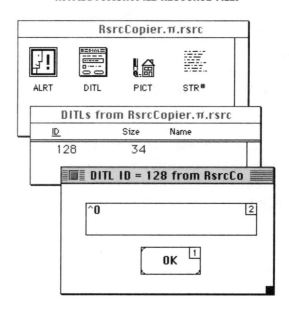

FIGURE 6.15 THE DITL RESOURCE USED BY THE CREATERSRCFILE PROGRAM.

RsrcCopier uses a STR# resource to decide which resource file to open. This is the same technique used in this chapter's MultipleRsrcFiles program. Figure 6.16 shows that the picture will be copied to a resource file named MyAddToRsrcFile. The PICT that it copies is shown in Figure 6.17.

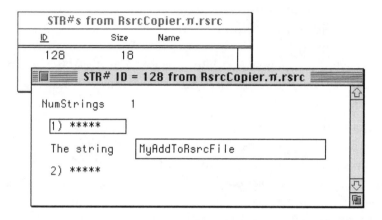

FIGURE 6.16 A STR# RESOURCE HOLDS THE NAME OF THE RESOURCE FILE THAT WILL RECEIVE THE COPIED RESOURCE.

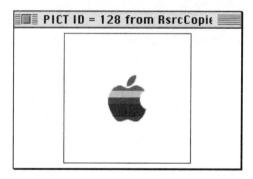

FIGURE 6.17 THE PICT RESOURCE THAT WILL BE COPIED FROM THE RSRCCOPIER APPLICATION AND ADDED TO THE MYADDTORSRCFILE RESOURCE FILE.

DetachResource() and ReleaseResource() Explained

As you'll see when you study the RsrcCopier source code listing, RsrcCopier makes a call to the Toolbox routine DetachResource().

Since the differences between DetachResource() and the more commonly used Toolbox function ReleaseResource() can be confusing, this section delves into the purposes of these two routines.

When a resource fork is opened, whether an application's fork or a resource file's fork, all of the resources in that fork are not loaded into memory. Instead, only resources with their preload attribute set get loaded. Additionally, resources are loaded individually as calls are made to Toolbox routines such as Get1Resource() and GetNewWindow(). What *is* always loaded into memory when a resource fork is opened is a *resource map*.

When a resource fork is opened, there are two resource maps for that fork. The first resides on disk, in the resource file. This map holds the disk location of each resource in the file. The second resource map is the one that gets loaded into memory. This map is made up of a series of handles—one handle for each resource. Except for resources that are marked as preloaded, these handles are initially set to nil. Figure 6.18 shows a resource fork being opened by an application. In this example, the resource fork holds two resources: a PICT resource with an ID of 128 and a snd resource with an ID of 9000. Assuming that the PICT resource is marked as preloaded and the snd resource isn't, only a copy of the picture data will be loaded into memory. Figure 6.19 shows that the handle for the PICT resource is set to point to this loaded data, while the handle for the snd resource remains nil.

Preloading a resource isn't the only way resource data makes its way into memory. When an application makes a call to a routine such as Get1Resource() the specified resource will get loaded—if it isn't already in memory. When that happens, the resource map handle for that one resource will change from nil to a handle that leads to the resource data.

The handles in the resource map in memory are used by the Resource Manager, rather than directly by the application. As objects in memory are moved about during the normal course of memory compaction, the resource map allows the Resource Manager to keep track of things. In order for an application to get a handle to a resource in memory, it must declare a handle variable and make a call to a Toolbox routine.

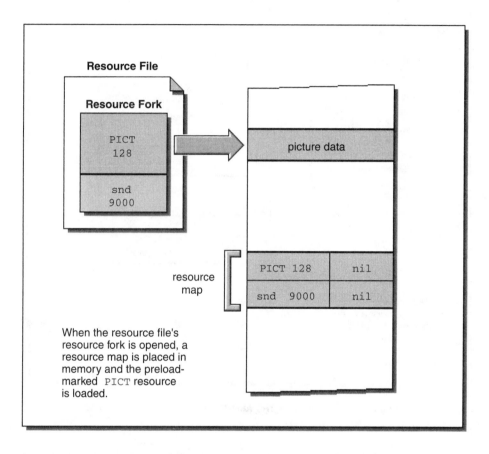

Resource File

Resource Fork

PICT
128

snd
9000

picture data

PICT 128 | nil

snd 9000 | nil

resource
map

When the resource file's resource fork is opened, a resource map is placed in memory and the preload-marked PICT resource is loaded.

**FIGURE 6.18 A RESOURCE FILE WITH ITS PRELOADED-MARKED
PICT RESOURCE BEING LOADED INTO MEMORY.**

For the PICT example discussed here, a call to GetPicture() would return a handle to the PICT in memory:

```
PicHandle    pict_handle;

pict_handle = GetPicture( pict_id );
```

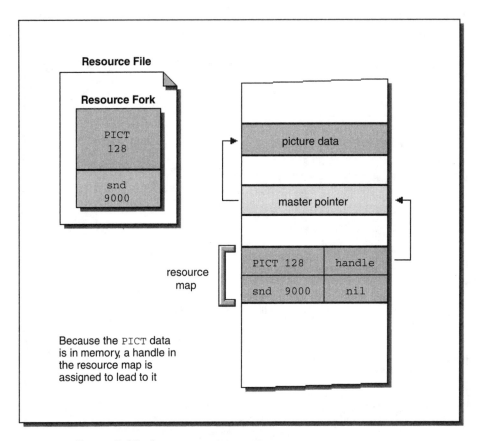

**FIGURE 6.19 A HANDLE IN THE RESOURCE MAP IS SET TO LEAD TO
THE PRELOADED PICTURE DATA.**

If the picture data *isn't* in memory, it will be loaded and both the
resource map handle and the application-defined handle will be set to
lead to this data. If the picture data *is* in memory, perhaps from being
preloaded, there's no need to load the data again. Instead, the application handle will just be set to the value of the resource map handle that
leads to the picture data. Figure 6.20 shows that once an application
declares a handle and makes a call to a resource-loading routine, there
are two handles leading to the resource data.

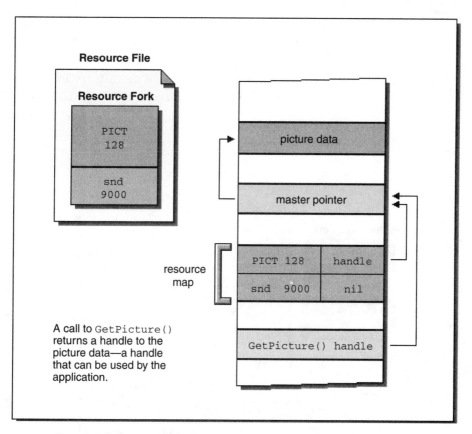

FIGURE 6.20 AN APPLICATION CAN DECLARE ITS OWN HANDLE VARIABLE
THAT WILL LEAD TO THE RESOURCE DATA.

When an application is through with resource data, it can make a call to the Toolbox routine ReleaseResource() to free the memory that holds the data:

```
PicHandle   pict_handle;

pict_handle = GetPicture( pict_id );

// draw the picture

ReleaseResource( (Handle)pict_handle );
```

331

A call to ReleaseResource() frees memory by setting the resource's master pointer to nil. Setting the master pointer to nil invalidates all handles that lead to the resource data. That means that both the resource map handle and the application-defined handle are invalid (see Figure 6.21). If the resource data is again needed, another Toolbox call will have to be made to load it.

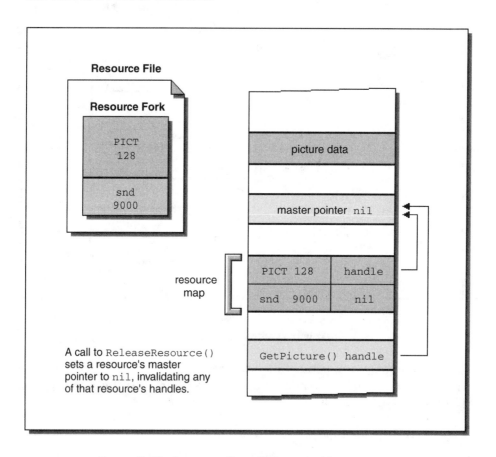

Resource File

Resource Fork

PICT
128

snd
9000

picture data

master pointer nil

resource
map

| PICT 128 | handle |
| snd 9000 | nil |

A call to ReleaseResource() sets a resource's master pointer to nil, invalidating any of that resource's handles.

GetPicture() handle

FIGURE 6.21 A CALL TO RELEASERESOURCE() **INVALIDATES ALL HANDLES THAT LEAD TO THE RESOURCE.**

When an application is finished using a resource, and no longer needs a handle to that resource, a call to ReleaseResource() should be made.

The Toolbox contains a companion routine to ReleaseResource() that is named DetachResource(). DetachResource() sets a resource map handle to nil, but doesn't release the resource data from memory and doesn't affect application-defined handles to the resource data. This situation is shown in Figure 6.22.

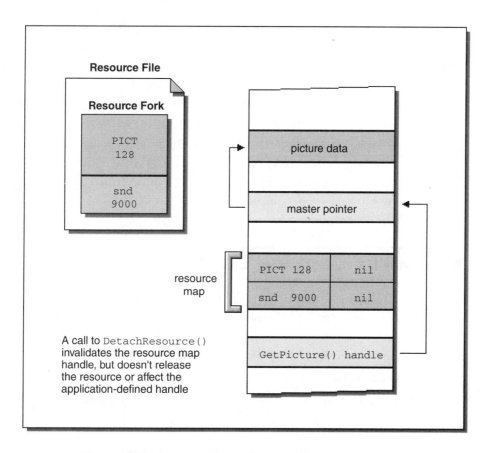

Resource File

Resource Fork

PICT
128

snd
9000

picture data

master pointer

resource
map

| PICT 128 | nil |
| snd 9000 | nil |

GetPicture() handle

A call to DetachResource() invalidates the resource map handle, but doesn't release the resource or affect the application-defined handle

FIGURE 6.22 A CALL TO DETACHRESOURCE() **INVALIDATES ONLY THE RESOURCE MAP HANDLE THAT LEADS TO THE RESOURCE.**

Why would an application need to set a resource map handle to nil, yet keep a valid application-defined handle? In most programming scenarios, it doesn't. But for the few cases when a program wants to access resource data "behind the back" of the Resource Manager, this step is necessary. One such case is in the copying of resources—something the RsrcCopier program does. To add a resource to a resource fork, the Toolbox routine `AddResource()` is called. `AddResource()` accepts a handle to the data in memory that is to be added to a resource fork. `AddResource()` imposes one important stipulation on the handle it works with, however. The handle must *not* be a resource handle. This is where the call to `DetachResource()` comes in. By setting the resource map handle to `nil`, the Resource Manager no longer recognizes the resource data in memory. Yet the application handle can still be used to access this resource data. To the application and the Resource Manager, this resource data is nothing more than any arbitrary bytes of data.

The call to `DetachResource()` seems like a sneaky way to get the call to `AddResource()` to work, and it is. But it is an important part of resource copying, and it is a step you shouldn't omit. In the next section, you'll see the source code—complete with a call to `DetachResource()`—that performs the resource copy.

Resource Copying Code

RsrcCopier uses the following general strategy to copy the PICT resource that is in its resource fork to the resource fork of an existing resource file:

1. Open the resource fork of the existing resource file.

2. Mark the application's resource fork as the current resource file.

3. Obtain a handle to the resource to copy.

4. Mark the open resource file's resource fork as the current resource file.

5. Verify that a resource of the same type and ID as the resource to copy isn't present.

6. Add the resource to the open resource file's resource fork.

7. Save the change that was made to the resource fork.

8. Close the resource fork of the existing resource file.

RsrcCopier uses a routine named `Open_Resource_File()` to open the resource fork of the MyAddToRsrcFile resource file. This routine relies on a call to the Toolbox function `FSpOpenResFile()` to open the fork. This version of `Open_Resource_File()` is identical to the version developed in this chapter's MultipleRsrcFiles program.

After the resource fork has been opened, RsrcCopier calls a function named `Copy_Rsrc_From_File_To_File()`. This function calls quite a few Toolbox routines, many of which may be new to you. Take a look at the function, then read the walk-through that follows.

```
void  Copy_Rsrc_From_File_To_File( ResType res_type,
                                   short   res_ID,
                                   short   from_ref_num,
                                   short   to_ref_num )
{
   Handle    app_handle;
   short     the_ID;
   ResType   the_type;
   Str255    res_name;
   short     res_attributes;
   Handle    test_handle;

   UseResFile( Appl_Rsrc_Fork_Ref_Num );

   app_handle = Get1Resource( COPY_RES_TYPE, COPY_RES_ID );

   GetResInfo( app_handle, &the_ID, &the_type, res_name );
   res_attributes = GetResAttrs( app_handle );
   DetachResource( app_handle );

   UseResFile( File_Rsrc_Fork_Ref_Num );

   test_handle = Get1Resource( res_type, res_ID );
   if ( test_handle == nil )
   {
      ParamText( "\pResource added.", "\p", "\p", "\p" );
      Alert( ALERT_ID, nil );
   }
   else
   {
      ParamText( "\pError. Resource not added - may already exist.",
               "\p", "\p", "\p" );
```

```
      Alert( ALERT_ID, nil );
      ExitToShell();
   }

   AddResource( app_handle, res_type, res_ID, res_name );
   SetResAttrs( app_handle, res_attributes );
   ChangedResource( app_handle );
   WriteResource( app_handle );
   ReleaseResource( app_handle );
}
```

Copy_Rsrc_From_File_To_File() is written such that it can copy any one resource from one file to another. Passing the resource type and ID lets the routine know which resource to look for. Passing the reference numbers of the fork to copy from and the fork to copy to allows the routine to be used with any two resource forks. Here are the parameters to the function:

```
void  Copy_Rsrc_From_File_To_File( ResType res_type,
                                   short   res_ID,
                                   short   from_ref_num,
                                   short   to_ref_num )
```

RsrcCopier defines constants for both the type and ID of the resource to copy. After you've successfully run the program, try changing the type and ID to match those of any other resource in the application's resource fork. Then recompile the program and run it again. Afterward, open the MyAddToRsrcFile to verify that the resource was added.

```
#define     COPY_RSRC_TYPE      'PICT'
#define     COPY_RSRC_ID        128
```

The Copy_Rsrc_From_File_To_File() routine expects both of the resource forks involved in the copy to be open. RsrcCopier defines a variable to hold a reference number to each of these forks:

```
short  Appl_Rsrc_Fork_Ref_Num;
short  File_Rsrc_Fork_Ref_Num = 0;
```

Here's how RsrcCopier calls the Copy_Rsrc_From_File_To_File() function:

```
Copy_Rsrc_From_File_To_File( COPY_RSRC_TYPE, COPY_RSRC_ID,
                             Appl_Rsrc_Fork_Ref_Num,
                             File_Rsrc_Fork_Ref_Num );
```

`Copy_Rsrc_From_File_To_File()` calls `UseResFile()` to make
the application's resource fork current. Then it calls `Get1Resource()`
to load the PICT resource from the application fork and to obtain a handle to the resource code:

```
Handle    app_handle;

UseResFile( Appl_Rsrc_Fork_Ref_Num );

app_handle = Get1Resource( res_type, res_ID );
```

**By the way, the 1 in the name of a Toolbox routine like
`Get1Resource()` is referring to the fact that the Toolbox
will only look in one resource file—the current one—to find
the specified resource. A call to** `GetResource()`, **on the
other hand, will result in a search of all open resource
forks.**

N O T E

The program defines constants for the type and the ID of the resource to
copy, but it doesn't define a constant for the third identifying feature of a
resource—its name. Many programmers don't name their resources,
even though resource editors easily allow them to. So RsrcCopier doesn't
assume a resource is named. When it comes time to add the resource to a
resource file, however, that piece of information becomes important. A
call to the Toolbox routine `GetResInfo()` takes care of things here.
Given a handle to a resource, `GetResInfo()` returns the resource's
type, ID, and name. Since the resource type and ID were passed in to
`Copy_Rsrc_From_File_To_File()`, the values that `GetResInfo()`
returns for these two identifiers will be ignored.

```
short     the_ID;
ResType   the_type;
Str255    res_name;

GetResInfo( app_handle, &the_ID, &the_type, res_name );
```

At this point, the program has the type, ID, and name of the resource to copy. It also has a handle to the resource. This still isn't enough information, though. Every resource has attributes associated with it, whether the resource is purgeable, locked, preloaded, and so forth. A call to the Toolbox routine `GetResAttrs()` gets all of this information and returns it in the bits of a 2-byte short variable:

```
short   res_attributes;

res_attributes = GetResAttrs( app_handle );
```

With all of the information about the resource to copy gathered, the PICT resource needs to be detached—as discussed at length in the previous section:

```
DetachResource( app_handle );
```

Next, the current resource fork needs to be changed from the application fork to the resource file fork:

```
UseResFile( File_Rsrc_Fork_Ref_Num );
```

Before adding the resource to the resource fork, the routine verifies that a resource of the same type and ID as the resource to copy isn't present. This is accomplished by calling `Get1Resource()`. Hopefully, a resource with the same type and ID isn't present in the destination fork. If that's the case, `Get1Resource()` will of course fail in its attempt to get the resource and return a value of `nil`. A check of this handle's value will determine if the copying routine should carry on with the resource add (handle is `nil`, resource not present), or exit (handle not `nil`, resource already exists).

```
test_handle = Get1Resource( res_type, res_ID);
if ( test_handle == nil )
   // display alert with "success" message
else
   // display alert with "failed" message
   // exit
```

N O T E

There is another approach that you can use to handle the case of duplicate resource IDs. As you've seen, if the test handle isn't `nil`**, then the resource already exists. Instead of exiting, you can request that the system issue a new ID with the** `Unique1ID()` **function. This routine returns an ID for the resource type passed to it—an ID that isn't used in the open resource fork. Here's a snippet that uses** `Unique1ID()`**:**

```
short  new_res_ID;

test_handle = Get1Resource( COPY_RES_TYPE, COPY_RES_ID );
if ( test_handle != nil )
   new_res_ID = Unique1ID( res_type );

// now add resource to fork
```

To add the resource to the open resource file's resource fork, a call is made to `AddResource()`. This routine requires a handle to the resource data in memory and the type, ID, and name of the resource. After that, the resource attributes are set with a call to `SetResAttrs()`:

```
AddResource( app_handle, res_type, res_ID, res_name );
SetResAttrs( app_handle, res_attributes );
```

When the resource fork of the resource file was opened, its resource map was placed in memory. Now, a new resource has been added to this resource fork, but the resource map hasn't been made aware of this change. To update the resource map, a call to the Toolbox routine `ChangedResource()` is made:

```
ChangedResource( app_handle );
```

At this point, the resource code has be added to the resource fork, but the addition hasn't been saved to disk. A call to the Toolbox function `WriteResource()` takes care of that task:

```
WriteResource( app_handle );
```

Finally, the handle to the resource code can be released using a call to `ReleaseResource()`. Recall that the previous call to `DetachResource()` did set the resource map handle to `nil`, but didn't release the resource code from memory.

```
ReleaseResource( app_handle );
```

The RsrcCopier Source Code Listing

RsrcCopier defines four routines aside from the `main()` function. One is the ever-present `Initialize_Toolbox()`. The other two, `Open_Resource_File()` and `Close_Resource_File()`, are identical to the routines of like name that were developed for the MultipleRsrcFiles program earlier in this chapter.

```
//_____
//                                    function prototypes

void    Initialize_Toolbox( void );
void    Open_Resource_File( short, short );
void    Close_Resource_File( short * );
void    Copy_Rsrc_From_File_To_File( ResType, short, short, short );


//_____
//                                    #define directives

#define     ALERT_ID                128
#define     STR_LIST_ID             128
#define     RSRC_FILE_STR_INDEX       1

#define     COPY_RSRC_TYPE          'PICT'
#define     COPY_RSRC_ID            128


//_____
//                                    declare global variables

short   Appl_Rsrc_Fork_Ref_Num;
short   File_Rsrc_Fork_Ref_Num = 0;
```

```
//_____
//                                                    main()

void  main( void )
{
   Initialize_Toolbox();

   Appl_Rsrc_Fork_Ref_Num = CurResFile();

   Open_Resource_File( STR_LIST_ID, RSRC_FILE_STR_INDEX );

   Copy_Rsrc_From_File_To_File( COPY_RSRC_TYPE, COPY_RSRC_ID,
                                Appl_Rsrc_Fork_Ref_Num,
                                File_Rsrc_Fork_Ref_Num );

   Close_Resource_File( &File_Rsrc_Fork_Ref_Num );
}


//_____
//                                        open a resource file

void  Open_Resource_File( short rsrc_str_ID_num, short str_index
)
{
   Str255  rsrc_file_name;
   short   vol_ref;
   long    dir_ID;
   FSSpec  rsrc_FSSpec;

   GetIndString( rsrc_file_name, rsrc_str_ID_num, str_index );

   vol_ref = 0;
   dir_ID  = 0;

   FSMakeFSSpec( vol_ref, dir_ID, rsrc_file_name, &rsrc_FSSpec );

   File_Rsrc_Fork_Ref_Num = FSpOpenResFile( &rsrc_FSSpec,
                                            fsCurPerm );

   if ( File_Rsrc_Fork_Ref_Num == -1 )
      ExitToShell();

   UseResFile( File_Rsrc_Fork_Ref_Num );
}
```

```
//_____
//  copy a single resource from one resource file to another

void  Copy_Rsrc_From_File_To_File( ResType res_type,
                                   short    res_ID,
                                   short    from_ref_num,
                                   short    to_ref_num )
{
   Handle    app_handle;
   Str255    res_name;
   short     res_attributes;
   Handle    test_handle;
   ResType   the_type;
   short     the_ID;

   UseResFile( from_ref_num );

   app_handle = Get1Resource( res_type, res_ID );

   GetResInfo( app_handle, &the_ID, &the_type, res_name );
   res_attributes = GetResAttrs( app_handle );
   DetachResource( app_handle );

   UseResFile( to_ref_num );

   test_handle = Get1Resource( res_type, res_ID );
   if ( test_handle == nil )
   {
      ParamText( "\pResource added.", "\p", "\p", "\p" );
      Alert( ALERT_ID, nil );
   }
   else
   {
      ParamText( "\pError. Resource not added - may already exist.",
                 "\p", "\p", "\p" );
      Alert( ALERT_ID, nil );
      ExitToShell();
   }

   AddResource( app_handle, res_type, res_ID, res_name );
   SetResAttrs( app_handle, res_attributes );
   ChangedResource( app_handle );
   WriteResource( app_handle );
   ReleaseResource( app_handle );

   UseResFile( Appl_Rsrc_Fork_Ref_Num );
}
```

```
//_____
//                              close a resource file

void  Close_Resource_File( short *file_ref_num )
{
   CloseResFile( *file_ref_num );

   *file_ref_num = 0;

   UseResFile( Appl_Rsrc_Fork_Ref_Num );
}
```

WORKING WITH A PREFERENCES FILE

Almost all professional-grade Macintosh applications have a preferences file that is stored in the Preferences folder of the System Folder. This file is never accessed directly by the application's users. Instead, the application itself opens and reads information from within this file. Depending on the information that a program needs, this can be done when the program is launched or at any time during its execution. When a program first starts, the preferences file may be accessed so that the application can determine user preferences such as the font in which text should be displayed. Later, the program may again access the same preferences file to determine which radio buttons should be turned on when a dialog box opens.

There's a lot of background information that you'll need to be responsible for knowing before you can jump right into writing an application that uses a preferences file. Fortunately, you already have a working knowledge of all of the techniques that go into the writing of this type of program. From the Chapter 5 section "Using Custom Resource Templates" you know how to create your own resource type using a custom resource and template resource. You've also seen how to read that information into program. Here, the custom resource will hold the preferences for the application. From this chapter's "Working with Multiple Resource Files" section you know how to store a resource in a separate resource file, and then how to have an application open this file's resource fork and load its resource. From reading this chapter's "Dynamically Creating a New

Resource File" and "Dynamically Copying a Resource to Another File" sections, you have the information needed to be able to give your program the ability to recreate a preferences file should an uniformed user inadvertently delete the existing preferences file. You'll do this by storing a copy of the preferences resource in the application's resource fork. Then you'll be able to create a new resource file and copy the resource information from the application's fork to the resource file's fork.

In this section, you'll see the source code for a program named PrefUser. PrefUser is an application that opens a dialog box like the one pictured in Figure 6.23. When the dialog box opens, the application will also open the program's preferences file to determine what values to give the dialog box items. The PrefUser preferences file holds four pieces of information: the string to display in the edit text box, the state of each of the two radio buttons, and the state of the one check box.

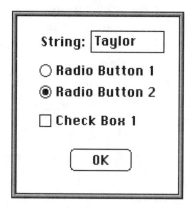

FIGURE 6.23 THE RESULT OF RUNNING THE PREFUSER PROGRAM.

PrefUser reads in the dialog box settings information from the preferences file, stores that information in four global variables, and closes the preferences file. Using the values in the global variables, the dialog box items are set. After that, the user is free to set the values of the dialog items by clicking on them. When finished, the user clicks **OK** to dismiss the dialog box. Before the dialog box is closed, the preferences file will again be accessed—this time to write the new dialog box item values back to the file.

The PrefUser Resources

PrefUser requires two resource files. Like most Mac programs, it needs a project resource file to hold the resources that will become part of the application. It also needs a resource file to serve as the preferences file. Figure 6.24 shows the PrefUser preferences file after it has been created by the application.

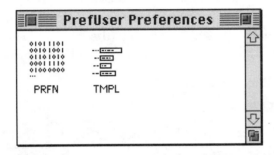

FIGURE 6.24 THE RESOURCES IN THE PREFUSER PREFERENCES PREFERENCES FILE.

The preferences file needs just two resources: a resource to hold the preferences data and a template that defines how that data looks in the resource editor. The template was created first. Selecting **Create New Resource** from the Resource menu brought up the Select New Type dialog box. The TMPL type was selected, and the dialog box was dismissed. Selecting **Get Resource Info** from the Resource menu allows the TMPL ID and name to be edited. The ID is arbitrary, but the name isn't; it has to match the name that will be given to the resource type that will hold the preferences data. That resource type will be named PRFN, so that's the name that has been given to this TMPL resource.

The preferences file will hold information about the three items and the string that will appear in the PrefUser dialog box. In the application, the three items will be set using calls to `SetDialogItem()`. A value of 1 turns on the item, a value of 0 turns off the item. The program will use a `Str255` variable to keep track of the string that gets drawn in the dialog box. Peeking ahead to the source code, you can see the data structure that will be used to hold the preferences information:

```
typedef  struct
{
   short   rad_1_val;
   short   rad_2_val;
   short   chk_1_val;
   Str255  name_str;
} PrefRecord, *PrefPtr, **PrefHandle;
```

Figure 6.25 shows the TMPL resource. It shows that the three dialog box item values will appear in the PRFN resource as DWRD items. Recall that DWRD represents a decimal word, or two bytes. Because the program will use a Str255 variable to hold the string, the TMPL resource defines the fourth PRFN resource item as a PSTR, that is, a Pascal string.

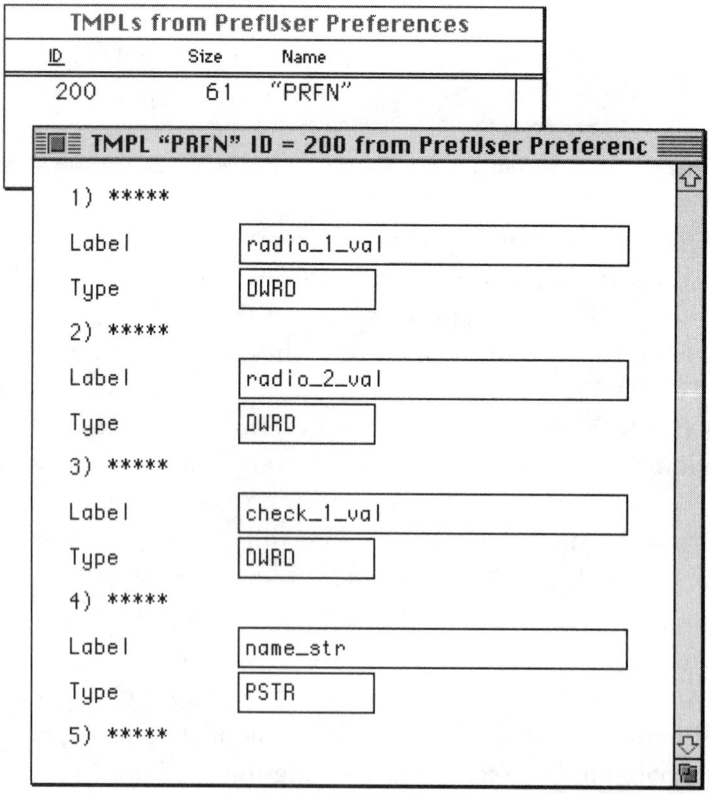

FIGURE 6.25 THE TMPL RESOURCE USED BY THE PREFERENCES RESOURCE.

With the template created, it's time to enter the preferences data. Once again **Create New Resource** is selected from the Resource menu. Then **PRFN** is typed in the edit box of the Select New Type dialog box. A click on **OK** creates a resource of this type and opens it up using the TMPL template. Figure 6.26 shows how the PRFN resource looks with values entered in it. When the PrefUser reads in this information, it will use `SetControlValue()` to turn the top radio button off, the bottom radio button on, and the check box off. Then it will make a call to `SetDialogItemText()` to write the string "Taylor" to the edit text item.

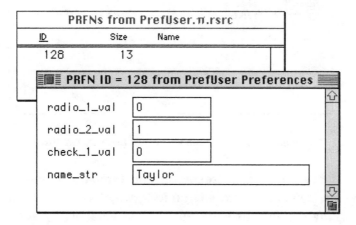

FIGURE 6.26 THE PRFN RESOURCE, AS IT LOOKS WHEN OPENED WITH THE TMPL RESOURCE PRESENT.

The second resource file that PrefUser needs is the application project resource file (see Figure 6.27).

Just like the preferences file, the project resource file has a PRFN and TMPL resource. In fact, using my resource editor, I copied these two resources directly from the PrefUser Preferences resource file and pasted them in the project resource file. It's interesting to note that this pair of resources may or may not be used by the application. Earlier in this chapter, you saw how to write an application that was capable of creating a new resource file. You also saw that it is possible to copy a resource from one resource fork to another. These two techniques will be used by the

PrefUser application only if the program cannot find the preferences file in the Preferences folder. In the unlikely case that the user moved, renamed, or deleted the preferences file, PrefUser will create a new, empty resource file and place it in the Preferences folder. Then it will copy the backup PRFN and TMPL resources held in the application resource fork and add them to the new preferences file.

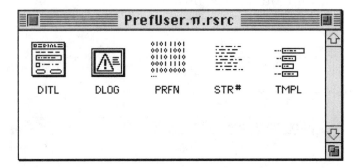

FIGURE 6.27 THE RESOURCES IN THE RESOURCE FILE USED BY THE PREFUSER PROJECT.

If the preferences resource and template resource exist in the application's resource fork, why have a preferences file? Why not just use the application versions to keep track of preferences? Because if it is at all avoidable, an application's resources shouldn't be altered. If a preferences file gets corrupted, it's an easy matter to replace it. If an application gets corrupted, it may not be as easy a task to restore.

Before opening its preferences file, PrefUser needs to know the file's name. This string is kept in a STR# resource. Figure 6.28 shows the name of the file that PrefUser will expect to find in the Preferences folder.

By convention, the name of an application's preferences file should be the name of the application followed by the word "Preferences." This isn't a requirement, but rather an Apple recommendation.

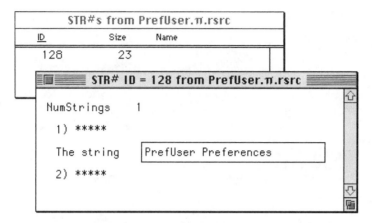

FIGURE 6.28 A STR# RESOURCE HOLDS THE NAME OF THE
PREFERENCES FI LE USED BY THE PREFUSER PROGRAM.

PrefUser displays a Modal dialog box that is defined by a DLOG and
DITL resource. Figure 6.29 shows the DITL.

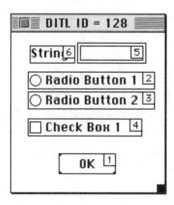

FIGURE 6.29 THE DITL RESOURCE USED BY THE PREFUSER PROGRAM.

Using a Preferences File to Set Dialog Box Items

When you run PrefUser, you'll see the dialog box that was pictured in
Figure 6.23. A call to a routine named Open_Dialog() brings this dialog box to life. Here's a look at the tasks Open_Dialog() takes care of:

```
void  Open_Dialog( void )
{
   // Open the dialog box

   // Access the preferences file to get dialog item values

   // Set the dialog item values using the
   // preferences information

   // Loop until done
   //     ModalDialog()
   //     Handle click on an item
   //     If item is OK button, get the final value of each item
   // End loop

   // Save the preferences back to the preferences file

   // Dispose of the dialog box
}
```

Much of the code that makes up Open_Dialog() involves the handling of a mouse click on one of the enabled items in the dialog box. This code, which is in a while loop and centers around a call to ModalDialog(), is very basic stuff. Of far more interest is the code that precedes and follows the loop.

Immediately after opening the dialog box with a call to GetNewDialog(), Open_Dialog() calls Get_Dialog_P refer-ences(). This routine opens the PrefUser Preferences resource file so that the dialog box item settings can be determined. Things aren't quite that simple, however, because there's a possibility that an attempt to open the preferences file could fail.

Get_Dialog_Preferences() relies on one, or possibly two, other application-defined routines to open the file. Figure 6.30 shows the routines that may become involved in the opening of the preferences file.

The code that makes up Open_Preferences_File() is very similar to the code in the Open_Resource_File() found in this chapter's MultipleRsrcFiles program. Open_Preferences_File() has two notable differences from Open_Resource_File(), however. First, it doesn't assume that the file to open is in the same directory as the application.

Instead, it assumes it can be found in the Preferences folder in the System Folder. So instead of assigning a value of 0 to both the volume reference number and the directory ID, `Open_Preferences_File()` makes a call to the Toolbox routine `FindFolder()`.

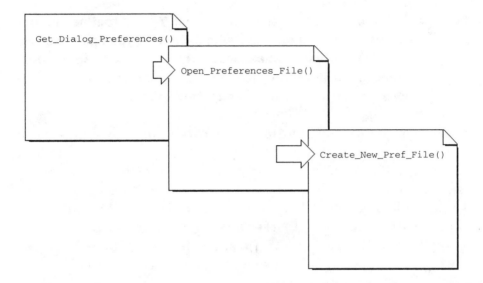

FIGURE 6.30 THE CHAIN OF CALLS FOLLOWED WHEN OPENING THE PREFERENCES FILE.

The `FindFolder()` routine is used to obtain path information to the Preferences folder, Apple Menu Items folder, Control Panels folder, and other system directories. The first parameter to `FindFolder()` is the reference number of the volume that holds the folder in question. System-related folders should of course be on the startup disk, so the Apple-defined constant `kOnSystemDisk` can be used here. To determine which folder to search for, `FindFolder()` accepts an Apple-defined constant as its second parameter. The third parameter, which can be another Apple-defined constant—specifies whether or not a new folder of this name should be created if an existing one can't be found. In return for this information, `FindFolder()` will fill the fourth and fifth parameters with the volume reference number and directory ID of the sought-after folder. Here's what a call to `FindFolder()` looks like:

```
short   vol_ref;
long    dir_ID;

FindFolder( kOnSystemDisk, kPreferencesFolderType,
            kDontCreateFolder, &vol_ref, &dir_ID );
```

NOTE FindFolder() **is another System 7–only routine. If your program is to run on Macs with System 6, you can't use this function. Instead, you can instruct the user to keep the preferences file in the application's directory. Then set the volume reference number and directory ID to 0.**

Aside from the call to FindFolder(), the only other difference between PrefUser's Open_Preferences_File() routine and MultipleRsrcFiles's Open_Resource_File() function comes in the handling of a failed attempt to open the resource file. Earlier you saw that Open_Resource_File() simply calls ExitToShell() to return to the Finder. The Open_Preferences_File() function handles things in a much more graceful manner by calling Create_New_ Pref_File() to create and open a new preferences file. Here's a look at Open_Preferences_ File():

```
short   Open_Preferences_File( void )
{
    Str255  pref_file_name;
    short   vol_ref;
    long    dir_ID;
    FSSpec  pref_FSSpec;
    short   file_ref_num;

    GetIndString( pref_file_name, STR_LIST_ID, PREF_STR_INDEX );

    FindFolder( kOnSystemDisk, kPreferencesFolderType,
                kDontCreateFolder, &vol_ref, &dir_ID );

    FSMakeFSSpec( vol_ref, dir_ID, pref_file_name, &pref_FSSpec );

    file_ref_num = FSpOpenResFile( &pref_FSSpec, fsCurPerm );

    if ( file_ref_num == -1 )
```

```
      file_ref_num = Create_New_Pref_File( pref_FSSpec );

   return ( file_ref_num );
}
```

If the attempt to find and open an existing preferences file fails, Open_Preferences_File() calls Create_New_Pref_File(). This function is very similar to the Copy_Rsrc_From_File_To_File() routine found in this chapter's RsrcCopier program. Create_New_ Pref_File() differs only in the respect that it doesn't assume two resource forks are open. Instead, it makes a call to FSpCreateRes File() to create a new resource file in the Preferences folder. Then, like Copy_Rsrc_From_File_To_File(), Create_New_Pref_File() copies a single resource from the application's resource fork to the resource file.

```
short  Create_New_Pref_File( FSSpec pref_FSSpec )

{
   short      file_ref_num;
   Handle     app_handle;
   short      res_ID;
   ResType    res_type;
   Str255     res_name;
   short      res_attributes;

   UseResFile( Appl_Rsrc_Fork_Ref_Num );

   app_handle = Get1Resource( PREF_RES_TYPE, PREF_RES_ID );

   GetResInfo( app_handle, &res_ID, &res_type, res_name );
   res_attributes = GetResAttrs( app_handle );
   DetachResource( app_handle );

   FSpCreateResFile( &pref_FSSpec, 'RSED', 'rsrc', smSystemScript );
   file_ref_num = FSpOpenResFile( &pref_FSSpec, fsCurPerm );
   UseResFile( file_ref_num );

   AddResource( app_handle, res_type, res_ID, res_name );
   ChangedResource( app_handle );
   WriteResource( app_handle );
   ReleaseResource( app_handle );
```

```
    return ( file_ref_num );
}
```

If `Open_Preferences_File()` succeeds in finding the preference
file, it opens it. If it fails, it calls `Create_New_Pref_File()` to create a
new resource file, open it, and copy the backup version of the PRFN
resource to that file. In either case, `Open_Preferences_File()` will
end up with a reference number to the open preferences file. It's this
number that is returned to `Get_Dialog_Preferences()`. Once
`Get_Dialog_Preferences()` has that number, it can make a call to
`UseResFile()` to set the current resource fork to the preferences file.
The data in the PRFN resource is then accessed and assigned to the global variables: `Radio_1_Val`, `Radio_2_Val`, `Check_1_Val`, and
`Name_String`:

```
data_handle = Get1Resource( PREF_RES_TYPE, PREF_RES_ID );

Radio_1_Val = (**(PrefHandle)data_handle).rad_1_val;
Radio_2_Val = (**(PrefHandle)data_handle).rad_2_val;
Check_1_Val = (**(PrefHandle)data_handle).chk_1_val;

source_str = (**(PrefHandle)data_handle).name_str;
byte_count = (**(PrefHandle)data_handle).name_str[0] + 1;
BlockMoveData( source_str, Name_String, byte_count );
```

If you need a refresher on just how the previous lines work, refer to the
description of the TemplateUser program in Chapter 5. If you're satisfied
with the explanation that `Get1Resource()` loads the PRFN resource and
double-indirection is then used to access each data element, then take a look
at the complete listing for the `Get_Dialog_Preferences()` routine.

```
#define    PREF_RES_TYPE     'PRFN'
#define    PREF_RES_ID         128

short      Radio_1_Val;      // global variables
short      Radio_2_Val;      //         |
short      Check_1_Val;      //         |
StringPtr  Name_String;      //        _v_
```

```
void  Get_Dialog_Preferences( void )
{
    short       pref_ref_num;
    Handle      data_handle;
    StringPtr   source_str;
    Size        byte_count;

    pref_ref_num = Open_Preferences_File();

    UseResFile( pref_ref_num );

    data_handle = Get1Resource( PREF_RES_TYPE, PREF_RES_ID );

    Radio_1_Val = (**(PrefHandle)data_handle).rad_1_val;
    Radio_2_Val = (**(PrefHandle)data_handle).rad_2_val;
    Check_1_Val = (**(PrefHandle)data_handle).chk_1_val;

    source_str = (**(PrefHandle)data_handle).name_str;
    byte_count = (**(PrefHandle)data_handle).name_str[0] + 1;
    BlockMoveData( source_str, Name_String, byte_count );

    CloseResFile( pref_ref_num );
}
```

With the preferences read into global variables, it's a simple matter to set the dialog box items to their appropriate values. Open_Dialog() calls Set_Initial_Dialog_Values() to handle this task. Set_ Initial_Dialog_Values() in turn relies on the Toolbox functions GetDialogItem(), SetControlValue(), and SetDialogItem Text() to set the values of the two radio buttons, the one check box, and the edit text item.

```
void Set_Initial_Dialog_Values( DialogPtr dlog )
{
    Handle  hand;
    short   type;
    Rect    box;

    GetDialogItem( dlog, RADIO_1_ITEM, &type, &hand, &box );
    SetControlValue( (ControlHandle)hand, Radio_1_Val );

    GetDialogItem( dlog, RADIO_2_ITEM, &type, &hand, &box );
    SetControlValue( (ControlHandle)hand, Radio_2_Val );
```

```
GetDialogItem( dlog, CHECK_1_ITEM, &type, &hand, &box );
SetControlValue( (ControlHandle)hand, Check_1_Val );

GetDialogItem( dlog, STRING_ITEM, &type, &hand, &box );
SetDialogItemText( hand, Name_String );
}
```

Once the dialog box items are set, Open_Dialog() enters the familiar while loop that most dialog boxes use to handle user mouse clicks on enabled items. When the user finally clicks on **OK**, a call is made to Get_Final_Dialog_Values():

```
case OK_ITEM:
    done = true;
    Get_Final_Dialog_Values( the_dialog );
    break;
```

Because Open_Dialog() doesn't keep track of the values of items as they are selected or deselected, this routine is needed to save the final dialog box item values to the global variables.

```
void Get_Final_Dialog_Values( DialogPtr dlog )
{
    Handle  hand;
    short   type;
    Rect    box;

    GetDialogItem( dlog, RADIO_1_ITEM, &type, &hand, &box );
    Radio_1_Val = GetControlValue( (ControlHandle)hand );

    GetDialogItem( dlog, RADIO_2_ITEM, &type, &hand, &box );
    Radio_2_Val = GetControlValue( (ControlHandle)hand );

    GetDialogItem( dlog, CHECK_1_ITEM, &type, &hand, &box );
    Check_1_Val = GetControlValue( (ControlHandle)hand );

    GetDialogItem( dlog, STRING_ITEM, &type, &hand, &box );
    GetDialogItemText( hand, Name_String );
}
```

Open_Dialog() ends by saving the values of the dialog box items to the preferences file and then disposing of the dialog box. The Save_

`Dialog_Preferences()` function begins by opening the preferences file. The Toolbox function `NewHandleClear()` is then called to allocate and clear (zero out) a block of memory the size of the PRFN resource. Then the values of the dialog box items are written to the memory that this handle leads to. This is essentially the reverse of the operations that were performed to read the PRFN values into memory when the dialog box was opened.

```
new_data_handle = NewHandleClear( sizeof( PrefRecord ) );

(**(PrefHandle)new_data_handle).rad_1_val = Radio_1_Val;
(**(PrefHandle)new_data_handle).rad_2_val = Radio_2_Val;
(**(PrefHandle)new_data_handle).chk_1_val = Check_1_Val;

source_str = Name_String;
byte_count = Name_String[0] + 1;
BlockMoveData( source_str,
               (**(PrefHandle)new_data_handle).name_str,
               byte_count );
```

Next, a handle to the PRFN resource is obtained. Before saving the new data, the old PRFN resource will be deleted. A call to `GetResInfo()` gets the name of the old resource, and a call to `GetResAttrs()` saves its attributes. Then the old PRFN is deleted using a call to `RemoveResource()`.

```
Handle   old_data_handle;
Handle   new_data_handle;

old_data_handle = Get1Resource( PREF_RES_TYPE, PREF_RES_ID );

GetResInfo( old_data_handle, &res_ID, &res_type, res_name );

res_attributes = GetResAttrs( old_data_handle );
RemoveResource( old_data_handle );
```

Finally, the new PRFN resource is added and the new resource is saved to disk with a call to `WriteResource()`:

```
AddResource( new_data_handle, res_type, res_ID, res_name );
SetResAttrs( new_data_handle, res_attributes );
WriteResource( new_data_handle );
```

Here's a look at the Save_Dialog_Preferences() routine. Note that while working with the new resource handle, the handle is locked in memory. That's because the Toolbox routine RemoveResource() may move or purge memory. Because the handle new_data_handle is used before and after the call to RemoveResource(), the memory it leads to should be locked in place so that the handle correctly leads to it regardless of any memory shifting that might take place.

NOTE The other resource-related routines in this chapter don't move memory. For other routines, refer to the appropriate volume in the new *Inside Macintosh* series of books. These books give a description of every Toolbox routine. If a routine may move memory, that fact will be mentioned in the routine description.

```
void   Save_Dialog_Preferences( void )
{
    short       pref_ref_num;
    Handle      old_data_handle;
    Handle      new_data_handle;
    short       res_ID;
    ResType     res_type;
    Str255      res_name;
    short       res_attributes;
    StringPtr   source_str;
    Size        byte_count;

    pref_ref_num = Open_Preferences_File();

    UseResFile( pref_ref_num );

    new_data_handle = NewHandleClear( sizeof( PrefRecord ) );
    HLock( new_data_handle );
        (**(PrefHandle)new_data_handle).rad_1_val = Radio_1_Val;
        (**(PrefHandle)new_data_handle).rad_2_val = Radio_2_Val;
        (**(PrefHandle)new_data_handle).chk_1_val = Check_1_Val;

    source_str = Name_String;
    byte_count = Name_String[0] + 1;
    BlockMoveData( source_str,
                   (**(PrefHandle)new_data_handle).name_str,
                   byte_count );
```

```
    old_data_handle = Get1Resource( PREF_RES_TYPE, PREF_RES_ID );

    GetResInfo( old_data_handle, &res_ID, &res_type, res_name );

    res_attributes = GetResAttrs( old_data_handle );
    RemoveResource( old_data_handle );
    AddResource( new_data_handle, res_type, res_ID, res_name );
    WriteResource( new_data_handle );
  HUnlock( new_data_handle );

    ReleaseResource( new_data_handle );

    CloseResFile( pref_ref_num );

    UseResFile( Appl_Rsrc_Fork_Ref_Num );
}
```

The PrefUser Source Code Listing

This chapter ends with a look at the listing for this book's longest program. Since you've seen `Initialize_Toolbox()` and the utility routines `Set_Radio_Buttons()` and `Set_Check_Box()` numerous
times already, they've been omitted from this listing.

```
//_____
//                                      #include directives

#include <Folders.h>  // holds the definition for FindFolder()


//_____
//                                      function prototypes
void    Initialize_Toolbox( void );
void    Open_Dialog( void );
void    Get_Final_Dialog_Values( DialogPtr );
void    Set_Initial_Dialog_Values( DialogPtr );
void    Get_Dialog_Preferences( void );
void    Save_Dialog_Preferences( void );
short   Open_Preferences_File( void );
short   Create_New_Pref_File( FSSpec );
void    Set_Radio_Buttons( DialogPtr, short *, short );
short   Set_Check_Box( DialogPtr, short );
```

```
//_____
//                                              #define directives

#define        DLOG_ID              128
#define          OK_ITEM             1
#define          RADIO_1_ITEM        2
#define          RADIO_2_ITEM        3
#define          CHECK_1_ITEM        4
#define          STRING_ITEM         5

#define        STR_LIST_ID          128
#define        PREF_STR_INDEX        1

#define        PREF_RES_TYPE       'PRFN'
#define        PREF_RES_ID          128


//_____
//                                          define data structures

typedef   struct
{
   short    rad_1_val;
   short    rad_2_val;
   short    chk_1_val;
   Str255   name_str;
} PrefRecord, *PrefPtr, **PrefHandle;


//_____
//                                       declare global variables

short        Radio_1_Val;
short        Radio_2_Val;
short        Check_1_Val;
StringPtr    Name_String;
short        Appl_Rsrc_Fork_Ref_Num;


//_____
//                                                        main()

void   main( void )
{
   Initialize_Toolbox();
```

```
    Appl_Rsrc_Fork_Ref_Num = CurResFile();
    Name_String = (StringPtr)NewPtr( sizeof( Str255 ) );

    Open_Dialog();
}


//_____
//                                          open a display dialog

void  Open_Dialog( void )
{
    DialogPtr   the_dialog;
    Boolean     done = false;
    short       the_item;
    short       new_radio;
    short       old_radio;

    the_dialog = GetNewDialog( DLOG_ID, nil, (WindowPtr)-1L );

    Get_Dialog_Preferences();

    Set_Initial_Dialog_Values( the_dialog );

    if ( Radio_1_Val == 1 )            // Determine which radio
        old_radio = RADIO_1_ITEM;      // button is on and call
    else if ( Radio_2_Val == 1 )       // that button the old
        old_radio = RADIO_2_ITEM;      // radio button

    ShowWindow( the_dialog );
    SetPort( the_dialog );

    while ( done == false )
    {
        ModalDialog( nil, &the_item );

        switch ( the_item )
        {
            case RADIO_1_ITEM:
                new_radio = RADIO_1_ITEM;
                Set_Radio_Buttons( the_dialog, &old_radio, new_radio );
                break;

            case RADIO_2_ITEM:
                new_radio = RADIO_2_ITEM;
```

```
                  Set_Radio_Buttons( the_dialog, &old_radio, new_radio );
                  break;

            case CHECK_1_ITEM:
               new_radio = CHECK_1_ITEM;
               Set_Check_Box( the_dialog, the_item );
               break;

            case OK_ITEM:
               done = true;
               Get_Final_Dialog_Values( the_dialog );
               break;
         }
      }

   Save_Dialog_Preferences();

   DisposDialog( the_dialog );
}


//_____
//                      get dialog settings from preferences file

void  Get_Dialog_Preferences( void )
{
   short       pref_ref_num;
   Handle      data_handle;
   StringPtr   source_str;
   Size        byte_count;

   pref_ref_num = Open_Preferences_File();

   UseResFile( pref_ref_num );

   data_handle = Get1Resource( PREF_RES_TYPE, PREF_RES_ID );

   Radio_1_Val = (**(PrefHandle)data_handle).rad_1_val;
   Radio_2_Val = (**(PrefHandle)data_handle).rad_2_val;
   Check_1_Val = (**(PrefHandle)data_handle).chk_1_val;

   source_str = (**(PrefHandle)data_handle).name_str;
   byte_count = (**(PrefHandle)data_handle).name_str[0] + 1;
   BlockMoveData( source_str, Name_String, byte_count );

   CloseResFile( pref_ref_num );
}
```

```
//_____
//                                  open the preferences file

short  Open_Preferences_File( void )
{
   Str255  pref_file_name;
   short   vol_ref;
   long    dir_ID;
   FSSpec  pref_FSSpec;
   short   file_ref_num;

   GetIndString( pref_file_name, STR_LIST_ID, PREF_STR_INDEX );

   FindFolder( kOnSystemDisk, kPreferencesFolderType,
               kDontCreateFolder, &vol_ref, &dir_ID );

   FSMakeFSSpec( vol_ref, dir_ID, pref_file_name, &pref_FSSpec );

   file_ref_num = FSpOpenResFile( &pref_FSSpec, fsCurPerm );

   if ( file_ref_num == -1 )
      file_ref_num = Create_New_Pref_File( pref_FSSpec );

   return ( file_ref_num );
}


//_____
//                          create preference file if none exists

short  Create_New_Pref_File( FSSpec pref_FSSpec )

{
   short       file_ref_num;
   Handle      app_handle;
   short       res_ID;
   ResType     res_type;
   Str255      res_name;
   short       res_attributes;

   UseResFile( Appl_Rsrc_Fork_Ref_Num );

   app_handle = Get1Resource( PREF_RES_TYPE, PREF_RES_ID );

   GetResInfo( app_handle, &res_ID, &res_type, res_name );
   res_attributes = GetResAttrs( app_handle );
   DetachResource( app_handle );
```

```
    FSpCreateResFile( &pref_FSSpec, 'RSED', 'rsrc', smSystemScript );
    file_ref_num = FSpOpenResFile( &pref_FSSpec, fsCurPerm );
    UseResFile( file_ref_num );

    AddResource( app_handle, res_type, res_ID, res_name );
    SetResAttrs( new_data_handle, res_attributes );
    ChangedResource( app_handle );
    WriteResource( app_handle );
    ReleaseResource( app_handle );

    return ( file_ref_num );
}


//_____
//                    set dialog item values when dialog opens

void Set_Initial_Dialog_Values( DialogPtr dlog )
{
    Handle  hand;
    short   type;
    Rect    box;

    GetDialogItem( dlog, RADIO_1_ITEM, &type, &hand, &box );
    SetControlValue( (ControlHandle)hand, Radio_1_Val );

    GetDialogItem( dlog, RADIO_2_ITEM, &type, &hand, &box );
    SetControlValue( (ControlHandle)hand, Radio_2_Val );

    GetDialogItem( dlog, CHECK_1_ITEM, &type, &hand, &box );
    SetControlValue( (ControlHandle)hand, Check_1_Val );

    GetDialogItem( dlog, STRING_ITEM, &type, &hand, &box );
    SetDialogItemText( hand, Name_String );
}


//_____
//                    get dialog item values when user is done

void Get_Final_Dialog_Values( DialogPtr dlog )
{
    Handle  hand;
    short   type;
    Rect    box;

    GetDialogItem( dlog, RADIO_1_ITEM, &type, &hand, &box );
```

```
    Radio_1_Val = GetControlValue( (ControlHandle)hand );

    GetDialogItem( dlog, RADIO_2_ITEM, &type, &hand, &box );
    Radio_2_Val = GetControlValue( (ControlHandle)hand );

    GetDialogItem( dlog, CHECK_1_ITEM, &type, &hand, &box );
    Check_1_Val = GetControlValue( (ControlHandle)hand );

    GetDialogItem( dlog, STRING_ITEM, &type, &hand, &box );
    GetDialogItemText( hand, Name_String );
}


//_____
//                  save dialog settings from preferences file
void  Save_Dialog_Preferences( void )
{
    short        pref_ref_num;
    Handle       old_data_handle;
    Handle       new_data_handle;
    short        res_ID;
    ResType      res_type;
    Str255       res_name;
    short        res_attributes;
    StringPtr    source_str;
    Size         byte_count;

    pref_ref_num = Open_Preferences_File();

    UseResFile( pref_ref_num );

    new_data_handle = NewHandleClear( sizeof( PrefRecord ) );
    HLock( new_data_handle );
        (**(PrefHandle)new_data_handle).rad_1_val = Radio_1_Val;
        (**(PrefHandle)new_data_handle).rad_2_val = Radio_2_Val;
        (**(PrefHandle)new_data_handle).chk_1_val = Check_1_Val;

        source_str = Name_String;
        byte_count = Name_String[0] + 1;
        BlockMoveData( source_str,
                       (**(PrefHandle)new_data_handle).name_str,
                       byte_count );

        old_data_handle = Get1Resource( PREF_RES_TYPE, PREF_RES_ID );

        GetResInfo( old_data_handle, &res_ID, &res_type, res_name );
```

```
        res_attributes = GetResAttrs( old_data_handle );
        RemoveResource( old_data_handle );
        AddResource( new_data_handle, res_type, res_ID, res_name );
        WriteResource( new_data_handle );
    HUnlock( new_data_handle );

    ReleaseResource( new_data_handle );

    CloseResFile( pref_ref_num );

    UseResFile( Appl_Rsrc_Fork_Ref_Num );
}
```

CHAPTER SUMMARY

Resources are housed in resource forks. A resource fork may be a part of an application or a part of a different type of file, such as a document file. If your application will make extensive use of resources—especially large snd or PICT resources, you might consider using one or more resource files. By using the Toolbox routine UseResFile( ), your application will be able to access the resources in these files just as it would resources in its own resource fork. The advantage comes when you need to revise the program. Because the resources are external, you'll be able to distribute a small application.

An application can create a new, empty resource file "on the fly" by making a call to the Toolbox routine FSpCreateResFile( ). This techniques is important when your application has to replace a damaged or missing resource file that it was expecting to work with.

Applications have the ability to copy resources from one resource fork to another. This is done by first calling Get1Resource( ) to obtain a handle to the resource to copy. After that, the Toolbox routine AddResource( ) is used to add the resource to a different resource fork.

A preferences file is a must for any program that is to be commercial grade. This file holds the settings that a user has made to the program and allows these settings to be restored each time the program is run. A preferences file is a resource file with a custom resource in it. This custom resource holds all of the preferences settings that the program is to track. When information from this file is needed by the application, the resource fork of the file is opened and the preferences information is read into memory. Once in memory, the application can use a handle to the data in assignment statements.

Chapter

7

More Mac Programming Techniques

FILES

The Standard File Package is a set of routines that handles the user interface when a user saves or opens a document. In this chapter, you'll see how to use these functions to display the standard Open dialog box that allows a user to select a file to open. Once a file selection has been made, the work of reading the files data to memory and then displaying that data in a window begins. This chapter demonstrates how to use several File Manager routines to get this task completed—for both PICT and TEXT files.

Opening an existing file is usually only half of the file managing tasks of which an application is capable. After a user has created a new document and drawn or written to it, your application should be able to let the user save that document to a file on disk. In this chapter, you'll see how to use the Standard File Package to display the standard Save dialog box to give the user the opportunity to name and save a document. Here, you'll again see how to work with both PICT and TEXT files.

OPENING A NEW DOCUMENT

An application may work with both documents and files—the two aren't the same. A program that makes use of a **New** command in a File menu creates a new document, usually an empty window based on a WIND resource. If that same application has a **Save** (or **Save As**) menu item, that document can be saved to disk as a file. When the application terminates, the document will cease to exist, while the file will remain present on disk.

If you've ever written a Mac application that opens a new window, you've essentially created a document. In that case, you may be tempted to skip this section, but please don't. The techniques used here will be expanded upon a little later in this chapter, when opening existing files and saving new files are discussed.

This section's NewDocument program opens a new window and draws a picture in it (see Figure 7.1). If this simple program implemented menus, it would have a **New** menu item that called the application's `Do_New_Picture_Document()` function to handle the task of opening the window. Instead, the NewDocument program simply makes the call from `main()`.

FIGURE 7.1 **THE RESULT OF RUNNING NEWDOCUMENT.**

NewDocument requires just two resources: a WIND and a PICT. The WIND has an ID of 128 and can be of any size. The PICT has an ID of 128 and will be used as the picture that gets drawn in the program's window. Figure 7.2 shows the project's resource file and the PICT resource.

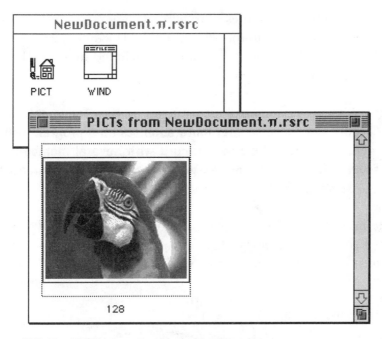

FIGURE 7.2 THE PICT RESOURCE IN THE NEWDOCUMENT PROJECT RESOURCE FILE.

Windows and Document Records

In order for your application to be capable of having more than one window open at one time, you'll need a scheme that allows your program to keep track of the contents of each window. That way, when a window needs updating (or needs to be saved to disk or printed), the correct window contents will be used. One such scheme is to define a document record data type. This data type will hold all the information about any one of a program's windows. For the NewDocument program, there's only one item that needs to be kept track of for any window—a handle to the picture that will appear in the window:

```
typedef  struct
{
   PicHandle  the_pict;

} WindowData, *WindowDataPtr, **WindowDataHandle;
```

The previous definition defines a structure of type WindowData, as well as a pointer and a handle to this structure. NewDocument will use on the data type and the handle, so the pointer is included here simply for the sake of completeness.

 While the document record used by NewDocument contains only one member, your more sophisticated program will most likely have a document record with several members. Later N O T E **in this chapter, this structure will grow to include three members.**

After defining the new data structure, you can use a call to NewHandle Clear() to allocate a block of memory the size of the data structure and return a handle to that memory. That's what is being done in this snippet:

```
WindowDataHandle  the_data;

the_data = (WindowDataHandle)NewHandleClear( sizeof( WindowData ) );
```

To assign a value to the structure's one member, dereference the handle twice. Here the PicHandle member is being set to nil to show that the member hasn't yet been assigned to a picture:

```
(**the_data).the_pict = nil;
```

NewDocument wraps the above code into a routine named Do_New_ Picture_Document(). This function opens a new window, allocates memory for a new document record, and then makes a call to SetWRefCon() to bind the window and record together. When finished, the routine returns a pointer to the new window.

```
WindowPtr  Do_New_Picture_Document( void )
{
   WindowPtr          the_window;
   WindowDataHandle   the_data;

   the_window = GetNewWindow( WIND_ID, nil, (WindowPtr)-1L );

   the_data = (WindowDataHandle)NewHandleClear(sizeof(WindowData ) );
   (**the_data).the_pict = nil;

   SetWRefCon( the_window, (long)the_data );

   return ( the_window );
}
```

Before the Toolbox function SetWRefCon() gets called, a window has been loaded into memory and a handle has been created to point to a section of memory the size of a WindowData structure. But there is no connection between the window and the memory allocated for the data structure. It's the call to SetWRefCon() that ties the data held in the WindowData structure to the new window. It does this by storing a handle to the data in the refCon field of a window.

A WindowPtr always points to a WindowRecord. The 4-byte refCon field of a WindowRecord can be used to hold a pointer to supplemental data for the window. Here, that supplemental data is the application-defined WindowData struct. Figure 7.3 shows how the call to SetWRefCon() associates the data of a WindowData structure with one particular window.

Another method for keeping track of a window's contents is to make use of the windowPic **field of the** WindowRecord, **as described in Chapter 8. That technique, however, is useful only when a window contains a picture. The technique described here can also be used for a window that holds text, as you'll see later in this chapter.**

If a program makes use of multiple windows, it's a simple matter to find the data that goes with any one window. First, obtain a pointer to the window in question. In almost all cases, the window that is to be worked with is the front window:

```
WindowPtr  the_window;
// do stuff here
the_window = FrontWindow();
```

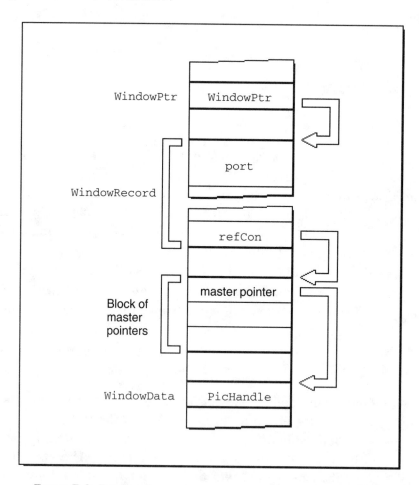

FIGURE 7.3 THE NEWDOCUMENT PROGRAM USES A WINDOW RECORD'S REFCON FIELD AS A HANDLE TO A PICTURE.

Next, get the value of the refCon field from the WindowRecord that the WindowPtr points to. Use the Toolbox routine GetWRefCon():

```
long  wind_ref_con;

wind_ref_con = GetWRefCon( the_window );
```

Earlier, the refCon field was assigned to hold a handle to a document record for this one window. That means the value of wind_ref_con is a handle. Before using the handle, it needs to be typecast to a WindowDataHandle:

```
WindowDataHandle  the_data;
the_data = (WindowDataHandle)wind_ref_con;
```

Now, the data in the document record can be accessed. For NewDocument, that data is a handle to a picture. To associate a picture with a window, the Add_Picture_Data_To_Document() routine is used. Pass this function a pointer to a window and a handle to a picture, and the routine will store the handle in the window's document record:

```
void  Add_Picture_Data_To_Document( WindowPtr the_window,
                                     PicHandle the_picture )
{
   WindowDataHandle  the_data;
   long              wind_ref_con;

   wind_ref_con = GetWRefCon( the_window );

   the_data = (WindowDataHandle)wind_ref_con;

   (**the_data).the_pict = the_picture;
}
```

Any time a window needs to have the proper picture drawn to it, the PicHandle in the window's document record can be used. The previous steps are used to retrieve the handle to the document record, and then the picture handle is obtained from that record:

```
WindowDataHandle  the_data;
long              wind_ref_con;
PicHandle         the_picture;

wind_ref_con = GetWRefCon( the_window );
```

```
the_data = (WindowDataHandle)wind_ref_con;
the_picture = (**the_data).the_pict;
```

A rectangle the size of the picture is then set, and the picture is drawn. The NewDocument routine `Update_Window()` follows all of these steps to update the window whose pointer is passed in:

```
void  Update_Window( WindowPtr the_window )
{
    WindowDataHandle  the_data;
    long              wind_ref_con;
    PicHandle         the_picture;
    Rect              pict_rect;
    short             pict_width;
    short             pict_height;

    SetPort( the_window );

    wind_ref_con = GetWRefCon( the_window );

    the_data = (WindowDataHandle)wind_ref_con;

    the_picture = (**the_data).the_pict;

    pict_rect   = (**the_picture).picFrame;
    pict_width  = pict_rect.right - pict_rect.left;
    pict_height = pict_rect.bottom - pict_rect.top;
    SetRect( &pict_rect, 0, 0, pict_width, pict_height );
    DrawPicture( the_picture, &pict_rect );
}
```

The NewDocument Source Code Listing

The NewDocument program opens a new window, creates a document record for the window, fills the `PicHandle` member of that record with a handle to a picture, and then resizes the window to the size of that picture. To end the program, just click the mouse.

The only routine not discussed is `Size_Picture_Window()`. This function uses the size of a window's picture to determine the size of the window, and to then show the previously invisible window.

```
//_____
//                                      function prototypes

void        Initialize_Toolbox( void );
WindowPtr   Do_New_Picture_Document( void );
void        Add_Picture_Data_To_Document( WindowPtr, PicHandle );
void        Size_Picture_Window( WindowPtr );
void        Update_Window( WindowPtr );


//_____
//                                      #define directives

#define     WIND_ID           128
#define     PARROT_PICT_ID    128


//_____
//                                      define data structures

typedef   struct
{
   PicHandle   the_pict;

} WindowData, *WindowDataPtr, **WindowDataHandle;


//_____
//                                                    main()

void  main( void )
{
   WindowPtr   the_window;
   PicHandle   the_picture;

   Initialize_Toolbox();

   the_window = Do_New_Picture_Document();
   the_picture = GetPicture( PARROT_PICT_ID );

   Add_Picture_Data_To_Document( the_window, the_picture );
   Size_Picture_Window( the_window );

   Update_Window( the_window );

   while ( !Button() )
      ;
}


//_____
//                                      create a new, empty file
```

```
WindowPtr  Do_New_Picture_Document( void )
{
    WindowPtr          the_window;
    WindowDataHandle   the_data;

    the_window = GetNewWindow( WIND_ID, nil, (WindowPtr)-1L );

    the_data = (WindowDataHandle)NewHandleClear(sizeof(WindowData ));
    (**the_data).the_pict = nil;

    SetWRefCon( the_window, (long)the_data );
    return ( the_window );
}

//_____
//                              fill file data for one window

void  Add_Picture_Data_To_Document( WindowPtr the_window,
                                    PicHandle the_picture )
{
    WindowDataHandle   the_data;
    long               wind_ref_con;

    wind_ref_con = GetWRefCon( the_window );

    the_data = (WindowDataHandle)wind_ref_con;

    (**the_data).the_pict = the_picture;
}

//_____
//          resize newly opened window to the size of picture

void  Size_Picture_Window( WindowPtr the_window )
{
    WindowDataHandle   the_data;
    long               wind_ref_con;
    PicHandle          the_picture;
    Rect               pict_rect;
    short              pict_width;
    short              pict_height;

    wind_ref_con = GetWRefCon( the_window );

    the_data = (WindowDataHandle)wind_ref_con;

    the_picture = (**the_data).the_pict;
    pict_rect   = (**the_picture).picFrame;
    pict_width  = pict_rect.right - pict_rect.left;
```

```
    pict_height = pict_rect.bottom - pict_rect.top;
    SetRect( &pict_rect, 0, 0, pict_width, pict_height );
    SizeWindow( the_window, pict_width, pict_height, false );
    ShowWindow( the_window );
}

//_____
//                                          update one window
void  Update_Window( WindowPtr the_window )
{
    WindowDataHandle   the_data;
    long               wind_ref_con;
    PicHandle          the_picture;
    Rect               pict_rect;
    short              pict_width;
    short              pict_height;

    SetPort( the_window );
    wind_ref_con = GetWRefCon( the_window );

    the_data = (WindowDataHandle)wind_ref_con;

    the_picture = (**the_data).the_pict;
    pict_rect   = (**the_picture).picFrame;
    pict_width  = pict_rect.right - pict_rect.left;
    pict_height = pict_rect.bottom - pict_rect.top;
    SetRect( &pict_rect, 0, 0, pict_width, pict_height );
    DrawPicture( the_picture, &pict_rect );
}
```

OPENING AN EXISTING PICT FILE

The NewDocument example demonstrates how to open a window and then use that window as a document. But it doesn't work with files. In this section, you'll see how to open an existing PICT file.

Opening a file doesn't show its contents on screen. To do that, you read the file contents to memory and then display this stored information in a window—a document. In this section, you'll see how to open and read a PICT file, and to display the resulting picture in a window. Later in this chapter, you'll see how to follow similar steps to read and display the contents of a TEXT file.

The OpenPICTfile program uses the standard Get File dialog box to display a list of available PICT files. The included disk has a few example

PICT files, or you can create your own using a graphics program. Figure 7.4 shows the standard Get File dialog box.

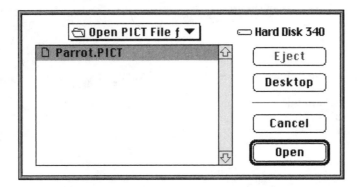

**FIGURE 7.4 THE STANDARD GET FILE DIALOG BOX—
A PART OF THE STANDARD FILE PACKAGE.**

After clicking the **Open** button or double-clicking on the name of a PICT file, the OpenPICT file program opens (but doesn't show) a new, empty window, and reads the PICT data from the file. The program then sizes the window to the size of the picture, makes the window visible, and finally displays the picture in it. For the included Parrot.PICT file, the result will look like that shown in Figure 7.5.

**FIGURE 7.5 OPENING A PICT FILE WITH OPENPICTFILE DISPLAYS
THE CONTENTS OF THE FILE IN A WINDOW.**

The OpenPICTfile project requires just a single resource: a WIND that will serve as the document window. Since the picture to display will be read in from an existing file, no PICT resource is needed. Figure 7.6 shows the project resource file.

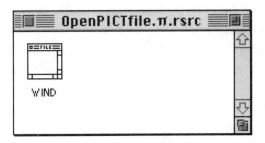

FIGURE 7.6 THE OPENPICTFILE PROJECT RESOURCE FILE CONSISTS OF JUST A SINGLE WIND RESOURCE.

Reading and Displaying the Contents of a PICT File

To allow a user to open any PICT file in any folder, or directory, you'll use the Standard Get dialog box—also referred to as the Open dialog box. A call to the Toolbox routine `StandardGetFile()` displays the dialog box pictured in Figure 7.4.

```
SFTypeList        type_list = { 'PICT', 0, 0, 0 };
StandardFileReply  reply;

StandardGetFile( nil, 1, type_list, &reply );
```

The first three parameters are used to tell the File Manager which types of files to display in the dialog box *display list*. `StandardGetFile()` can easily display four different types of files. If your application is capable of opening more than four different types, you'll need to pass a pointer to a filter function as the first parameter. Since the OpenPICTfile program only works with one file type (PICT files), I'll pass `nil` here. The second parameter tells how many types of files to display, while the third parameter specifies each type. You can fill the `SFTypeList` when you declare it, as I've done here. Surround the type in single quotes, and for unused type simply supply a 0:

```
SFTypeList  type_list = { 'PICT', 0, 0, 0 };
```

The last parameter to StandardGetFile() is a pointer to a variable of type StandardFileReply. When the user clicks on the **Open** or **Cancel** buttons in the standard Get File dialog box, the File Manager will fill the members of the StandardFileReply structure. From the universal header file StandardFile.h, here's how the StandardFileReply structure looks:

```
struct StandardFileReply
{
    Boolean      sfGood;
    Boolean      sfReplacing;
    OSType       sfType;
    FSSpec       sfFile;
    ScriptCode   sfScript;
    short        sfFlags;
    Boolean      sfIsFolder;
    Boolean      sfIsVolume;
    long         sfReserved1;
    short        sfReserved2;
};
```

The example programs in this chapter will make use of just two of the StandardFileReply members: sfGood and sfFile. By examining the value of sfGood, your program can determine if the user clicked on the **Open** button (sfGood will be true) or the **Cancel** button (sfGood will be false). To open the selected file, your program will need an FSSpec—a *file system specification*—for that file. The file system specification is the standardized way of specifying the name and location (path) of a Macintosh file. The sfFile field of the StandardFileReply supplies this FSSpec.

To open a selected file, use the Toolbox routine FSpOpenDF(). Pass this function a pointer to the file's FSSpec, a permission level, and a pointer to a variable of type short:

```
short  pict_ref_num;

FSpOpenDF( &reply.sfFile, fsRdPerm, &pict_ref_num );
```

FSpOpenDF() will find the requested file and open its data fork. If a permission level of fsRdPerm is specified, your application will only be able to read the file. The five Apple-defined permission levels are as follows:

```
#define     fsCurPerm        0    // whatever permission is
                                  // allowed
#define     fsRdPerm         1    // read permission
#define     fsWrPerm         2    // write permission
#define     fsRdWrPerm       3    // exclusive read/write
                                  // permission
#define     fsRdWrShPerm     4    // shared read/write permission
```

After opening the file, FSpOpenDF() returns a file reference number to your program. It is this number that your application will then use to refer to the file, as shown here in calls to the Toolbox routines GetEOF() and SetFPos():

```
long  file_length;
GetEOF( pict_ref_num, &file_length );
SetFPos( pict_ref_num, fsFromStart, 512 );
```

GetEOF() is used to get the size (in bytes) of the contents of a file. SetFPos() is used to move the file mark—the position marker used to keep track of the current position to read from or write to—to a particular byte location in a file. All PICT files have a 512-byte header that is used in different ways by different applications. These first 512 bytes hold data unrelated to the picture data, so you'll want to move the file mark past them before starting to read the picture data. The fsFromStart constant used in the call to SetFPos() tells the function to count from the start of the file.

The total length of the file was found by GetEOF() and is held in the variable file_length. The actual size of the picture is this total size minus the 512-byte header:

```
Size  pict_size;

pict_size = file_length - 512;
```

At this point, the file is open and all of the information necessary to read its contents has been obtained. Before beginning the read, I'll make a call to `NewHandleClear()` to allocate an area of memory the size of the picture and to return a handle to this area:

```
Handle  temp_handle = nil;

temp_handle = NewHandleClear( pict_size );
```

The Toolbox routine `FSRead()` is used to read in the file data. Pass this function the reference number of the file to read from, a pointer to the number of bytes to read, and a pointer to a buffer to read to:

```
HLock( temp_handle );
   FSRead( pict_ref_num, &pict_size, *temp_handle );
HUnlock( temp_handle );
```

The above code uses the temporary handle as the buffer to read to. Since `temp_handle` is a handle—and `FSRead()` requires a pointer buffer—I've dereferenced it once. Since a handle is relocatable, I've also taken the precaution of locking it during the move.

After the call to `FSRead()` is complete, `temp_handle` is a handle to the picture data. Now it's a simple matter to typecast this generic handle to a `PicHandle`:

```
PicHandle  the_picture;

the_picture = ( PicHandle )temp_handle;
```

At this point, the application has a `PicHandle` that can used as any other picture handle is used. It can be used in a call to `DrawPicture()`, or it can be stored in the `the_pict` field of a window's document record.

In the OpenPICTfile program, all of the code necessary to open a PICT file is packaged in a routine named `Load_Picture_From_PICT_File()`. `Load_Picture_From_PICT_File()` accepts a `WindowPtr` as its only parameter. After the user chooses a PICT file to open, this window pointer will be used in a call to `SetWTitle()` to change the document window's title to that of the file being opened. After opening the picture file, Load_Picture_From_PICT_File( ) doesn't do anything with the picture. Instead, it returns the picture data to the calling routine.

```
PicHandle  Load_Picture_From_PICT_File( WindowPtr the_window )
{
    SFTypeList          type_list = { 'PICT', 0, 0, 0 };
    StandardFileReply   reply;
    short               pict_ref_num;
    long                file_length;
    Size                pict_size;
    Handle              temp_handle = nil;
    PicHandle           the_picture;

    StandardGetFile( nil, 1, type_list, &reply );

    if ( reply.sfGood == false )
        ExitToShell();

    SetWTitle( the_window, reply.sfFile.name );

    FSpOpenDF( &reply.sfFile, fsRdPerm, &pict_ref_num );

    GetEOF( pict_ref_num, &file_length );
    SetFPos( pict_ref_num, fsFromStart, 512 );

    pict_size = file_length - 512;

    temp_handle = NewHandleClear( pict_size );

    HLock( temp_handle );
        FSRead( pict_ref_num, &pict_size, *temp_handle );

    HUnlock( temp_handle );
    the_picture = ( PicHandle )temp_handle;

    return ( the_picture );
}
```

The OpenPICTfile Source Code Listing

OpenPICTfile uses all of the routines found in the NewDocument example—only Load_Picture_From_PICT_File( ) is new. OpenPICTfile begins by making a call to `Do_New_Picture_Document( )` to open a new, empty window and a new document record. It then stores a handle to the window's document record in the `WindowRecord refCon` field.

The last section's NewDocument program used a PICT resource as the source of the picture to display. Here, OpenPICTfile uses the picture found in a PICT file. After `Load_Picture_From_PICT_File( )` returns a `PicHandle` to `main( )`, the program finishes up just as it did in NewDocument. First, `Add_Picture_Data_To_Document( )` adds the `PicHandle` to the window's document record. Then `Size_Picture_Window( )` resizes the window to fit the picture and shows the window. Finally, `Update_Window( )` displays the picture.

For simplicity, OpenPICTfile doesn't implement menus. Instead, the Open dialog box will appear when the program launches. If you add an **Open** menu item to the File menu of one of your programs, handle that menu selection by calling `Load_Picture_From_PICT_File( )`, `Add_Picture_Data_To_Document( )`, and `Size_Picture_Window( )`.

After selecting a PICT file, OpenPICTfile displays that file's picture in a document window. To end the program, just click the mouse button.

```
//_____
//                                              function prototypes

void        Initialize_Toolbox( void );
WindowPtr   Do_New_Picture_Document( void );
PicHandle   Load_Picture_From_PICT_File( WindowPtr );
void        Add_Picture_Data_To_Document( WindowPtr, PicHandle );
void        Size_Picture_Window( WindowPtr );
void        Update_Window( WindowPtr );

//_____
//                                              #define directives

#define     WIND_ID         128

//_____
//                                              define data structures
typedef  struct
{
   PicHandle  the_pict;

} WindowData, *WindowDataPtr, **WindowDataHandle;
```

```
//_____
//                                                        main()

void  main( void )
{
    WindowPtr   the_window;
    PicHandle   the_picture;

    Initialize_Toolbox();

    the_window = Do_New_Picture_Document();

    the_picture = Load_Picture_From_PICT_File( the_window );

    Add_Picture_Data_To_Document( the_window, the_picture );

    Size_Picture_Window( the_window );

    Update_Window( the_window );

    while ( !Button() )
        ;
}

//_____
//             get a handle to a picture from a PICT document

PicHandle  Load_Picture_From_PICT_File( WindowPtr the_window )
{
    SFTypeList          type_list = { 'PICT', 0, 0, 0 };
    StandardFileReply   reply;
    short               pict_ref_num;
    long                file_length;
    Size                pict_size;
    Handle              temp_handle = nil;
    PicHandle           the_picture;

    StandardGetFile( nil, 1, type_list, &reply );

    if ( reply.sfGood == false )
        ExitToShell();

    SetWTitle( the_window, reply.sfFile.name );

    FSpOpenDF( &reply.sfFile, fsRdPerm, &pict_ref_num );

    GetEOF( pict_ref_num, &file_length );
    SetFPos( pict_ref_num, fsFromStart, 512 );
```

```
    pict_size = file_length - 512;

    temp_handle = NewHandleClear( pict_size );

    HLock( temp_handle );
        FSRead( pict_ref_num, &pict_size, *temp_handle );
    HUnlock( temp_handle );

    the_picture = ( PicHandle )temp_handle;

    return ( the_picture );
}

//_____
//                                    create a new, empty file

WindowPtr  Do_New_Picture_Document( void )
{
    WindowPtr           the_window;
    WindowDataHandle    the_data;

    the_window = GetNewWindow( WIND_ID, nil, (WindowPtr)-1L );

    the_data= (WindowDataHandle)NewHandleClear(sizeof(WindowData) );
    (**the_data).the_pict = nil;

    SetWRefCon( the_window, (long)the_data );

    return ( the_window );
}

//_____
//                              fill file data for one window

void  Add_Picture_Data_To_Document( WindowPtr the_window,
                                    PicHandle the_picture )
{
    WindowDataHandle  the_data;
    long              wind_ref_con;

    wind_ref_con = GetWRefCon( the_window );

    the_data= (WindowDataHandle)wind_ref_con;

    (**the_data).the_pict = the_picture;
}
```

```
//_____
//          resize newly opened window to the size of picture

void  Size_Picture_Window( WindowPtr the_window )
{
   WindowDataHandle  the_data;
   long              wind_ref_con;
   PicHandle         the_picture;
   Rect              pict_rect;
   short             pict_width;
   short             pict_height;

   wind_ref_con = GetWRefCon( the_window );

   the_data = (WindowDataHandle)wind_ref_con;

   the_picture = (**the_data).the_pict;

   pict_rect   = (**the_picture).picFrame;
   pict_width  = pict_rect.right - pict_rect.left;
   pict_height = pict_rect.bottom - pict_rect.top;
   SetRect( &pict_rect, 0, 0, pict_width, pict_height );
   SizeWindow( the_window, pict_width, pict_height, false );
   ShowWindow( the_window );
}

//_____
//                                      update one window

void  Update_Window( WindowPtr the_window )
{
   WindowDataHandle  the_data;
   long              wind_ref_con;
   PicHandle         the_picture;
   Rect              pict_rect;
   short             pict_width;
   short             pict_height;

   SetPort( the_window );

   wind_ref_con= GetWRefCon( the_window );

   the_data= (WindowDataHandle)wind_ref_con;

   the_picture = (**the_data).the_pict;
```

```
    pict_rect   = (**the_picture).picFrame;
    pict_width  = pict_rect.right - pict_rect.left;
    pict_height = pict_rect.bottom - pict_rect.top;
    SetRect( &pict_rect, 0, 0, pict_width, pict_height );
    DrawPicture( the_picture, &pict_rect );
}
```

Saving a Document to a PICT File

In this chapter's "Opening a New Document" section, a document was created, but no files were involved. Then in this chapter's "Opening an Existing PICT File" section, a document was created from an existing file. In neither case, however, was a file *created*. Now that you know how to create a document, and you've worked with document records, you're ready to see how to save the contents of a document to a file.

The SavePICTfile program is an expanded version of NewDocument. SavePICTfile uses the routines found in NewDocument to open a new, empty document and to then draw a picture in it. As in NewDocument, SavePICTfile gets the picture from a PICT resource in the application's resource fork.

After opening the document and displaying a picture in it, SavePICTfile posts the standard Save dialog box (see Figure 7.7.)

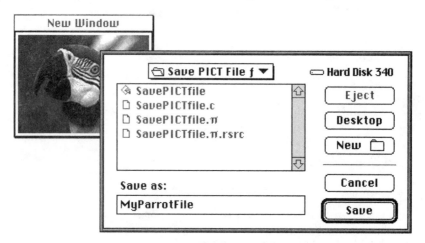

FIGURE 7.7 THE STANDARD SAVE FILE DIALOG BOX—
A PART OF THE STANDARD FILE PACKAGE.

The standard Save dialog box allows the user to supply a name for the file that is to be created. If the user types in the name of an existing file, the File Manager will display the Name Conflict Alert box (see Figure 7.8.)

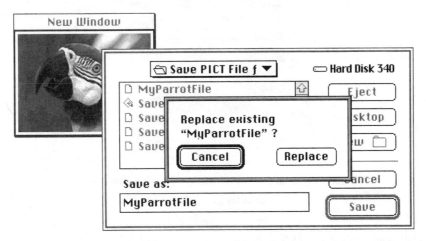

FIGURE 7.8 THE NAME CONFLICT ALERT BOX, A PART OF THE STANDARD FILE PACKAGE.

After quitting SavePICTfile, you'll see a new PICT file. If you double-click on it, the Finder will display the alert box shown in Figure 7.9. SavePICTfile doesn't support the opening of PICT files, so you'll have to open your newly created file from an application that does. Apple's simple text editing program TeachText is capable of displaying a PICT file, so go ahead and click on the **OK** button in the alert box. When you do, you'll see the PICT file opened in a TeachText document like the one shown in Figure 7.10.

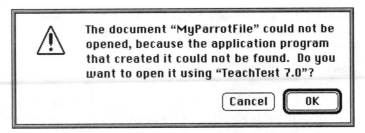

**FIGURE 7.9 DOUBLE-CLICKING ON A PICT FILE CREATED BY
SAVEPICTFILE DISPLAYS THIS ALERT.**

FIGURE 7.10 A PICT FILE CREATED BY SAVEPICTFILE CAN BE OPENED USING TEACHTEXT.

SavePICTfile requires the same two resources that the NewDocument project used: a PICT and a WIND. The OpenPICTfile resource file is shown in Figure 7.11.

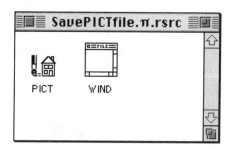

FIGURE 7.11 THE RESOURCES FOR THE SAVEPICTFILE PROJECT.

Expanding the Document Record

Until a user saves a document, there is no file associated with that document. Once a document is saved, you'll want to enable that document to keep track of the file it was saved to. If your program allows a document to be edited, the user may want to save the document several times during the execution of the application. If the document keeps track of the file it's been saved to, each additional save that is performed will be easy to perform.

Any information that is to be tied to a particular document can be kept in the document record. To this point, that record has consisted of just a PicHandle that is used to keep track of the picture that is currently displayed in the document:

```
typedef   struct
{
   PicHandle   the_pict;

} WindowData, *WindowDataPtr, **WindowDataHandle;
```

To keep track of a file, I'll add two more fields to the document record—one for the file's reference number and the other for an FSSpec for the file:

```
typedef   struct
{
   PicHandle   the_pict;
   long        file_ref_num;
   FSSpec      file_FSSpec;

} WindowData, *WindowDataPtr, **WindowDataHandle;
```

When a new, empty document is created, the file reference number should be set to 0 to show that there is no file paired with this document. Later, when the user saves the document, the file reference number will be changed to a nonzero value. Here's the SavePICTfile version of Do_New_Picture_Document( ). There's only one new line of code in the routine, which is shown in bold type.

```
WindowPtr  Do_New_Picture_Document( void )
{
   WindowPtr           the_window;
   WindowDataHandle    the_data;

   the_window = GetNewWindow( WIND_ID, nil, (WindowPtr)-1L );
```

```
the_data = (WindowDataHandle)NewHandleClear(sizeof(WindowData ));
(**the_data).the_pict = nil;
(**the_data).file_ref_num = 0;

 SetWRefCon( the_window, (long)the_data);

 return ( the_window );
}
```

Saving a Document with "Save As"

Application's use much of the same code to handle **Save As** and **Save** menu selections. The primary differences are that a **Save As** command will display the standard Put dialog box—also called the Save dialog box— while the **Save** command won't. Additionally, a **Save As** menu selection may require the creation of a new file, while a **Save** menu selection does not. In this section you'll see how to handle a **Save As** menu item selection. The next section illustrates the handling of the **Save** menu item.

To allow the user to choose the name of the file to save a document's contents to, have your application post the Save dialog box. A call to the Toolbox routine `StandardPutFile()` will display the dialog box pictured in Figure 7.7:

```
StandardFileReply  the_reply;

StandardPutFile( "\pSave as:", "\pUntitled", &the_reply );
```

The first parameter to `StandardPutFile()` is the string that will appear just over the text item in the Open dialog box. The second parameter is the default string that will appear in the text item—it's the name the file will be given if the user clicks on the **Save** button without first typing in a file name. The final parameter is a pointer to a `StandardFileReply` variable. After the user clicks the **Save** button, the File Manager will fill this variable will information about the newly created file.

Now it's up to your application to determine *what* is to be saved. By convention, a **Save** or **Save As** menu selection is used to save the front-most window. A call to `FrontWindow()` returns a pointer to that window.

Then, as was done in previous examples, a handle to the document record for that window is obtained:

```
WindowPtr          the_window;
long               wind_ref_con;
WindowDataHandle   the_data;

the_window = FrontWindow();
wind_ref_con = GetWRefCon( the_window );
the_data = (WindowDataHandle)wind_ref_con;
```

Now it's time to create a new, empty file. A call to `FSpCreate()` takes care of this task. Before making this call, however, verify that the user isn't replacing an existing file of the same name. If the user is, then there's no need to create a new file—the original file can be used.

```
if ( the_reply.sfReplacing == false )
    FSpCreate( &the_reply.sfFile, 'svpf', 'PICT', smSystemScript );
```

The first parameter to `FSpCreate()` is a pointer to the `FSSpec` to be filled by the File Manager. Because the File Manager just created the new file, it knows (and can return) this file name and directory information to the application. The second and third parameters to `FSpCreate()` are the file's creator and file type. Here, svfp was chosen to represent "save picture file"—your creator type can of course differ. To save a document as a PICT file, the third parameter must be PICT. The last parameter to `FSpCreate()` is the script system to be used to display the file's name. Use the system script here.

The document record, as defined in the SavePICTfile program, has two members devoted to keeping track of the file associated with a document. One of those members is the file's `FSSpec`. At this point, that member should be set to the `FSSpec` that was returned by `FSpCreate()`:

```
(**the_data).file_FSSpec = the_reply.sfFile;
```

Next, check to verify that there isn't already an open file associated with the document. If there is, close it now with a call to `FSClose()`.

```
if ( (**the_data).file_ref_num != 0 )
   FSClose( (**the_data).file_ref_num );
```

Recall that when a new document is opened, the application-defined routine Do_New_Picture_Document() sets the file_ref_num field of the document record to 0. If that field isn't 0 at this point, then an open file already exists for this document.

Now it's time to open the new file. A call to FSpOpenDF() opens the data fork—that's where the picture data will be written to:

```
short   ref_num;

FSpOpenDF( &(**the_data).file_FSSpec, fsRdWrPerm, &ref_num );
```

The first parameter to FSpOpenDF() is a pointer to the FSSpec of the file to open. The second parameter is the permission level for the file; make sure this permission level includes write privileges so that the application can write the picture data to it. The last parameter to FSpOpenDF() is a pointer to a short variable. FSpOpenDF() will assign this variable a reference number for the opened file.

At this point, a file is created and opened, so it's safe to say that the document that is about to be saved now has a file associated with it. Set the document record file_ref_num member to the value returned by FSpOpenDF():

```
(**the_data).file_ref_num = ref_num;
```

Now is the time to write the data to the new file. This task requires a little effort, so I'll wrap the data-writing code in another application-defined routine—one named Write_PICT_Data_To_File(). Before moving onto that function, take a look at how the above code has been grouped into a function named Handle_Save_As_Choice():

```
void  Handle_Save_As_Choice( void )
{
   WindowPtr             the_window;
   long                  wind_ref_con;
```

```
WindowDataHandle    the_data;
StandardFileReply   the_reply;
short               ref_num;

StandardPutFile( "\pSave as:", "\pUntitled", &the_reply );

if ( the_reply.sfGood == false )
   return;

the_window = FrontWindow();
wind_ref_con = GetWRefCon( the_window );
the_data = (WindowDataHandle)wind_ref_con;

SetWTitle( the_window, the_reply.sfFile.name );
if ( the_reply.sfReplacing == false )
   FSpCreate( &the_reply.sfFile, 'svpf', 'PICT',
              smSystemScript );

(**the_data).file_FSSpec = the_reply.sfFile;
if ( (**the_data).file_ref_num != 0 )
   FSClose( (**the_data).file_ref_num );

FSpOpenDF( &(**the_data).file_FSSpec, fsRdWrPerm, &ref_num );

(**the_data).file_ref_num = ref_num;

Write_PICT_Data_To_File( the_window );
}
```

You've seen that a picture can be stored as either a PICT resource or a PICT file. If it is a PICT resource, it exists in the resource fork of a file. Often that file is an application-file—a Mac program.

To read a picture stored in a PICT resource, you open a resource fork (or use the already-open application resource fork) and make a call to GetPicture( ). To write a PICT resource to a resource fork, you again open a resource fork and then use a series of Toolbox routines that includes AddResource( ) and WriteResource( ). Chapter 6 described this process.

To read a picture stored in a PICT file, you open a file's data fork, not its resource fork. Then you read the picture data. Reading a picture from a PICT file isn't as easy as simply making a call to GetPicture( ) because each PICT file has a 512-byte header that must be taken into consideration. After that, a call to `FSRead()` reads in the picture data. Reading PICT files was discussed earlier in this chapter. To write a picture to a PICT file, the 512-byte header must again be considered. Next, the picture information held in memory (and referenced by a `PicHandle`) must be written to the file. Figure 7.12 shows the layout of the disk memory a PICT file occupies.

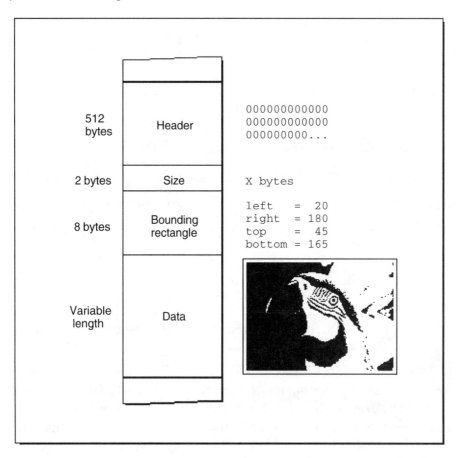

FIGURE 7.12 THE PARTS OF A PICT FILE AS THEY APPEAR IN MEMORY.

To decide which picture to write to disk, you'll again rely on the data in the front window—the picture in the active document. Get that window's `refCon` value to use as the handle to the document record, then dereference that handle to get a handle to the picture in that window:

```
WindowDataHandle   the_data;
long               wind_ref_con;
PicHandle          the_picture;

wind_ref_con = GetWRefCon( the_window );

the_data = (WindowDataHandle)wind_ref_con;
the_picture = (**the_data).the_pict;
```

The routine that writes the picture data to a file will be called after the file has been created. That means the file will be open, and its reference number will be held in the document record belonging to the window that holds the picture. The file reference number will be needed in subsequent Toolbox calls, so retrieve it now:

```
short   ref_num;

ref_num = (**the_data).file_ref_num;
```

The picture header, size, bounding rectangle, and data are all written to a file's data fork using calls to FSWrite(). Before making the first call to FSWrite(), set the file marker to the start of the file:

```
SetFPos( ref_num, fsFromStart, 0 );
```

A picture's 512-byte header is used to store application-specific information about the picture. If your application ignores this header, as many programs do, fill each byte with a 0. One way to do this is to set a long variable (4 bytes) to a value of 0, then loop 128 times. Each pass through the loop should write these 4-bytes of zeros to the file. After 128 passes through the loop, the file will contain 512 zeros. FSWrite() accepts a pointer to data as its third parameter, so you'll want to set up the loop as follows:

```
long   num_bytes;
long   zero_data;

num_bytes = 4;
zero_data = 0L;
for ( i = 1; i <= 128; i++ )
   FSWrite( ref_num, &num_bytes, &zero_data );
```

399

After writing the header, write the picture's size, bounding rectangle, and data to the file. You won't have to manually calculate these individual values—they're all held in the `Picture` structure that the picture's `PicHandle` leads to in memory. Because of this, all of a picture's information can be written to disk using a single call to `FSWrite()`. Before doing so, make a call to `GetHandleSize()` to get the size, in bytes, of the picture:

```
num_bytes = GetHandleSize( (Handle)the_picture );
FSWrite( ref_con, &num_bytes, (Ptr)(*the_picture) );
```

Pictures that are created on a Macintosh computer that isn't using Color QuickDraw and pictures created in a basic graphics port (as opposed to a color graphics port) are considered version 1 pictures. These picture types are always 32 KB or less in size. For pictures of this type, the memory model shown in Figure 7.12 applies. Color or grayscale pictures—version 2 pictures—can be larger than 32 KB. For this type of picture, the 2-byte picture size is ignored. As you've just seen, whether a document's picture is version 1 or version 2, its information can be written by first making a call to `GetHandleSize()`. This Toolbox routine returns the size in bytes of the object that a handle references. The subsequent call to `FSWrite()` then writes all of the picture information to the `ref_con` file. Figure 7.13 summarizes the writing of a picture to a file.

When finished writing, call `SetEOF()` to resize the file to the number of bytes that have just been written to it. For a picture, the size will be the size of the picture plus the 512-byte header:

```
SetEOF( ref_con, num_bytes + 512 );
```

Next, call `GetVRefNum()` to determine the volume containing the file. When passed a file reference number, `GetVRefNum()` returns a volume reference number. The volume reference number is needed in the subsequent call to the `FlushVol()` Toolbox function. `FlushVol()` flushes a volume. The data that was written using `FSWrite()` was placed in a memory buffer. `FlushVol()` ensures that this data goes from the buffer to disk. `FlushVol()` also updates the file's descriptive information contained on the disk.

400

```
GetVRefNum( ref_con, &vol_ref_num );
FlushVol( nil, vol_ref_num );
```

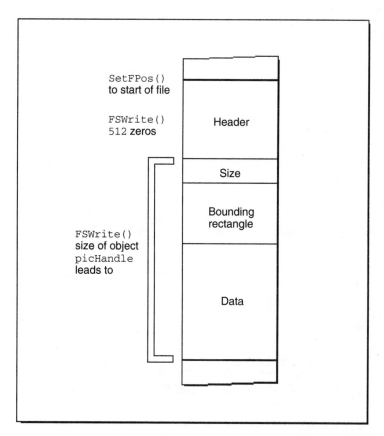

FIGURE 7.13 FSWRITE() IS USED TO WRITE THE PICTURE HEADER AND DATA TO A FILE.

Here's a look at all of the above code, grouped into the Write_PICT_ Data_To_File() function. Recall that this routine will be invoked at the end of Handle_Save_As_Choice(), that is, the function that creates a new file and opens its data fork.

```
void  Write_PICT_Data_To_File( WindowPtr the_window )
{
   WindowDataHandle    the_data;
   long                wind_ref_con;
   PicHandle           the_picture;
```

```
   short              ref_num;
   long               num_bytes;
   long               zero_data;
   short              vol_ref_num;
   int                i;

   wind_ref_con = GetWRefCon( the_window );

   the_data = (WindowDataHandle)wind_ref_con;

   the_picture = (**the_data).the_pict;
   ref_num = (**the_data).file_ref_num;

   SetFPos( ref_num, fsFromStart, 0 );

   num_bytes = 4;
   zero_data = 0L;
   for ( i = 1; i <= 128; i++ )
      FSWrite( ref_num, &num_bytes, &zero_data );

   num_bytes = GetHandleSize( (Handle)the_picture );
   FSWrite( ref_con, &num_bytes, (Ptr)(*the_picture) );

   SetEOF( ref_con, num_bytes + 512 );
   GetVRefNum( ref_con, &vol_ref_num );
   FlushVol( nil, vol_ref_num );
}
```

Saving a Document With "Save"

Once a user has saved a file using the File menu **Save As** item, subsequent saves are easier to perform; there's no need to post the Save dialog box or create a new file.

When the user selects the **Save** menu item from your program, first check to see if the frontmost window has been saved. You can do this by checking the value of the file_ref_num field of the window's document record. When the document record was created in Do_New_ Picture_Document(), this field was set to 0. Its value doesn't change until the document is first saved and a new file is created and associated with the document. If file_ref_num *isn't* 0, call Write_PICT_ Data_To_File() to save the window's data to the existing and open file. If the file_ref_num *is* 0, the window's data has never been saved.

In that case, treat the **Save** selection as a **Save As** choice, and call `Handle_Save_As_Choice( )`.

```
if ( (**the_data).file_ref_num != 0 )
   Write_PICT_Data_To_File( the_window );
else
   Handle_Save_As_Choice();
```

The SavePICTfile Source Code Listing

SavePICTfile uses the routines from past programs to open a new window and initialize its document record. It then loads a PICT resource and draws the picture to the window. SavePICTfile doesn't implement menus, so after opening a new window, a call to `Handle_Save_As_ Choice( )` is made to mimic a user's selection of **Save As** from a menu.

After saving the document, the program waits for a click of the mouse button. When that happens, SavePICTfile doesn't terminate. Instead, a call to `Handle_Save_Choice( )` is made. This allows you to verify that `Handle_Save_Choice( )` doesn't post the Save dialog box once a document has been saved. After the second save, again click the mouse button to end the program.

You can be sure that the second save is really taking place in any one of three ways:

N O T E

1. After clicking the mouse button the first time, listen to your Mac as it accesses the hard drive during the writing of the file.

2. After saving the file the first time (by typing a file name in the Save dialog box and clicking the save button), wait a minute or two before clicking the mouse. Once you do click the mouse, the file will again be saved. This second save will mark the existing file as modified. You can verify that the file was modified by clicking once on it in the Finder and then selecting Get Info from the Finder's File menu. Figure 7.14 shows an example of a file's different Created and Modified times.

3. Use your compiler's debugger during the compile of the SavePICTfile source code. Step through the code to see that Handle_Save_Choice( ) executes as expected.

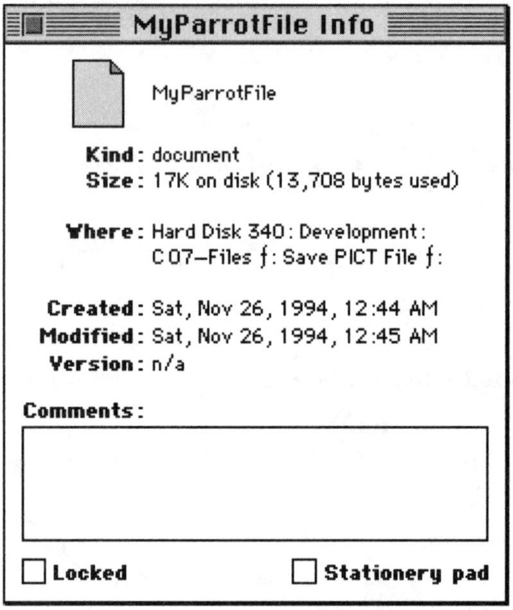

FIGURE 7.14 PAUSING BETWEEN SAVES DURING THE RUNNING OF SAVEPICTFILE RESULTS IN A FILE WITH DIFFERENT CREATED AND MODIFIED TIMES.

```
//_____
//                                         function prototypes

void       Initialize_Toolbox( void );
WindowPtr  Do_New_Picture_Document( void );
void       Add_Picture_Data_To_Document( WindowPtr, PicHandle );
void       Size_Picture_Window( WindowPtr );
void       Update_Window( WindowPtr );
void       Handle_Save_As_Choice( void );
void       Handle_Save_Choice( void );
void       Write_PICT_Data_To_File( WindowPtr );

//_____
//                                         #define directives
```

```
#define      WIND_ID           128
#define      PARROT_PICT_ID    128

//_____
//                                     define data structures

typedef  struct
{
   PicHandle   the_pict;
   long        file_ref_num;
   FSSpec      file_FSSpec;

} WindowData, *WindowDataPtr, **WindowDataHandle;

//_____
//                                                    main()

void  main( void )
{
   WindowPtr   the_window;
   PicHandle   the_picture;

   Initialize_Toolbox();

   the_window = Do_New_Picture_Document();

   the_picture = GetPicture( PARROT_PICT_ID );

   Add_Picture_Data_To_Document( the_window, the_picture );

   Size_Picture_Window( the_window );

   Update_Window( the_window );

   Handle_Save_As_Choice();

   Update_Window( the_window );

   while ( !Button() )
      ;

   Handle_Save_Choice();

   while ( !Button() )
      ;
}
```

```
//_____
//                                              save file

void   Handle_Save_Choice( void )
{
   WindowPtr          the_window;
   long               wind_ref_con;
   WindowDataHandle   the_data;

   the_window = FrontWindow();
   wind_ref_con = GetWRefCon( the_window );

   the_data = (WindowDataHandle)wind_ref_con;

   if ( (**the_data).file_ref_num != 0 )
      Write_PICT_Data_To_File( the_window );
   else
      Handle_Save_As_Choice();
}


//_____
//                 display the "Save As" dialog box, save file

void   Handle_Save_As_Choice( void )
{
   WindowPtr          the_window;
   long               wind_ref_con;
   WindowDataHandle   the_data;
   StandardFileReply  the_reply;
   short              ref_num;

   StandardPutFile( "\pSave as:", "\pUntitled", &the_reply );

   if ( the_reply.sfGood == false )
      return;

   the_window = FrontWindow();
   wind_ref_con = GetWRefCon( the_window );
   the_data = (WindowDataHandle)wind_ref_con;

   SetWTitle( the_window, the_reply.sfFile.name );

   if ( the_reply.sfReplacing == false )
      FSpCreate( &the_reply.sfFile, 'svpf', 'PICT',
              smSystemScript );

   (**the_data).file_FSSpec = the_reply.sfFile;
```

```
   if ( (**the_data).file_ref_num != 0 )
      FSClose( (**the_data).file_ref_num );

   FSpOpenDF( &(**the_data).file_FSSpec, fsRdWrPerm, &ref_num );

   (**the_data).file_ref_num = ref_num;

   Write_PICT_Data_To_File( the_window );
}

//_____
//                          write 'PICT' data to an open file

void  Write_PICT_Data_To_File( WindowPtr the_window )
{
   WindowDataHandle    the_data;
   long                wind_ref_con;
   PicHandle           the_picture;
   short               ref_num;
   long                num_bytes;
   long                zero_data;
   short               vol_ref_num;
   int                 i;

   wind_ref_con = GetWRefCon( the_window );

   the_data = (WindowDataHandle)wind_ref_con;

   the_picture = (**the_data).the_pict;
   ref_num = (**the_data).file_ref_num;

   SetFPos( ref_num, fsFromStart, 0 );

   num_bytes = 4;
   zero_data = 0L;
   for ( i = 1; i <= 128; i++ )
      FSWrite( ref_num, &num_bytes, &zero_data );

   num_bytes = GetHandleSize( (Handle)the_picture );
   FSWrite( ref_con, &num_bytes, (Ptr)(*the_picture) );

   SetEOF( ref_con, num_bytes + 512 );
   GetVRefNum( ref_con, &vol_ref_num );
   FlushVol( nil, vol_ref_num );
}
```

```
//_____
//                              create a new, empty file

WindowPtr  Do_New_Picture_Document( void )
{
   WindowPtr            the_window;
   WindowDataHandle     the_data;

   the_window = GetNewWindow( WIND_ID, nil, (WindowPtr)-1L );

   the_data= (WindowDataHandle)NewHandleClear(sizeof(WindowData) );
   (**the_data).the_pict = nil;
   (**the_data).file_ref_num = 0;

   SetWRefCon( the_window, (long)the_data);

   return ( the_window );
}

//_____
//                              fill file data for one window

void  Add_Picture_Data_To_Document( WindowPtr the_window,
                                    PicHandle the_picture )
{
   WindowDataHandle  the_data;
   long              wind_ref_con;

   wind_ref_con = GetWRefCon( the_window );

   the_data= (WindowDataHandle)wind_ref_con;

   (**the_data).the_pict = the_picture;
}

//_____
//         resize newly opened window to the size of picture

void  Size_Picture_Window( WindowPtr the_window )
{
   WindowDataHandle  the_data;
   long              wind_ref_con;
   PicHandle         the_picture;
   Rect              pict_rect;
   short             pict_width;
   short             pict_height;

   wind_ref_con = GetWRefCon( the_window );

   the_data = (WindowDataHandle)wind_ref_con;
```

```
    the_picture = (**the_data).the_pict;

    pict_rect   = (**the_picture).picFrame;
    pict_width  = pict_rect.right - pict_rect.left;
    pict_height = pict_rect.bottom - pict_rect.top;
    SetRect( &pict_rect, 0, 0, pict_width, pict_height );
    SizeWindow( the_window, pict_width, pict_height, false );
    ShowWindow( the_window );
}

//_____
//                                          update one window

void  Update_Window( WindowPtr the_window )
{
    WindowDataHandle   the_data;
    long               wind_ref_con;
    PicHandle          the_picture;
    Rect               pict_rect;
    short              pict_width;
    short              pict_height;

    SetPort( the_window );

    wind_ref_con = GetWRefCon( the_window );

    the_data = (WindowDataHandle)wind_ref_con;

    the_picture = (**the_data).the_pict;

    pict_rect   = (**the_picture).picFrame;
    pict_width  = pict_rect.right - pict_rect.left;
    pict_height = pict_rect.bottom - pict_rect.top;
    SetRect( &pict_rect, 0, 0, pict_width, pict_height );
    DrawPicture( the_picture, &pict_rect );
}
```

OPENING AN EXISTING TEXT FILE

In this section, you'll see how to open, read, and display the contents of a
TEXT file. If you've skipped any of the previous sections in this chapter,
you'll want to go back and read through them now. Many of the techniques and Toolbox routines used to open a file that holds text are the
same as those used to open a file that holds a picture. Those that are will
be touched on only lightly here.

The OpenTEXTfile program uses the same standard Open dialog box that OpenPICTfile used; it's shown in Figure 7.15. The included disk has an example text file that OpenTEXTfile can work with. OpenTEXTfile can also be used to open any other text file, including source code files.

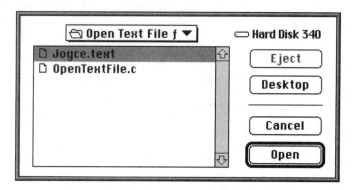

FIGURE 7.15 THE STANDARD OPEN DIALOG BOX USED BY THE OPENTEXTFILE PROGRAM.

After clicking the **Open** button, the OpenTEXTfile program opens a new, empty window. The program then reads the TEXT data from the selected file and displays it in the new window. If OpenTEXTfile is used to open the Joyce.text TEXT file, the window will look like that shown in Figure 7.16.

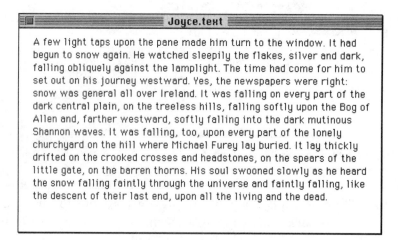

FIGURE 7.16 A TEXT FILE OPENED BY THE OPENTEXTFILE PROGRAM.

OpenTEXTfile uses just a single resource—a WIND with an ID of 128. The program won't resize the window, so I've set the WIND resource to create a window large enough to display much or all of a small text file.

For simplicity, OpenTEXTfile displays the text of the file it opens in a window of fixed size. The techniques presented here will also work in more sophisticated applications, such as those that use windows that grow and windows with scroll bars.

N O T E

The Text Window Document Record

For a window that holds a picture, the document record structure, which can hold any data pertinent to the type of document an application uses, might look like this:

```
typedef  struct
{
   PicHandle  the_pict;
   long       file_ref_num;
   FSSpec     file_FSSpec;

} WindowData, *WindowDataPtr, **WindowDataHandle;
```

For a window that holds text, there's no need to have a PicHandle field in the document record. Instead, a text edit handle would be more appropriate. The other two fields—the file reference number and the file system specification—would still be applicable. Here's the version of the document record used by the OpenTEXTfile program:

```
typedef  struct
{
   TEHandle  the_text;
   long      file_ref_num;
   FSSpec    file_FSSpec;

} WindowData, *WindowDataPtr, **WindowDataHandle;
```

411

NOTE

What about a program that can open more than one type of window? If your program is capable of opening both a graphics window and a text window, your program might define a couple of constants that will be used when distinguishing between window types:

```
#define    PICT_WIND    1
#define    TEXT_WIND    2
```

Then, the document record structure might look like this:

```
typedef  struct
{
    short      wind_type;
    PicHandle  the_pict;
    TEHandle   the_text;
    long       file_ref_num;
    FSSpec     file_FSSpec;

} WindowData, *WindowDataPtr, **WindowDataHandle;
```

Here, the same structure can be used for either window type. When a new graphics document is opened (with, perhaps, a New Picture Window menu selection), the wind_type **field can be set to** PICT_WIND. **The** TEHandle **field will go unused for the graphics window. If the user opens a new text document (with a New Text Window menu selection), the program will set the** wind_type **member to** TEXT_WIND, **and the** PicHandle **member will be left unused.**

Reading and Displaying the Contents of a TEXT File

Before opening an existing text file, a new window in which to display the text should be opened. Do_New_Text_Document() takes care of that task. This routine is analogous to the Do_New_Picture_Document() function that you just saw in the previous example program—SavePICTfile. In fact, only one line from that routine has been modified in order to come up with the Do_New_Text_Document() function. That line appears in bold font:

```
WindowPtr  Do_New_Text_Document( void )
{
    WindowPtr           the_window;
    WindowDataHandle    the_data;

    the_window = GetNewWindow( WIND_ID, nil, (WindowPtr)-1L );

    the_data = (WindowDataHandle)NewHandleClear(sizeof(WindowData ));
    (**the_data).the_text = nil;
    (**the_data).file_ref_num = 0;

    SetWRefCon( the_window, (long)the_data );

    return ( the_window );
}
```

Do_New_Picture_Document() initialized the document record PicHandle field to nil. In the OpenTEXTfile program, the document record has a TEHandle field in place of the PicHandle member. Do_New_Text_Document() initializes the TEHandle field to nil.

With a new empty window open, it's time to allow the user to select a text file to open. In preparation for this, a new TEHandle should be created. To do that, set a destination rectangle, a view rectangle, and then call TENew():

```
TEHandle  the_TEtext;
Rect      dest_rect;
Rect      view_rect;

SetPort( the_window );
SetRect( &dest_rect, 20, 20, 460, 260 );
view_rect = dest_rect;

the_TEtext = TENew( &dest_rect, &view_rect );
```

When a program creates an edit record, as TENew() does, two rectangles need to be set. One of them, the destination rectangle, is the area in which the text is drawn. The other, the view rectangle, is the area in which the displayed text will be displayed. While the boundaries of these two rectangles are often the same, Figure 7.17 shows that they don't have to be.

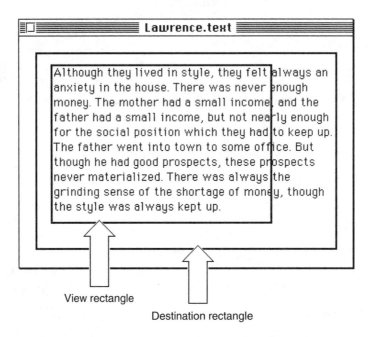

Although they lived in style, they felt always an anxiety in the house. There was never enough money. The mother had a small income, and the father had a small income, but not nearly enough for the social position which they had to keep up. The father went into town to some office. But though he had good prospects, these prospects never materialized. There was always the grinding sense of the shortage of money, though the style was always kept up.

View rectangle

Destination rectangle

FIGURE 7.17 AN EXAMPLE OF A VIEW RECTANGLE AND A DESTINATION RECTANGLE THAT AREN'T THE SAME.

If the view rectangle is set smaller than the destination rectangle, as shown in Figure 7.17, the text outside of the view rectangle will not be displayed. Figure 7.18 shows how the Lawrence.text window would look using the rectangles shown in Figure 7.17.

After creating the new text edit record and receiving a handle to it, call StandardGetFile() to display the standard Open dialog box. Tell the File Manager to display only text files by setting the SFTypeList to TEXT:

```
SFTypeList        type_list = { 'TEXT', 0, 0, 0 };
StandardFileReply  reply;

StandardGetFile( nil, 1, type_list, &reply );
```

```
┌─────────────────────────────────────────────┐
│ ▦▦ ▦▦▦▦▦▦▦▦▦ Lawrence.text ▦▦▦▦▦▦▦▦▦▦ │
├─────────────────────────────────────────────┤
│                                               │
│    Although they lived in style, they felt    │
│    anxiety in the house. There was never      │
│    money. The mother had a small income       │
│    father had a small income, but not nea     │
│    for the social position which they had      │
│    The father went into town to some off      │
│    though he had good prospects, these pr     │
│    never materialized. There was always       │
│    grinding sense of the shortage of mone     │
│    the style was always kept up.              │
│                                               │
│                                               │
│                                               │
└─────────────────────────────────────────────┘
```

FIGURE 7.18 THE DISPLAYED TEXT, USING THE RECTANGLES IN FIGURE 7.17.

As you did when opening a PICT file, call FSpOpenDF() to open the TEXT file's data fork, then call GetEOF() to determine the length of the file. A call to SetFPos() sets the file mark to the start of the file, ready for reading. GetEOF() and SetFPos() are the same Toolbox routines used when working with a PICT file. Here, the only difference is that the last parameter to SetFPos() should be 0, not 512—there's no 512-byte header to skip in a text file as there is in a PICT file.

```
short   text_ref_num;
long    file_length;

FSpOpenDF( &reply.sfFile, fsRdPerm, &text_ref_num );


GetEOF( text_ref_num, &file_length );
SetFPos( text_ref_num, fsFromStart, 0 );
```

A call to FSRead() will read in the text from the text file and store it in a buffer. Declare a generic pointer variable to serve as the buffer, then allocate memory for the buffer using a call to NewPtr(). Then read in the text with a call to FSRead().

```
Ptr   text_buffer;

text_buffer = NewPtr( file_length );

FSRead( text_ref_num, &file_length, text_buffer );
```

To move the text from the buffer to the TEHandle variable the_TEtext, call TESetText(). This Toolbox function copies text that is in a buffer and stores it in the text edit record referenced by a TEHandle. The first parameter to TESetText() is a pointer to the buffer, and the third parameter is the TEHandle. The second parameter is the number of bytes to copy.

```
HLock( (Handle)the_TEtext );
   TESetText( text_buffer, file_length, the_TEtext );
HUnlock( (Handle)the_TEtext );
```

The OpenTEXTfile program wraps the above code into a routine named Load_TEtext_From_TEXT_Doc(). After creating a new, empty document, Load_TEtext_From_TEXT_Doc() is called to open a TEXT file, read in the text it contains, and return a handle to that text to main(). Here's a snippet that is a part of OpenTEXTfile's main() function:

```
WindowPtr   the_window;
TEHandle    the_TEtext;

the_window = Do_New_Text_Document();

the_TEtext = Load_TEtext_From_TEXT_Doc( the_window );
```

Here's a look at the complete Load_TEtext_From_TEXT_Doc() routine:

```
TEHandle  Load_TEtext_From_TEXT_Doc( WindowPtr the_window )
{
    SFTypeList          type_list = { 'TEXT', 0, 0, 0 };
    StandardFileReply   reply;
    short               text_ref_num;
    long                file_length;
    Ptr                 text_buffer;
```

```
TEHandle            the_TEtext;
Rect                dest_rect;
Rect                view_rect;

SetPort( the_window );
SetRect( &dest_rect, 20, 20, 460, 260 );
view_rect = dest_rect;

the_TEtext = TENew( &dest_rect, &view_rect );

StandardGetFile( nil, 1, type_list, &reply );

if ( reply.sfGood == false )
   ExitToShell();

SetWTitle( the_window, reply.sfFile.name );

FSpOpenDF( &reply.sfFile, fsRdPerm, &text_ref_num );

GetEOF( text_ref_num, &file_length );
SetFPos( text_ref_num, fsFromStart, 0 );

text_buffer = NewPtr( file_length );

FSRead( text_ref_num, &file_length, text_buffer );

HLock( (Handle)the_TEtext );
   TESetText( text_buffer, file_length, the_TEtext );
HUnlock( (Handle)the_TEtext );

return ( the_TEtext );
}
```

At this point, OpenTEXTfile has a window open and a TEHandle that references the text from a file, but the two aren't associated with one another. A call to Add_Text_Data_To_Document() takes care of that. This function is almost identical to the Add_Picture_Data_To_Document() routine that you saw in the OpenPICTfile program. OpenTEXTfile needs to associate

```
void  Add_Text_Data_To_Document( WindowPtr the_window,
                                 TEHandle  the_TEtext )
{
   WindowDataHandle  the_data;
   long              wind_ref_con;
```

```
   wind_ref_con = GetWRefCon( the_window );

   the_data = (WindowDataHandle)wind_ref_con;

   (**the_data).the_text = the_TEtext;
}
```

To update a window that has text in it, use the Toolbox routine
TEUpdate(). TEUpdate() needs the portRect of the window that
needs updating. You can dereference a WindowPtr to get its port rectangle, then use the & operator on the portRect—TEUpdate() requires
a pointer. The second parameter to TEUpdate() should be a text edit
handle to the text that is to be drawn.

```
WindowPtr   the_window
TEHandle    the_TEtext;

TEUpdate( &(*the_window).portRect, the_TEtext );
```

OpenTEXTfile calls the application-defined routine Update_Window()
to redraw the contents of a document window. Like the OpenPICTfile
version of this function, this new version first gets a handle to the window's document record. The document record's TEHandle field holds
the handle to the window's text, so that's the field that's accessed by
Update_Window():

```
void  Update_Window( WindowPtr the_window )
{
   WindowDataHandle   the_data;
   long               wind_ref_con;
   TEHandle           the_TEtext;

   SetPort( the_window );

   wind_ref_con = GetWRefCon( the_window );

   the_data = (WindowDataHandle)wind_ref_con;

   the_TEtext = (**the_data).the_text;

   EraseRect( &(*the_window).portRect );
   TEUpdate( &(*the_window).portRect, the_TEtext );
}
```

The OpenTEXTfile Source Code Listing

OpenTEXTfile works in much the same way as this chapter's OpenPICTfile does. Figure 7.19 shows the `main()` routine for each; you should examine the figure and make a line-by-line comparison to see just how similar the two programs are.

```
void  main( void )
{
    WindowPtr   the_window;
    PicHandle   the_picture;

    Initialize_Toolbox();
    the_window = Do_New_Picture_Document();
    the_picture = Load_Picture_From_PICT_File( the_window );
    Add_Picture_Data_To_Document( the_window, the_picture );
    Size_Picture_Window( the_window );
    Update_Window( the_window );
    while ( !Button() )
        ;
}
```

```
void  main( void )
{
    WindowPtr   the_window;
    TEHandle    the_TEtext;

    Initialize_Toolbox();
    the_window = Do_New_Text_Document();
    the_TEtext = Load_TEtext_From_TEXT_Doc( the_window );
    Add_Text_Data_To_Document( the_window, the_TEtext );
    ShowWindow( the_window );
    Update_Window( the_window );
    while ( !Button() )
        ;
}
```

FIGURE 7.19 THE OPENTEXTFILE PROGRAM RUNS MUCH LIKE THE OPENPICTFILE PROGRAM.

After initializing the Toolbox, OpenTEXTfile calls `Do_New_Text_Document()` to open an empty window and create a document record for that window. A call to `Load_TEtext_From_TEXT_Doc()` displays the standard Open dialog box, opens a TEXT file, reads the file's text to memory, and returns a `TEHandle to main()`. Next, `Add_Text_Data_To_Document()` is called to assign this `TEHandle` to the text handle field of the window's document record. Then, the window (which was opened but not yet displayed) is shown. A call to Update_Window( ) then writes the document's text to the window. The program ends when the mouse button is clicked.

```
//_____
//                                          function prototypes

void        Initialize_Toolbox( void );
TEHandle    Load_TEtext_From_TEXT_Doc( WindowPtr );
WindowPtr   Do_New_Text_Document( void );
void        Add_Text_Data_To_Document( WindowPtr, TEHandle );
void        Update_Window( WindowPtr );

//_____
//                                          #define directives

#define     WIND_ID             128

//_____
//                                          define data structures

typedef  struct
{
   TEHandle  the_text;
   long      file_ref_num;
   FSSpec    file_FSSpec;

} WindowData, *WindowDataPtr, **WindowDataHandle;

//_____
//                                                    main()

void  main( void )
{
   WindowPtr  the_window;
   TEHandle   the_TEtext;

   Initialize_Toolbox();

   the_window = Do_New_Text_Document();

   the_TEtext = Load_TEtext_From_TEXT_Doc( the_window );

   Add_Text_Data_To_Document( the_window, the_TEtext );

   ShowWindow( the_window );

   Update_Window( the_window );
```

```
    while ( !Button() )
        ;
}

//_____
//                  create a new text edit handle, add test text

TEHandle   Load_TEtext_From_TEXT_Doc( WindowPtr the_window )
{
    SFTypeList          type_list = { 'TEXT', 0, 0, 0 };
    StandardFileReply   reply;
    short               text_ref_num;
    long                file_length;
    Ptr                 text_buffer;
    TEHandle            the_TEtext;
    Rect                dest_rect;
    Rect                view_rect;

    SetPort( the_window );
    SetRect( &dest_rect, 20, 20, 460, 260 );
    view_rect = dest_rect;

    the_TEtext = TENew( &dest_rect, &view_rect );

    StandardGetFile( nil, 1, type_list, &reply );

    if ( reply.sfGood == false )
        ExitToShell();

    SetWTitle( the_window, reply.sfFile.name );

    FSpOpenDF( &reply.sfFile, fsRdPerm, &text_ref_num );

    GetEOF( text_ref_num, &file_length );
    SetFPos( text_ref_num, fsFromStart, 0 );

    text_buffer = NewPtr( file_length );

    FSRead( text_ref_num, &file_length, text_buffer );

    HLock( (Handle)the_TEtext );
        TESetText( text_buffer, file_length, the_TEtext );
    HUnlock( (Handle)the_TEtext );

    return ( the_TEtext );
}
```

```
//_____
//                                     create a new, empty file

WindowPtr  Do_New_Text_Document( void )
{
   WindowPtr         the_window;
   WindowDataHandle  the_data;

   the_window = GetNewWindow( WIND_ID, nil, (WindowPtr)-1L );

   the_data = (WindowDataHandle)NewHandleClear(sizeof(WindowData ));
   (**the_data).the_text = nil;
   (**the_data).file_ref_num = 0;

   SetWRefCon( the_window, (long)the_data );

   return ( the_window );
}

//_____
//                                    fill file data for one window

void  Add_Text_Data_To_Document( WindowPtr the_window,
                                 TEHandle  the_TEtext )
{
   WindowDataHandle  the_data;
   long              wind_ref_con;

   wind_ref_con = GetWRefCon( the_window );

   the_data = (WindowDataHandle)wind_ref_con;

   (**the_data).the_text = the_TEtext;
}

//_____
//                                        update one window

void  Update_Window( WindowPtr the_window )
{
   WindowDataHandle  the_data;
   long              wind_ref_con;
   TEHandle          the_TEtext;

   SetPort( the_window );

   wind_ref_con = GetWRefCon( the_window );
```

```
the_data = (WindowDataHandle)wind_ref_con;

the_TEtext = (**the_data).the_text;

EraseRect( &(*the_window).portRect );
TEUpdate( &(*the_window).portRect, the_TEtext );
}
```

SAVING A DOCUMENT TO A TEXT FILE

If you understood this chapter's SavePICTfile program, you're a good ways into understanding SaveTEXTfile. SavePICTfile opened a new window, added a picture to it, and then displayed the standard Save dialog box so that the user could save the document to a PICT file. SaveTEXTfile follows a similar course—it opens a new window, adds a little text to the window, then displays the same Save dialog box (see Figure 7.20) to let the user save the document to a TEXT file.

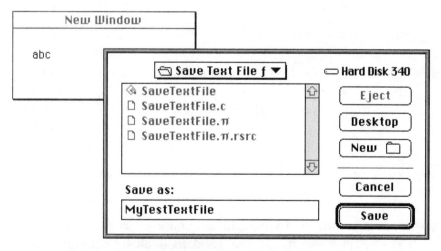

**FIGURE 7.20 THE STANDARD SAVE DIALOG BOX DISPLAYED
BY THE SAVETEXTFILE PROGRAM.**

After running SaveTEXTfile, a new TEXT file will be in the Save Text File ƒ folder. You can open it with any text editor, including TeachText. When you do, you'll see a document with the string "abc" in it.

SaveTEXTfile needs just a single WIND as its only resource. If your application supports text windows with scroll bars, you'll want to add those CNTL resources as well.

Adding Text to a Document

Before saving a document as a text file, the document of course needs to have text in it. SaveTEXTfile creates a new text edit record and then adds some test characters to the record. This snippet, which is identical to code found in OpenTEXTfile, allocates memory for a new text edit record and returns a TEHandle to the program:

```
TEHandle    the_TEtext;
Rect        dest_rect;
Rect        view_rect;

SetPort( the_window );
SetRect( &dest_rect, 20, 20, 100, 50 );
view_rect = dest_rect;

the_TEtext = TENew( &dest_rect, &view_rect );
```

OpenTEXTfile uses the Toolbox routine TEKey() to add three characters to the text edit record. The first parameter to TEKey() is the character to add to the record, and the second parameter is a TEHandle to that record:

```
TEKey( 'a', the_TEtext );
TEKey( 'b', the_TEtext );
TEKey( 'c', the_TEtext );
```

If your program supports user-entered text, it will look for keyDown **events and respond to each by calling** TEKey(). **See** *Inside Macintosh: Text* **for a description of how to write** NOTE **a routine that can be used in a text editor.**

SaveTEXTfile uses a routine named Create_New_TEtext() to create the text edit record and add the characters to it. When complete, Create_New_TEtext() returns the TEHandle to the calling routine.

```
TEHandle  Create_New_TEtext( WindowPtr the_window )
{
   TEHandle  the_TEtext;
   Rect      dest_rect;
   Rect      view_rect;

   SetPort( the_window );
   SetRect( &dest_rect, 20, 20, 100, 50 );
   view_rect = dest_rect;

   the_TEtext = TENew( &dest_rect, &view_rect );

   TEKey( 'a', the_TEtext );
   TEKey( 'b', the_TEtext );
   TEKey( 'c', the_TEtext );

   return ( the_TEtext );
}
```

After opening a new, empty window, SaveTEXTfile's main() routine calls
Create_New_TEtext() to create the new text edit record. Then a call
to Add_Text_Data_To_Document() sets the TEHandle field of the
window's document record is set to this text edit record. The Update_
Window() function then draws the text to the window. The source code
for both Add_Text_Data_To_Document() and Update_Window()
are identical to the versions of these functions found in the OpenTEXTfile
example. Here's the snippet from main() that handles these chores:

```
WindowPtr  the_window;
TEHandle   the_TEtext;

the_window = Do_New_Text_Document();
ShowWindow( the_window );

the_TEtext = Create_New_TEtext( the_window );

Add_Text_Data_To_Document( the_window, the_TEtext );

Update_Window( the_window );
```

Saving a TEXT Document with "Save As"

Earlier in this chapter, when discussing the saving of a document as a
PICT file, the Handle_Save_As_Choice() routine was developed.

There, I said that the function would be written in such a way that only minimal changes would have to be made to it in order to save a document to a file type other than PICT. Here you'll see that this is indeed the case.

`Handle_Save_As_Choice()` displays the standard Save dialog box to let the user name the TEXT file. Then, a handle to the document's data is obtained so that the file reference number can be saved to it. From the SavePICTfile example, you've already seen all of the code necessary to do this:

```
WindowPtr            the_window;
long                 the_ref_con;
WindowDataHandle     the_data;
StandardFileReply    the_reply;

StandardPutFile( "\pSave as:", "\pUntitled", &the_reply );

if ( the_reply.sfGood == false )
   return;

the_window = FrontWindow();
the_ref_con = GetWRefCon( the_window );
the_data = (WindowDataHandle)the_ref_con;
```

Next, the new file is created with a call to `FSpCreate()`. Here the creator may differ from SavePICTfile and the file type will be TEXT instead of PICT.

```
FSpCreate( &the_reply.sfFile, 'svtf', 'TEXT', smSystemScript );
```

NOTE Notice that I say that the creator *may* differ. Remember, an application's creator is the 4-character name that differentiates the application from other programs and is set in your development environment. If your application creates files, it should give them the same creator type as the application so that the Finder will know that these files "belong" to your program. If your program saves both PICT files and TEXT files, then the calls to `FSpCreate()` will have the same creator (to match the application creator), but different file type names—one will be PICT, the other TEXT.

After saving the file system specification, opening the file's data fork, and then saving the file reference number, Handle_Save_As_Choice() calls an application-defined routine that does the actual writing of the window's contents to the file. The following is the SaveTEXTfile version of Handle_Save_As_Choice(). The differences from the previous version (found in SavePICTfile) have been marked in bold type.

```
void  Handle_Save_As_Choice( void )
{
    WindowPtr           the_window;
    long                the_ref_con;
    WindowDataHandle    the_data;
    StandardFileReply   the_reply;
    short               ref_num;

    StandardPutFile( "\pSave as:", "\pUntitled", &the_reply );

    if ( the_reply.sfGood == false )
        return;

    the_window = FrontWindow();
    the_ref_con = GetWRefCon( the_window );
    the_data = (WindowDataHandle)the_ref_con;

    SetWTitle( the_window, the_reply.sfFile.name );

    if ( the_reply.sfReplacing == false )
        FSpCreate( &the_reply.sfFile, 'svtf', 'TEXT',
                smSystemScript );

    (**the_data).file_FSSpec = the_reply.sfFile;

    if ( (**the_data).file_ref_num != 0 )
        FSClose( (**the_data).file_ref_num );

    FSpOpenDF( &(**the_data).file_FSSpec, fsRdWrPerm, &ref_num );

    (**the_data).file_ref_num = ref_num;

    Write_Text_Data_To_File( the_window );
}
```

In SavePICTfile, the routine that wrote the data to disk was Write_ Picture_ Data_To_File(). Here, the function is Write_Text_

Data_To_File(). While these two routines differ, many of the Toolbox functions they use are the same.

Write_Text_Data_To_File() begins by getting a handle to the document record of the window that is to be saved to a file. The document record holds the window's text in a TEHandle, and it's this text that is to be saved.

```
WindowDataHandle   the_data;
long               wind_ref_con;
short              ref_num;
TEHandle           TE_handle;

wind_ref_con = GetWRefCon( the_window );

the_data = (WindowDataHandle)wind_ref_con;

ref_num = (**the_data).file_ref_num;

TE_handle = (**the_data).the_text;
```

A TEHandle is a handle to a TERec—a structure that has 30 fields. The TERec, or text edit record, contains all of the information about a block of text. You've already altered the values of two of these fields once you've used the TENew() routine—it sets the destRect (destination rectangle) and viewRect (view rectangle) fields for the text edit record. The hText field is a generic handle to the actual text that can be edited. This is the text that will be written to the text file. The hText handle will also be used as the buffer in a call to FSWrite().

```
Handle  text_buffer;

text_buffer = (**TE_handle).hText;
```

The FSWrite() function needs to know the number of bytes of information to write. The teLength field of the TERec holds this value:

```
long  num_bytes;

num_bytes = (**TE_handle).teLength;
```

Now, it's time for the write. Set the file mark to the start of the file and write the text:

```
SetFPos( ref_num , fsFromStart, 0 );

FSWrite( ref_num , &num_bytes, (*text_buffer) );
```

Finally, end by calling SetEOF() to resize the file to the number of bytes written, GetVRefNum() to determine the volume that holds the file, and FlushVol() to flush the volume:

```
short  vol_ref_num;

SetEOF( ref_num , num_bytes );
GetVRefNum( ref_num , &vol_ref_num );
FlushVol( nil, vol_ref_num );
```

Here's a look at the entire Write_Text_Data_To_File() function:

```
void  Write_Text_Data_To_File( WindowPtr the_window )
{
   WindowDataHandle  the_data;
   long              wind_ref_con;
   short             ref_num;
   long              num_bytes;
   TEHandle          TE_handle;
   Handle            text_buffer;
   short             vol_ref_num;

   wind_ref_con = GetWRefCon( the_window );

   the_data = (WindowDataHandle)wind_ref_con;

   ref_num = (**the_data).file_ref_num;

   TE_handle = (**the_data).the_text;
   text_buffer = (**TE_handle).hText;
   num_bytes = (**TE_handle).teLength;

   SetFPos( ref_num, fsFromStart, 0 );

   FSWrite( ref_num, &num_bytes, (*text_buffer) );
```

```
        SetEOF( ref_num, num_bytes );
        GetVRefNum( ref_num, &vol_ref_num );
        FlushVol( nil, vol_ref_num );
}
```

The SaveTEXTfile Source Code Listing

SaveTEXTfile runs much as SavePICTfile. After opening a new, empty window and adding text to it, the program gives the user the opportunity to
provide a name for the file that the document will be saved as. A new file is
then created and saved to disk by the call to Do_Save_As_Choice().
When the user clicks the mouse button, Do_Save_Choice() is called to
again save the file—this time without use of the standard Save dialog box.
After one more mouse click, the program terminates.

```
//_____
//                                           function prototypes

void        Initialize_Toolbox( void );
WindowPtr   Do_New_Text_Document( void );
TEHandle    Create_New_TEtext( WindowPtr );
void        Add_Text_Data_To_Document( WindowPtr, TEHandle );
void        Update_Window( WindowPtr );
void        Handle_Save_As_Choice( void );
void        Handle_Save_Choice( void );
void        Write_Text_Data_To_File( WindowPtr );

//_____
//                                           #define directives

#define     WIND_ID           128

//_____
//                                           define data structures

typedef  struct
{
    TEHandle    the_text;
    long        file_ref_num;
    FSSpec      file_FSSpec;

} WindowData, *WindowDataPtr, **WindowDataHandle;
```

```
//_____
//                                                      main()

void  main( void )
{
   WindowPtr   the_window;
   TEHandle    the_TEtext;

   Initialize_Toolbox();

   the_window = Do_New_Text_Document();
   ShowWindow( the_window );

   the_TEtext = Create_New_TEtext( the_window );

   Add_Text_Data_To_Document( the_window, the_TEtext );

   Update_Window( the_window );

   Handle_Save_As_Choice();

   Update_Window( the_window );

   while ( !Button() )
      ;

   Handle_Save_Choice();

   while ( !Button() )
      ;
}

//_____
//                create a new text edit handle, add test text

TEHandle  Create_New_TEtext( WindowPtr the_window )
{
   TEHandle    the_TEtext;
   Rect        dest_rect;
   Rect        view_rect;

   SetPort( the_window );
   SetRect( &dest_rect, 20, 20, 100, 50 );
   view_rect = dest_rect;

   the_TEtext = TENew( &dest_rect, &view_rect );
```

```
   TEKey( 'a', the_TEtext );
   TEKey( 'b', the_TEtext );
   TEKey( 'c', the_TEtext );

   return ( the_TEtext );
}

//_____
//                                                  save file

void  Handle_Save_Choice( void )
{
   WindowPtr         the_window;
   long              the_ref_con;
   WindowDataHandle  the_data;

   the_window = FrontWindow();
   the_ref_con = GetWRefCon( the_window );
   the_data = (WindowDataHandle)the_ref_con;

   if ( (**the_data).file_ref_num != 0 )
      Write_Text_Data_To_File( the_window );
   else
      Handle_Save_As_Choice();
}

//_____
//              display the "Save As" dialog box, save file

void  Handle_Save_As_Choice( void )
{
   WindowPtr         the_window;
   long              the_ref_con;
   WindowDataHandle  the_data;
   StandardFileReply the_reply;
   short             ref_num;

   StandardPutFile( "\pSave as:", "\pUntitled", &the_reply );

   if ( the_reply.sfGood == false )
      return;

   the_window = FrontWindow();
   the_ref_con = GetWRefCon( the_window );
   the_data = (WindowDataHandle)the_ref_con;

   SetWTitle( the_window, the_reply.sfFile.name );
```

```
   if ( the_reply.sfReplacing == false )
      FSpCreate( &the_reply.sfFile, 'svtf', 'TEXT',
                 smSystemScript );

   (**the_data).file_FSSpec = the_reply.sfFile;

   if ( (**the_data).file_ref_num != 0 )
      FSClose( (**the_data).file_ref_num );

   FSpOpenDF( &(**the_data).file_FSSpec, fsRdWrPerm, &ref_num );

   (**the_data).file_ref_num = ref_num;

   Write_Text_Data_To_File( the_window );
}

//_____
//                              write 'TEXT' data to an open file

void  Write_Text_Data_To_File( WindowPtr the_window )
{
   WindowDataHandle   the_data;
   long               wind_ref_con;
   short              ref_num;
   long               num_bytes;
   TEHandle           TE_handle;
   Handle             text_buffer;
   short              vol_ref_num;

   wind_ref_con = GetWRefCon( the_window );

   the_data = (WindowDataHandle)wind_ref_con;

   ref_num = (**the_data).file_ref_num;

   TE_handle = (**the_data).the_text;
   text_buffer = (**TE_handle).hText;
   num_bytes = (**TE_handle).teLength;

   SetFPos( ref_num , fsFromStart, 0 );

   FSWrite( ref_num , &num_bytes, (*text_buffer) );

   SetEOF( ref_num , num_bytes );
   GetVRefNum( ref_num , &vol_ref_num );
   FlushVol( nil, vol_ref_num );
}
```

```
//_____
//                                    create a new, empty file

WindowPtr  Do_New_Text_Document( void )
{
   WindowPtr         the_window;
   WindowDataHandle  the_data;

   the_window = GetNewWindow( WIND_ID, nil, (WindowPtr)-1L );

   the_data = (WindowDataHandle)NewHandleClear(sizeof(WindowData ));
   (**the_data).the_text = nil;
   (**the_data).file_ref_num = 0;

   SetWRefCon( the_window, (long)the_data );

   return ( the_window );
}


//_____
//                                    fill file data for one window

void  Add_Text_Data_To_Document( WindowPtr the_window,
                                 TEHandle  the_TEtext )
{
   WindowDataHandle  the_data;
   long              wind_ref_con;

   wind_ref_con = GetWRefCon( the_window );

   the_data = (WindowDataHandle)wind_ref_con;

   (**the_data).the_text = the_TEtext;

}


//_____
//                                    update one window

void  Update_Window( WindowPtr the_window )
{
   WindowDataHandle  the_data;
   long              wind_ref_con;
   TEHandle          TE_handle;

   SetPort( the_window );

   wind_ref_con = GetWRefCon( the_window );
```

434

```
    the_data = (WindowDataHandle)wind_ref_con;

    TE_handle = (**the_data).the_text;

    EraseRect( &(*the_window).portRect );
    TEUpdate( &(*the_window).portRect, TE_handle );
}
```

CHAPTER SUMMARY

In an application, any window can be considered a document. If you define a structure that serves as a document record, you can keep track of individual documents so that your program can treat each individually. The primary things you'll want to keep track of in a document record are the contents of the document, such as a handle to the picture or text it holds, and information necessary to save the document as a file. This file information includes a file system specification, or FSSpec, for the file so that your application can find the file by its file path. The other piece of file-related information to keep in the document record is a file reference number so that the application can keep track of which (of possibly several) open file it should work with.

To open an existing file, your program can use the StandardGetFile() function. This routine displays the standard Open dialog box that lets the user select a file from a list of files. Once selected, a file can be opened and its contents read by using File Manager routines such as FSRead().

To save a document as a file, use the Toolbox routine StandardPut File(). This function displays the standard Save dialog box that allows the user to provide a name for the file that will hold the contents of a document. After that, File Manager routines like FSWrite() should be used to write the document contents to the disk file.

Chapter

8

PRINTING

In the previous chapter, you saw how to use files to provide users of your Macintosh applications with the means to save program output. In this chapter, you'll see how to add a second data-saving feature to your Mac applications. By adding printing capabilities, both text and graphics can be sent to any printer that's attached to the user's computer.

In this chapter, you'll see how to display the two standard printing dialog boxes found in many Mac programs. The Printing Style dialog box allows the user to select page preferences such as page orientation. The Printing Job dialog box lets the user specify the print quality and the page range. Both of these dialog boxes can be brought to the screen using Printing Manager routines that work for all printers that come with a Macintosh printer driver.

Here, you'll see how to give your programs the power to print a picture stored in a resource file or a picture that is in its own PICT file. You'll also see how text that exists as static text in an application's resource fork can be brought into a program as a string and sent to the printer.

ABOUT PRINTING

When an application includes the ability to print files, it relies on the *Printing Manager.* Just like the other system software managers, you'll use the Printing Manager functions to standardize the way your application looks and works.

The Printer Resource File

Like other Toolbox managers, the Printing Manager is a collection of system software routines. Unlike the other managers, the code that makes up each routine *isn't* found in ROM or in the System File. Rather, the Toolbox printing routines are nothing more than empty shells. When your application makes a call to a Toolbox printing function, the program is directed to code that exists in a *printer resource file.*

When an application calls a routine from a manager *other* than the Printing Manager, the program jumps to Toolbox code in ROM or in the System File. The code that makes up that one routine—whatever routine it is—is then carried out. If the call is to, say, Line(100, 0), QuickDraw draws a line 100 pixels long to the current port. This is true regardless of what kind of monitor is hooked up to the Macintosh. For printers, this "one generic code works on all" principle doesn't apply. There are countless third-party printers that can be hooked up to a Macintosh, and no uniform standard of how Toolbox calls should be handled by a printer. So Apple leaves it up to the manufacturer of each printer to supply the code that makes the printing functions work.

Every printer that works with a Macintosh comes supplied with a printer resource file. This file, which is placed in the Extensions folder in the System Folder, holds the code that actually carries out Printing Manager routines. The file, which has a name that often includes the name of the printer, must be present in order for the printer to function. Figure 8.1 shows several icons in an Extension folder. The four icons in the top row are each printer resource files.

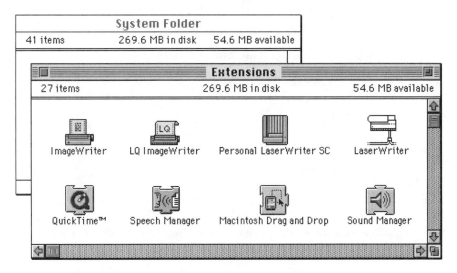

FIGURE 8.1 EXTENSIONS FOLDER ICONS, INCLUDING FOUR PRINTER RESOURCE FILE ICONS.

As you can see from Figure 8-1, the Extensions folder can hold more than one printer resource file. Since each type of printer has its own printer resource file, and since a Macintosh can have more than one printer connected to it, a Mac can have more than one printer resource file. The printer (and thus the printer resource file) that a Macintosh uses is governed by the Chooser program in the Apple menu.

The printer resource file holds several resource types. Resources of type PDEF are printer definition functions—they hold the compiled code that executes when a Printing Manager function is called. Figure 8.2 shows some of the PDEF resources found in a printer resource file named DW 3.1 (Serial). This file comes bundled with the Hewlett Packard DeskWriter printers.

What happens when a Mac application makes a call to a Printing Manager routine? The call is routed to the printer resource file. There, the code that makes up one of the many PDEF resources is loaded and executed. Figure 8.3 illustrates this sequence of events.

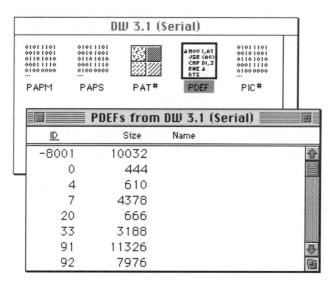

FIGURE 8.2 A PRINTER RESOURCE FILE CONTAINS NUMEROUS PDEF RESOURCES.

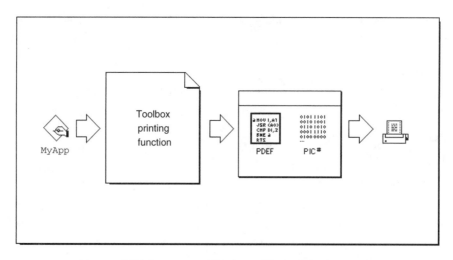

FIGURE 8.3 A CALL TO A PRINTING MANAGER FUNCTION IS CARRIED OUT BY CODE IN A PDEF RESOURCE.

By having each printer manufacturer support all the same Printing Manager routines, the burden of worrying about which printer is connected to a user's system is lifted from the Macintosh software developer. When you write an application that calls Printing Manager routines, you won't have to consider the type of printer that any one user might have. Instead, just make the function call. It will be up to the printer resource file to handle that function call as is appropriate for that printer.

As an example of how the programmer is shielded from printer specifics, consider the Printing Manager function that displays the familiar *Style dialog box* that is displayed when a user selects the **Page Setup** menu item found in the File menu of many programs. The Printing Manager function `PrStlDialog()` is responsible for posting this dialog box—an example of which is shown in Figure 8.4. This figure shows the dialog box displayed by the printer resource file for one of the Hewlett Packard DeskWriter printers. Though the Style dialog box looks similar for different printers, it is not identical. That's because the code that displays the dialog box, and the DITL resource that defines its look, is a part of each printer resource file, not a part of the Macintosh ROM or System File. Figure 8.5 shows the DITL resource for the Style dialog box displayed for a Hewlett Packard DeskWriter printer. Notice that this DITL is present in the printer resource file for the HP printer.

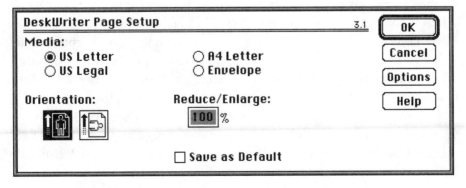

FIGURE 8.4 A TYPICAL PRINTING STYLE DIALOG BOX.

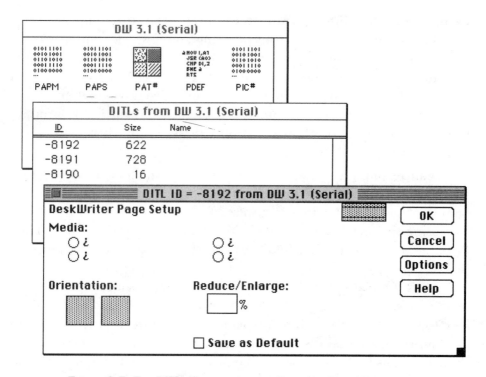

FIGURE 8.5 THE DITL THAT DEFINES THE PRINTING STYLE DIALOG BOX
IS FOUND IN THE PRINTING RESOURCE FILE.

The Printer Driver Resource

When a Toolbox printing routine like `PrStlDialog()` is called, it's the PDEF code in the printer resource file that actually gets executed. Many printing routines, like `PrStlDialog()`, don't perform any printing. When it does come time to do the actual printing, it's another printer resource file resource that does the low-level work of translating QuickDraw routines to instructions recognized by a printer. It's a driver resource that handles this task of communicating with the printer. Each printer resource file has a DRVR resource with an ID of -8192, usually named .XPrint (see Figure 8.6).

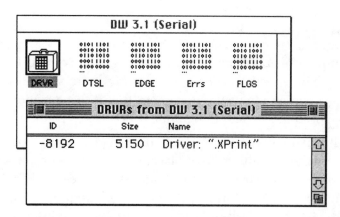

FIGURE 8.6 THE .XPRINT DRVR RESOURCE COMMUNICATES WITH THE PRINTER.

PRINTING MANAGER FUNCTIONS

Like all of the Toolbox managers, the Printing Manager consists of a wealth of functions. But to get started with printing, you'll need to use only a handful of them. In this section, you'll see the source code for a program named MinimalPrint. When executed, this application prints a string of text and a diagonal line (see Figure 8.7). To accomplish this, MinimalPrint uses the nine Printing Manager routines that you'll find in every Mac program that has the ability to print.

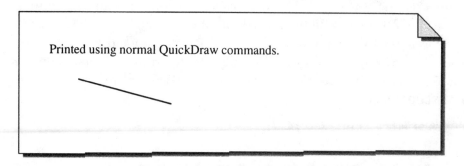

FIGURE 8.7 THE OUTPUT FROM THE MINIMALPRINT PROGRAM—A PRINTED PAGE.

The Print Record

Before printing, your application must create a print record. This record holds information specific to the printer being used, such as its resolution, and information about the document that is to be printed, such as scaling, page orientation, and the number of copies to print.

In C, the print record is represented by a `struct` of the type `TPrint`. Before any printing takes place, your application must allocate memory for a `TPrint` structure and obtain a handle—a `THPrint` handle—to that memory. You can make a call to the Memory Manager routine `NewHandle()` or `NewHandleClear()` to accomplish this. Include the size of a print record as the parameter and cast the returned generic pointer to a `THPrint` handle:

```
THPrint  Print_Record;

Print_Record = (THPrint)NewHandleClear( sizeof( TPrint ) );
```

The _T_ in THPrint stands for _type_ and the _H_ stands for _handle_. You'll see this notation used throughout the functions of the Printing Manager. This naming convention (called Hungarian notation) was used by the Apple programmers initially involved in writing the Printing Manager. Elsewhere in this chapter, you'll see _P_ for _pointer_ and _Pr_ for _printer_.

After creating a new print record, call the Printing Manager routine `PrintDefault()` to fill the record with default values. These values will serve as initial values until the user selects **Page Setup** and **Print** from the File menu of your application. The values entered in the corresponding dialog boxes will overwrite some or all of the values supplied by `PrintDefault()`:

```
PrintDefault( Print_Record );
```

The MinimalPrint Source Code Listing

Normally, you'll find the source code listing for an example program given at the end of the section. Because MinimalPrint is such a short listing, I'll provide the source code right up front. After the listing, I'll give a thorough walk-through.

Aside from `main()`, there's only one application-defined function—the same `Initialize_Toolbox()` routine you're accustomed to seeing. Since it's just a "copy and paste" routine, I've omitted its listing here.

```
#include <Printing.h>

void  main( void )
{
   THPrint     Print_Record;
   TPPrPort    printer_port;
   TPrStatus   printer_status;

   Initialize_Toolbox();

   Print_Record = (THPrint)NewHandleClear( sizeof( TPrint ) );

   PrOpen();

   PrintDefault( Print_Record );

   PrStlDialog( Print_Record );

   PrJobDialog( Print_Record );

   printer_port = PrOpenDoc( Print_Record, nil, nil );

   PrOpenPage( printer_port, nil );
      TextFont( times );
      TextSize( 14 );
      MoveTo( 10, 20 );
      DrawString( "\pPrinted using normal QuickDraw commands." );
      MoveTo( 50, 50 );
      Line( 100, 30 );
   PrClosePage( printer_port );

   PrCloseDoc( printer_port );

   PrClose();
}
```

The Basic Printing Manager Functions

Now that you know that the code used to execute Printing Manager functions resides in a resource file, you shouldn't be surprised to learn that this resource file must be opened before its code can be accessed. The Printing Manager function `PrOpen()` prepares the current printer resource file for use. The current printer is whichever printer was last selected in the Chooser program found in the Apple menu. Preparation consists of opening both the Printing Manager and the printer resource file for the current printer. When finished with the resource file, a call to `PrClose()` closes the Printing Manager and the printer resource file.

Your application *must* balance a call to `PrOpen()` **with a call to** `PrClose().`

T I P

`PrOpenDoc()` initializes a *printing graphics port*. This graphics port isn't associated with any window—it's associated with the printer. When a window's graphics port is current (by way of a call to `SetPort()`), drawing takes place on the screen. When a printing graphics port is current (by way of a call to `PrOpenDoc()`), drawing operations are routed to the printer. Once a printing graphics port is current, all QuickDraw commands are sent to the printer.

When passed a handle to a print record, `PrOpenDoc()` allocates a new printing graphics port and returns a `TPPrPort` to the application. The `TPPrPort` is a pointer to a printing graphics port. `PrOpenDoc()` requires a second and third parameter, each of which can normally be set to `nil`. The second parameter can be used when an application wants to pass in a pointer to an existing printing graphics port, and the third parameter can be used to allocate a particular area in memory to serve as an input and output buffer.

`PrCloseDoc()` closes a printing graphics port. Make a single call to `PrCloseDoc()` after the last page of a document has been sent to the printer. Pass `PrCloseDoc()` the pointer to the printing graphics port that was returned by `PrOpenDoc()`. The `PrCloseDoc()` call balances the earlier call to `PrOpenDoc()`.

`PrOpenPage()` is used to begin printing a single page of a document. Pass `PrOpenPage()` the pointer to the printing graphics port that was obtained in the `PrOpenDoc()` call. The second parameter is used only for deferred printing—a delayed printing feature that is normally used only on older printers. You can usually set this parameter to `nil`. After a call to `PrOpenPage()` is made, all of the QuickDraw commands necessary to output one page of a document should be made. After that, call `PrClosePage()`.

PrClosePage() signals the end of the current page. Once a call to `PrClosePage()` is made, the Printing Manager will stop accumulating QuickDraw calls. `PrClosePage()` requires a single parameter—the pointer to the printing graphics port that was returned by `PrOpenDoc()`.

You've probably noticed the pairing between "open" and "close" Printing Manager functions. As shown in Figure 8.8, you'll want to balance `PrOpen()`, `PrOpenDoc()`, and `PrOpenPage()` with their closing counterparts.

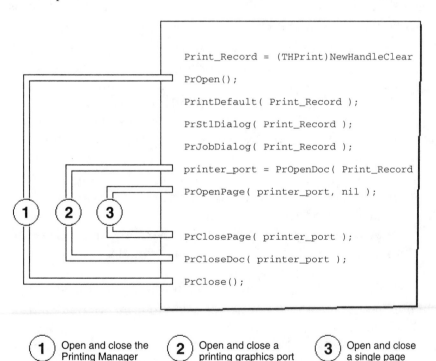

```
Print_Record = (THPrint)NewHandleClear

PrOpen();

PrintDefault( Print_Record );

PrStlDialog( Print_Record );

PrJobDialog( Print_Record );

printer_port = PrOpenDoc( Print_Record

PrOpenPage( printer_port, nil );


PrClosePage( printer_port );

PrCloseDoc( printer_port );

PrClose();
```

(1) Open and close the Printing Manager   (2) Open and close a printing graphics port   (3) Open and close a single page

FIGURE 8.8 EACH PRINTING MANAGER OPEN FUNCTION IS PAIRED WITH A CLOSE ROUTINE.

Besides the open and close calls, the MinimalPrint source code relies on a few other Printing Manager routines. The first is PrDefault(), which you've already seen. PrDefault() initializes the members (such as print resolution) of a TPrint record. The values used in the initialization are dependent on the current printer driver and come from the driver's resource file. PrDefault() requires a single parameter—a handle to a TPrint record.

Before printing, you'll want to give the user the opportunity to specify printing style options. A call to PrStlDialog() displays a Style dialog box that allows the user to do just that. If your application has a **Page Setup** menu item, make a call to PrStlDialog() in response to a user's selection of this menu item. For simplicity, MinimalPrint doesn't include any menus, so the program simply brings this dialog box up near the start of the program. As discussed earlier, the Style dialog box is defined in the resource file of the printer driver, so its exact look is dependent on the printer in use.

The PrStlDialog() function requires a handle to a TPrint record as its one parameter. If the user clicks the style dialog box **OK** button, the values entered in that dialog box (such as page orientation) will be placed in the **TPrint** record. PrStlDialog() will then return a value of true. If the user clicks the **Cancel** button, the TPrint record will be unaffected and the routine will return a value of false.

Your application *must* make a call to PrOpen() before attempting to call any other Printing Manager routines, including PrStlDialog(). If your application is supposed to open the Style dialog box, but doesn't, you probably failed to include a call to PrOpen() in the program.

Displaying the Style dialog box saves document printing information, but not the number of copies or the range of pages to print. To do that, call PrJobDialog(). This routine will display the printing *Job dialog box*. Like the Style dialog box, the Job dialog box is defined in the printer resource file. A call to PrJobDialog() should be made in response to a user's selection of the **Print** menu item in your application.

PrJobDialog() accepts a handle to a `TPrint` record as its only parameter. A mouse click on the dialog box's **OK** button results in the values in the dialog box (such as number of copies to print) being entered into the `TPrint` record. `PrJobDialog()` then returns a value of `true` to the application. A click on the dialog box's **Cancel** button leaves the `TPrint` record untouched and returns a value of `false` to the program.

Again, make sure that a call to `PrOpen()` is present somewhere in your application's source code before calling a Printing Manager routine.

T I P

About half of the code in MinimalPrint is devoted to the open and close routines. Figure 8.9 adds remarks to the remaining lines of code in MinimalPrint.

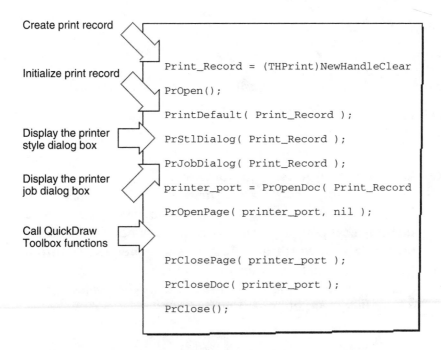

```
Create print record                 Print_Record = (THPrint)NewHandleClear

Initialize print record             PrOpen();

                                    PrintDefault( Print_Record );

Display the printer                 PrStlDialog( Print_Record );
style dialog box

                                    PrJobDialog( Print_Record );

Display the printer                 printer_port = PrOpenDoc( Print_Record
job dialog box
                                    PrOpenPage( printer_port, nil );

Call QuickDraw
Toolbox functions

                                    PrClosePage( printer_port );

                                    PrCloseDoc( printer_port );

                                    PrClose();
```

FIGURE 8.9 THE BASIC PRINTING MANAGER FUNCTIONS INCLUDE CALLS TO INITIALIZE PRINTING AND DISPLAY THE PRINTING DIALOG BOXES.

Running MinimalPrint

When you run MinimalPrint, you'll first see the Style dialog box. Figure 8.10 shows a typical example. You can change the page orientation and, if your printer supports it, set the page reduction or enlargement percentage. After pressing the **OK** button, you'll see the Job dialog box (Figure 8.11 gives an example). Here, you set the print quality. Because MinimalPrint only calls `PrOpenPage()` and `PrClosePage()` one time, only one page will be printed, regardless of any values you enter in the Page Range edit boxes. After pressing the **OK** button, MinimalPrint will print a single page. The contents of the page are defined by the code between the `PrOpenPage()` and `PrClosePage()` calls. Though it isn't necessary, I've indented the code between these calls to add some emphasis to just where the printing code is located.

```
PrOpenPage( printer_port, nil );
   TextFont( times );
   TextSize( 14 );
   MoveTo( 10, 20 );
   DrawString( "\pPrinted using normal QuickDraw commands." );
   MoveTo( 50, 50 );
   Line( 100, 30 );
PrClosePage( printer_port );
```

N O T E Experiment with the code between `PrOpenPage()` and `PrClosePage()`. **Add a few more QuickDraw calls, then compile and run the program. As you do this, keep in mind that a typical printer considers one page to be approximately 560 pixels in width and 720 pixels in height. Entering QuickDraw commands (such as** `MoveTo()` **or** `SetRect()`**) that fall out of this range will result in text or objects that get partially printed—or not printed at all.**

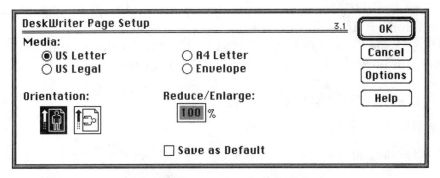

FIGURE 8.10 MINIMALPRINT DISPLAYS THE PRINTING STYLE DIALOG BOX
SIMILAR TO THIS HP DESKWRITER VERSION.

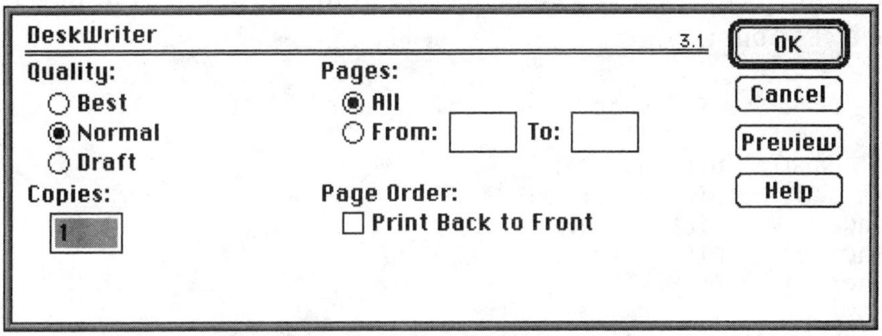

FIGURE 8.11 MINIMALPRINT DISPLAYS A PRINTING JOB DIALOG BOX,
LIKE THIS HP DESKWRITER VERSION.

Printing Pictures

As long as a printing graphics port is current—rather than a "normal" graphics port—QuickDraw calls will be routed to the printer. To print text you can use DrawString(), and to print graphics you can use calls to such routines as Line(), FrameRect(), and FillRect(). To print more sophisticated graphics, you can use a call to DrawPicture() to print any picture that's saved as a PICT resource.

The PrintPICT program listing that appears a few pages ahead is a derivation of MinimalPrint. Instead of a few QuickDraw calls between `PrOpenPage()` and `PrClosePage()`, PrintPICT calls an application-defined routine named `Draw_Stuff_To_Port()`:

```
PrOpenPage( printer_port, nil );

Draw_Stuff_To_Port( pict_ID );

PrClosePage( printer_port );
```

Using the passed-in picture ID, `Draw_Stuff_To_Port()` first gets a handle to a PICT resource. Then the function sets a boundary rectangle to hold the picture and draws the picture to the current port using a call to `DrawPicture()`:

```
void  Draw_Stuff_To_Port( short pict_ID )
{
   PicHandle   pict_handle;
   Rect        pict_rect;
   short       pict_width;
   short       pict_height;
   short       L, R, T, B;

   pict_handle = GetPicture( pict_ID );

   pict_rect = (**pict_handle).picFrame;
   pict_width  = pict_rect.right - pict_rect.left;
   pict_height = pict_rect.bottom - pict_rect.top;

   L = 75;
   R = L + pict_width;
   T = 50;
   B = T + pict_height;
   SetRect( &pict_rect, L, T, R, B );

   DrawPicture( pict_handle, &pict_rect );

   ReleaseResource( (Handle)pict_handle );
}
```

The `picFrame` field holds a rectangle that serves as the boundary of the retrieved PICT. From that rectangle the width and height of the picture are extracted. Using these values, a rectangle can be established such that the picture can be printed to any part of the page. The `Draw_Stuff_To_Port()` function will place the picture 75 pixels in and 50 pixels down on the page. Because the (0, 0) coordinate of a page doesn't appear in the very upper-left corner of a page, the picture will actually be set in and down a little. As shown in Figure 8.12, printers generally leave about a quarter of an inch margin on a page.

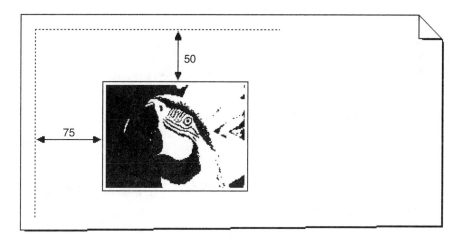

FIGURE 8.12 PRINTERS LEAVE A SMALL MARGIN ON EACH SIDE OF A PRINTED PAGE.

You may have noticed that the `Draw_Stuff_To_Port()` routine doesn't call any Printing Manager functions. That means that this same routine can be used to draw to either

NOTE **a window or a printer. Whichever port is active at the time of the call will receive the output. That means this one routine could be used to update a window and send its contents to a printer. If a call to `Draw_Stuff_To_Port()` was preceded by a call to `SetPort()`, the picture would be drawn to the active window rather than to the printer:**

```
WindowPtr  the_window;

the_window = GetNewWindow( 128, nil, (WindowPtr)-1L );
SetPort( the_window );
Draw_Stuff_To_Port( 128);
```

The PrintPICT includes all of the basic Printing Manager function calls that you saw in the MinimalPrint listing. Only one of these calls differs here—the call to `PrJobDialog()`. This function returns a value—a value that was ignored in MinimalPrint. The returned `Boolean` value signals whether or not the Job dialog box **OK** button was clicked. If it wasn't, then the user canceled printing. The simplistic PrintPICT program handles this case by terminating. If the **OK** button was clicked, a value of `true` will be returned by `PrJobDialog()` and the program will continue:

```
Boolean    do_print;

// Other Printing Manager calls here

do_print = PrJobDialog( Print_Record );

if ( do_print == false )
   ExitToShell() ;
```

If you followed MinimalPrint, the rest of PrintPICT will look very familiar to you. Here's the listing:

```
//_____
//                                                      main()

void  main( void )
{
   THPrint     Print_Record;
   TPPrPort    printer_port;
   TPrStatus   printer_status;
   Boolean     do_print;
   short       pict_ID = 128;

   Initialize_Toolbox();

   Print_Record = (THPrint)NewHandleClear( sizeof( TPrint ) );

   PrOpen();

   PrintDefault( Print_Record );

   PrStlDialog( Print_Record );
```

```
   do_print = PrJobDialog( Print_Record );

   if ( do_print == false )
      ExitToShell() ;

   printer_port = PrOpenDoc( Print_Record, nil, nil );

   PrOpenPage( printer_port, nil );

   Draw_Stuff_To_Port( pict_ID );

   PrClosePage( printer_port );

   PrCloseDoc( printer_port );

   PrClose();
}


//_____
//                      QuickDraw commands to be sent to a port
void  Draw_Stuff_To_Port( short pict_ID )
{
   PicHandle   pict_handle;
   Rect        pict_rect;
   short       pict_width;
   short       pict_height;
   short       L, R, T, B;

   pict_handle = GetPicture( pict_ID );

   pict_rect = (**pict_handle).picFrame;
   pict_width  = pict_rect.right - pict_rect.left;
   pict_height = pict_rect.bottom - pict_rect.top;

   L = 30;
   R = L + pict_width;
   T = 50;
   B = T + pict_height;
   SetRect( &pict_rect, L, T, R, B );

   DrawPicture( pict_handle, &pict_rect );

   ReleaseResource( (Handle)pict_handle );
}
```

Printing a Document

The two printing example programs you've seen so far don't use windows. Instead, words and graphics mysteriously appear on a printed page. To the user, there's no apparent origin of the graphics that get printed. A more realistic use of printing would be for an application to send the contents of a window to the printer; the PrintPICTdoc program does that.

When PrintPICTdoc runs, the user sees the standard Get File dialog box discussed in Chapter 7. And again as in Chapter 7, the dialog box is used here to open a PICT file. Figure 8.13 shows the dialog box with the names of three sample PICT files.

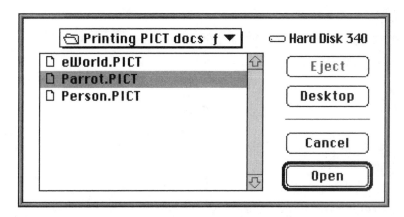

FIGURE 8.13 PrintPICTdoc displays the standard Get File dialog box to allow the user to open a PICT file.

Selecting a file to open brings a window to the screen. It holds the contents of the PICT file. After the window opens, the Style dialog box appears. Clicking its OK button brings up the Printing Job dialog box (see Figure 8.14).

Clicking the **OK** button dismisses the Job dialog box. Then the contents of the window are sent to the printer.

456

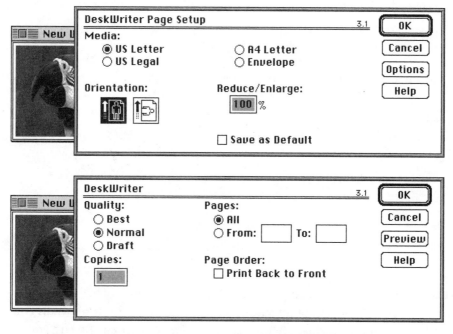

FIGURE 8.14 PRINTPICTDOC DISPLAYS FIRST THE STYLE DIALOG BOX,
THEN THE JOB DIALOG BOX.

N O T E The purpose of PrintPICTdoc is to demonstrate how the contents of a window can be printed. To keep things straightforward, there isn't much of an interface. To see a document printing example that includes a menu and multiple, movable windows, keep reading this chapter!

Walking Through PrintPICTdoc

PrintPICTdoc consists of main() and several short application-defined routines. Here's the listing for main():

```
void  main( void )
{
   WindowPtr  the_window;
```

```
    PicHandle  the_picture;

    Initialize_Toolbox();
    Initialize_Printing();

    the_picture = Load_Picture_From_PICT_Doc();
    Open_Picture_Display_Window( the_picture );

    PrOpen();
    PrStlDialog( Print_Record );
    PrClose();

    the_window = FrontWindow();
    Do_Print_Window( the_window );

    while ( !Button() )
        ;
}
```

`main()` begins by initializing the Toolbox and a print record. Initializing the print record consists of allocating memory for it and setting the record members to default values. A new routine, `Initialize_Printing()`, takes care of this.

```
void  Initialize_Printing( void )
{
    Print_Record = (THPrint)NewHandleClear( sizeof( TPrint ) );
    PrOpen();
    PrintDefault( Print_Record );
    PrClose();
}
```

Notice that `Initialize_Printing()` nests the call to `PrintDefault()` between calls to `PrOpen()` and `PrClose()`. Remember, the printer resource file must be open before a Printing Manager call can be made. In previous examples, `PrOpen()` was called at the start of the program and `PrClose()` was called at the end. While that approach works for both simple and large applications, for the larger application you might want to consider the tactic used here.

When an application launches, its application fork is opened by the system. When PrOpen( ) is called, the printer resource file is opened. At that point, the program has two resource files open. When making certain Toolbox calls, this has to be kept in mind. Most Toolbox functions that use resources search all open resource files and search the current resource file first. If the printer resource file is open, it will be included in the search. Since different resources of the same type can have the same ID (provided they reside in different resource files), your application could end up using the wrong resource. Additionally, a call to Get1Resource( ), which searches only the current resource file, could fail to find a specified resource if the printer resource file is current rather than the application resource fork. If you close the printing resource after using it, you usually won't have to be concerned with which file is current.

With initialization complete, main( ) calls Load_Picture_From_ PICT_Doc( ) to display the standard Get File dialog box. After a PICT file selection is made, the routine loads the picture and returns a handle to it. After that, main( ) passes this PicHandle to a routine named Open_Picture_Display_Window( ):

```
the_picture = Load_Picture_From_PICT_Doc();
Open_Picture_Display_Window( the_picture );
```

Open_Picture_Display_Window( ) uses the picFrame field of the Picture record to get the size of the picture. Then it opens a window, displays the picture that the_picture references, and resizes the window so that it is the same size as the picture. Open_Picture_ Display_Window( ) uses a handy Toolbox routine named SetWindow Pic( ) to draw the picture to the window. When SetWindowPic( ) is passed a pointer to a window and a handle to a picture, it establishes a link between the two. It does this by adding the picture handle to the windowPic field of the WindowRecord that the window pointer points to. Once that is done, updating the window is no longer a concern of the programmer. Instead, the Window Manager will redraw the picture any time the window needs updating.

```
void  Open_Picture_Display_Window( PicHandle the_picture )
{
   Rect        pict_rect;
   short       pict_width;
   short       pict_height;
   WindowPtr   the_window;

   pict_rect = (**the_picture).picFrame;
   pict_width  = pict_rect.right - pict_rect.left;
   pict_height = pict_rect.bottom - pict_rect.top;

   the_window = GetNewWindow( WIND_ID, nil, (WindowPtr)-1L );
   SetWindowPic( the_window, the_picture );
   SetPort( the_window );
   SizeWindow( the_window, pict_width, pict_height, false );
   ShowWindow( the_window );
}
```

The functionality of Load_Picture_From_PICT_Doc() **and** Open_Picture_Display_Window() **could easily have been combined into one routine. That is, a single function** N O T E **could have loaded the picture and then opened a window and displayed that picture. By using two functions, though, things are kept more generic, which is a desirable feature. Now** Open_Picture_Display_Window() **can be used to display any picture, whether that picture is from a PICT document that was opened or from a PICT resource in a resource file.** Open_Picture_Display_Window() **doesn't care where the** PicHandle **it uses comes from. And while PrintPICTdoc doesn't use** Open_Picture_Display_Window() **in these different ways, the application that you Copy and Paste the routine to might!**

After a window has been opened, main() calls PrStlDialog() to display the Style dialog box. After the Style dialog box is dismissed, a routine named Do_Print_Window() is called to print the contents of the window. This routine looks similar to the main() routine of the simpler MinimalPrint program presented earlier in this chapter.

```
void  Do_Print_Window( WindowPtr the_window )
{
   TPPrPort    printer_port;
   TPrStatus   printer_status;
   Boolean     do_print;

   PrOpen();

   do_print = PrJobDialog( Print_Record );

   if ( do_print == false )
      return ;

   printer_port = PrOpenDoc( Print_Record, nil, nil );

   PrOpenPage( printer_port, nil );

   Draw_Stuff_To_Port( the_window );

   PrClosePage( printer_port );

   PrCloseDoc( printer_port );

   PrClose();
}
```

Do_Print_Window( ) is designed to print the contents of a window, so it accepts a WindowPtr as its only parameter. Before calling Do_Print_Window( ), main( ) uses the Toolbox routine FrontWindow( ) to get a pointer to the window. In a Macintosh application that has multiple windows open, it's the front window that gets printed. Though PrintPICTdoc only opens a single window, the call to FrontWindow( ) hints at how an application that works with multiple windows determines which window should get printed.

To specify what is to be printed, Do_Print_Window( ) relies on the familiar Draw_Stuff_To_Port( ) routine. In this version of the function, the contents of a window are sent to the printer. To get a handle to the picture to draw to the printing graphics port, Draw_Stuff_To_Port( ) relies on a routine that is the companion to SetWindowPic( )GetWindowPic( ). When passed a WindowPtr, GetWindowPic( ) returns the PicHandle that is found in the window's windowPic field. After that, it's a simple matter to get the framing rectangle and use that Rect in a call to DrawPicture( ).

```
void  Draw_Stuff_To_Port( WindowPtr the_window )
{
   PicHandle  the_picture;
   Rect       pict_rect;

   the_picture = GetWindowPic( the_window );
   pict_rect = (**the_picture).picFrame;

   DrawPicture( the_picture, &pict_rect );
}
```

The PrintPICTdoc Source Code Listing

Because PrintPICTdoc uses only one resource, a WIND that defines the window that will hold the picture, the project's resource file wasn't shown here. Instead, it's time to take a look at the PrintPICTdoc source code.

```
//_____
//                                    #include directives

#include <Printing.h>


//_____
//                                    function prototypes

void       Initialize_Toolbox( void );
void       Initialize_Printing( void );
PicHandle  Load_Picture_From_PICT_Doc( void );
void       Open_Picture_Display_Window( PicHandle );
void       Do_Print_Window( WindowPtr );
void       Draw_Stuff_To_Port( WindowPtr );


//_____
//                                    #define directives

#define    WIND_ID         128


//_____
//                                    global variables

THPrint  Print_Record;
```

```
//_____
//                                                   main()

void  main( void )
{
   WindowPtr   the_window;
   PicHandle   the_picture;

   Initialize_Toolbox();
   Initialize_Printing();

   the_picture = Load_Picture_From_PICT_Doc();
   Open_Picture_Display_Window( the_picture );

   PrOpen();
   PrStlDialog( Print_Record );
   PrClose();

   the_window = FrontWindow();
   Do_Print_Window( the_window );

   while ( !Button() )
      ;
}


//_____
//                                      set up a print record

void  Initialize_Printing( void )
{
   Print_Record = (THPrint)NewHandleClear( sizeof( TPrint ) );
   PrOpen();
   PrintDefault( Print_Record );
   PrClose();
}


//_____
//             get a handle to a picture from a PICT document

PicHandle  Load_Picture_From_PICT_Doc( void )
{
   SFTypeList          type_list = { 'PICT', 0, 0, 0 };
   StandardFileReply   reply;
   short               pict_ref_num = 0;
   long                file_length;
```

```
   Size              pict_size;
   Handle            temp_handle = nil;
   PicHandle         the_picture;

   StandardGetFile( nil, 1, type_list, &reply );

   if ( reply.sfGood == false )
      ExitToShell();

   FSpOpenDF( &reply.sfFile, fsRdPerm, &pict_ref_num );

   GetEOF( pict_ref_num, &file_length );
   SetFPos( pict_ref_num, fsFromStart, 512 );

   pict_size = file_length - 512;

   temp_handle = NewHandleClear( pict_size );

   HLock( temp_handle );
      FSRead( pict_ref_num, &pict_size, *temp_handle );
   HUnlock( temp_handle );

   the_picture = ( PicHandle )temp_handle;

   return ( the_picture );
}


//_____
//                          open a document and display a picture

void  Open_Picture_Display_Window( PicHandle the_picture )
{
   Rect       pict_rect;
   short      pict_width;
   short      pict_height;
   WindowPtr  the_window;

   pict_rect = (**the_picture).picFrame;
   pict_width  = pict_rect.right - pict_rect.left;
   pict_height = pict_rect.bottom - pict_rect.top;

   the_window = GetNewWindow( WIND_ID, nil, (WindowPtr)-1L );
   SetWindowPic( the_window, the_picture );
   SetPort( the_window );
   SizeWindow( the_window, pict_width, pict_height, false );
   ShowWindow( the_window );
```

```
   DrawPicture( the_picture, &pict_rect );
}



//_____
//                               handle a print request
void  Do_Print_Window( WindowPtr the_window )
{
   TPPrPort    printer_port;
   TPrStatus   printer_status;
   Boolean     do_print;

   PrOpen();

   do_print = PrJobDialog( Print_Record );

   if ( do_print == false )
      return ;

   printer_port = PrOpenDoc( Print_Record, nil, nil );

   PrOpenPage( printer_port, nil );

   Draw_Stuff_To_Port( the_window );

   PrClosePage( printer_port );

   PrCloseDoc( printer_port );

   PrClose();
}



//_____
//                  QuickDraw commands to be sent to a port
void  Draw_Stuff_To_Port( WindowPtr the_window )
{
   PicHandle   the_picture;
   Rect        pict_rect;

   the_picture = GetWindowPic( the_window );
   pict_rect = (**the_picture).picFrame;

   DrawPicture( the_picture, &pict_rect );
}
```

MULTIPLE WINDOWS AND PRINTING

Now that you have a firm grasp of which Printing Manager routines are the primary ones, and how those functions are used, it's time to take a look at printing in a "real" Macintosh application. PrintPICTdocII is a program that, like its predecessor PrintPICTdoc, opens a PICT file and displays the file's picture in a window. This new version of the program, however, also includes a menu bar, allows for multiple, draggable windows to be open, and supports printing of those windows. Figure 8.15 shows PrintPICTdocII with three picture windows open at the same time.

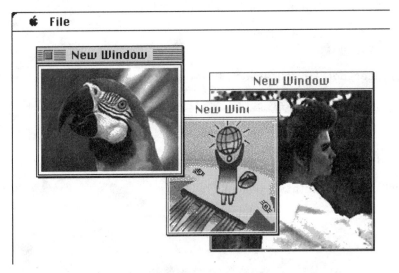

FIGURE 8.15 **PrintPICTdocII** ALLOWS MULTIPLE WINDOWS
TO BE OPEN AT ANY GIVEN TIME.

PrintPICTdocII has a File menu with five items. The **Open** item displays the standard Get File dialog box that lets the user select a PICT file to open. The **Close** item closes the active window. **Page Setup** displays the Printing Style dialog box, while **Print** displays the Printing Job dialog box and sends the contents of the active window to the printer. The last item, **Quit**, ends the program. Figure 8.16 shows the PrintPICTdocII File menu. The right side of the figure shows what the menu looks like when no windows are open.

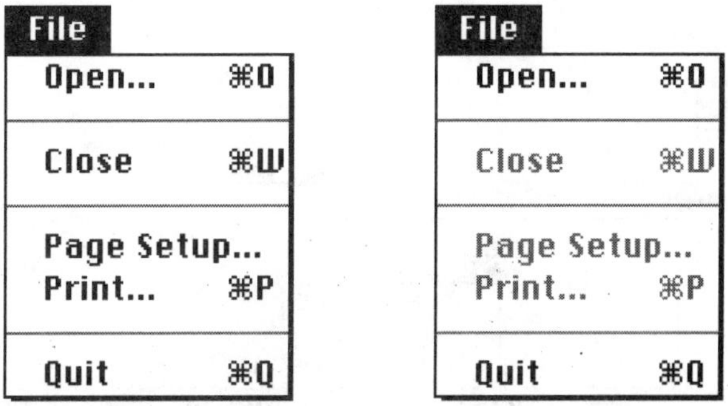

File	
Open...	⌘O
Close	⌘W
Page Setup...	
Print...	⌘P
Quit	⌘Q

File	
Open...	⌘O
Close	⌘W
Page Setup...	
Print...	⌘P
Quit	⌘Q

FIGURE 8.16 THE PRINTPICTDOCII FILE MENU HAS ITEMS THAT WILL
DIM WHEN NO DOCUMENTS ARE OPEN.

The PrintPICTdocII Resources

PrintPICTdocII requires just a few resources. Two MENU resources (see Figure 8.17) define the applications menus. The one MBAR resource pictured in Figure 8.18 groups those menus together to form a single menu bar. The last resource is a WIND with an ID of 128. Since the program will resize the window to match the size of the picture it displays, its resource size is unimportant.

The PrintPICTdocII Interface

To work with menus and windows, PrintPICTdocII relies on several routines that aren't printing related, which I will describe in this section. Here's a look at how things get started:

```
void  main( void )
{
    Initialize_Toolbox();

    Initialize_Printing();

    Set_Up_Menu_Bar();

    while ( All_Done == false )
        Handle_One_Event();
}
```

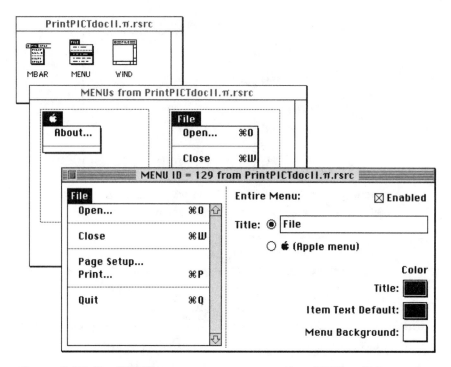

FIGURE 8.17 THE **MENU** RESOURCE USED FOR THE **PRINTPICTDOCII** FILE MENU.

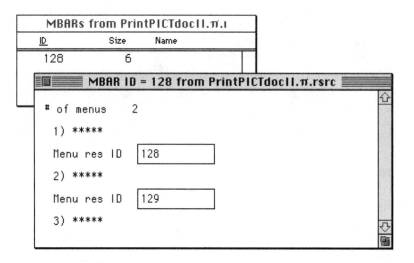

FIGURE 8.18 THE **MBAR** RESOURCE USED TO DEFINE THE MENUS
IN THE **PRINTPICTDOCII** MENU BAR.

The first three routines provide basic program set up. `Initialize_Toolbox()` and `Initialize_Printing()` you've seen before. `Set_Up_Menu_Bar()` loads the MBAR resource, sets it up, then displays the menu bar at the top of the screen. After that, the never-ending event loop starts to cycle, calling `Handle_One_Event()` each time.

```
void  Handle_One_Event( void )
{
   Adjust_Menus();

   WaitNextEvent( everyEvent, &The_Event, 15L, 0L );

   switch ( The_Event.what )
   {
      case mouseDown:
         Handle_Mouse_Down();
         break;

      case keyDown:
         Handle_Keystroke();
         break;
   }
}
```

`Handle_One_Event()` begins by calling `Adjust_Menus()` to either enable or disable the **File** menu items. If a window is open, then the **Close**, **Page Setup**, and **Print** items should be active. If no windows are open, then these items of course do not apply—and should be dimmed. `Adjust_Menus()` bases its decision on whether to enable or dim the menu items on the result of a call to the Toolbox routine `FrontWindow()`. If `FrontWindow()` returns `nil`, there are no open windows, and the items should be disabled.

While each call to `Handle_One_Event()` captures the most recent event (by means of `WaitNextEvent()`), PrintPICTdocII only responds to `mouseDown` and `keyDown` events. If the event is a mouse button click, `Handle_Mouse_Down()` is called to drop a menu, or select, move, or close a window—whichever is appropriate based on the cursor location at the time of the mouse click. If the event involves a key press instead, `Handle_Keystroke()` is called to determine if the user has pressed a menu command key equivalent. If that is the case, `Handle_Keystroke()` treats the key press as a menu selection.

If a mouse click involves a menu item, `Handle_Menu_Choice()` will be called. This function in turn calls `Handle_Apple_Choice()` or `Handle_File_Choice()`—whichever is appropriate.

Because the previous routines consist of code basic to most Mac programs, I didn't include their listings here in the discussion. Instead, refer to the source code listing several pages ahead. To make up for the omission, Figure 8.19 provides a flow diagram of how these routines interact.

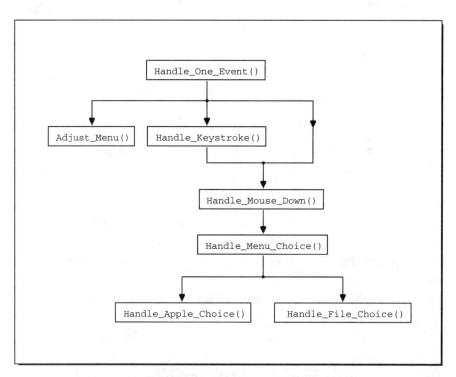

FIGURE 8.19 THE PRINTPICTDOCII EVENT LOOP AND
THE HIERARCHY OF ROUTINES IT INVOKES.

Handling Selections from the File Menu

When the user selects an item from the File menu, `Handle_File_Choice()` gets called. You should be able to quickly recognize the code under each `case` label; you've seen it all before in this chapter.

```
void  Handle_File_Choice( short the_item )
{
   WindowPtr   the_window;
   PicHandle   the_picture = nil;

   switch ( the_item )
   {
      case OPEN_ITEM:
         the_picture = Load_Picture_From_PICT_Doc();
         if ( the_picture != nil )
            Open_Picture_Display_Window( the_picture );
         break;

      case CLOSE_ITEM:
         the_window = FrontWindow();
         CloseWindow( the_window );
         break;

      case PAGE_SETUP_ITEM:
         PrOpen();
         PrStlDialog( Print_Record );
         PrClose();
         break;

      case PRINT_ITEM:
         the_window = FrontWindow();
         Do_Print_Window( the_window );
         break;

      case QUIT_ITEM:
         All_Done = true;
         break;
   }
}
```

If the user selects **Open** from the File menu, the Load_Picture_From_PICT_Doc() and Open_Picture_Display_Window() routines are called. These two functions are responsible for loading a user-selected PICT to memory and then displaying that picture in a new window. This version of Load_Picture_From_PICT_Doc() is identical to the previous one, with the exception of one line. Instead of calling ExitTo Shell() if the user clicks the **Cancel** button in the standard Get File dialog box, Load_Picture_From_PICT_Doc() returns a value of nil to the calling function:

```
if ( reply.sfGood == false )
   return ( nil );
```

The result is that the_picture variable in `Handle_File_Choice()` gets a value of `nil`, and call to `Open_Picture_Display_Window()` is skipped. If the user went ahead and selected a PICT file to open, the routine to open the picture display window will be called. Incidentally, `Open_Picture_Display_Window()` is identical to the earlier version that you saw.

```
case OPEN_ITEM:
   the_picture = Load_Picture_From_PICT_Doc();
   if ( the_picture != nil )
      Open_Picture_Display_Window( the_picture );
   break;
```

To handle a **Page Setup** selection, the Printing Manager routine `PrStl Dialog()` is called. Since the printer resource file isn't being left open for the duration of the program, it's necessary to first open it:

```
case PAGE_SETUP_ITEM:
   PrOpen();
   PrStlDialog( Print_Record );
   PrClose();
   break;
```

A menu choice of **Print** results in a call to `Do_Print_Window()`. But first, the active window is determined through a call to `FrontWindow()`. The result of that call is passed to `Do_Print_Window()`. `Do_Print_Window()` looks just as it did earlier in this chapter—it displays the Job dialog box and calls `Draw_Stuff_To_Port()` to dump the picture to the printer.

```
case PRINT_ITEM:
   the_window = FrontWindow();
   Do_Print_Window( the_window );
   break;
```

The code used to handle the **Close** and **Quit** menu items should be self-explanatory.

The PrintPICTdocII Source Code Listing

The following is the complete source code listing for the PrintPICTdocII example.

```
//_____
//                                          #include directives

#include <Printing.h>


//_____
//                                          function prototypes
void        Initialize_Toolbox( void );
void        Initialize_Printing( void );
void        Set_Up_Menu_Bar( void );
PicHandle   Load_Picture_From_PICT_Doc( void );
void        Open_Picture_Display_Window( PicHandle );
void        Do_Print_Window( WindowPtr );
void        Draw_Stuff_To_Port( WindowPtr );
void        Handle_One_Event( void );
void        Handle_Keystroke( void );
void        Handle_Mouse_Down( void );
void        Handle_Menu_Choice( long );
void        Handle_Apple_Choice( short );
void        Handle_File_Choice( short );
void        Adjust_Menus( void );


//_____
//                                          #define directives

#define     WIND_ID                 128

#define     MENU_BAR_ID             128

#define     APPLE_MENU_ID           128
#define         SHOW_ABOUT_ITEM         1

#define     FILE_MENU_ID            129
#define         OPEN_ITEM               1
#define         CLOSE_ITEM              3
#define         PAGE_SETUP_ITEM         5
#define         PRINT_ITEM              6
```

```
#define        QUIT_ITEM                 8


//_____
//                                      global variables

THPrint      Print_Record;
Boolean      All_Done = false;
EventRecord  The_Event;


//_____
//                                              main()

void  main( void )
{
   Initialize_Toolbox();

   Initialize_Printing();

   Set_Up_Menu_Bar();

   while ( All_Done == false )
      Handle_One_Event();
}


//_____
//                              set up a print record

void  Initialize_Printing( void )
{
   Print_Record = (THPrint)NewHandleClear( sizeof( TPrint ) );
   PrOpen();
   PrintDefault( Print_Record );
   PrClose();
}


//_____
//                              set up menu bar and menus

void  Set_Up_Menu_Bar( void )
{
   Handle      menu_bar_handle;
   MenuHandle  apple_menu_handle;
```

```
    menu_bar_handle = GetNewMBar( MENU_BAR_ID );

    SetMenuBar( menu_bar_handle );
    DisposHandle( menu_bar_handle );

    apple_menu_handle = GetMHandle( APPLE_MENU_ID );
    AddResMenu( apple_menu_handle, 'DRVR' );

    DrawMenuBar();
}


//_____
//              get a handle to a picture from a PICT document
PicHandle  Load_Picture_From_PICT_Doc( void )
{
    SFTypeList          type_list = { 'PICT', 0, 0, 0 };
    StandardFileReply   reply;
    short               pict_ref_num = 0;
    long                file_length;
    Size                pict_size;
    Handle              temp_handle = nil;
    PicHandle           the_picture;

    StandardGetFile( nil, 1, type_list, &reply );

    if ( reply.sfGood == false )
        return ( nil );

    FSpOpenDF( &reply.sfFile, fsRdPerm, &pict_ref_num );

    GetEOF( pict_ref_num, &file_length );
    SetFPos( pict_ref_num, fsFromStart, 512 );

    pict_size = file_length - 512;

    temp_handle = NewHandleClear( pict_size );

    HLock( temp_handle );
        FSRead( pict_ref_num, &pict_size, *temp_handle );
    HUnlock( temp_handle );

    the_picture = ( PicHandle )temp_handle;

    return ( the_picture );
}
```

```
//_____
//                        open a document and display a picture

void  Open_Picture_Display_Window( PicHandle the_picture )
{
   Rect        pict_rect;
   short       pict_width;
   short       pict_height;
   WindowPtr   the_window;

   pict_rect = (**the_picture).picFrame;
   pict_width  = pict_rect.right - pict_rect.left;
   pict_height = pict_rect.bottom - pict_rect.top;

   the_window = GetNewWindow( WIND_ID, nil, (WindowPtr)-1L );
   SetWindowPic( the_window, the_picture );
   SetPort( the_window );
   SizeWindow( the_window, pict_width, pict_height, false );
   ShowWindow( the_window );

   DrawPicture( the_picture, &pict_rect );
}


//_____
//                                      handle a print request

void  Do_Print_Window( WindowPtr the_window )
{
   TPPrPort    printer_port;
   TPrStatus   printer_status;
   Boolean     do_print;

   PrOpen();

   do_print = PrJobDialog( Print_Record );

   if ( do_print == false )
      return ;

   printer_port = PrOpenDoc( Print_Record, nil, nil );

   PrOpenPage( printer_port, nil );

   Draw_Stuff_To_Port( the_window );
```

```
   PrClosePage( printer_port );

   PrCloseDoc( printer_port );

   PrClose();
}



//_____
//                    QuickDraw commands to be sent to a port

void  Draw_Stuff_To_Port( WindowPtr the_window )
{
   PicHandle  the_picture;
   Rect       pict_rect;

   the_picture = GetWindowPic( the_window );
   pict_rect = (**the_picture).picFrame;

   DrawPicture( the_picture, &pict_rect );
}



//_____
//                                          handle one event

void  Handle_One_Event( void )
{
   Adjust_Menus();

   WaitNextEvent( everyEvent, &The_Event, 15L, 0L );

   switch ( The_Event.what )
   {
      case keyDown:
         Handle_Keystroke();
         break;

      case mouseDown:
         Handle_Mouse_Down();
         break;
   }
}
```

```
//_____
//                              enable/disable File menu items

void  Adjust_Menus( void )
{
   WindowPtr    the_window;
   MenuHandle   file_menu_handle;

   file_menu_handle = GetMHandle( FILE_MENU_ID );

   the_window = FrontWindow();

   if ( the_window == nil )
   {
      DisableItem( file_menu_handle, CLOSE_ITEM );
      DisableItem( file_menu_handle, PAGE_SETUP_ITEM );
      DisableItem( file_menu_handle, PRINT_ITEM );
   }
   else
   {
      EnableItem( file_menu_handle, CLOSE_ITEM );
      EnableItem( file_menu_handle, PAGE_SETUP_ITEM );
      EnableItem( file_menu_handle, PRINT_ITEM );
   }
}


//_____
//                                      handle a keystroke

void  Handle_Keystroke( void )
{
   short  chr;
   long   menu_choice;

   chr = The_Event.message & charCodeMask;

   if ( ( The_Event.modifiers & cmdKey ) != 0 )
   {
      if ( The_Event.what != autoKey )
      {
         menu_choice = MenuKey( chr );
         Handle_Menu_Choice( menu_choice );
      }
   }
}
```

```
//_____
//                         handle a click of the mouse button

void   Handle_Mouse_Down( void )
{
   WindowPtr   the_window;
   short       the_part;
   long        menu_choice;

   the_part = FindWindow( The_Event.where, &the_window );

   switch ( the_part )
   {
      case inMenuBar:
         menu_choice = MenuSelect( The_Event.where );
         Handle_Menu_Choice( menu_choice );
         break;

      case inSysWindow:
         SystemClick( &The_Event, the_window );
         break;

      case inDrag:
         DragWindow( the_window, The_Event.where,
                     &qd.screenBits.bounds );
         break;

      case inGoAway:
         if ( TrackGoAway( the_window, The_Event.where ) )
            CloseWindow( the_window );
         break;

      case inContent:
         if ( the_window != FrontWindow() )
            SelectWindow( the_window );
         break;
   }
}


//_____
//                            handle a click in the menu bar

void   Handle_Menu_Choice( long  menu_choice )
{
   short   the_menu;
```

```
    short   the_menu_item;

    if ( menu_choice != 0 )
    {
       the_menu = HiWord( menu_choice );
       the_menu_item = LoWord( menu_choice );

       switch ( the_menu )
       {
          case APPLE_MENU_ID:
             Handle_Apple_Choice( the_menu_item );
             break;

          case FILE_MENU_ID:
             Handle_File_Choice( the_menu_item );
             break;
       }
       HiliteMenu(0);
    }
}


//_____
//                                handle a click in the Apple menu

void  Handle_Apple_Choice( short the_item )
{
    Str255        desk_acc_name;
    short         desk_acc_number;
    MenuHandle    apple_menu_handle;

    switch ( the_item )
    {
       case SHOW_ABOUT_ITEM :
          SysBeep( 1 );
          break;

       default :
          apple_menu_handle = GetMHandle( APPLE_MENU_ID );
          GetItem( apple_menu_handle, the_item, desk_acc_name );
          desk_acc_number = OpenDeskAcc( desk_acc_name );
          break;
    }
}
```

```
//_____
//                                    handle a click in the File menu

void  Handle_File_Choice( short the_item )
{
    WindowPtr   the_window;
    PicHandle   the_picture = nil;

    switch ( the_item )
    {
        case OPEN_ITEM:
            the_picture = Load_Picture_From_PICT_Doc();
            if ( the_picture != nil )
                Open_Picture_Display_Window( the_picture );
            break;

        case CLOSE_ITEM:
            the_window = FrontWindow();
            CloseWindow( the_window );
            break;

        case PAGE_SETUP_ITEM:
            PrOpen();
            PrStlDialog( Print_Record );
            PrClose();
            break;

        case PRINT_ITEM:
            the_window = FrontWindow();
            Do_Print_Window( the_window );
            break;

        case QUIT_ITEM:
            All_Done = true;
            break;
    }
}
```

PRINTING DIALOG ITEM TEXT

Several types of Mac applications display information by the "screen-full," as does the program in Figure 8.20. This example, which teaches the fundamentals of Mac programming, is like many other software tutorials and other educational applications. It allows a user to flip through screens (windows or dialog boxes) of information at his or her own pace.

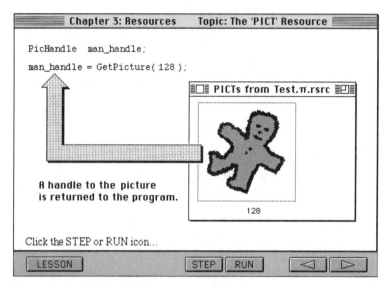

FIGURE 8.20 A TYPICAL ELECTRONIC TUTORIAL.

Programs like the one shown in Figure 8.20 would benefit from having a **Print Page** button or menu item. That would allow the user to dump any page of information to the printer. The PrintDITLscreens program that is presented in this section does just that. Figure 8.21 shows one of the program's three screens.

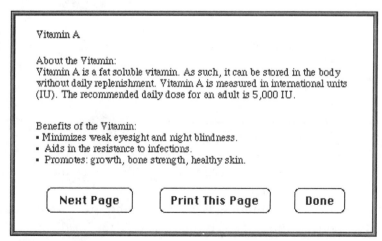

FIGURE 8.21 THE RESULT OF RUNNING THE PRINTDITLSCREENS PROGRAM.

The PrintDITLscreens program is capable of displaying what appears to be three screens of information. The program accomplishes this by leaving the same dialog box on the screen and simply "swapping" DITL resources—a technique discussed at length in Chapter 5. Each time the user clicks the **Next Page** button, a different DITL resource is used to display the static text. After the third screen is reached, the program cycles back to the first screen. The three buttons at the bottom of the dialog box are in the base DITL, so they are present on each "page."

When the user of PrintDITLscreens presses the **Print This Page** button, the text that is currently in the dialog box gets printed. For the first screen of information, the output would look like the page shown in Figure 8.22.

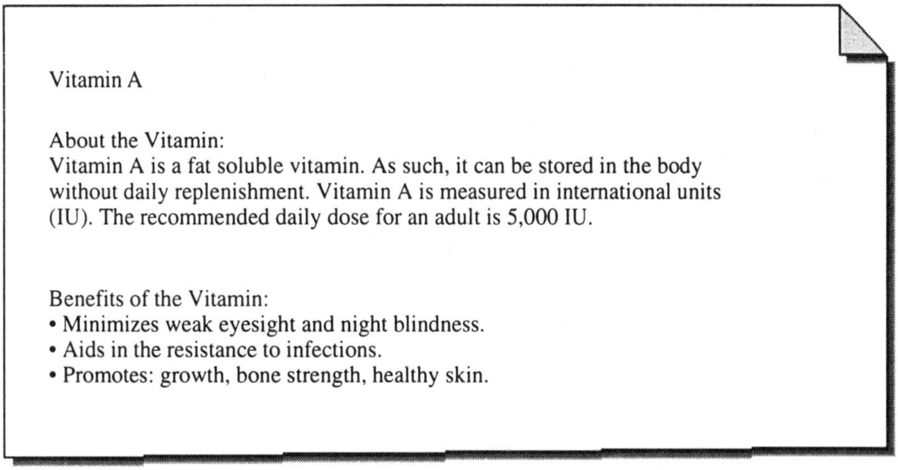

Vitamin A

About the Vitamin:
Vitamin A is a fat soluble vitamin. As such, it can be stored in the body without daily replenishment. Vitamin A is measured in international units (IU). The recommended daily dose for an adult is 5,000 IU.

Benefits of the Vitamin:
• Minimizes weak eyesight and night blindness.
• Aids in the resistance to infections.
• Promotes: growth, bone strength, healthy skin.

FIGURE 8.22 EXAMPLE HARD-COPY OUTPUT FROM THE PRINTDITLSCREENS PROGRAM.

The PrintDITLscreens Resources

PrintDITLscreens needs a single DLOG resource and four DITL resources. Figure 8.23 shows the DLOG resource as it looks with the base DITL—the DITL that will always be present in the dialog box. Figure 8.24 shows a list of the four DITL resources, along with a look at DITL 128, the base item list.

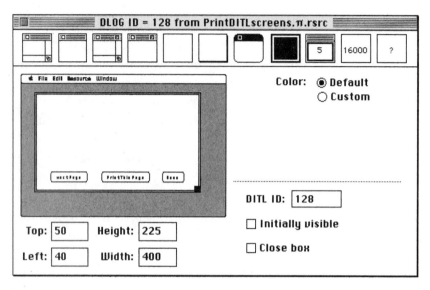

FIGURE 8.23 THE DLOG RESOURCE USED BY THE PRINTDITLSCREENS PROGRAM.

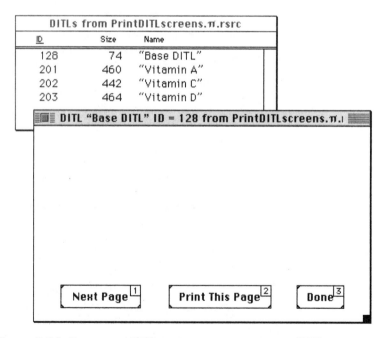

FIGURE 8.24 THE LIST OF DITL RESOURCES AND THE BASE DITL USED BY THE
PRINTDITLSCREENS PROGRAM.

Figure 8.25 shows what one of the three overlay DITL resources looks like—DITL 128. For readability, the program will display the text items of the dialog box in Times font rather than the system font. To make editing the DITL easier, I've selected the **View As** menu item from ResEdit's DITL menu and selected Times from the pop-up menu. That causes ResEdit to display the static text items in this one DITL in the Times font, providing a "what you see is what you get" view of the text items. Figure 8.26 shows the ResEdit DITL menu, while Figure 8.27 shows the dialog box that appears when **View As** is selected from that menu.

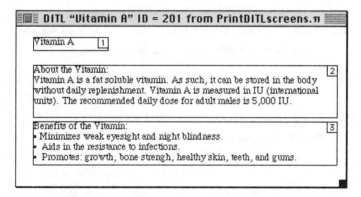

FIGURE 8.25 ONE OF THE THREE OVERLAY DITL RESOURCES USED BY THE PRINTDITLSCREENS PROGRAM.

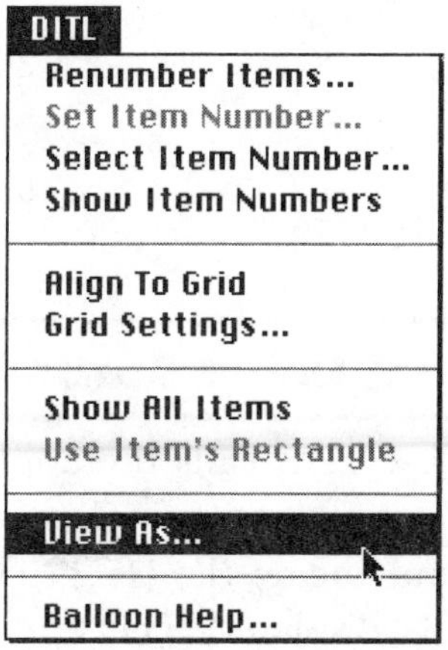

FIGURE 8.26 THE RESEDIT VIEW AS MENU ITEM IN THE DITL MENU.

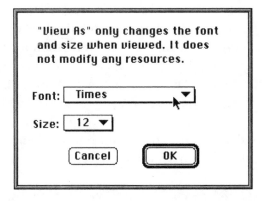

FIGURE 8.27 SELECTING THE VIEW AS MENU ITEM ALLOWS THE LOOK
OF TEXT IN A **DITL** RESOURCE TO BE CHANGED.

The base DITL is always present in the DLOG, and its items will be recognized by the PrintDITLscreens program as items 1, 2, and 3. At any time, PrintDITLscreens will also overlay one of the other three DITL resources onto the dialog box as well. Each of those three DITL resources consists of three static text items—the page title and two items that hold information about a particular vitamin. When added to the three base DITL items already in the dialog records list of items, these three items will be recognized by the program as items 4, 5, and 6. When referring to these items, the PrintDITLscreens source code uses these six #define directives:

```
#define      NEXT_PAGE_ITEM            1
#define      PRINT_PAGE_ITEM           2
#define      DONE_ITEM                 3
#define      PAGE_TITLE_TEXT_ITEM      4
#define      PAGE_TEXT_1_ITEM          5
#define      PAGE_TEXT_2_ITEM          6
```

Printing Lines of Text Using Static Text Items

Upon running, PrintDITLscreens calls the application-defined routine Open_Dialog() to set the display font to Times and open the dialog box that holds the base DITL and one overlay DITL. The dialog box opens with the first overlay (DITL 201) displayed. The current_overlay variable keeps track of the displayed DITL.

```
#define      OVERLAY_1_DITL_ID       201

Handle   item_list_handle;
short    current_overlay;

SetDAFont( times );  // set font to Times rather than system font

The_Dialog = GetNewDialog( DLOG_ID, nil, (WindowPtr)-1L );

item_list_handle = Get1Resource( 'DITL', OVERLAY_1_DITL_ID );
AppendDITL( The_Dialog, item_list_handle, overlayDITL );
ReleaseResource( item_list_handle );

current_overlay = OVERLAY_1_DITL_ID;

ShowWindow( The_Dialog );
SetPort( The_Dialog );
```

If the user clicks on the **Next Page** button, `Open_Dialog()` calculates how many items are currently in the dialog box and shortens the dialog item list so that it reflects only the number of items in the base DITL. Then the DITL ID value held in `current_overlay` is incremented for use in the next "page." If the user is already at the last page, the DITL ID is set to the first overlay DITL, so the program returns to the first page of information. The DITL resource is then retrieved, and its items are appended to the item list. For more information on `ShortenDITL()` and `AppendDITL()`, and this DITL switching technique, refer back to Chapter 5.

```
case NEXT_PAGE_ITEM:
   total_items = CountDITL( The_Dialog );
   ShortenDITL( The_Dialog, total_items - NUM_BASE_ITEMS );

   if ( current_overlay == LAST_OVERLAY )
      current_overlay = OVERLAY_1_DITL_ID;
   else
      ++current_overlay;

   item_list_handle = Get1Resource( 'DITL', current_overlay );
   AppendDITL( The_Dialog, item_list_handle, overlayDITL );
   ReleaseResource( item_list_handle );
   break;
```

If the user clicks on the **Print This Page** button, the text that is currently displayed in the dialog box will be sent to the user's printer. A routine named Do_Print_Window() sees to that:

```
case PRINT_PAGE_ITEM:
   Do_Print_Window();
   break;
```

The Do_Print_Window() function calls all of the basic Printing Manager functions such as PrOpen() and PrOpenDoc(). It doesn't, however, make a call to PrJobDialog(). While it is a courtesy to the user, displaying the Printing Job dialog box is not necessary to cause printing to begin—a call to PrOpenPage() does that. Do_Print_Windows() skips the Job dialog box and goes right to the call to PrOpenPage(). As usual, it's the Draw_Stuff_To_Port() function that defines what it is that gets printed. Here's that the PrintDITLscreens version of that function:

```
void  Draw_Stuff_To_Port( void )
{
   Handle  hand;
   short   type;
   Rect    box;
   Str255  dlog_string;
   short   text_y;

   TextFont( times );
   TextSize( 12 );

   GetDialogItem( The_Dialog, PAGE_TITLE_TEXT_ITEM, &type, &hand,
               &box );
   GetDialogItemText( hand, dlog_string );

   text_y = START_TEXT_Y;
   MoveTo( START_TEXT_X, text_y );
   DrawString( dlog_string );

   text_y = START_TEXT_Y + ( 2 * LINE_SPACING_TEXT );
   MoveTo( START_TEXT_X, text_y );
   Break_Text_Into_Lines( PAGE_TEXT_1_ITEM, text_y );

   text_y = START_TEXT_Y + ( 8 * LINE_SPACING_TEXT );
```

```
   MoveTo( START_TEXT_X, text_y );
   Break_Text_Into_Lines( PAGE_TEXT_2_ITEM, text_y );
}
```

Draw_Stuff_To_Port( ) begins by setting the text to 12 point Times.
Earlier, Open_Dialog( ) set the text to Times with a call to SetDAFont( ).
Because font changes that are made *before* a call to PrOpenPage( ) don't
affect text sent to the printer, it is necessary to use calls like TextFont( )
and TextSize( ) within the routine that draws to the printer graphics port.

After setting the text, the next two lines of code get the text from the
fourth item (PAGE_TITLE_TEXT_ITEM) in the dialog box item list:

```
#define     PAGE_TITLE_TEXT_ITEM          4

Handle   hand;
short    type;
Rect     box;
Str255   dlog_string;

GetDialogItem( The_Dialog, PAGE_TITLE_TEXT_ITEM, &type, &hand,
               &box );
GetDialogItemText( hand, dlog_string );
```

In Figure 8.28 you'll notice that each of the three overlay DITL resources
are set up in the same way—the first item is a title for the page, the second item holds text that describes a vitamin, and the third item contains
text that covers benefits of a vitamin. By keeping the items in each overlay DITL consistent, a single routine (Draw_Stuff_To_Port( )) can
be used to send the text of any one DITL to the printer.

After getting the text in the first DITL item (which, when added to
the base items, is the fourth item in the list), Draw_Stuff_To_Port( )
moves the graphics pen to the upper-left corner of the printing graphics
port and draws the text:

```
#define     START_TEXT_X           0
#define     START_TEXT_Y          20

short    text_y;

text_y = START_TEXT_Y;
```

```
MoveTo( START_TEXT_X, text_y );
DrawString( dlog_string );
```

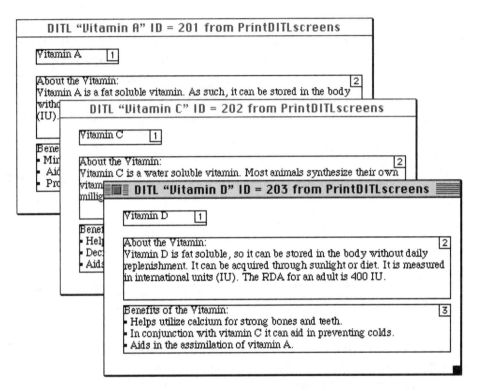

FIGURE 8.28 EACH OF THE THREE OVERLAY **DITL** RESOURCES
CONTAINS THREE STATIC TEXT ITEMS.

After drawing the title (such as "Vitamin A"), the graphics pen is moved back to the left side of the port and down a couple of lines. Then a routine named Break_Text_Into_Lines() is called to retrieve the text from the second static text item and to send that text to the printer:

```
#define    LINE_SPACING_TEXT      15
#define    PAGE_TEXT_1_ITEM        5

text_y = START_TEXT_Y + ( 2 * LINE_SPACING_TEXT );
MoveTo( START_TEXT_X, text_y );
Break_Text_Into_Lines( PAGE_TEXT_1_ITEM, text_y );
```

As its first parameter, `Break_Text_Into_Lines()` receives the item number of the dialog item text to retrieve. In this example, the item is the second static text item from the overlay DITL—the fifth item including the base DITL items. The second parameter is the vertical pixel distance that the pen should be moved from the top of the port before drawing begins.

`Break_Text_Into_Lines()` begins by retrieving the text from the dialog box item and saving that text to an `Str255` variable:

```
Handle  hand;
short   type;
Rect    box;
Str255  dlog_string;

GetDialogItem( The_Dialog, dlog_item, &type, &hand, &box );
GetDialogItemText( hand, dlog_string );
```

If the program next attempted to write the string directly to the printer, the text would flow off the right side of the page. While the text that makes up the words of a static text item may appear to occupy several lines, it is really just a single string. The boundaries of the static text item, as defined in the DITL in the resource file, determine how the text looks on screen, but it doesn't break up the text into individual lines. As part of the solution to this dilemma, I've added carriage returns after each line of text in each static text item, as shown for item number 2 in Figures 8.29 and 8.30.

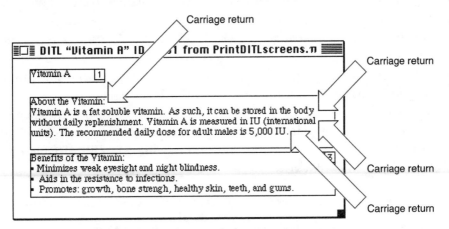

FIGURE 8.29 Each line in a single static text item is separated from other lines by a carriage return.

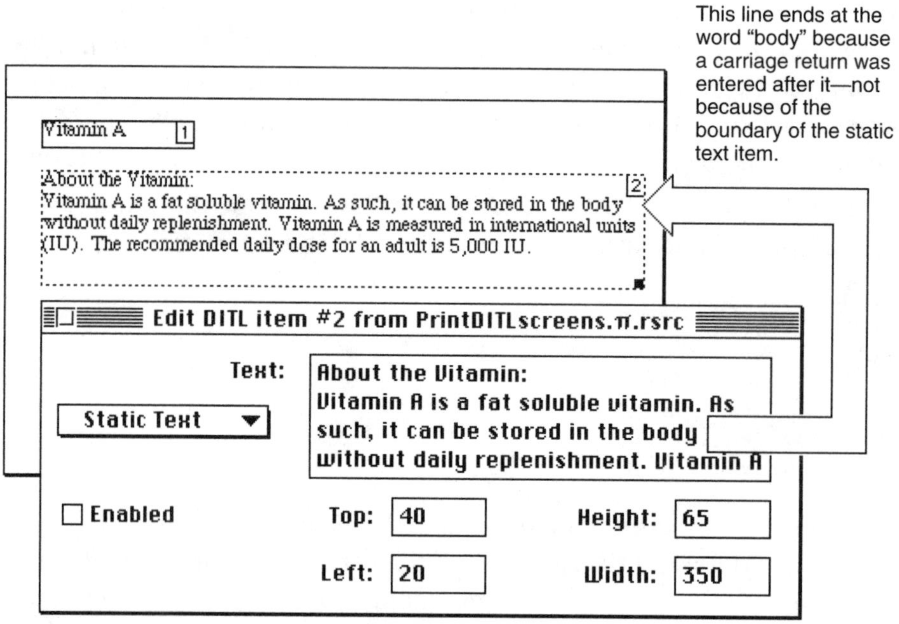

This line ends at the word "body" because a carriage return was entered after it—not because of the boundary of the static text item.

FIGURE 8.30 CARRIAGE RETURNS IN DITL STATIC TEXT ITEMS ARE ADDED IN THE STATIC TEXT EDITOR.

Before writing the retrieved string to the printing port, `Break_Text_Into_Lines()` divides the string into several smaller strings. The start and end of each of these substrings are determined by the carriage returns in the static text item string. `Break_Text_Into_Lines()` finds the length of the entire string, in characters, then uses a `for` loop to check each character in the string, searching for the carriage returns. Each time a carriage return is found, the text from the last carriage return to the newly found carriage return is printed. This is done by copying these characters from the entire static text string to a temporary string, then making a call to `DrawString()`. In brief, here's how one `Str255` variable gets broken up into lines of text:

```
Get the length of the static text string

Begin loop, one iteration for each character in the string
    If character is ASCII 13 (return character),
    end of a line is found
```

```
    Starting char of line is the last return character, + 1
    Ending char of the line is the current return character
    Copy these characters to a temporary string
    Draw the temporary string to the printing port
    Position the graphics pen for the next line of text
End loop
```

The PrintDITLscreens Source Code Listing

When you run PrintDITLscreens, you'll see a dialog box like the one in Figure 8.31. If you'd like to write an electronic tutorial, PrintDITLscreens might be a good place to start. It uses DITL overlays, as described in Chapter 5, to change the information in the dialog box. By creating several more DITL resources, any amount of information could be easily conveyed to the user. To give the program a better interface, you could add a File menu that holds the **Page Setup** item found in most applications that allow printing. With a menu in place, the **Print This Page** button could be replaced with a **Print Page** menu item. The dialog box could be made modeless, and different dialog boxes could be provided for different topics, such as one for vitamins and one for minerals. Finally, you could get rid of the drab buttons and replace them with custom controls, as was done in Chapter 2. The results of these improvements could be a program like the one pictured in Figure 8.32.

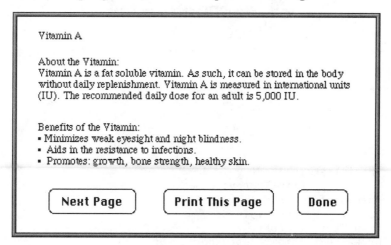

FIGURE 8.31 THE RESULT OF RUNNING THE PRINTDITLSCREENS PROGRAM.

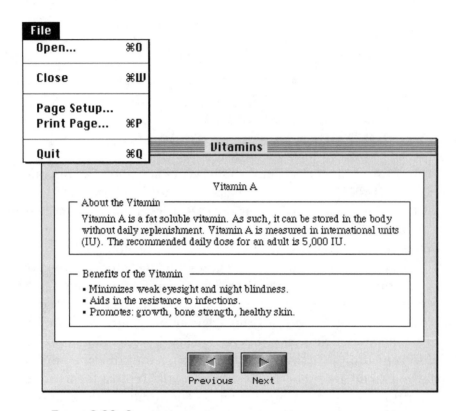

FIGURE 8.32 ONE POSSIBLE RESULT OF RUNNING AN ENHANCED VERSION
OF THE **PRINTDITL**SCREENS PROGRAM.

```
//_____
//                                              #include directives

#include <Printing.h>


//_____
//                                              function prototypes

void   Initialize_Toolbox( void );
void   Initialize_Printing( void );
void   Open_Dialog( void );
void   Do_Print_Window( void );
void   Draw_Stuff_To_Port( void );
void   Break_Text_Into_Lines( short, short );
void   Copy_Part_Of_String( Str255, Str255, short, short );
```

```
//_____
//                                    #define directives

#define        DLOG_ID                      128
#define            NEXT_PAGE_ITEM           1
#define            PRINT_PAGE_ITEM          2
#define            DONE_ITEM                3

#define        NUM_BASE_ITEMS               3

#define        OVERLAY_1_DITL_ID            201
#define        LAST_OVERLAY                 203
#define        PAGE_TITLE_TEXT_ITEM         4
#define        PAGE_TEXT_1_ITEM             5
#define        PAGE_TEXT_2_ITEM             6

#define        START_TEXT_X                 0
#define        START_TEXT_Y                 20
#define        LINE_SPACING_TEXT            15


//_____
//                                         global variables

THPrint    Print_Record;
DialogPtr  The_Dialog;


//_____
//                                               main()

void   main( void )
{
    Initialize_Toolbox();

    Initialize_Printing();

    Open_Dialog();
}


//_____
//                                    set up a print record

void   Initialize_Printing( void )
{
    Print_Record = (THPrint)NewHandleClear( sizeof( TPrint ) );
    PrOpen();
```

```
    PrintDefault( Print_Record );
    PrClose();
}


//_____
//                                        open a display dialog

void  Open_Dialog( void )
{
    Boolean     done = false;
    short       the_item;
    Handle      item_list_handle;
    short       current_overlay;
    short       total_items;

    SetDAFont( times );

    The_Dialog = GetNewDialog( DLOG_ID, nil, (WindowPtr)-1L );

    item_list_handle = Get1Resource( 'DITL', OVERLAY_1_DITL_ID );
    AppendDITL( The_Dialog, item_list_handle, overlayDITL );
    ReleaseResource( item_list_handle );

    current_overlay = OVERLAY_1_DITL_ID;

    ShowWindow( The_Dialog );
    SetPort( The_Dialog );

    while ( done == false )
    {
        ModalDialog( nil, &the_item );

        switch ( the_item )
        {
            case NEXT_PAGE_ITEM:
                total_items = CountDITL( The_Dialog );
                ShortenDITL( The_Dialog, total_items - NUM_BASE_ITEMS );

                if ( current_overlay == LAST_OVERLAY )
                    current_overlay = OVERLAY_1_DITL_ID;
                else
                    ++current_overlay;

                item_list_handle = Get1Resource( 'DITL',
                                                 current_overlay );
                AppendDITL( The_Dialog, item_list_handle, overlayDITL );
                ReleaseResource( item_list_handle );
```

```
                break;

            case PRINT_PAGE_ITEM:
                Do_Print_Window();
                break;

            case DONE_ITEM:
                done = true;
                break;
        }
    }

    DisposDialog( The_Dialog );

    SetDAFont( systemFont );
}
```

```
//_____
//                                 handle a print request

void  Do_Print_Window( void )
{
    TPPrPort    printer_port;
    TPrStatus   printer_status;

    PrOpen();

    printer_port = PrOpenDoc( Print_Record, nil, nil );

    PrOpenPage( printer_port, nil );

    Draw_Stuff_To_Port();

    PrClosePage( printer_port );

    PrCloseDoc( printer_port );

    PrClose();
}
```

```
//_____
//                     QuickDraw commands to be sent to a port

void  Draw_Stuff_To_Port( void )
{
    Handle  hand;
```

```
   short   type;
   Rect    box;
   Str255  dlog_string;
   short   text_y;

   TextFont( times );
   TextSize( 12 );

   GetDialogItem( The_Dialog, PAGE_TITLE_TEXT_ITEM, &type, &hand,
               &box );
   GetDialogItemText( hand, dlog_string );

   text_y = START_TEXT_Y;
   MoveTo( START_TEXT_X, text_y );
   DrawString( dlog_string );

   text_y = START_TEXT_Y + ( 2 * LINE_SPACING_TEXT );
   MoveTo( START_TEXT_X, text_y );
   Break_Text_Into_Lines( PAGE_TEXT_1_ITEM, text_y );

   text_y = START_TEXT_Y + ( 8 * LINE_SPACING_TEXT );
   MoveTo( START_TEXT_X, text_y );
   Break_Text_Into_Lines( PAGE_TEXT_2_ITEM, text_y );
}


//_____
//         Break one Str255 string into several lines of text

void  Break_Text_Into_Lines( short dlog_item, short text_y )
{
   Handle  hand;
   short   type;
   Rect    box;
   Str255  dlog_string;
   short   str_length;
   short   start_char;
   short   end_char;
   int     i;
   short   count;
   char    the_chr;
   Str255  line_string;

   GetDialogItem( The_Dialog, dlog_item, &type, &hand, &box );
   GetDialogItemText( hand, dlog_string );

   str_length = dlog_string[0];
```

```
      count = 0;
      start_char = 1;

      for ( i = 1; i <= str_length; i++ )    // go through entire
                                             // string
      {
         ++count;

         the_chr = dlog_string[i];

         if ( the_chr == 13 )
         {
            end_char = i;
            Copy_Part_Of_String( line_string, dlog_string,
                                 start_char, end_char );
            DrawString( line_string );

            start_char = end_char + 1;
            text_y += LINE_SPACING_TEXT;
            MoveTo( START_TEXT_X, text_y );
            count = 0;
         }

      }
}


//_____
//              copy a portion of one string to another string

void  Copy_Part_Of_String( Str255 dst,
                           Str255 src,
                           short   start_char,
                           short   end_char )
{
   int  i, j;

   j = 1;
   for ( i = start_char; i <= end_char; i++ )
   {
      dst[j] = src[i];
      j++;
   }
   dst[0] = ( end_char - start_char ) + 1;
}
```

CHAPTER SUMMARY

The functions that make up the Macintosh system software Printing Manager are actually found in the printer resource file that accompanies every printer that is compatible with the Macintosh. Because it is the printer vendor that is responsible for the implementation of each of the Printing Manager routines, the printing dialog boxes vary from one printer to another. The Printing Style dialog box is used to set the page orientation and the reduction/enlargement scale. You'll use the `PrStlDialog()` to bring this dialog box to the screen. The Printing Job dialog box lets the user specify the number of copies and the quality of the printed page. This dialog box is posted using the `PrJobDialog()` routine.

Printing is accomplished by sending QuickDraw routines not to a normal graphics port, but to a printing graphics port instead. After initializing the Printing Manager with a call to `PrOpen()`, this specialized graphics port is opened by way of a call to `PrOpenDoc()`. After invoking `PrOpenPage()`, all subsequent calls to QuickDraw routines are sent to the printer rather than the screen. It is the printer driver software that interprets these calls and does the actual printing.

Appendix

A

More Mac Programming Techniques

Errors

Whether you use the Symantec or Metrowerks compiler, you're apt to
run into an error somewhere in your programming endeavors. This
appendix covers the errors that you could encounter as you work on projects of the types described in this book.

SYMANTEC AND CODE RESOURCE ERRORS

If you're using the Symantec C++ compiler and you get errors while
working on a code resource project, check out the pages in the following
sections.

ResEdit Crash While Working with CNTL Resources

After a CDEF code resource is compiled and built in the THINK Project Manager, a resource editor is used to copy the resource from its own file and to paste it directly into the application's resource fork. Figure A.1 shows this technique. Using this approach (as do the examples in this book), you shouldn't encounter any ResEdit-related problems.

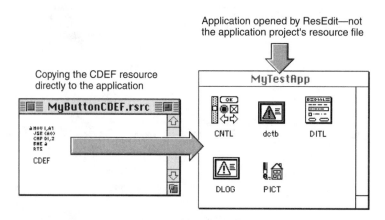

FIGURE A.1 COPYING A CDEF FROM A RESOURCE FILE AND PASTING IT DIRECTLY INTO AN APPLICATION.

A second way to work with a CDEF is to copy the CDEF code resource into the application project resource file (projectname.π.rsrc) before the application is built. Then, when you build the application in the THINK Project Manager, the linker will merge the project resource file, including the CDEF resource, into the application. In Figure A.2, this approach is being used.

If you use this second approach, and ResEdit is your resource editor, you could lead to a crash while working in ResEdit. If you copy the CDEF to the application project's resource file and then quit ResEdit, you'll be safe. If, however, you start to edit either a CNTL resource or a Control item in a DITL resource, ResEdit may unexpectedly quit. For this reason, the book uses the method of working on the application project's resource file *without* the CDEF pasted into it.

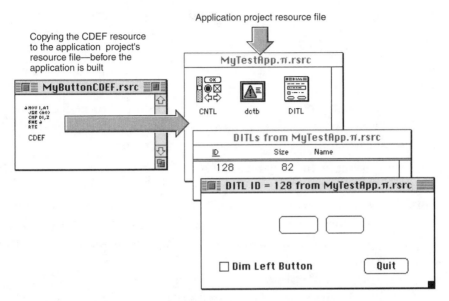

FIGURE A.2 COPYING A **CDEF** FROM A RESOURCE FILE AND PASTING IT INTO THE PROJECTS RESOURCE FILE.

Slider Control Freezes in Built Application

If you build an application that uses a slider CDEF code resource, you should be able to drag the slider thumb back and forth along the full length of the slider control. If at some point the thumb freezes and can't be moved, you'll need to modify the application project's resource file and rebuild the application. This problem is a ResEdit bug and is related to the DITL Control item that holds the slider control.

Open the application project's resource file (projectname.π.rsrc) using ResEdit and open the DITL resource. Move the Control item a few pixels in any direction. Save the file and quit ResEdit. Rebuild the application in the THINK Project Manager.

Global Variables Don't Hold Values

The Mac operating system locates an application's global variables by keeping track of where they're located in memory. To do this, it holds a pointer to the start of the globals. This pointer is kept in the A5 register. Since a code resource is usually used by an application, the code resource cannot use this same register to hold a pointer to its own set of global variables. If you attempt to declare a global variable in a code resource, you'll find that it won't hold a value that is assigned to it. To overcome this obstacle and to allow a code resource to declare global variables, the Symantec compilers let you devote a register other than A5 as the pointer to a global variable space—the A4 register.

Before working with global variables in a code resource, you'll need to set up the A4 register. When the main() function of a code resource begins to execute, register A0 holds the starting address of the code resource. That address needs to be moved in to A4. Once that happens, the operating system will be able to locate any global variables that the code resource has declared.

To set up the A4 register, call the routines RememberA0() and SetUpA4() as the first lines of code in main(). These two functions are Symantec-defined routines—they aren't part of the Mac Toolbox. Their definitions are in the Symantec SetUpA4.h header file, so you'll need to include that header in your code resource. Just before exiting main(), call the Symantec routine RestoreA4(). Below is a snippet that shows how the sequence of calls looks in a 'cdev' code resource. The same format would apply to any other code resource type as well.

```
#include   <SetUpA4.h>

short   Num_Strings;   // global variable: use anywhere in the 'cdev'

pascal   CDEVHandle   main( short          message,
                            short          item,
                            short          num_items,
                            short          control_panel_ID,
                            EventRecord    *the_event,
                            CDEVHandle     cdev_storage,
                            DialogPtr      the_dialog )
{
   RememberA0();
   SetUpA4();

   switch ( message )
   {
```

```
    // okay to use Num_Strings here or
    // in any routine called by main().
  }

  RestoreA4();

  return ( cdev_storage );
}
```

For a complete example of how the A4 register and global variables are used, see the Appendix A—Errors ƒ folder. In there you'll find a Control Panel code resource example named GlobalData in the Code Resources ƒ folder. That example uses a global variable, as well as a string literal—another source of data errors in a code resource. The GlobalData control panel is shown in Figure A.3.

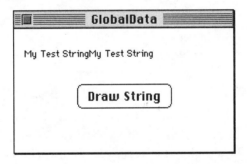

FIGURE A.3   THE RESULT OF RUNNING THE GLOBALDATA PROGRAM.

Strings Contain Garbage Characters

To use strings in a code resource, you'll have to first set up the A4 register, as discussed in the "Global Variables Don't Hold Values" section of this appendix. Refer to that section for more information on the A4 register.

In a code resource, a string literal will consist of random garbage—even after being given a value in a #define directive or an assignment statement. Once the A4 register is set up, however, the characters that make up a string will be preserved. The following snippet shows how the A4 register is set up and how a string can be used in a cdev resource. This technique works for any other code resource type as well.

```
#include   <SetUpA4.h>

#define    TEST_DRAW_STR    "\pMy Test String"

pascal  CDEVHandle  main( short        message,
                          short        item,
                          short        num_items,
                          short        control_panel_ID,
                          EventRecord  *the_event,
                          CDEVHandle   cdev_storage,
                          DialogPtr    the_dialog )
{
   RememberA0();
   SetUpA4();

   switch ( message )
   {
      // okay to use TEST_DRAW_STR here or
      // in any routine called by main().
   }

   RestoreA4();

   return ( cdev_storage );
}
```

For a complete example, see the Appendix A—Errors ƒ folder. Look in the Code Resources ƒ folder to find a control panel code resource example named GlobalData. That example uses a string literal in a #define directive. It also shows how a global variable can be used in a code resource.

Multisegment Project Error

Code resources are generally small in size—usually well below the 32KB size limit of a segment. For that reason, segmentation rarely becomes an issue for code resources. If you do decide to create a multisegment code resource, the Symantec compiler will respond with the error message shown in Figure A.4

If you need to create a code resource that consists of more than one segment—as the one shown in Figure A.5 does—you'll need to let the THINK Project Manager know of your intentions.

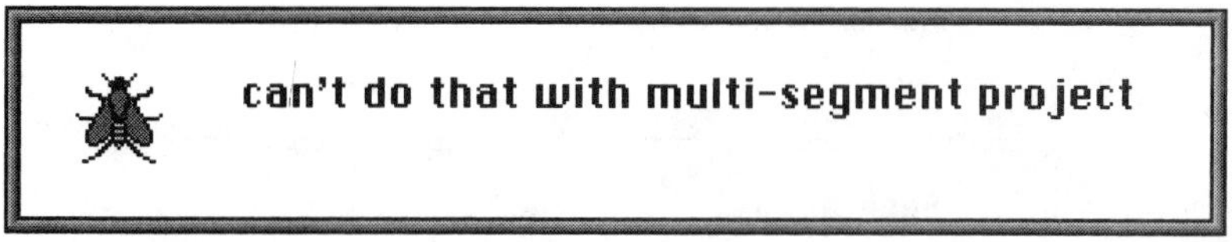

 can't do that with multi-segment project

FIGURE A.4 THE SYMANTEC ERROR WHEN TRYING TO BUILD A CODE RESOURCE GREATER THAN 32 KB IN SIZE.

Before compiling a multisegment code resource project, select **Set Project Type** from the Project menu. Then check the **Multisegment** checkbox, as shown in Figure A.6.

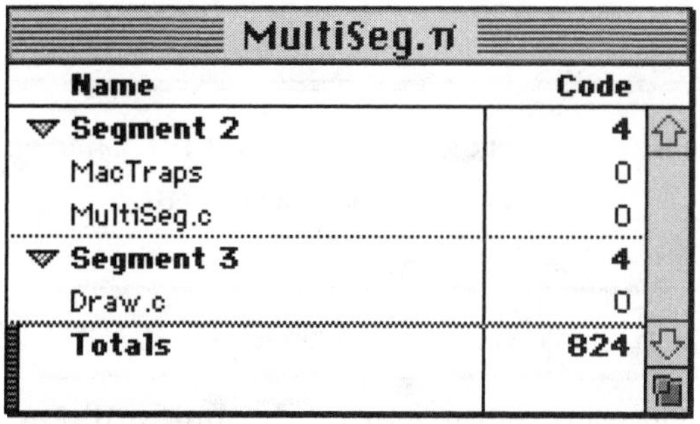

MultiSeg.π	
Name	**Code**
▽ **Segment 2**	4
MacTraps	0
MultiSeg.c	0
▽ **Segment 3**	4
Draw.c	0
Totals	**824**

FIGURE A.5 A SYMANTEC CODE RESOURCE PROJECT THAT CONSISTS OF MORE THAN ONE SEGMENT.

Once this checkbox is checked, you can compile and build the code resource—without regard for the number of segments it's made up of.

For an example of a control panel resource that uses two segments, refer to the Appendix A—Errors ƒ folder. Look in the Code Resources ƒ folder to find the control panel code resource example named MultiSeg. That example uses both a global variable and a string literal in two source code files. The source code for the MultiSeg cdev is identical to that of the GlobalData cdev discussed in the "Global Variables Don't Hold Values" section of this appendix. The only difference is that MultiSeg uses two segments.

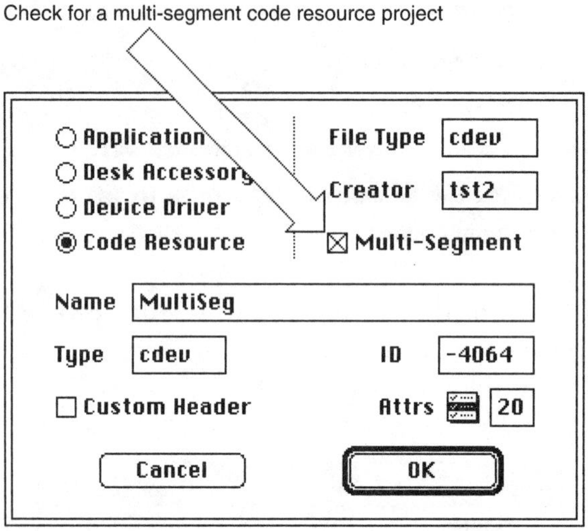

Check for a multi-segment code resource project

**FIGURE A.6 MARKING A SYMANTEC CODE RESOURCE PROJECT
TO BE MORE THAN ONE SEGMENT.**

METROWERKS AND CODE RESOURCE ERRORS

If you use a Metrowerks CodeWarrior compiler and you get errors when you're working on a code resource project, read the pages in the following sections.

ResEdit Crash While Working with CNTL Resources

After a CDEF code resource is compiled and built in CodeWarrior, a resource editor is used to copy the resource from its own file and to paste it directly into the application's resource fork. This technique is shown in Figure A.7. Using this approach (as the examples in this book do), you shouldn't encounter any ResEdit-related problems.

A second way to work with a CDEF is to copy the CDEF code resource into the application project resource file (projectname.µ.rsrc) before the application is built. Then, when you build the application in CodeWarrior, the linker will merge the project resource file, including the CDEF resource, into the application. In Figure A.8, this approach is being used.

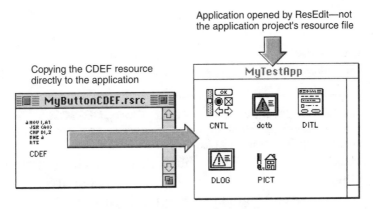

FIGURE A.7 COPYING A CDEF FROM A RESOURCE FILE

AND PASTING IT DIRECTLY INTO AN APPLICATION.

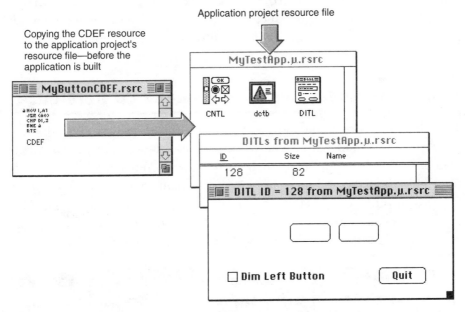

FIGURE A.8 COPYING A CDEF FROM A RESOURCE FILE AND

PASTING IT INTO THE A PROJECT'S RESOURCE FILE.

If you use this second approach, and ResEdit is your resource editor, you could lead to a crash while working in ResEdit. If you copy the CDEF to the application project's resource file and then quit ResEdit, you'll be safe. If, however, you start to edit either a CNTL resource or a Control item in a DITL resource, ResEdit may unexpectedly quit. For this reason, the book uses the method of working on the application project's resource file *without* the CDEF pasted into it.

Slider Control Freezes in Built Application

If you build an application that uses a slider CDEF code resource, you should be able to drag the slider thumb back and forth along the full length of the slider control. If at some point the thumb freezes and can't be moved, you'll need to modify the application project's resource file and rebuild the application. This problem is a ResEdit bug and is related to the DITL Control item that holds the slider control.

Open the application project's resource file (projectname.π.rsrc) using ResEdit and open the DITL resource. Move the Control item a few pixels in any direction. Save the file and quit ResEdit. Rebuild the application in Metrowerks.

Link Error: Illegal Single Segment 32-Bit Reference

The Metrowerks compilers give you three different object code options for a project: **Small**, **Smart**, and **Large** code. Newly created projects default to the Smart option, which allows call references to be outside of the 16-bit offset range limit imposed by the **Small** code model. This works fine for application projects, but not for code resource projects. If a Metrowerks code resource isn't set to the **Small** code model, a build of the code resource will result in error messages like the ones in Figure A.9.

```
┌─────────────────────── Message Window ───────────────────────┐
│ ●● Errors : 5    ◇◇ Warnings : 0    Infos : 0                 │
│ ●● Link Error   : LinkError:MyMDEF.c: 'main' has illegal single segment 32-bit refe│
│                                                              │
│ ●● Link Error   : LinkError:MyMDEF.c: 'main' has illegal single segment 32-bit refe│
└──────────────────────────────────────────────────────────────┘
```

FIGURE A.9 LINK ERROR MESSAGES WHEN A METROWERKS CODE RESOURCE
IS BUILT USING THE INCORRECT CODE MODEL.

For all of the Metrowerks code resources covered in this book (MDEF, CDEF, and cdev), you'll need to make sure that the Code Model is set to **Small** in the Processor panel of the Preferences dialog box, as shown in Figure A.10. To make this change, select **Preferences** from the Edit menu. Then click on the Processor icon to display the Processor Info panel. Choose **Small** from the Code Model pop-up menu.

Code Model must be set to Small for code resources

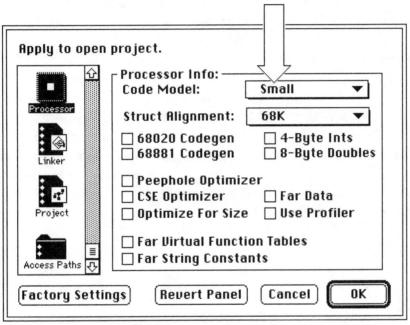

FIGURE A.10 USING THE METROWERKS PREFERENCES DIALOG BOX TO MARK A CODE RESOURCE TO USE THE SMALL CODE MODEL.

Global Variables Don't Hold Values

The Mac operating system locates an application's global variables by keeping track of where they're located in memory. To do this, it holds a pointer to the start of the globals. This pointer is kept in the A5 register. Since a code resource is usually used by an application, the code resource cannot use this same register to hold a pointer to its own set of global variables. If you attempt to declare a global variable in a code resource, you'll find that it won't hold a value that is assigned to it. To overcome this obstacle and allow a code resource to declare global variables, the Metrowerks compilers let you devote a register other than A5 as the pointer to a global variable space—the A4 register.

Before working with global variables in a code resource, you'll need to set up the A4 register. When the main() function of a code resource begins to execute, register A0 holds the starting address of the code resource. That address needs to be moved in to A4. Once that happens, the operating system will be able to locate any global variables that the code resource has declared.

To set up the A4 register, call the routine SetCurrentA4() as the first lines of code in main(). This function is a Metrowerks-defined routine—it isn't part of the Macintosh Toolbox. Its definition is in the Metrowerks A4Stuff.h header file, so you'll need to include that header in your code resource. Just before exiting main(), call the Metrowerks routine SetA4(). Below is a snippet that shows how the sequence of calls looks in a cdev code resource. The same format would apply to any other code resource type as well.

```
#include  <A4Stuff.h>

short  Num_Strings;   // global variable: use anywhere in the 'cdev'

pascal  CDEVHandle  main( short        message,
                          short        item,
                          short        num_items,
                          short        control_panel_ID,
                          EventRecord  *the_event,
                          CDEVHandle   cdev_storage,
                          DialogPtr    the_dialog )
{
   long  save_A4;

   save_A4 = SetCurrentA4();

   switch ( message )
   {
      // okay to use Num_Strings here or
      // in any routine called by main().
```

```
    }

    SetA4( save_A4 );

    return ( cdev_storage );
}
```

For a complete example of how the A4 register and global variables are used, see the Appendix B—Errors ƒ folder. In there, you'll find a control panel code resource example named GlobalData in the Code Resources ƒ folder. That example uses a global variable, as well as a string literal—another source of data errors in a code resource. The GlobalData control panel is shown in Figure A.11.

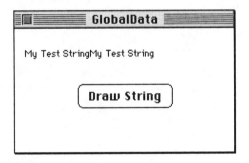

FIGURE A.11 THE RESULT OF RUNNING THE GLOBALDATA PROGRAM.

Strings Contain Garbage Characters

To use strings in a code resource you'll have to first set up the A4 register, as discussed in the "Global Variables Don't Hold Values" section of this appendix. Refer to that section for more information on the A4 register.

In a code resource, a string literal will consist of random garbage—even after being given a value in a #define directive or an assignment statement. Once the A4 register is set up, however, the characters that make up a string will be preserved. The following snippet shows how the A4 register is set up and how a string can be used in a cdev resource. This technique works for any other code resource type as well.

```
#include   <A4Stuff.h>

#define    TEST_DRAW_STR    "\pMy Test String"

pascal   CDEVHandle  main( short       message,
                          short       item,
                          short       num_items,
                          short       control_panel_ID,
                          EventRecord *the_event,
                          CDEVHandle  cdev_storage,
                          DialogPtr   the_dialog )
{
   long  save_A4;

   save_A4 = SetCurrentA4();

   switch ( message )
   {
      // okay to use TEST_DRAW_STR here or
      // in any routine called by main().
   }

   SetA4( save_A4 );

   return ( cdev_storage );
}
```

For a complete example, see the Appendix A—Errors *f* folder. Look in the Code Resources *f* folder to find a control panel code resource example named GlobalData. That example uses a string literal in a #define directive. It also shows how a global variable can be used in a code resource.

Multisegment Project Error

Code resources are generally small in size—usually well under the 32KB size limit of a segment. For that reason, segmentation rarely becomes an issue for code resources. If you do decide to create a multisegment code resource, the Metrowerks compiler will respond with the error message shown in Figure A.12.

Link Error: Code resource cannot have more than one segment.

OK

FIGURE A.12 THE METROWERKS ERROR WHEN TRYING TO BUILD
A CODE RESOURCE GREATER THAN **32 KB** IN SIZE.

If you need to create a code resource that consists of more than one segment, as the one shown in Figure A.13 does—you'll need to let the CodeWarrior compiler know of your intentions.

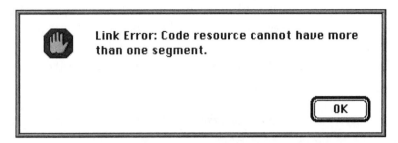

File	Code	Data		
▽ **Segment 1**	**0**	**0**	▣	⇧
MultiSeg.c	0	0	• ▣	
MacOS.lib	0	0	▣	
▽ **Segment 2**	**0**	**0**	▣	
Draw.c	0	0	• ▣	⇩
3 file(s)	**0**	**0**		▥

MultiSeg.μ

FIGURE A.13   A METROWERKS CODE RESOURCE PROJECT THAT
CONSISTS OF MORE THAN ONE SEGMENT.

Before compiling a multisegment code resource project, select **Preferences** from the Edit menu. Click on the **Project** icon to display the Project panel in the dialog box. Then check the **Multi Segment** checkbox, as shown in Figure A.14.

Once this checkbox is checked, you can compile and build the code resource, without regard for the number of segments it's made up of.

For an example of a control panel resource that uses two segments, refer to the Appendix A—Errors *f* folder. Look in the Code Resources *f* folder to find the control panel code resource example named MultiSeg.

That example uses both a global variable and a string literal in two source code files. The source code for the MultiSeg cdev is identical to that of the GlobalData cdev discussed in the "Global Variables Don't Hold Values" section of this appendix. The only difference is that MultiSeg uses two segments.

Check for a multi segment code resource project

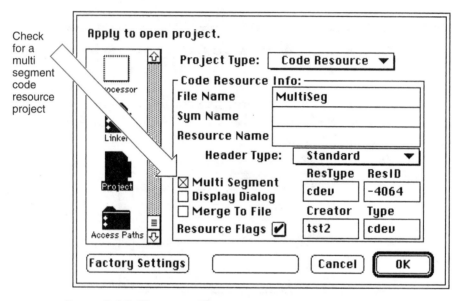

FIGURE A.14 MARKING A METROWERKS CODE RESOURCE PROJECT TO BE MORE THAN ONE SEGMENT.

SYSTEM CRASHES: ERRORS AT RUNTIME

If a project successfully compiles, but crashes when you run the application that you built from the project, you'll want to read the following pages. Figure A.15 shows two of the error messages you could encounter.

Routines Available Only in System 7

Some Toolbox routines are available only on Macs running a version of System 7. The following five System 7-only functions are used in this book's examples:

```
AppendDITL()
ShortenDITL()
FindFolder()
StandardGetFile()
StandardPutFile()
```

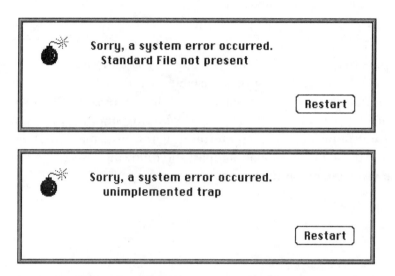

FIGURE A.15 RUNTIME ERROR MESSAGES RESULTING FROM APPLICATIONS THAT USE ROUTINES NOT FOUND ON PRE–SYSTEM 7 MACS.

If you run a program and you get the bomb alert, with a "Standard File not present" error message, then it's likely that the application called either `StandardGetFile()` or `StandardPutFile()` while running on a Mac with a pre-System 7 operating system. If the alert has an "unimplemented trap" error message, than several Toolbox calls could be suspect. For the examples in this book, `AppendDITL()`, `ShortenDITL()`, and `FindFolder()` are System 7–only routines that will result in this error message when an application they appear in is run on a machine using a version of System 6.

You can check the user's machine to verify it is running System 7 by making a call to the Toolbox function `Gestalt()`. But first, make sure that `Gestalt()` itself is present—it's not found on early Macintosh models or early systems. A call to `SysEnvirons()` returns information about the host machine in a `SysEnvRec` variable. If the `machineType` field of this record is less than 0, the host machine is old. And, if the systemVersion is less than 0x0607, the host machine is running a version of system software older than 6.0.7. If your application is running on a machine that matches one or both of these descriptions, there's a chance your application may crash.

If the machine is not old, and it's running a version of system software 6.0.7 or newer, move onto the next test. Call the Gestalt() function, passing a *selector code* of gestaltSystemVersion. In return, Gestalt() will set the response variable to a hex value representing the system running on the host machine. If this value is 0x0700 or greater, the Mac has a version of System 7. The following snippet is an example of how your application might determine if the host machine is running System 7. If the program makes it past the following tests without exiting, a version of System 7 is in use.

```
#include <GestaltEqu.h>

SysEnvRec   mac_info;
OSErr       err;
long        response;

SysEnvirons( curSysEnvVers, &mac_info );

if ( (mac_info.machineType < 0) ||
     (mac_info.systemVersion < 0x0607) )
   ExitToShell();

err = Gestalt(gestaltSystemVersion, &response);

if ( err == noErr )
{
   if ( response < 0x0700 )
      ExitToShell();
}
else
   ExitToShell();
```

Index

More Mac Programming Techniques